The Apocalypse in the Early Middle Ages

D1649049

This ground-breaking study reveals the distinctive impact of apocalyptic ideas about time, evil and power on Church and society in the Latin West, *c.* 400–*c.* 1050. Drawing on evidence from late antiquity, the Frankish kingdoms, Anglo-Saxon England, Spain and Byzantium and sociological models, James Palmer shows that apocalyptic thought was a more powerful part of mainstream political ideologies and religious reform than many historians believe. Moving beyond the standard 'Terrors of the Year 1000', *The Apocalypse in the Early Middle Ages* opens up broader perspectives on heresy, the Antichrist and Last World Emperor legends, chronography, and the relationship between eschatology and apocalypticism. In the process, it offers reassessments of the worlds of Augustine, Gregory of Tours, Bede, Charlemagne and the Ottonians, providing a wide-ranging and up-to-date survey of medieval apocalyptic thought. This is the first full-length English-language treatment of a fundamental and controversial part of medieval religion and society.

JAMES T. PALMER is Lecturer in Mediaeval History at the University of St Andrews.

The Apocalypse in the Early Middle Ages

James T. Palmer

CAMBRIDGE
UNIVERSITY PRESS

CAMBRIDGE
UNIVERSITY PRESS

University Printing House, Cambridge CB2 8BS, United Kingdom

Cambridge University Press is part of the University of Cambridge.

It furthers the University's mission by disseminating knowledge in the pursuit of education, learning and research at the highest international levels of excellence.

www.cambridge.org
Information on this title: www.cambridge.org/9781107449091

© James T. Palmer 2014

First published 2014

A catalogue record for this publication is available from the British Library

ISBN 978-1-107-08544-2 Hardback
ISBN 978-1-107-44909-1 Paperback

To Sophie and Audrey

Contents

Figures

Maps

Acknowledgements

I started out researching and planning this book shortly after I moved to the University of St Andrews back in 2007. My postdoctoral research on time in the early Middle Ages, generously funded by a Leverhulme Early Career Fellowship at the University of Nottingham, had drawn me into the subject of the apocalyptic and I was surprised that there was no sustained, coherent treatment of it for my period. I committed to teaching a third-year option on apocalyptic traditions from Rome to Joachim of Fiore and began piecing together ideas of my own, with not a little help from my students. For the academic season 2011/12 the AHRC gave me invaluable support with a research fellowship which allowed me to spend more time in libraries and to begin the process of writing up – a process aided by institutional leave from the School of History the following year. Invaluable time dedicated to the book was afforded by an ERASMUS exchange at the University of Oslo with Jón Viðar Sigurðsson, in 2011, and by a visiting fellowship at Virginia Tech in 2013, generously supported by the Residential College at West Ambler Johnston Hall, Ben Sax, and my indulgent host Matt Gabriele.

I incurred a great deal of academic debt in the period in which this book was produced. Colleagues in the School of History, St Andrews, were always supportive and encouraging. One could not hope to work in a more stimulating and friendly environment. Within that collective brilliance, a few individuals need to be thanked for their direct input. Simon MacLean kindly read most of the book in draft and gave much useful advice. Justine Firnhaber-Baker and Alex Woolf patiently listened to me talking about it at length and made many suggestions, some followed, others not. Tim Greenwood helped me to straighten up Chapter 4, and both he and Paul Magdalino helpfully talked through various aspects of eastern apocalyptic thought with me. John Hudson was an excellent nominated mentor for the AHRC, which is to say he said encouraging things but let me get on with it. The enthusiastic postgraduate community in St Andrews has also been a continuous source of support, tea and cake. It is a great sadness that, from among them, Berenike Walburg never got to see this book, but I hope she would have appreciated the efforts to look East 'to the really interesting stuff'.

Outside the School, a special thanks needs to be expressed to Helen Foxhall Forbes, who carefully went through the whole draft manuscript before its initial submission and helped me to improve and sharpen up my ideas throughout. The two anonymous readers were magnificent and put in great care and effort in preparing reports to bring the best out of the finished volume. I also benefited from having Clemens Gantner, Simon Loseby, Rick Sowerby and Jo Story cast critical eyes over individual chapters. The remaining mistakes really are my own to bear. I have enjoyed being part of overlapping networks of scholars with related interests, and warmly thank Christopher Bonura, Lizzie Boyle, Katy Cubitt, Peter Darby, Sarah Foot, Matt Gabriele, Anke Holdenried, Mayke de Jong, Richard Landes, Rob Meens, Marco Mostert, Levi Roach, Jay Rubenstein, Felicitas Schmieder, Faith Wallis, Immo Warntjes, Brett Whalen, Steve White and Veronika Wieser for numerous conversations and emails which have helped to propel things forwards. (Sorry if I missed anyone out – I will make it up to you.) Individual elements of the book were tried out on audiences in London, Frankfurt, Utrecht, Blacksburg (Virginia Tech), Paris (IMS), Nottingham, Sheffield and, of course, Leeds and Kalamazoo, with many positive lessons learned along the way. Staff in the various libraries I worked in – in London, Paris, Berlin, Oxford, Cambridge and St Andrews – made my task much easier and I am grateful to all. And I must not forget to acknowledge my debt to the staff at Cambridge University Press, and in particular Liz Friend-Smith and Amanda George, who were encouraging from the beginning and saw that everything got done. I would also like to thank Annie Jackson for her sterling work as my copy-editor.

Finally, I must express my gratitude to those 'outside' the academic universe who made everything possible. My parents, Jan and Trevor, have been there beyond the call of duty more times than I can count. Christine and the Money family have always been patient and supportive even when they didn't have to be. On the other side of the water, the Firnhabers, Bakers and Oslunds have been wonderfully welcoming. At home, Sophie and Audrey have been the most inspiring source of joy and happiness, making all those early starts worth it. And then there's Justine, again – someone who has made anything and everything feel possible.

Abbreviations

AASS	*Acta Sanctorum*
CCCM	Corpus Christianorum, continuatio mediaevalis
CCSL	Corpus Christianorum, series latina
CLA	*Codices latini antiquiores: A Palaeographical Guide to Latin Manuscripts Prior to the Ninth Century*, ed. E. A. Lowe
DA	*Deutsches Archiv für Erforschung des Mittelalters*
EHR	*English Historical Review*
EME	*Early Medieval Europe*
JEH	*Journal of Ecclesiastical History*
MGH	Monumenta Germaniae Historica
AA	Auctores antiquissimi
Cap.	Capitula regum Francorum
Conc.	Concilia
Epp. (Sel.)	Epistolae (selectae in usum scholarum)
Libri mem.	Libri memoriales
LL	Leges
QQ zur Geistesgesch.	Quellen zur Geistesgeschichte des Mittelalters
SRG	Scriptores rerum Germanicarum in usum scholarum separatism editi
SRM	Scriptores rerum Merovingicarum
SS	Scriptores
P&P	*Past and Present*
PL	Patrologia Latina
SC	Sources chrétiennes
TRHS	*Transactions of the Royal Historical Society*

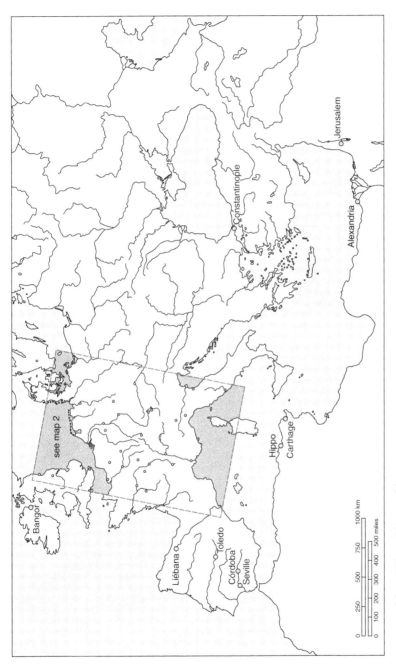

Map 1 The wider world

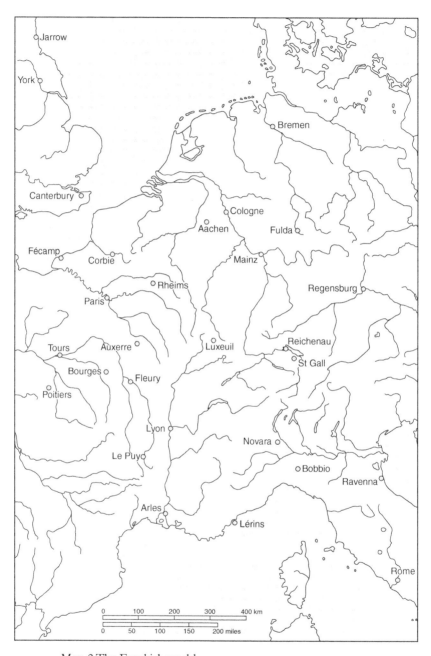

Map 2 The Frankish world

Introduction: how the world ends

In 557 the great imperial city of Constantinople was devastated by an earthquake. Here was a city founded two hundred years earlier to be a truly Christian place, at the time under the dominance of the powerful and long-lived emperor Justinian I (r. 527–65). But, as the monumental Hagia Sophia built by the emperor partially collapsed, people panicked. Rumours circulated that the world was nearly at its end and self-proclaimed prophets caused terror by preaching about worse things to come. Had Christ himself not foretold of earthquakes in the Last Days (Matt. 24.7; Mark 13.8; Luke, 21.11)? Agathias, a lawyer in the city, despaired at how easily people had been wound up by such nonsense, which he found often accompanied these kinds of disasters. He also noted that the people of the city reformed their lives: 'suddenly all were honest in their business dealings, so that even public officials, putting aside their greed, dealt with lawsuits according to the law.'[1] Hymns were sung, gifts were given to the Church, people lived better lives. The fear of imminent judgement had reformed society – or at least would have done, had people not reverted to their old ways as soon as things had calmed down (Proverbs 26.11).

Agathias's story treats us to a drama which is resoundingly human and modern despite its distance to us in time. In many crises, big or small, people are unsettled and seek to change their lives, as they hope to understand the higher reasons for what is going on. Apocalypticism has repeated, if not enduring, resonance for human societies. It reveals much about how people understand the world and their place in it. As Frank Kermode observed, it is almost natural for human beings to anticipate endings when they tell stories about the world.[2] The way a narrative resolves can legitimise or subvert the route there, so a life of

---

[1] Agathias, *Historiae*, V. 5, ed. R. Keydell (Berlin, 1967), pp. 169–70, quoted in P. Magdalino, 'The History of the Future and Its Uses: Prophecy, Policy and Propaganda', in R. Beaton and C. Rouché (eds.), *The Making of Byzantine History. Studies Dedicated to Donald M. Nicol on His Seventieth Birthday* (Aldershot, 1993), pp. 3–34 at p. 6.
[2] F. Kermode, *The Sense of an Ending: Studies in the Theory of Fiction* (London, 1967).

suffering can be made good by a finale of peace and joy but it can be made more tragic if the ending resounds with hopelessness, fear and torment. And since everyone has an ending, even if the end of time or the world is too abstract to conceptualise fully, then it really is a universal in human experience. Johannes Fried expressed this in no uncertain terms for the Middle Ages: 'the end of time was *the* fundamental interpretative category for all humanity, belief, knowledge and action, even if it was not always and by everyone and in every deed made explicit.'[3] Agathias may have shaken his head at the popular response to the earthquake, but he understood all too well that he was observing a common human dynamic, framed in this case by (mis)understandings of scripture.

Not everyone was as dismissive as our Constantinopolitan lawyer. All Christians knew that the End was promised – it is just that no one knew *when* it would come, not least because scripture stated that only God could know that (Matt. 24.36; Mark, 17.32; Acts 1.7). There would be signs including wars, tribulations and earthquakes, adding up to 'perilous times' (2 Tim. 3.1). There would be many 'antichrists' (1 John 2.18) and, once there had been a 'falling away' of political power, the Son of Perdition himself – Antichrist – would come (2 Thess. 2.3). But whether people lived to witness the End Times themselves, or died beforehand, everyone was going to have to face the Last Judgement. Such inevitability meant that many people channelled fear rather than dismissing it, because there was a pastoral imperative to get people to prepare themselves and for society to be judged. Apocalypse and Judgement were reasons to act and, consequently, things which could be employed to persuade people into action.[4] Neither denial nor fatalism is an appropriate response. This is why Apocalypse remains such a central theme in analyses of environmental change, global economic crises or terrorism – the penalties for inaction are doom.[5]

---

[3] J. Fried, *Aufstieg aus dem Untergang. Apokalyptisches Denken und die Entstehung der modernen Naturwissenschaft im Mittelalter* (Munich, 2001), p. 37: 'Endzeit war die fundamentale Deutungskatagorie alles Menschen, des Glaubens, der Wissenschaften, des Handelns, auch wenn es nicht immer und von jedermann bei jedem Tun explizit wurde.' Possibly the best introductory survey of apocalyptic thought in the early Middle Ages is J. Flori, *L'Islam et la fin des temps. L'interprétation prophétique des invasions musulmanes dans la chrétienté médiévale* (Paris, 2007). See also the essays in R. Emmerson and B. McGinn (eds.), *The Apocalypse in the Middle Ages* (Ithaca, NY, 1992), J. A. Aertsen and M. Pickavé (eds.), *Ende und Vollendung. Eschatologische Perspektiven im Mittelalter* (Berlin and New York, 2002), A. Gow, R. Landes and D. C. van Meter (eds.), *The Apocalyptic Year 1000: Religious Expectation and Social Changes 950–1050* (Oxford, 2003), and R. E. Guglielmetti (ed.), *L'apocalisse nel medioevo* (Florence, 2011).

[4] F. Borchardt, *Doomsday Speculation as a Strategy of Persuasion* (Lewiston, NY, 1990).

[5] V. Wieser, C. Zolles, C. Feik, M. Zolles and L. Schlöndorff (eds.), *Abendländische Apokalyptik. Kompendium zur Genealogie der Endzeit* (Berlin, 2013)

The thesis of the present book then is this: apocalyptic thought in the early Middle Ages was commonplace and mainstream, and an important factor in the way that people conceptualised, stimulated and directed change. It was not solely the marginal and extremist way of thinking nearly all modern scholars imagine. Apocalyptic thought, understood properly, essentially becomes a powerful part of reform discourse about how best to direct people – individually and collectively – towards a better life on Earth. Even when people saw divine punishment, maybe in attacks by Huns or raids by Vikings, they felt compelled to change behaviour, rather than to wallow in fatalistic self-pity.[6] The apocalyptic, then, is a heightened engagement with the problem of the limited chances one has to 'get it right' before one is judged. It is, as Stephen O'Leary recognised, a mode of argument, and one which makes sense of key problems in human experience (the existence of evil, the mystery of time, the problem of authority).[7] But, by that very definition, it is also a living body of ideas which changes in response to how the general theory meets the historically specific, such as in the way the scripture resonates differently with each social and political upheaval. I shall refrain from making any regrettable claims that this was a 'definitive period' in European/ world history because the devil is in the detail: this is a case study of the interplay between big ideas and action, not an exercise in teleological thinking.

Why might the End have come? In the history of Christianity and Christendom, the simple answer is that it was promised – first by Christ himself, then in the revelation of John of Patmos, and in apocrypha such as the Revelation of Thomas.[8] But the End did not come soon enough, which led to repeated crises of interpretation. What did the eschatological and apocalyptic promises in the Bible really mean? At the same time as they dealt with this issue, early Christians experienced other crises and challenges: persecution, institutionalisation, codification, schism. Christianity only even became dominant in Roman society long after emperors were Christians from the early fourth century, with plenty of 'Roman' pagans still active in the public life of the empire a century later. And then new challenges appeared: the Western Empire grew weak and gave way to new 'barbarian' kingdoms; plague more than decimated the population of Europe throughout the sixth century; the rise of Islam and the Arab caliphates redrew the political and religious map in the seventh;

---

[6] J. T. Palmer, 'Apocalyptic Outsiders and Their Uses in the Early Medieval West' (forthcoming).

[7] S. O'Leary, *Arguing the Apocalypse: A Theory of Millennial Rhetoric* (Oxford, 1994).

[8] M. Himmelfarb, *The Apocalypse: A Brief History* (Chichester, 2010); E. Pagels, *Revelations: Visions, Prophecy, and Politics in the Book of Revelation* (New York, 2012).

and then in the eighth century, Charlemagne reinvented empire in the West through conquest and propaganda, but ended his days anxious and introspective. Apocalyptic thought shaped and fed off all of these things.

If Charlemagne's empire represented any kind of 'high point' in Europe's early medieval history, it was one with little comfort. People worried about whether it was possible to calculate the proximity of the End. People certainly worried about Vikings and heretics and other outsiders who might have been challenges foretold. As the unity of empire fell away again once more, there were concerns about signs, strange natural occurrences, dreams, and the fate of the soul in the afterlife. By the tenth century, political continuity seemed to be a good barrier to the coming of Antichrist, but such continuity was in short supply. The 'transformation of the Year 1000' was also the 'crisis of the Year 1000', with violence, invasion, succession disputes and new mobilisations of popular piety. The world changed, and changed often; and as it did so people drew on apocalyptic hopes and fears, from emperors and kings down to peasant farmers. The history of early medieval apocalyptic thought is also the history of the early Middle Ages.

Debating the apocalyptic

Few historians have ever succeeded in discussing the apocalyptic dynamics of the early Middle Ages without controversy. The historiography on the 'Terrors of the Year 1000', following Edward Peters's classification, can be divided into three broad schools, two of which place apocalypticism centrally in medieval history, and one which denies its importance.[9] The first of the apocalyptic schools propounds the 'strong thesis', in which 1000 marked a clear dividing line in history, with widespread apocalyptic anxiety beforehand giving way to relief afterwards. According to Daniel Milo, the seminal formulation of this idea was largely due to Jules Michelet in the 1830s, in particular as he responded to the revolution of 1830.[10] In no small part Michelet, like many after him, was led to his interpretation of the period by Ralph Glaber's complex *Five Books of History*, although it represents only one extreme take on the early eleventh century. Significant refinement was provided by the 'weak thesis', so-called because it concerns a wider date range – 979 to 1042

---

[9] E. Peters, 'Mutations, Adjustments, Terrors, Historians, and the Year 1000', in M. Frassetto, *The Year 1000: Religious and Social Response to the Turning of the First Millennium* (New York, 2002), pp. 9–28.

[10] D. Milo, 'L'an mil: un problème d'historiographie moderne', *History and Theory*, 27.3 (1988), 261–81 at p. 278. See J. Michelet, *History of France*, trans. W. K. Kelly (London, 1844), pp. 336–40.

in Fried's version – in which heightened interest in apocalyptic thought fed into a panorama of political, social and religious change.[11] It was first developed by Henri Focillon in 1952 in a study of early medieval art and its contexts, but the thesis found its most profound and wide-ranging exposition in Johannes Fried's 1989 article 'Endzeiterwartung um die Jahrtausendwende' ('Awaiting the End of Time around the Turn of the Year 1000').[12] Many more have followed Fried's lead, most prominently Richard Landes in his studies of millenarian movements and apocalyptic chronography.[13] Variations of the 'weak thesis' have also been important in studies of Byzantine apocalypticism.

There is a long history of challenging the work of scholars who have studied the apocalyptic. From 1873, and the publication of François Plaine's 'Les prétendues terreurs de l'an mille', we can see what Peters labelled the 'strong counter-thesis'. Plaine opened the issue by subjecting a wider selection of sources than earlier historians to critical analysis – although fewer than Fried and others a century later – and he concluded that there was little evidence of widespread interest in the Year 1000. 'In a word, the terrors of the Year 1000 are nothing more or less than a myth.'[14] This theme was taken up by Pietro Orsi in Italy, Heinrich von Eicken in Germany, and George Lincoln Burr in the United States, the latter summarising the terrors as 'only a nightmare of modern scholars'.[15] The mood

[11] The reason for this extended range for the millennium of the Incarnation and of the Passion is that 979 represents the earliest contemporaries might have dated the Incarnation, while 1042 represented the latest that they might have placed the Passion. For a good study of the relevant chronological inquiries – but passing over issues of apocalypse – see P. Verbist, *Duelling with the Past: Medieval Authors and the Problem of the Christian Era, c. 990–1135* (Turnhout, 2010).

[12] H. Focillon, *L'an mil* (Paris, 1952) [*The Year 1000*, trans. F. Wieck (New York, 1969), pp. 39–72]; J. Fried, 'Endzeiterwartung um die Jahrtausendwende', *DA*, 45.2 (1989), 385–473. Professor Fried's important article is translated into English as 'Awaiting the End of Time around the Year 1000', in Gow, Landes and van Meter, *The Apocalyptic Year 1000*, pp. 16–63, but I will refer to the original German version throughout this book because only there do you get the full references.

[13] R. Landes, 'Lest the Millennium Be Fulfilled: Apocalyptic Expectations and the Pattern of Western Chronography, 100–800 CE', in W. Verbeke, D. Verhelst, and A. Welkenhuysen (eds.), *The Use and Abuse of Eschatology in the Middle Ages* (Leuven, 1988), pp. 137–211; '*Millenarismus absconditus*: L'historiographie augustinienne et l'An Mil', *Le Moyen Âge*, 98 (1992), 355–77; 'Sur les traces du Millennium: La via negativa', *Le Moyen Âge*, 99 (1993), 5–26; *Relics, Apocalypse, and the Deceits of History: Ademar of Chabannes (989–1034)* (Cambridge, MA, 1995); *Heaven on Earth: The Varieties of the Millennial Experience* (Oxford, 2011).

[14] F. Plaine, 'Les prétendues terreurs de l'an mille', *Revue des questions historiques*, 13 (1873), 145–64 at p. 164: 'En un mot, les terreurs de l'an 1000 ne sont ni plus ni moins qu'un mythe.'

[15] G. L. Burr, 'The Year 1000 and the Antecedents of the Crusades', *American Historical Review*, 6.3 (1901), 429–39 (quotation at p. 438). H. von Eicken, 'Die Legende von der Erwartung des Weltunterganges und der Wiederkehr Christi im Jahre 1000', *Forschungen*

of the 'strong counter-thesis' has been no less pronounced in the writings of critics of the 'weak thesis'. Most notably, Sylvain Gouguenheim's *Les fausses terreurs de l'an mil* (1999) offered point-by-point challenges to Fried's and Landes's 'over-interpretation' of the sources, and the tendency of both to join up isolated references into a coherent whole and to read between the lines.[16] The warning to be careful is of course essential but, as Fried argued at length, Gouguenheim's strictures remain intellectually problematic, and his non-apocalyptic readings of sources are not always more convincing.[17]

These theses, although principally concerned with France and Germany in the Year 1000, are indicative of the ways in which apocalyptic tradition is approached by early medieval historians more generally. The clearest, and in some ways quietest, divide is between scholars who believe apocalyptic tradition was widely influential and those who pass over it altogether for whatever reason. A good example in scholarship on the Carolingian world concerns the imperial coronation of Charlemagne on Christmas Day, 800. In 1978 Juan Gil, combining the prevailing chronological tradition that 800 was the 6,000th year of the world with the logic of literalist readings of scripture which claimed the world would last only 6,000 years, argued that there was clearly an eschatological setting for Charlemagne's actions.[18] But while prominent 'weak thesis' historians – Fried, Landes, Brandes – have supported and developed this idea, there has been little engagement from historians specialising in other aspects of Carolingian history, with silence on the matter, for example, in the cultural and political biographies of the emperor by Rosamond McKitterick (2008) and Matthias Becher (1999; second edition 2007).[19] Such absences are not the products of ignorance or neglect, but rather of the wealth of source material which has led some historians to prioritise other factors (ambition, conquest, economic change). For Peter Brown's

---

zur Deutschen Geschichte, 23 (1883), 303–18; P. Orsi, *L'anno mille: Saggio di critica storica* (Turin, 1887).

[16] S. Gouguenheim, *Les fausses terreurs de l'an mil: Attente de la fin des temps ou approfondissement de la foi* (Paris, 1999), pp. 52–63.

[17] J. Fried, 'Die Endzeit fest im Griff des Positivismus? Zur Auseinandersetzung mit Sylvain Gouguenheim', *Historische Zeitschrift*, 275 (2002), 281–322. See also R. Landes, 'The *Terribles espoirs* of 1000 and the Tacit Fears of 2000', in Gow, Landes and van Meter, *The Apocalyptic Year 1000*, pp. 3–16 at p. 4 and dismissive footnotes throughout his 'The Fear'.

[18] J. Gil, 'Los terrores del ano 6000', in *Actas del simposio para el estudio de los codices del 'Comentario al apocalypsis' de Beato de Liebana* (Madrid, 1978), pp. 217–47.

[19] M. Becher, *Karl der Große* (2nd edn, Munich, 2007); R. McKitterick, *Charlemagne: The Formation of a European Identity* (Cambridge, 2008). Note even the silence of Henry Mayr-Harting in his 'Charlemagne, the Saxons, and the Imperial Coronation of 800', *EHR*, 111.444 (1996), 1113–33, despite his interest in later (Ottonian) eschatology and apocalypticism.

study of the formation of Christendom, apocalyptic tradition was but one voice of many; but with a more institutional perspective, such as Chris Wickham's, these voices naturally seem barely audible at all.[20] Buried within Gouguenheim's position is the weaker truism that the apocalyptic was not always important in every way – but Fried allowed for that, as we have seen, and it does not mean that it was unimportant.

As characterised so far, the 'counter-thesis' position sounds largely negative, when in practice many of its implications can be pursued productively. Simon MacLean, for example, has argued persuasively that modern scholars on both sides focus on debating whether or not the sources contain literal interpretations of apocalyptic tradition; often, he suggested instead, the ideologies and rhetoric employed could be more revealing of the strategies of authors, expectations of audiences and the nature of various discourses in general.[21] References to antichrists in Adso's *Letter on the Origins of Antichrist* (*c.* 950) and Wulfstan of York's *Sermon of the Wolf* (1009, revised in 1014), for MacLean, reveal much about how calls to action against opponents were framed by scripture.[22] A variation of the theme is provided by Dominique Barthélemy, who interpreted Bernard of Angers' reference to 'antichrists' in the early eleventh century as a mere dramatisation of claims against St Foy of Conques and the eventual come-uppance of the claimants.[23] Pursued carefully, as in these cases, attention to rhetorical strategy illuminates the ways in which apocalyptic thought was adopted in situations which do not seem to be apocalyptic, millenarian or eschatological beyond a superficial level. The danger is to expect that apocalyptic in extant sources works only at a rhetorical level, and indeed MacLean warns that 'the rhetorical baby should not be thrown out with the bathwater'.[24] Sometimes the sources will work like Barthélemy's example; sometimes they will seem in context to reflect something that fits Fried's model.

There is a fourth position which requires outlining, not least because it is the one I find resonates best with the source material. In 1995, Bernard McGinn argued that the defining characteristic of early medieval apocalyptic was a persistent sense of 'psychological imminence' rather than

[20] P. Brown, *The Rise of Western Christendom: Triumph and Diversity AD 200–1000* (2nd edn, Oxford, 2003); C. Wickham, *Framing the Early Middle Ages: Europe and the Mediterranean, 400–800* (Oxford, 2005).

[21] S. MacLean, 'Apocalypse and Revolution: Europe around the Year 1000', *EME*, 15.1 (2007), 86–106 at pp. 100–5.

[22] Ibid., p. 102; S. MacLean, 'Reform, Queenship and the End of the World in Tenth-Century France: Adso's "Letter on the Origin and Time of the Antichrist"', *Revue Belge de Philologie et d'Histoire*, 86 (2008), 645–75, esp. pp. 653–8.

[23] D. Barthélemy, 'Antichrist et blasphémateur', *Médiévales*, 37 (1999), 57–70 at pp. 68–9.

[24] MacLean, 'Apocalypse and Revolution', p. 105.

'chronological imminence'.[25] By this, he meant that the Augustinian warnings against prediction meant not a de-eschatologising of ways of thinking, but rather a more radical mode of thought in which Judgement might come at any moment, with action (Church reform, invasion, etc.) pursued accordingly. A particular attraction of this point of view is that it explains the consistency of apocalyptic tradition across *and between* key dates (500, 800, 1000) and it begins to make sense of personal eschatologies and responses to specific events or processes which lie significantly outwith the obvious markers of 'chronological imminence'. Dates can be meaningful within this framework, as Paul Magdalino has argued occurs in Byzantine apocalyptic tradition; their significance, however, is defined by the nature of psychological imminence not the date alone.[26] A similar way of understanding late antique tradition was sketched by R. A. Markus, who illustrated his point with reference to Gregory the Great, who neither observed calendrical calculations nor combated vulgar beliefs about the End, but who rather expressed a 'sense of urgency and the conviction that his world could not be taken for granted. Its very instability and the fragility of civilized order demand constant effort of imagination, of understanding and enterprise.'[27]

Resources for exploring the devotional and intellectual parameters of apocalyptic tradition in the early Middle Ages are well served by attention to the theology and philosophy of the early Church. The thought of the North African bishop Augustine of Hippo is the most thoroughly explored in this context, including important analysis from Markus and Paula Fredriksen.[28] Other individuals to receive sustained treatment

---

[25] B. McGinn, 'The End of theWorld and the Beginning of Christendom', in M. Bull (ed.), *Apocalypse Theory and the End of theWorld* (Oxford, 1995), pp. 58–89.
[26] Magdalino, 'The History of the Future'; idem, 'The Year 1000 in Byzantium', in P. Magdalino (ed.), *Byzantium in the Year 1000* (Leiden, 2002), pp. 233–70; idem, 'The End of Time in Byzantium', in W. Brandes and F. Schmieder (eds.), *Endzeiten: Eschatologie in den monotheistischen Weltreligionen* (Berlin, 2008), pp. 119–34. See also W. Brandes, 'Anastasios ὁ Δίκορος. Endzeiterwartung und Kaiserkritik in Byzanz um 500 n.Chr.', *Byzantinische Zeitschrift*, 90 (1997), 24–63 and 'Liudprand von Cremona (*Legatio* Cap. 39–40) und eine bisher unbeachtete West-Östliche Korrespondenz über die Bedeutung des Jahres 1000 A.D.', *Byzantinische Zeitschrift*, 93 (2000), 435–63.
[27] R. A. Markus, 'Living within Sight of the End', in C. Humphrey and M. Ormrod (eds.), *Time in the MedievalWorld* (York, 2001), pp. 23–34 at p. 34. In many respects this principle can be seen at work in other recent studies of medieval apocalyptic including: B. Whalen, *Dominion of God: Christendom and Apocalypse in the Middle Ages* (Cambridge, MA, 2009); M. Gabriele, *An Empire of Memory: The Legend of Charlemagne, the Franks and Jerusalem before the First Crusade* (Oxford, 2011); J. Rubenstein, *Armies of Heaven: The First Crusade and the Quest for Apocalypse* (Philadelphia, PA, 2011).
[28] R. A. Markus, *Saeculum: History and Society in the Theology of St Augustine* (Cambridge, 1970); P. Fredriksen, 'Apocalypse and Redemption in Early Christianity: From John of Patmos to Augustine of Hippo', *Vigiliae Christianae*, 45.2 (1991), 151–83, reworked in

include Gregory the Great, Bede and John Scottus Eriugena.[29] Far more attention has been devoted to later figures beyond the scope of the present study, such as Hildegard of Bingen, Rupert of Deutz and Joachim of Fiore.[30] Certain themes in theology have been charted through the period in question, most notably with Brian Daley's study of hope,[31] and numerous examinations of interpretations of the figure of Antichrist.[32] Trends in biblical exegesis have also been analysed in general in ways which affect our subject.[33] The challenge posed by Fried's 'Endzeiterwartung' in particular is to take the currents in the writings which have formed the basis of these kinds of studies and to trace the ways in which they intersect with political, social and, in both cases, devotional activity. In many ways the interesting question is not whether there was evidence of apocalypticism in the early Middle Ages – there is – but why people invoked apocalyptic thought when they did in the context of a range of political and cultural processes.

A question of methodology

A survey of historiographical moods will only take us so far because we need to begin to outline the kinds of interpretative tools available and appropriate to the task. Sociology, anthropology and religious studies

'Tyconius and Augustine on the Apocalypse', in Emmerson and McGinn, *The Apocalypse in the Middle Ages*, pp. 20–37.

[29] On Gregory see R. A. Markus, *Gregory the Great and His World* (Cambridge, 1997), ch. 4. On Bede, P. Darby, *Bede and the End of Time* (Farnham, 2012) and the introduction to F. Wallis, *Bede: Commentary on Revelation* (Liverpool, 2013). On Eriugena, J. McEvoy and M. Dunne (eds.), *History and Eschatology in John Scottus Eriugena and His Time* (Leuven, 2002), pp. 3–29.

[30] M. Reeves, *The Influence of Prophecy in the Later Middle Ages: A Study in Joachimism* (Oxford, 1969); A. Williams (ed.), *Prophecy and Millenarianism: Essays in Honour of Marjorie Reeves* (London, 1980); S. Flanagan, *Hildegard of Bingen, 1098–1179: A Visionary Life* (2nd edn, London 1998); B. Newman (ed.), *Voice of the Living Light: Hildegard of Bingen and Her World* (Berkeley, CA, 1998); J. van Engen, *Rupert of Deutz* (Berkeley, CA, 1983).

[31] B. Daley, *The Hope of the Early Church: A Handbook of Patristic Eschatology* (Cambridge, 1991).

[32] H. D. Rauh, *Das Bild des Antichrist im Mittelalter: Von Tyconius zum deutschen Symbolismus* (Münster, 1973); D. Verhelst, 'La préhistoire des conceptions d'Adson concernant l'Antichrist', *Recherches de théologie ancienne et médiévale*, 40 (1973), 52–103; R. Emmerson, *Antichrist in the Middle Ages: A Study of Medieval Apocalypticism, Art and Literature* (Manchester, 1981); B. McGinn, *Antichrist: Two Thousand Years of the Human Fascination with Evil* (San Francisco, CA, 1994); K. Hughes, *Constructing Antichrist: Paul, Biblical Commentaries, and the Development of Doctrine in the Middle Ages* (Washington, DC, 2005).

[33] Fredriksen, 'Tyconius and Augustine on the Apocalypse'; E. A. Matter, 'The Apocalypse in Early Medieval Exegesis', in Emmerson and McGinn, *The Apocalypse in the Middle Ages*, pp. 38–50; Wallis, *Bede: Commentary on Revelation*, pp. 5–22.

can provide a rich world of case studies and models which might help to shed light on the ways in which apocalyptic movements work. It has been a notable feature of Richard Landes's work, most overwhelmingly in his 2011 book *Heaven on Earth*, that many of his lines of argument stem from understandings about how 'millennial movements' work in general, and how cults deal with both prophecy and prophecy failure. Such trails can be productive as long as we avoid the Landesian temptation to engage in 'Jurassic Park' anthropology and to start filling in missing dinosaur DNA (e.g., silences in eighth-century chronicles) with frog DNA (e.g., appeals to what would happen in 1950s' UFO cults). Any study which concerns itself with cross-cultural comparisons does need to make allowance for difference as well as similarity, because the logic of ideas and actions cannot always be constant when their context is invariably different from one instance to the next.[34] But far from comparative history being an empty pursuit, it can lead us towards two useful things: first, it allows us to begin to identify distinctiveness and similitude in the societies we are going to study, and second, it can help us to draw up the *questions* we might ask of our material, even if it cannot tell us the answers in advance.

Before we can even begin that task, we need to be careful about our terminology. Time and time again, it transpires that words like 'millennialism' do not quite mean what people take them to mean at first sight; some words take on new meanings, and some words are just uncommon. The word 'eschatology' can be taken as being the study of Last Things, pursued on the assumption that all people are mortal, all earthly things will wither, and that there will be a Day of Judgement.[35] 'Apocalypticism' stands as a subsection of eschatology – so much so that it is not always possible to distinguish the two – because it is the belief that that End is imminent. This is the meaning of 'apocalyptic' which resonates best with popular usage, where it often means something catastrophically bad, either en route to a very final ending or else preceding a post-apocalyptic dystopia. One might talk of *the* Apocalypse. We must bear in mind, however, that in eschatology and apocalypse a believer can be *hopeful* that the End is to hand, because it will bring resolution and an end to suffering, and might even usher in some kind of paradise. Moreover, the word 'apocalypse' itself actually means 'revelation'. In the last book of the New Testament, John of Patmos did not 'see the Apocalypse', but rather had various truths about future things

[34] C. Wickham, 'Problems in Doing Comparative History', in P. Skinner (ed.), *Challenging the Boundaries of Medieval History* (Turnhout, 2009), pp. 5–28.
[35] J. Walls (ed.), *The Oxford Handbook of Eschatology* (Oxford, 2008).

revealed to him.[36] We will return to 'millennialism' shortly; but for now it is important to bear in mind a certain amount of semantic range that needs to be treated with caution.

It is necessary alongside these common terms to be aware of types of apocalypse. The most useful basic distinction focuses on individual and communal experience, which can be labelled 'moral' or 'individual apocalypse', and 'political' or 'collective apocalypse' respectively.[37] 'Moral apocalypse' concerns individual mortality, responsibility and accountability for sin, and the fate of the soul on death. In the sources for this book, the most dramatic examples revolve around death-bed visions of the afterlife, which could then be used as moral lessons – guides to what would happen to the good or bad on death, and therefore also an exhortation for people to correct their behaviour.[38] Such things were, of course, also mainstays of preaching, penitentials and church art – and, as we shall see, they could be highly political in tone.[39] 'Political apocalypse', by contrast, spoke about the fate of the community as a whole. There remained, of course, elements of moral apocalypse because it was often the responsibility of large-scale organisations (the Church, the empire) to keep people on the right course; but the focus was more on society's sins, punishments and rewards as a whole, which led naturally to an interest in the fate of the world in the End Times. It is in this kind of context that we find most speculation about sequences of empires, kings or times, which will have widespread implications for the Last Judgement and its timing.

With some of these basic distinctions and definitions set up, it is necessary to turn to some of the subjects which have dominated modern scholarship on apocalypticism: millenarian movements, the problem of prophecy failure, the relationship between apocalyptic thought and reason, and the authority of apocalyptic thought. These themes will return time and time again in the sources and our analysis, but here I offer a brief but critical survey of the key points:

---

[36] Take care also with the word 'apocrypha', which means 'secrets' or similar things. It is often used to denote something which is not genuine.

[37] J. Baun, *Tales from Another Byzantium: Celestial Journey and Local Community in the Medieval Greek Apocrypha* (Cambridge, 2007); eadem, 'The Moral Apocalypse in Byzantium', in A. Baumgarten (ed.), *Apocalyptic Time* (Leiden, 2000), pp. 241–67.

[38] P. Dinzelbacher, *Die Jenseitsbrücke im Mittelalter* (Vienna, 1973); C. Carozzi, *Le voyage de l'âme dans l'Au-delà d'après la littérature latine (Vᵉ–VIIIᵉ siècle)* (Rome, 1994); I. Moreira, *Heaven's Purge: Purgatory in Late Antiquity* (Oxford, 2010).

[39] W. Levison, 'Die Politik in den Jenseitsvisionen des frühen Mittelalter', in his *Aus rheinischer und fränkischer Frühzeit* (Düsseldorf, 1948), pp. 229–46; P. E. Dutton, *The Politics of Dreaming in the Carolingian Empire* (Lincoln, NE, 1994).

Millennialism/millenarianism

Because 'millenarianism' is often to do with popular movements and revolts rather than the institutional Church, it has been a popular 'sociological' subject for investigation. ('Millenarianism' and 'millennialism' are basically the same word, the first derived from French, the latter from Latin). The root of the name comes from those who believed in a literal and earthly realisation of Rev. 20.4 and 20.6, which refer to a thousand-year-long reign of Christ and his saints. Few millenarian groups as defined by modern scholars would fit this category. Instead, they are millenarian in a 'liberal' sense. Catherine Wessinger, an expert on millennialism in modern North America, defines it as follows:

> Millennialism is the audacious human hope that in the imminent future there will be a transition – either catastrophic or progressive – to a 'collective salvation', which will be accomplished by a divine or superhuman agent and/or humans working in accordance with a divine or superhuman plan.[40]

Such a definition is deliberately designed to take account of a wide range of millennial movements and phenomena, embracing both movements which seek to destroy the current order in order to establish a new one (catastrophic millennialism) and those which seek to reform the existing order more peacefully (progressive millennialism). There is a range of further factors which are often cited to identify millenarian beliefs. Norman Cohn's much-cited five-point list posits that there will be belief that salvation will be (1) collective, (2) terrestrial, (3) imminent, (4) total, and (5) accomplished by agencies which are consciously regarded as supernatural.[41] An extended list was proposed by Richard Landes which resonates with analysis of millenarian groups generally by highlighting (1) ecstatic frenzy, (2) the prominent role of women, (3) a charismatic leader, (4) a movement that is popular, radical and hostile to institutional hierarchies, and (5) a steadfastness in believing these things.[42]

Millenarianism provides an important counterpoint to apocalypticism. It is itself 'apocalyptic' in the sense that it is revelatory and revolves around the transformation of the earthly life, but in the process it is nominally more hopeful and revolutionary. In early medieval Christianity, as

[40] C. Wessinger, 'Millennialism in Cross-Cultural Perspective', in C. Wessinger (ed.), *The Oxford Handbook of Millennialism* (Oxford, 2011), pp.3–26 at p. 3. See also her formal definition on p. 5.
[41] N. Cohn, *In Pursuit of the Millennium: Revolutionary Millenarians and Mystical Anarchists of the Middle Ages* (2nd edn, London, 1970), p. 15.
[42] Landes, '*Millenarismus absconditus*', pp. 376–7; Wessinger, 'Millennialism', pp. 6–9.

in modern Christianity, there was no shortage of people who hoped for the End of the earthly life so that they could move into a transcendental spiritual life with God – millenarianism did not have the monopoly on positive emotion. Perhaps the key difference lies in the degree of determination one could hope to exact over the future. In non-millenarian scenarios, believers were largely at the mercy of events they could not control, although in general this encouraged them to prepare their souls in anticipation of Judgement rather than to fall into fatalism or passivity. Millenarians, in contrast, sought to influence the way in which the future would unfold in relation to prophesied apocalyptic events, so effectively creating a kingdom on earth for themselves. Both models, then, agitated for some kind of response which would lead people to purify themselves and their communities, but what differed was how these responses fitted into a cosmic order of being.

Within the contrast just outlined, we begin to find the roots of a problematic issue: did the early medieval Church always act so differently from a millenarian movement as defined above?[43] As we shall see in Chapter 2 with Pope Gregory the Great (d. 604) and Bishop Gregory of Tours (d. 594), it is possible to find charismatic and popular leaders in the institutional Church who interpreted the word of God for their audiences, encouraged women to take an active role in Christian society and believed in collective salvation, an imminent and total transformation of the world, and the power of 'supernatural' intervention. The only things which were not 'millenarian' here were the hope for an earthly kingdom (although there was still commitment to reform on earth and a spiritual kingdom), an opposition to an institutional hierarchy (because they were it), and perhaps the ecstatic frenzy. On a superficial level at least, then, the early medieval Church can be read as a cult writ large in relation to millenarian analysis. This is where it has been particularly important, certainly since Cohn's work, to stress millenarianism as a populist non- or anti-institutional phenomenon, as Landes has done. But once we have drawn up this sense of opposition, it is imperative to take both sides into account. What happens if the institutional hierarchy is radically apocalyptic too, but in a different way? What happens if the charismatics or their ideas are absorbed into mainstream debates, as they were later in the case of Joachim of Fiore (d. 1201)? Millenarianism may stand as a cross-cultural phenomenon, but what it is acting against will introduce new and unpredictable variables.

---

[43] This is different in the later Middle Ages: R. E. Lerner, 'The Medieval Return to the Thousand-Year Sabbath', in Emmerson and McGinn, *The Apocalypse in the Middle Ages*, pp. 51–71.

In pursuing these issues, it is necessary not to define apocalypticism in terms which are exclusively millenarian or which only focus on one part of that spectrum. This is a widespread problem in the scholarship on medieval apocalyptic thought. Claude Carozzi, for instance, considered there to be two kinds of eschatology: an apocalyptic one essentially defined by 'millenarian' tendencies towards prediction, and one which embraced a timeless, penitential salvation for all.[44] This, as will be seen, dramatically underestimates the sheer variety of positions possible within eschatological and apocalyptic schema. The problem is apparent in Carozzi's work because, led by his definition, he moved to deny that there was any meaningful apocalyptic thought in the half-millennium after Augustine because there was little 'millenarianism' as he understood it. The argument, while raising interesting issues, does not stand up to scrutiny. A similar problem underpins Gouguenheim's critique of Fried and Landes, in which the author prioritised an 'everyday eschatology' in which 'imminence' played little part against predictive millenarian fears in AD 1000.[45] Yet it has to be recognised that belief in imminence was not exclusively millenarian, millenarian beliefs did not have to be attached to firm predictions about 'when' and the realities of 'everyday eschatology' would have left people confronting the certainty of their own mortality and Judgement even if the end of the world remained at some distance.

Personal eschatology is in many ways the body of thought which connects the individual to the universal, and thus stands apart from millenarianism's collectivity. As Carozzi stressed, between the fourth and ninth centuries liturgical cycles and penitential systems were developed which directly linked culpability, death and the eternal, emphasising a pastoral mood over a collective, apocalyptic one.[46] In both East and West, traditions flowered in which individuals reported back on the afterlife, the stories transmitted to remind people of what would happen to them after death on the basis of the life that they lived.[47] Such texts are themselves 'apocalyptic' in the sense that they are 'revelatory', and concern the route from Judgement to the hereafter. The difference between what would happen to an individual if they died the very next day, and what would happen to them if the world ended in a non-millenarian scenario, is quite

---

[44] C. Carozzi, *Apocalypse et salut dans le christianisme ancien et médiéval* (Paris, 1999), esp. p. 187.

[45] Gouguenheim, *Les fausses terreurs*, p. 56.

[46] Carozzi, *Apocalypse et salut*, pp. 62–7.

[47] Carozzi, *Le voyage de l'âme*; Baun, *Tales from Another Byzantium*; P. Brown, 'The Decline of the Empire of God: Amnesty, Penance, and the Afterlife from Late Antiquity to the Middle Ages', in C. W. Bynum and P. Freedman (eds.), *Last Things: Death and the Apocalypse in the Middle Ages* (Philadelphia, PA, 2000), pp. 41–59; the essays in P. Clarke and T. Claydon (eds.), *The Church, the Afterlife and the Fate of the Soul*, Studies in Church

minimal: they would be judged. Personal eschatologies and the urgency of apocalyptic anxiety in the Augustinian-Gregorian matrix complemented each other well because they focused on similar issues but from different directions. The interplay of these ideas requires as much attention as any assumed opposition in them.

Prophecy failure and expectation management

A central part of millenarian movements, but also a much wider issue, is how people deal with prophecy and any failure for prophecy to be realised. Mainstream medieval Christianity, as we saw above, was in no way insulated from the idea of prophecy because the Gospels themselves contained explicit statements about the future. Nevertheless, these were sufficiently vague as to resist predictive specificity, such as in Christ's statement on the Mount of Olives that 'nation shall rise against nation, and kingdom against kingdom, and there shall be famines and pestilence and earthquakes in diverse places' (Matt. 24.7). Which kingdoms and when? One would only know which instance of these factors combining was the definitive last one when it was occurring. Christian exegetes' interest in typological analysis of the Bible (see further below) helped to maintain a freshness of relevance, because prophecy could be redeployed to describe types of action in the world until it was finally fully realised. Such strategies of interpretation fed psychological imminence rather than defused it as they kept patterns of meaning and promise alive in the world. Prophecy could never fail – it could only be misunderstood.[48]

Before continuing we must address a point of ambiguity concerning the realisation of prophecy. The idea of 'realised eschatology' in the modern sense refers to the idea, first propounded by theologian C. H. Dodd in the 1930s, that the end prophesied by Christ was in fact fulfilled by his own ministry and, as a consequence, there was no end to time as such.[49] In discussions of early medieval apocalyptic thought, the term has been used differently to refer to the belief that prophecy was coming true in the unfolding of later history, especially through monastic order.[50] The

---

History 45 (Woodbridge, 2009); H. Foxhall Forbes, '*Diuiduntur in quattuor*: The Interim and Judgement in Anglo-Saxon England', *Journal of Theological Studies*, 61.2 (2010), 659–84.

[48] Useful framing for this thought can be found in R. Southern, 'Aspects of the European Tradition of Historical Writing: 3. History as Prophecy', *TRHS*, 5th series, 22 (1972), 159–80, although his separation of prophecy and apocalypse was too strong.

[49] C. H. Dodd, *The Parables of the Kingdom* (London, 1935), pp. 34–110 and his *The Interpretation of the Fourth Gospel* (Cambridge, 1953), pp. 165–6 and 446–7.

[50] D. Iogna-Prat, 'Le baptême du schéma des trois ordres fonctionnels. L'apport de l'école d'Auxerre dans la seconde moitié du IXe siècle', *Annales – économies, sociétés, civilisations,*

implication, at one level, is that apocalypticism was being defused by the application of typological or ecclesiological analysis of scripture to history itself. It is, however, by no means clear-cut that this was an anti-apocalyptic strategy in the same way that it was for Dodd, because the radical implication of Augustine's eschatology – at least as understood by writers such as Gregory the Great and Bede – was that there was both a typological patterning of meaning in history *and* an ending which could not be predicted on the basis of scripture. To put it another way: it is by no means explicit in the sources that beliefs in the 'realisation' of scripture and in apocalyptic imminence were mutually exclusive positions. Most people lived in the 'shadow of the end' while using the Bible to textualise the world around them, making the relationship between prophecy and text complicated.

If 'prediction' were difficult to establish on the basis of scripture, then it has serious implications for our understanding of the ways in which societies might deal with 'prophecy failure'. If the world was predicted to end in 1000 and it did not, or a new millennial kingdom was to be established which never materialised, how would people react? In their classic study of a UFO cult in the 1950s, Festinger, Riecken and Schachter formulated the idea of 'cognitive dissonance' in relation to crushed expectation (in the case of their subjects, that a flood would destroy the world on 21 December 1954).[51] Rather than accepting that beliefs had been proven false, people could be motivated to promote their ideas anew, and to find increased social support and thus affirmation of their beliefs (if, say, the world had been spared … for now). Subsequent studies have criticised the model of 'cognitive dissonance', however, not least because the beliefs of millenarian groups are generally too complex to accept simple disproval. Instead, as Melton and Tumminia have observed, groups undergo a process of 'adaptation, reaffirmation and reappraisal' in relation to their prophecies, using a range of interpretative strategies to address and explain the 'test' in ways which make sense of failure while preserving core beliefs.[52] 'Prophecy' could prove to be flexible, both as

41.1 (1986), 101–26, esp. p. 117. T. Head and R. Landes, 'Introduction', in T. Head and R. Landes (eds.), *The Peace of God: Social Violence and Religious Response Around the Year 1000* (Ithaca, NY, 1992), p. 12; G. Lobrichon, 'The Chiaroscuro of Heresy', in Head and Landes, *The Peace of God*, p. 98.

[51] L. Festinger, H. W. Riecken and S. Schachter, *When Prophecy Fails: A Social and Psychological Study of a Modern Group that Predicted the Destruction of the World* (London, 1964).

[52] J. G. Melton, 'Spiritualization and Reaffirmation: What Really Happens when Prophecy Fails', *American Studies*, 26 (1985), 17–29; D. Tumminia, 'How Prophecy Never Fails: Interpretative Reason in a Flying-Saucer Group', *Sociology of Religion*, 59.2 (1998), 157–70, and her *When Prophecy Never Fails: Myth and Reality in a Flying-Saucer Group* (Oxford, 2005).

groups moved forward in time beyond a prescribed date, and retrospect-ively as they revised the exact nature and implications of what they had previously believed.[53] In cases we will encounter in the present book, it will be clear that 'prophecy' was already so contested, and the basis for it so ambiguous, that even the dynamics of failure may have been flattened for the Middle Ages.[54]

One can perhaps say more about expectation management with regards to medieval prophecy than one can about cognitive dissonance. Richard Landes has led the way here with his sketch of how Church authorities sought a way of measuring time that could sidestep apocalyptic specula-tion.[55] This relied on the observation that there were efforts to recalculate time to postpone the arrival of the Year 6000, if only artificially – first when AMI (6000 = 500) was abandoned in the fourth century in favour of AMII (6000 = c. 799), and then when that was abandoned in the eighth century in favour of AMIII (6000 = AD 2048) or, for the first time, dating *anno Domini*. The net result for Landes was that people in the West did not have to confront the urgent apocalyptic implications of mainstream chronology head-on until 979–1033; while, for O'Leary, this showed how the End is always proclaimed in the context of communities who constantly have to 'reconceive and redefine [their] place in universal history in the face of the apparently endless extension of [their] earthly existence'.[56] There are problems with Landes's interpretation of the pat-tern, however, as factors divorced from apocalyptic speculation – Easter calculations, scholarly enquiry into chronology – tended to underpin the changes, and often they were far from comprehensively success-ful.[57] Nevertheless, the issue of how people dealt with future expecta-tions, apocalyptic or otherwise, remains an important area for further investigation.

A second model of expectation management proposed by Landes inadvertently highlights the need to pay more attention to the various strands of apocalyptic thought of the mainstream Church. The model essentially posits that the defining dynamic is between radical preachers

---

[53] S. O'Leary, 'When Prophecy Fails and When It Succeeds: Apocalyptic Prediction and the Re-entry into Ordinary Time', in A. I. Baumgarten (ed.), *Apocalyptic Time* (Leiden, 2000), pp. 341–62.

[54] Compare the 'waxing wave' diagram in Landes, *Heaven on Earth*, p. 53.

[55] Landes, 'Lest the Millennium Be Fulfilled'.

[56] O'Leary, *Arguing*, p. 50. Note that the situation in the East was markedly different: Magdalino, 'The History of the Future' and 'The Year 1000 in Byzantium'; Brandes, 'Anastasios ὁ Δίκορος' and 'Liudprand von Cremona'.

[57] J. T. Palmer, 'Calculating Time and the End of Time in the Carolingian World, c. 740–c. 820', *EHR*, 523 (2011), 1307–31; idem, 'The Ordering of Time', in Wieser *et al.*, *Abendländische Apokalyptik*, pp. 605–18.

who proclaim that the new morning is near (roosters) and the institutional hierarchy bent on silencing them (owls).[58] An element of danger is suggested, as the owls move to suppress the roosters so as to stop unrest, disappointment and a loss of authority. In part what this seeks to characterise is the way that millenarian apocalypticism in Cohn's formulation is rarely evident in the sources, assuming that it has been condemned through a consensus of silence.[59] Except, at best, this really is just about millenarianism again, because apocalypticism – the sense that the End is imminent – is scarcely suppressed in histories, letters, poems and art. There are three things in particular which complicate Landes's picture here: first, 'owls' are often rather noisy in the way that they combat unorthodox apocalyptic beliefs because they want people to hear and understand their arguments; second, many texts and ideas which were condemned or irregular were copied, preserved and generally archived for reference and study; and third, as indeed Landes allows, many owls were themselves deeply interested in apocalypticism. What we have, then, are two dynamics operating in parallel: a struggle for how to envisage the future, and a scholarly impulse to argue on the basis of catalogued knowledge.

Reason and irrationality

To complicate the picture further, it is necessary to take account of the role of reason in these competitive thought-worlds. Fried saw 'fear of the year 1000' as a tension between knowledge and ignorance ('Wissen und Nicht-Wissen'), which motivated people to dispel their anxiety through action (painting, preaching) and the application of reason. 'Reason', he argued, 'is given the task of conquering fear and sublimating it'.[60] This, as a statement, comes close to articulating the often-held assumption that apocalypticism is irrational if not just hysterical, and that its antithesis is therefore in knowledge and logic; yet this is not quite what Fried meant, or at least not in the way he developed his argument in his 2001 book, *Aufstieg aus dem Untergang*. Fried outlined two related processes at work: first, how anticipation of the End generated an anxiety which was

---

[58] First set out in R. Landes, 'Owls, Roosters, and Apocalyptic Time: A Historical Method for Reading a Refractory Documentation', *Union Seminary Quarterly Review*, 49 (1996), 165–85 and developed in Landes, *Heaven on Earth*, chs 2–3.

[59] Landes, 'Sur les traces du Millennium', p. 16 ('une conspiration du silence' – but in personal correspondence he affirms that it should be a 'consensus of silence' because he does not believe there were meetings behind closed doors and such).

[60] Fried, 'Endzeiterwartung', p. 472: 'Vernunft vermag die Angst zu bannen und zu sublimieren.'

a spur to action, and second, how the need to understand eschatology and combat mistaken beliefs about it required study of a broad range of disciplines covering matters of society, astronomy, logic and textual criticism.[61] This second dynamic of apocalyptic thought, Fried argued, was the primary motor behind the development of modern science precisely because of the imperative to comprehend God's word and world. Reason was not the antithesis of apocalyptic thought, but a mode of processing it effectively.

Again, we have an interpretation of the apocalyptic which exposes its discursive nature. One of Fried's key examples was the way in which St Augustine of Hippo dealt with apocalyptic anxieties and interpretations of apocalyptic scripture which he considered heretical, such as millenarianism.[62] Augustine's 'anti-apocalypticism' was developed and articulated, not as simple statements of dogma, but in a varied series of arguments with people whom he sought to persuade. This is an important point, often forgotten. Challenging heretics, pagans, and even friends, he needed to fight for each point, counter each objection, defend every interpretation, using letters, treatises and sermons. As a result, his ideas were transmitted enshrined as arguments and exhortations to strive to become more knowledgeable about relevant things, including false beliefs. It might be a mistake to assume that apocalyptic thought *always* drove learning, as it is often difficult to find even weak eschatological context in, say, computistical compendia, while, on other occasions, it is common to find apocalyptic speculation as a consequence rather than as a cause of developments in learning. Either way, the harmony of eschatological thinking with medieval scientific endeavour – something often thought preposterous – is now well attested through studies by Arno Borst, Bianca Kühnel and Immo Warntjes into Carolingian computistical compendia and related material.[63]

The power of Apocalypse

The last overarching consideration – but a central one – is how Apocalypse had any kind of efficacy in the early medieval world. The apocalyptic voice supposes authority and seeks to exert influence (remembering the insights of studies such as O'Leary's). 'Power' is, at its simplest, the

---

[61] Fried, *Aufstieg*, pp. 22–3 and 51–3.
[62] Ibid., pp. 47–51.
[63] A. Borst, *Die karolingische Kalenderreform*, MGH Schriften, 48 (Hanover, 1998), pp. 234–41 and 729–34; B. Kühnel, *The End of Time in the Order of Things* (Regensburg, 2003); I. Warntjes, 'A Newly Discovered Prologue of AD 699 to the Easter Table of Victorius of Aquitaine in an Unknown Sirmond Manuscript', *Peritia*, 21 (2010), 254–83.

capacity to make things happen and to make people behave in certain ways, be it in relation to kingship, law, military conflict or even the Last Judgement. It is not necessarily identical with the right to wield power because in so many instances those rights can be undermined by human weakness, subversion or competition between rival domains of power. Kings can lose authority; peasants can revolt; holy men and women can use charisma to fight secular politics. Strategies of legitimisation are therefore important to the ways in which influence over affairs is sought, although in many cases the ability to effect change in and of itself is legitimising. The three elements – real-world influence, the rights of power and strategies of legitimisation – and how they combine are crucial variables which can invite or be affected by the apocalyptic.

Let's begin by thinking about how this applies directly to the apocalyptic voice before turning to its realisation. As stated already, the central message of the apocalyptic and eschatological material that is the focus of this book is that change is necessary and sins must be accounted for before the End comes. Even where we might discern 'passive commentary' – a historian commenting darkly on events long past, for example – the acts of presentation and reflection involved in writing and reading encourage recognition of a gap in standards to be made good. The force of the argument, of course, comes from the authority of scripture, which can be cited to underpin interpretations of any situation or preferred course of action.[64] But even then, the application of scriptural authority relies upon the authority of interpretation, usually derived from education or divine inspiration, precisely because meaning is rarely transparent. Apocalyptic rhetoric can be invoked as a strategy of persuasion, but it is a course of action which must be accompanied by appeals to both the Word of God and the authority of human interpretation. None of this, of course, ensures the success of the rhetoric in achieving certain objectives, because the argument must be both understood and accepted by the audience. Communication must occur.

Sketched as above, there ought to be little about the apocalyptic voice which seems alien to the mechanics of pursuing power in the early Middle Ages. The power of persuasion is a natural complement and alternative to coercive forms of power.[65] Modern scholarship has placed great emphasis

---

[64] On authors and authority see M. Carruthers, *The Book of Memory: A Study of Memory in Medieval Culture* (2nd edn, Cambridge, 2008), pp. 236–7.

[65] On 'pastoral power' see P. Brown, *Through the Eye of a Needle: Wealth, the Fall of Rome, and the Making of Christianity, 350–550 AD* (Princeton, NJ, 2012), pp. 503–5. On more 'coercive' forms of power see T. N. Bisson, 'The "Feudal Revolution"', *P&P*, 142 (1994), 6–42; idem, *The Crisis of the Twelfth Century: Power, Lordship and the Origins of European Government* (Princeton, NJ, 2009). Bisson's original article sparked lively responses

on 'symbolic communication' in medieval politics, through which actors (kings, bishops, whoever) can seek to influence the attitudes of others by drawing on a shared repertoire of gestures and action.[66] A show of penitence by a king, as ably performed by Henry IV at Canossa in 1077 for the benefit of Pope Gregory VII, could force opponents to step back from a course of opposition triggered by past, unpopular actions.[67] It could be an attempt to control the conversation and direct the course of events, grounded in a particular understanding of part of Christian culture for which authority could be asserted, and realised publicly in a way which ensured communication. The case of political 'public' penance is resonant here because such penance drew on the same spectrum of corrective thought as the apocalyptic. And in a world of ritual 'textualised' by the Bible, as it surely was from *c*. 600, understanding of scripture had the power to shape public action, as Mayke de Jong has shown convincingly for the reign of Emperor Louis the Pious (d. 840).[68] Time and time again, as we shall see, Apocalypse informed part of the repertoire of early medieval politics.

And of course the power of Apocalypse went deep in society. In the opening example of Constantinople in 557, Agathias tells us of lawyers raising their standards, politicians shunning scandalous behaviour, people giving up the world for monastic orders and others giving gifts to churches or caring for the poor and the sick. This was a society mobilised, if only for a moment, to make a difference. Some of the consequences may have been far from negligible, too. The Church was wealthier, bolstered in numbers and being listened to, while the usual moral standards of society were suddenly questioned more fiercely by people who wanted to change.[69] It is hard to know how transformative these things were in the short term or beyond, but they at least highlight for a moment the potential for apocalyptic thought to open up shifts in wealth, resources and expectations.

---

from D. Barthélemy, T. Reuter, S. White and C. Wickham in *P&P*, 152 (1996) and 155 (1997).

[66] The starting point for such studies is G. Althoff, *Spielregeln der Politik im Mittelalter. Kommunikation in Frieden und Fehde* (Darmstadt, 1997) but see also P. Buc, *The Dangers of Ritual: Between Early Medieval Texts and Social Scientific Theory* (Princeton, NJ, 2001).

[67] T. Reuter, 'Contextualising Canossa: Excommunication, Penance, Surrender, Reconciliation', in J. Nelson (ed.), *Medieval Polities and Modern Mentalities* (Cambridge, 2006), pp. 147–66. See also C. Cubitt, 'The Politics of Remorse: Penance and Royal Piety in the Reign of Æthelred the Unready', *Historical Research*, 85.228 (2012), 179–92.

[68] M. de Jong, *The Penitential State: Authority and Atonement in the Age of Louis the Pious 814–840* (Cambridge, 2009).

[69] Magdalino, 'The History of the Future', p. 7, points out that it was in the year after the earthquake that Prokopios of Caesarea wrote his infamous political satire, *Anecdota*.

There were clear limits to the authority of Apocalypse in the period under consideration. The early Middle Ages witnessed little by the way of creative prophecy-making, and there was no figure to rival Hildegard of Bingen or Joachim of Fiore in the twelfth century with their divinely inspired interpretations of history, scripture or dreams. Authority came predominantly through textual authority and careful scholarly inquiry. Haimo of Auxerre's work built on that of Bede, which built on Primasius's, which built on Augustine's.[70] Apocalyptic thought was far from stagnant as ideas were processed through such chains – firstly, because the same idea resonated differently depending on context; and secondly, because the 'Augustinian-Gregorian matrix' represented a paradigm that had to be fleshed out, with concepts such as 'Antichrist' and 'purgation of sins' only sketchily defined early on. The development of the paradigm was, unsurprisingly, not controlled or predictable because of the ways in which ideas spread across vast distances. Even comparatively radical materials such as the sermon of Pseudo-Methodius gained authority because they were processed in the relatively controlled environments of monastic or cathedral libraries.

The corollary of this was that the paradigm's authority was in some sense 'unfalsifiable'. Prophecy was generally avoided except when used retrospectively to provide a diagnosis of recent events, which meant that few false predictions were made. Extending the accountability for sin into an elaborated penitential afterlife meant that no one would get away with their misdeeds, so preserving the authority of warnings. But most of all, the pursuit of typological and anagogical interpretations of the Bible, and the rejection of literalism, ensured that the unfolding of history was seen in terms of ahistorical themes at least as much as linear salvation history. No individual instance of invasion, persecution or a pseudo-prophet was enough in itself to 'fulfil' apocalyptic scripture because the meaning of the relevant passages would be repeated and memorialised through multiple instances. Only at the End, with the worst of all terrors and the reign of the Son of Perdition, Antichrist, would people be sure. In part, this may have served as a strategy to postpone the End indefinitely because it was possible for history to proceed without a sense of moral closure. But this also worked to maintain anxiety through uncertainty. If one could never really be sure whether ongoing trials and tribulations were the last ones or not, then the combination of tests and potential resonance could act as a potent force to stoke the fires of 'psychological imminence'.

---

[70] Matter, 'The Apocalypse'.

Overview

Already we have covered some significant ground. We have encountered a number of different schools of thought about the power of Apocalypse in the Middle Ages, and a number of different models and ideas which can be used to generate analysis. It is also evident, however, that there have been issues concerning acts of definition, methodology and selection of evidence which have led to a rather polarised debate. The purpose of this book, therefore, is to move things forward by providing a history of apocalyptic thought in the early Middle Ages which (a) embraces the variety, breadth and regional character of tradition, (b) seeks to contextualise the apocalyptic relative to other intellectual, social and political developments and (c) sketches the situational influence of Apocalypse on action and behaviour in whatever ways the source material suggests.

The history will unfold more or less in chronological order, with certain themes bracketing together material in each chapter. Chapters 1 and 2 explore how the traumatic shift from late Roman to the early post-Roman world defined what has been called 'the Augustinian-Gregorian matrix'. I start there rather than with Christ because this was the most crucial period for the repertoire of medieval apocalyptic ideas. Augustinian thought defeated 'literal' millenarianism, but left other issues concerning interpretation of invasion and time, particularly once Gregory the Great (and Gregory of Tours) had injected Augustine's thought with a greater sense of urgency. Chapter 3 examines the interplay between thought about 'personal eschatology' (purgation of sin, etc.) and thinking about calculating the End in the seventh and early eighth centuries, to show how non-millenarian apocalypticism continued to develop apace. A further non-Augustinian element is introduced in Chapter 4 in the shape of the sermon of Pseudo-Methodius (*c.* 690), which provided new ways of thinking about evil – this time the Saracens and Gog and Magog – and the role of empires in defeating it, notably with the last 'king of the Greeks or Romans'.

Chapters 5 to 7 explore a period of steady evolution in apocalyptic thought, but an evolution which was an integral part of radical and changing times. The fate of empires again features prominently. Chapter 5 focuses on the anomaly that was the Carolingian experiment, as Charlemagne's establishment of widespread unity of church and state threatened to surpass the fourth (and final) kingdom prophesied by Daniel. The challenge that any perceived Golden Age creates, however, is that everything thereafter announces decay. Chapters 6 and 7 chart the intensification of a politicised apocalyptic mood, founded on Carolingian dominance but then stoked by the failure of state action and Church reform to respond effectively to moral turpitude and invasions by Vikings and others. The consequences could be varied, embracing weakness and power. As we will see in Chapter 7, by *c.* 1000 this could mean repeated calls to reform in troubled England and ritualised displays of eschatologically inspired imperial authority in Ottonian Germany.

Chapter 7, in fact, aims to build on a number of observations from across the study to help move things beyond debate about whether or not people were afraid of the Year 1000. First, we have to accept that apocalypse is a varied and constantly changing cluster of thought-worlds which (unsurprisingly) affect individuals and societies in different ways. We will therefore take care to see what was 'new' in apocalyptic thought (Y1K, Sibylline traditions, heightened interest in Antichrist) and to see how these things affected situations in the Ottonian *Reich*, France and England differently. In the process, I hope we can also move beyond the simple equation of apocalyptic anxiety with social crisis which has sometimes affected debates on the 'Transformation of the Year 1000'. Because apocalypse was integral to the different Christian cultural matrices of the early Middle Ages, it played roles in crisis *and* in general expressions of piety *and* in efforts to articulate and exert power. From that perspective, this book argues, it is evident that apocalypse was not (just) about the imminence of the End, but very much about how one conceptualises and directs change in anticipation of the inevitable.

1   The end of civilisation (*c.* 380–*c.* 575)

Few periods defined medieval apocalypticism more than the waning of the Roman Empire in the West.[1] For that reason, we start here with the fourth century AD rather than with Christ himself.[2] The empire provided both a symbolic secular counterpoint to the Christian community, and a political body which it was prophesied had to fall before the End Times could begin. Sometimes the fate of the world already seemed inexorably bound to the successes and failures of the Roman world, and had for a long time, which meant that the profound crises which beset the Western Empire in the fourth and fifth centuries seemed to be of global importance. The migration and invasions of 'barbarian' groups, notably from the famous Gothic crossing of the Danube in 376 onwards, contributed to a destabilisation of political order and a cluster of anxieties about what it meant to be Roman and Christian. The cultural dissonance was pronounced. And when Rome itself was sacked in 410 by Alaric's Goths and in 455 by Genseric's Vandals, the cultural shock was muddied only a little by Alaric's and Genseric's adherence to a heretical form of Christianity and their pro-Roman ambitions. In the wake of such high drama, great patristic writers such as Augustine of Hippo and Jerome of Stridon began to set down strategies for understanding apocalyptic thought which responded to the changing worlds around them, while others saw nothing less than announcements of the approaching End

---

[1] For a useful guide to eschatology in this period see B. E. Daley, *The Hope of the Early Church: A Handbook of Patristic Eschatology* (Cambridge, 1991) and J. Flori, *L'Islam et la fin des temps. L'interprétation prophétique des invasions musulmanes dans la chrétienté médiévale* (Paris, 2007), pp. 65–108. There are many ways to understand the fall of Rome: B. Ward-Perkins, *The Fall of Rome and the End of Civilization* (Oxford, 2005) (it was terrible); P. Heather, *The Fall of the Roman Empire: A New History* (London, 2005) (the Huns did it); W. Goffart, *Barbarian Tides: The Migration Age and the Later Roman Empire* (Philadelphia, 2006) (it was relatively peaceful); G. Halsall, *Barbarian Migrations and the Roman West, 376–568* (Cambridge, 2007) (much was governed by internal fragmentation).

[2] For earlier interpretation of Apocalypse, see M. Himmelfarb, *The Apocalypse: A Brief History* (Chichester, 2010) and E. Pagels, *Revelations: Visions, Prophecy, and Politics in the Book of Revelation* (New York, 2012).

itself. These were, in the words of one observer, the prophesied 'perilous times' (*tempora periculosa* [2 Tim. 3.1]).[3]

The fall of Rome helped to establish questions in apocalyptic thought that would dominate debate across the early Middle Ages. How closely bound to the fate of the world were the successes or failures of empires and emperors? What did it mean in the scheme of things if outsiders ('barbarians', Jews) and inside enemies (heretics) were more successful than small-c catholic communities? Just who were 'Gog and Magog'? Did it matter that calamities occurred within sight of what many people considered to be the 6,000th year of the world? Could one predict when the End would come so readily? How did the souls of people who would not experience the End Times reach the Last Judgement? These were big, existential issues for Christians in the last days of the Western Roman Empire. And although it is often argued that Augustine's non-apocalyptic answers effectively satisfied everybody,[4] debate continued, with new circumstances and new ideas constantly challenging received wisdom.[5]

Trying to establish the place of apocalyptic thought within the fall of Rome is a daunting challenge in its own right. It takes us from abstract theology and anagogy to the ways in which people sought to change and reimagine the world – specifically in this chapter, from the eschatology of empire, to understandings of 'outsiders', the structure and meaning of time, and ultimately how one should approach the issue of 'Judgement'. Christians attended to these matters at the same time as they redefined many other aspects of their religion because, on the one hand, what counted as 'orthodoxy' was only slowly coalescing, while, on the other, the institutional Church was emerging as a major political player in the new social orderings of the day and it needed to adapt accordingly.[6] As Peter Brown has shown recently, these processes involved developing ideas of pastoral leadership and wealth management which directed

---

[3] Gildas, *De excidio et conquestu Britanniae*, c. 104, ed. T. Mommsen, MGH AA, 13 (Berlin, 1888), p. 81. For a good survey of apocalyptic mood in the period see T. E. Kitchen, 'Apocalyptic Perceptions of the Roman Empire in the Fifth Century', in V. Wieser, C. Zolles, C. Feik, M. Zolles and L. Schlöndorff (eds.), *Abendländische Apokalyptik. Kompendium zur Genealogie der Endzeit* (Berlin, 2013), pp. 641–60.

[4] S. Gouguenheim, *Les fausses terreurs de l'an mil* (Paris, 1999), pp. 67–8; C. Carozzi, *Apocalypse et salut dans le christianisme ancient et medieval* (Paris, 1999), pp. 56–8.

[5] R. Landes, 'Lest the Millennium be Fulfilled: Apocalyptic Expectations and the Pattern of Western Chronography, 100–800 CE', in W. Verbeke, D. Verhelst, and A. Welkenhuysen (eds.), *The Use and Abuse of Eschatology in the Middle Ages* (Leuven, 1988), pp. 137–211 at p. 158.

[6] A. Cain and N. Lenski (eds.), *The Power of Religion in Late Antiquity* (Aldershot, 2009).

social behaviour in new ways during a period of crisis.[7] The importance of
this can be drawn out further if the processes are seen to work alongside
those identified by Chris Wickham, which include the collapse in aristo-
cratic demand for luxury goods and a shift from the state's tax-exaction
towards local rent-extraction.[8] Likewise, we could bear in mind Guy
Halsall's analysis of the ways in which the experience of power became
more localised and experimental with the rise of pseudo-barbarian 'successor states'.[9] None of these processes need always implicate the others,
but they should at least be borne in mind together.

Let us draw out an early hypothesis to keep us focused: eschatological
thought during this period of great crisis and upheaval provided motivation and direction for positive human action. In all Christian theology –
even Augustine's – individual lives and human history were only ever
going to reach the same point, namely Judgement Day. Apocalyptic
thought helped many people to understand why history was unfolding
in the bloody way that it was, and it also gave them the spur to remember to reform themselves and the world around them in preparation for
Judgement. It explained and inspired. And it was a widespread part of
how Christians defined the new power of the Church in society more
generally. We might need to consider it as a mainstream issue with real
effects. What it was not, was the minority 'hysteria' some scholars have
assumed. We are not talking about a few uneducated and irrational
people, frenzied in the face of an ending they perceive but do not wish to
face, all turning to behave eccentrically. In what follows I do not claim
that apocalypse was *the* thing that defined the late Roman world. But its
impact, as we shall see, was far from ephemeral.

The eschatology of empire

We begin by considering how the Roman Empire gained Christian
eschatological dimensions. Early Christian writers, working under pagan
Roman domination, believed that the end of Rome would coincide with

---

[7] P. Brown, *Through the Eye of a Needle: Wealth, the Fall of Rome, and the Making of Christianity in the West, 350–550 AD* (Princeton, NJ, 2012). For background see his *The Rise of Western Christendom* (2nd edn, Oxford, 2003). See also R. A. Markus, *The End of Ancient Christianity* (Cambridge, 1990), esp. p. 217 where he emphasises the importance of diverting wealth to churches – a point now developed much further in I. Wood, 'Entrusting Western Europe to the Church, 400–750', *TRHS*, 6th series, 23 (2013), 37–73.

[8] C. Wickham, *Framing the Early Middle Ages: Europe and the Mediterranean, 400–800* (Oxford, 2005). A number of good responses were collected in *Journal of Agrarian Change*, 9.1 (2009).

[9] Halsall, *Barbarian Migrations.*

the end of the world to provide a clear sense of release from earthly persecution. Tertullian (fl. 200), one optimistic apocalyptic voice, justified saying prayers for the emperor on the grounds that it was only the empire which held back the end of all things.[10] A bleaker assessment, framed by the Diocletianic persecutions of Christians in *c.* 303–6, was offered by Lactantius, who argued that Rome was reaching its old age as an empire 'and what is left to follow old age but death?'[11] What is remarkable about Lactantius's work is how he brought non-Christian prophecies to bear on the matter, quoting the *Sibylline Oracles* and Hystaspes on Rome's inevitable demise in order to prove to his pagan detractors that Christianity was predicted by their prophets. New contexts generated variance. Nevertheless, the kind of account he gave of the End Times would become almost clichéd in its mixing of Old and New Testament themes: Rome's kingship would be split up, further division and fighting would occur, there would be earthquakes and terrible signs, and panic and a wailing and gnashing of teeth – but all, again, foreseen by the Sibyl as well as attested in scripture.[12] Lactantius, like Tertullian, did not wish the End to come quickly, but saw it as a terrible inevitability.

The future envisaged by Tertullian and Lactantius was complicated by the conversion of the Roman Empire to Christianity.[13] Legend held that Philip I 'the Arab' (244–9) was the first Christian emperor, but this seems unlikely and Christianity remained anyway a persecuted minority religion until the fourth century.[14] Then, in the space of a few short years, Christianity came into the mainstream following the battlefield conversion of Emperor Constantine (r. 306–38) in 312.[15] He encouraged others to convert, and quickly Christianity built up real political capital. Emperors followed Constantine's lead in being proactive about the promotion and defence of the religion, inspired by his leadership at the first ecumenical council, held in Nicaea in 325, and by his decision to found a new Christian capital at Byzanz, which he renamed Constantinople

[10] Tertullian, *Apologeticum*, 32. 1 and 39. 2, ed. E. Dekkers, CCSL, 1 (Turnhout, 1954), pp. 143 and 150. On Tertullian's millenarian apocalypticism see Daley, *The Hope*, pp. 34–7.
[11] Lactantius, *Divinae Institutiones*, VII. 15. 17, eds. E. Heck and A. Wlosok (Berlin, 2011), p. 700: 'quid restat nisi ut sequatur interitus senectutem'. See also VII. 15. 11, p. 698.
[12] Lactantius, *Divinae Institutiones*, VII. 16. 1–14, pp. 701–3.
[13] Brown, *The Rise of Western Christendom*, ch. 2; R. MacMullen, *Christianity and Paganism in the Fourth to Eighth Centuries* (New Haven, CT, 1997).
[14] Eusebius, *Historia ecclesiastica*, VI. 34, ed. E. Schwartz, Die Griechischen christlichen Schriftsteller der ersten drei Jahrhundert: Eusebius Werke, 2 (Leipzig, 1903), II. 588, 590 is the first reference to Philip's conversion.
[15] N. Lenski (ed.), *The Cambridge Companion to the Age of Constantine* (Cambridge, 2012), esp. the essays in Part II.

in 330. The empire which had seemed so at odds with Christianity now embraced it, and the fate of 'Church and State' proceeded, for a while at least, in partnership.[16] These were 'Christian times' and a cause for optimism.[17] And with that, the eschatology of empire had changed.

A pronounced consequence of these early developments was that Constantinople became the focus of a variety of prophecies and anxieties.[18] The now-lost 'Theodosian Sibyl' prophesied that the city would last only 60 years, and once that date (390) had passed the prediction was changed to 3 × 60 years in the *Oracle of Baalbek* (502–5) and 3 × 600 years in later recensions.[19] Yet it was perhaps the city's sense of pride, rather than its symbolic status, which dictated the threat as the Sibyl warned it not to boast. As Paul Magdalino has shown, Constantinople really came into its own once it could be seen as a 'New Jerusalem' after 500. Soon it seemed to surpass Jerusalem as the head of Christendom and it was even possible to imagine the Second Coming taking place in the Byzantine capital instead.[20] As Christianity spread outwards from the city, it also seemed that the apocalyptic missions to preach unto all corners of the world was being fulfilled (Matt. 24.14), which in turn drew further attention to the growing and singular importance of the city in unfolding apocalyptic drama in the world. Political power and cultural centrality changed the contours of the world so that a new city could take on a prophetic role.

Emperors themselves – often semi-religious imperial figures – were also becoming integrated into apocalyptic tradition. Hilary of Poitiers, for example, labelled the Arian Emperor Constantinius II (r. 334–61) 'Antichrist' for his persecution of Catholics.[21] Further 'apocalyptic'

---

[16] F. E. Cranz, '*De Civitate Dei*, XV, 2, and Augustine's Idea of the Christian Society', *Speculum*, 25.2 (1950), 215–25 at pp. 221–2.

[17] R. A. Markus, *Saeculum: History and Society in the Theology of St Augustine* (Cambridge, 1970), pp. 25–34.

[18] P. Magdalino, 'The History of the Future and Its Uses: Prophecy, Policy and Propaganda', in R. Beaton and C. Roueché (eds.), *The Making of Byzantine History. Studies Dedicated to Donald M. Nicol on His Seventieth Birthday* (Aldershot, 1993), pp. 3–34 esp. pp. 11–14. A. Berger, 'Das apokalyptische Konstantinopel. Topographisches in apokalyptischen Schriften der mittelbyzantinischen Zeit', in W. Brandes and F. Schmieder (eds.), *Endzeiten: Eschatologie in den monotheistischen Weltreligionen* (Berlin, 2008), pp. 135–57.

[19] *The Oracle of Baalbek*, ed. and trans. P. J. Alexander (Washington, DC, 1967), p. 25 (Greek p. 14), with discussion at pp. 41–2 and 54–5.

[20] Pseudo-Chrysostom, *Patrologia Graeca*, 61. 775–6, discussed in Magdalino, 'History of the Future', p. 12. Kosmas Indikopleustes, *Christian Topography*, II. 73–5, ed. and trans. W. Wolska-Conus, Sources chrétiennes, 141 (Paris, 1968), pp. 387–91.

[21] Hilary of Poitiers, *Contra Arianos*, c. 2 (PL, 10. 609–10); *De trinitate*, VI. 42 (PL, 10. 191); and especially the labelling of 'Constantius Antichristus' in *Contra Constantium imperatorem*, c. 5, PL, 10. 581.

imperial critique can be found in the *Oracle of Baalbek*, which gave a chilling portrayal of Emperor Anastasios (r. 491–518):

His name resembles the last day [*anastasis* = 'resurrection'] and begins with the eighteenth letter [sigma], but when he seizes his kingship, he will be called Anastasios. He is bald, handsome, his forehead (shines) like silver, he has a long right arm, he is noble, terrifying, high-souled and free and hates all the beggars. He will ruin many from among the people either lawfully or unlawfully and will depose those who observe godliness.[22]

There were other emperors prophesied to follow, yet these all belonged to a final 'ninth generation', leaving Anastasios as a clear symbol of the corruption of recent history giving way to the conflicts of the End Times. Such thinking paved the way for Prokopios's infamous private satire of Emperor Justinian (r. 527–65) as an antichrist-like Demon King – something doubly interesting, as Scott points out, for being a play on Justinian's own claims to a role leading society towards the Second Coming.[23] Apocalypse could be embraced for grandeur and to criticise. In doing so, however, Byzantine imperial apocalyptic ran directly against the de-eschatologising tendencies of writers in the West.

The Western tendencies in question had emerged only gradually in response to disenchantment about the power of the empire and its ability to represent those optimistic 'Christian Times'. There had been a long build-up of crises in the empire, with Gothic groups and then others crossing the Danube, sometimes settling, but sometimes upsetting the perceived status quo. There was a tangible sense of cultural dissonance, with the idea that social order was being upset and needed stabilising.[24] The quality of leadership offered to the Romans by the emperors had varied from Theodosius's force and vigour to his young son Honorius's lack of tact or engagement – a difference noted in the apocryphal *Revelation of Thomas* as an early sign of the coming Last Days.[25] The great turning

---

[22] *The Oracle of Baalbek*, pp. 27–8 (Greek, p. 9); W. Brandes, 'Anastasios ὁ Δίκορος. Endzeiterwartung und Kaiserkritik in Byzanz um 500 n.Chr.', *Byzantinische Zeitschrift*, 90 (1997), 24–63 at 53 and 57–60.

[23] Prokopios, *Anecdota*, 12. 14, ed. and trans. H. B. Dewing, Loeb Classical Library, 6 (Cambridge, MA, 1935), p. 148; 18. 1–4 and 36–7, pp. 210–12, 222–4. R. D. Scott, 'Malalas, *The Secret History*, and Justinian's Propaganda', *Dumbarton Oaks Papers*, 39 (1985), 99–109 at 108; Magdalino, 'History of the Future', pp. 7–8 ('[it] cannot be taken any more seriously than its scurrilous stories about Theodora's sex life'); Brandes, 'Anastasios ὁ Δίκορος', 43.

[24] J. T. Palmer, 'Apocalyptic Outsiders and Their Uses in the Early Medieval West', (forthcoming).

[25] A useful survey of events is provided in M. Kulikowski, *Rome's Gothic Wars: From the Third Century to Alaric* (Cambridge, 2007), ch. 8. For the prophecy see *Revelatio Thomae* (interpolated version), ed. F. Wilhelm, *Deutsche Legende und Legendare* (Leipzig, 1907),

point came in 410 when the Gothic leader Alaric, who had spent some time working as a mercenary against invaders, sought the title of *magister militum* ('master of the armies') and lands for his men from Honorius. After the emperor, hiding in the marshy retreats of Ravenna, had repeatedly refused to even discuss matters, Alaric led his men into Rome to seize its wealth with little resistance, and the 'barbarians' seemed to have made a mockery of a higher civilisation. One pagan, Rutilius, felt that Rome had been betrayed by the general Stilicho – who he also accused of burning the Sibylline books – but he also believed that it had the strength to rise again from its misfortunes.[26] As Rutilius and others began to blame weaknesses brought on by Christianity, Augustine began to formulate an epic response in the form of *On the City of God*.

Augustine had begun to lose faith in the optimism of 'Christian Times' well in advance of the sack of Rome, but such a concrete disaster focused his thoughts.[27] The resulting views expressed in *On the City of God* were fundamental to Latin apocalyptic thought on two fronts. Firstly, Augustine addressed an argument to pagans to the effect that pagan history was so full of catastrophes that events in 410 were not sufficiently unusual to suspect the vengeance of Jupiter.[28] By the same token, of course, this meant that Roman history was not Christian history – they had different courses which combined and separated at various points. Second, as a result of this, Augustine had to explain to Christian audiences what relevance the Roman Empire had in potential apocalyptic scenarios. Some people, for example, felt that St Paul had alluded to the collapse of the Roman Empire as a precursor to the arrival of Antichrist, and also that the empire embodied apocalyptic evil. Indeed, Augustine wrote, some people even believed that Emperor Nero would return because in his actions, persecuting Christians, he seemed to be an antichrist.[29] Such thinking, Augustine sighed, was absurd, and one ought to consider instead that Rome was just something that would step aside at the End (2 Thess. 2.7). In conclusions such as this, Augustine could

pp. 40*–42* at p. 41*: 'Subito exsurget rex prope suppremum tempus, amatur legis. Obtinebit imperium non multo duos filius relinquit. Primus per prima littera nuncupatur, secundus octavus. Primus ante secundum morietur.'

[26] Rutilius, *De reditu suo sive Iter Gallicum*, II, ed. E. Doblhofer (Heidelberg, 1972), pp. 138, 140.

[27] The essential starting point for studies here is Markus, *Saeculum*, esp. pp. 32–3 on his shift in attitude. See also P. Fredriksen, 'Apocalypse and Redemption in Early Christianity: From John of Patmos to Augustine of Hippo', *Vigiliae Christianae*, 45.2 (1991), 151–83 at pp. 165–6.

[28] The full argument is developed across Augustine, *De civitate Dei*, II–IV, eds. B. Dombart and A. Kalb, CCSL, 49 (Turnhout, 1955), pp. 34–127.

[29] Ibid., XX. 19, p. 732.

never quite escape the tendency in North African theology to draw clear distinctions between Church and state.[30] He was too impressed with the potential for the Church to be a force for good in the transitory politics of the world to see anything other than a complex 'mixed body' – but this did not mean that secular affairs were a good guide to the fate of the Church itself.

Augustine's political thought had important implications. The nature of the 'mixed body' meant that it was radically predisposed to action, because it could never be satisfied with itself.[31] The inherent tensions between spiritual ideals and pragmatic earthly action ensured that there was a perpetual drive to criticise and reform; the only state of perfection could come with Judgement Day and the removal of the corrupting sinfulness of human existence. This continual striving for perfection had other contributors, to be sure, but it was *On the City of God* which spoke most directly to future political leaders – most notably Charlemagne (d. 814) – about the need for continuous action in secular and religious affairs. We will see further below the apocalyptic dimension to this because, in attacking the impulse to predict the date of the End, Augustine opened up the similarly radical existential mode in which action was necessary because Judgement could come at any time. The only satisfactory end point and resolution for political action lay in its final conclusion.

People worried about the state of the empire regardless because of two prophetic passages in the Book of Daniel. Indeed, as Gerhard Podskalsky showed, these passages in Daniel formed the backbone of 'imperial eschatology' in the East, but it applies to the West too.[32] In the first part, Nabuchodonosor saw a statue made of four elements – gold, iron, bronze and clay – which Daniel interpreted as a succession of four kingdoms, the last of which would be given over to God (Dan. 2). The second dream was Daniel's own, in which he saw four terrible beasts come out of the sea; this again he interpreted as a succession of kingdoms (Dan. 7). Daniel identified the first as Nabuchodonosor's Babylon, but left the identity of the others necessarily open until St Jerome in 399 suggested that the second was Persia, the third Alexander's Macedonia, and fourth was the Roman Empire of his own day, weak and undone by civil war and the attacks of diverse barbarian peoples.[33] Paulus Orosius, Augustine's

---

[30] Markus, *Saeculum*, ch. 5; Fredriksen, 'Apocalypse and Redemption', pp. 155–60.

[31] Markus, *Saeculum*, pp. 168–73. See now also R. Corradini, 'Augustine's *eschaton*: Back to the Future', in Wieser *et al.*, *Abendländische Apokalyptik*, pp. 693–713.

[32] G. Podskalsky, *Byzantinische Reichseschatologie. Die Periodisierung der Weltgeschichte in den vier Grossreichen (Daniel 2 und 7) und dem tausendjährigen Friedensreihe (Apok. 20). Eine Motivgeschichtliche Untersuchung* (Munich, 1972).

[33] Jerome, *In Danielem*, I. ii. 31/35, ed. F. Glorius, CCSL, 75A (Turnhout, 1964), pp. 794–5; Daley, *The Hope*, pp. 101–2.

pupil, employed a similar scheme, but with Macedonia second, Carthage third and Rome fourth – and more importantly, he defined them by the four cardinal points rather than as a sequence, in order to soften Rome's eschatological significance.[34] Nevertheless, Orosius was one of the writers who was most important for putting forward a vision of Christian salvation history which was intimately entwined with Rome's, because Rome embraced and carried Christ's message.[35] In these two voices, Jerome's and Orosius's, a pessimistic and an optimistic view of recent history were set out.

The two voices can be best exemplified in relation to the sack of Rome. Here, Jerome was clearly the 'pessimist'. In his preface to his commentary on Ezekiel, he spoke of his anxiety – the way he flitted between hope and despair when he first heard the news whilst in Palestine, torturing himself as he considered the suffering of others, and how the Roman world had lost its head.[36] Antichrist, he was sure, was close.[37] But from this starting point he quickly began to mobilise the potential for disaster to highlight virtue and vice. In 412 he wrote to Principia in Rome, consoling her on the death of their friend Marcella during the sack.[38] Marcella, thought Jerome, had shown purity in dedicating her life to Christ, remaining unwed and promoting orthodoxy against the teachings of Jerome's friend-turned-enemy Rufinus. This purity clashed with standards in the city of Rome: 'a slander-loving community, filled as it formerly was with people from all parts and bearing the palm of wickednesses'.[39] In a letter to Gaudentius the following year, Jerome again contrasted the quest for perfection with the refusal of people to learn. 'Oh for shame,' he wrote, 'the whole world falls into ruin, but sins are not extinguished in us.'[40] Time was running short and Jerome had embraced a rhetoric to agitate for change.

As the 'optimist', Orosius was keen to downplay the singular importance of events. Although he described Rome besieged and in panic, he presented the Goths as generally respectful of Christian things – they were, after all, Christians themselves – even as they looted and sought

---

[34] Orosius, *Historiae adversus paganos*, II. 2. 2–4, ed. M.-P. Arnaud-Lindet (3 vols., Paris, 1990–1), I. 85–6. North was Macedonia, south Carthage, west Rome and east Babylon.

[35] Ibid., *Historiae*, VI. 1. 5–9, ed. Arnaud-Lindet, II. 163–4.

[36] Jerome, *In Hezechielem*, prol., ed. F. Glorie, CCSL, 75 (Turnhout, 1964), p. 3.

[37] Jerome, *Epistola*, no. 123. 15, ed. I. Hilberg, CSEL, 56. 2 (Vienna, 1996), p. 91.

[38] Jerome, *Epistola*, no. 127, pp. 145–56.

[39] Ibid., 127. 3, p. 147: 'in maledica civitate, et in urbe, in qua orbis quondam populus fuit, palmaque vitiorum.'

[40] Jerome, *Epistola*, no. 128. 5, p. 161: 'Pro nefas, orbis terrarum ruit et in nobis peccata non corruunt.'

gold and silver. His 'defence' of what happened rested on two things: first, that there had been no devastation on the scale of the fires in Rome in Caesar's time or Nero's, and second, not much had actually happened. Indeed, on this second point, Orosius wrote (perhaps with a touch of irony):

Although this deed is of recent memory, if anyone were to see the great numbers of Rome's population and listen to them, he would think, as they themselves say, that 'nothing had happened' ... unless he were to learn of it by chance from the few ruins which still remain from the fire![41]

The 'truth', as Orosius stressed as he came to the conclusion of his work, was that many terrible things had happened in history, but that they had all come to an end one way or another. This was unsurprisingly comforting for communities under siege for a long time to come, such as when Alfred the Great faced Viking attacks in the late ninth century.[42] But Orosius was not ambivalent about the End. On the contrary, he was quite clear that there would be unprecedented tribulation at the end of time when Antichrist came.[43] He just had not yet come.

Not all analysis of West Rome's fall was apocalyptic, but fall it did. With some hindsight Marcellinus Comes (d. 536), writing a Latin chronicle in Constantinople, noted that the 'Western kingdom' (*regnum Hesperium*) had essentially ended with the death of Aetius, the effective *magister militum*, in 454.[44] Peter Heather summarised what was happening as follows: 'the idea of Empire quickly became meaningless, since the centre no longer controlled anything that anyone wanted.'[45] Still, numerous 'barbarian' leaders treated with the Eastern emperors, with Odoacer and Theoderic of the Goths in Italy, and Clovis I of the Franks, each gaining honour and legitimisation as a result. Even when the daily reality of empire had started to fade in the West, the persistence of the Eastern entity and the allure of the ideal affected politics. The fall of Rome *in the imagination* was a long time coming.

[41] Orosius, *Historiae*, VII. 40. 1, ed. Arnaud-Lindet, III. 117: 'cuius rei quamuis recens memoria sit, tamen si quis ipsius populi Romani et multitudinem videat et vocem audiat, "nihil factum", sicut etiam ipsi fatentur, arbitrabitur; nisi aliquantis adhuc exsistentibus ex incdendio ruinis forte doceatur.'
[42] *The Old English Orosius*, ed. J. Bately, Early English Text Society Supplementary Series, 6 (Oxford, 1979).
[43] Orosius, *Historiae*, pref, 15–16 (ed. Arnaud-Lindet, I. 9); VII, 27. 15–16 (III. 74).
[44] Marcellinus Comes, *Chronicon*, ed. T. Mommsen, MGH AA, 11, p. 86. On the text see B. Croke, *Count Marcellinus and His Chronicle* (Oxford, 2001). Compare also the gloomy assessment of the state of the *respublica* in the Gallic Chronicle of 452, c. 138, ed. Mommsen, MGH AA, 9, p. 662.
[45] P. Heather, *The Goths* (Oxford, 1996), p. 189.

The apocalyptic Other vs the Roman Empire

The role of the pseudo-barbarians themselves in all this played to further aspects of apocalyptic thought. Had Christ not said that nation would rise against nation and kingdom against kingdom in the Last Days (Matt. 24.7; Mark 13.8; Luke 21.10)? And in Revelation did it not say that the peoples of Gog and Magog would accompany Satan in the last persecution (Rev. 20.7)? Outsiders had deep resonance, even if many had arrived a generation earlier as settlers rather than as invaders. Many saw the successes of Goths, Huns and others against the Romans as signs of punishment for sin, and the lines between that kind of 'Old Testament' thought and 'New Testament' apocalypse were hazy. To confuse matters further, many pseudo-barbarians actively became more Roman. In the middle of the fifth century, Gallo-Roman Sidonius Apollinaris wrote to his Frankish friend Arbogast saying that, although the law of the Romans faltered on the frontiers, the eloquence and style of its language were preserved by the Frank: 'Drinker of the Moselle, you belch the Tiber.'[46] Non-Romans could disrupt, but they could also create, the harmony and continuity people craved. The realities of increasingly localised power structures and identities meant that the clear distinction between Roman 'us' and barbarian 'them' was unsustainable. And from that point, the definition of apocalyptic outsiders was going to change too.

In apocalyptic terms, the complexity of West Rome's mutations unsurprisingly generated no single response. One can find examples of 'us-and-them' anxiety – one need look no further than the gloomy fifth-century chronicle of Hydatius of Lemica in north-west Spain, who narrated the Gothic and Suebian conquest of the Iberian peninsula up to 469. Amongst the terse descriptions of battles and betrayals, he established a portentous mood by referring to things such as the fulfilment of a prophecy of Daniel's in King Ataulf's marriage to Galla Placidia in 414, and to 'signs and prodigies' after a hard year for crops in 469.[47] He

---

[46] Sidonius Apollinaris, *Epistulae*, IV. 17, ed. C. Luetjohann, MGH AA, 8 (Berlin, 1887), p. 68: 'potor Mosellae Tiberim ructas'. On Sidonius: J. Harries, *Sidonius Apollinaris and the Fall of Rome, AD 407–485* (Oxford, 1994).

[47] Hydatius, *Chronicon*, ed. and trans. R. W. Burgess (Oxford, 1993), pp. 84 and 122. S. Muhlberger, *The Fifth-Century Chronicles: Prosper, Hydatius, and the Gallic Chronicler of 452* (Leeds, 1990), pp. 175–85; R. W. Burgess, 'From Gallia Romana to Gallia Gothica: The View from Spain', in J. Drinkwater and H. Elton (eds.), *Fifth-Century Gaul: A Crisis of Identity* (Cambridge, 1992), pp. 19–27; L. A. García Moreno, 'Expectatives milenaristas y escatolólgicas en la España tardoantigua (ss. V–VIII)', in *Spania. Estudis d'Antiguitat Tardana oferts en homenatge al professor Pere de Palol I Salellas* (Barcelona, 1996), pp. 103–9 at pp. 104–5; Kitchen, 'Apocalyptic Perceptions', pp. 649–53.

may also have expected the end of the world in 482.[48] But who was to say that the 'barbarians' were necessarily the 'enemy' in this process? Avitus of Vienne, early in the sixth century, saw no less trauma in the world: 'it is predicted in the Gospel about the end of the world: "nation shall rise against nation and kingdom against kingdom" – from these very signs of evil let us understand that the virtual end of the world is upon us.'[49] Yet in that case, he was actually writing to a 'barbarian' king, Gundobad of the Burgundians (d. 516), in response to a query from the king about how to interpret a passage from Micah. And even though he was worried here about the threat of heresy in the world – as a Catholic writing to an Arian – apocalyptic anxiety hardly dominated his mood.[50] Different circumstances and different people changed the logic of interpreting any non-Roman presence.

Apocalyptic rhetoric which urged reform in the face of crisis still had a clear role to play. Salvian of Marseilles, writing in the 440s, was at pains to argue that God was not indifferent to human affairs and was indeed judging Christians through events such as the invasions.[51] His *On the Governance of God* served as a lengthy polemic, designed to provoke reflection and correction in the face of tangible political struggle and excessive taxation policies. As such, the target was Christian morality, not the demonisation of the Other per se. Christian Romans shared many flaws with barbarians, such as greed, lewdness and infidelity, and often they could be worse even though – and perhaps because – they knew that they were inherently better than the Franks, Goths and Huns.[52] Similar themes abound in Gildas's *On the Ruin and Conquest of Britain*, written a generation or so later as the author retired from public life to live in a monastery. Britain had fallen into the hands of the Picts and Saxons, he argued, again because of the sins of the people and the poor and

---

[48] Burgess, *Hydatius*, pp. 31–3 draws attention to a marginal note in Berlin, Staatsbibliothek, Phillipps 1829, which shows that Hydatius knew a *Revelatio Thomae* which prophesied the end of the world nine jubilees after the Passion. This text is not identical with any extant *Revelatio Thomae* (see n. 25). See also Burgess's 'Hydatius and the Final Frontier: The Fall of the Roman Empire and the End of the World', in R. Mathiesen and H. Sivan (eds.), *Shifting Frontiers in Late Antiquity* (Aldershot, 1996), pp. 321–32.

[49] Avitus, *Epistula*, no. 22, ed. R. Peiper, MGH AA, 6. 2 (Berlin, 1883), pp. 54–5: 'nam in evangelio de fine saeculi praedictur: Exurgent gens contra gentem et regnum contra regnum, et ex ipsis matorum indiciis imminere iam paene mundi terminum colligamus' (D. Shanzer and I. N. Wood, *Avitus of Vienne: Letters and Selected Prose* (Liverpool, 2002), pp. 202–3).

[50] Compare, for instance, the discussion of heresy in Avitus, *Epistula*, no. 7, pp. 35–40.

[51] M. Maas, 'Ethnicity, Orthodoxy and Community in Salvian of Marseilles', in Drinkwater and Elton (eds.), *Fifth-Century Gaul*, pp. 275–84.

[52] Salvian, *De gubernatione Dei*, ed. C. Halm, MGH AA, 1. 1 (Berlin, 1877), esp. IV. 14, pp. 49–50.

disunited leadership provided by kings.[53] Notably, Gildas sought prophetic voices: not his own, but those from the Old Testament, such as
Isaiah, Jeremiah and Ezekiel, who foretold of the ills that would befall the
sinful.[54] Neither Salvian nor Gildas preached about the end of the world
in these texts, but their key 'revelation' was that Christians were being
punished by barbarians for their sins. Institutions and communities had
grown old and rotten. Judgement was being made. People needed to act
and to correct their behaviour and to improve.

   The works of Salvian and Gildas represented only one rhetorical strategy when it came to dealing with cultural dissonance. Quodvultdeus of
Carthage, a pupil of Augustine, wrote homilies in which he also addressed
his anger at the Vandalic raiders who tore through North Africa from 429
onwards, driving him into exile in Italy.[55] Such dislocation and related
signs, the bishop feared, might have been indicative of the coming of
Antichrist. The Goths may have been Gog and Magog from Revelation.[56]
But he did not repeat these ideas in his homilies, when addressing his flock
rather than his intellectual peers. There could be apocalyptic urgency,
for instance when he announced in *On the Cataclysm* that 'the day of
our redemption is close'.[57] In his eyes, however, the people responsible
for destruction, rape and torment were heretics and pagans (the Vandals
were Arian Christians); and Jewish communities were not blameless
either. His sermons addressed his enemies directly in the second person, calling out their doctrinal errors and encouraging them to correct
themselves. He added familiar laments about standards of Christian living, particularly surrounding the raucous behaviour at circuses.[58] The
important thing throughout is that, just because there are enemies in
what might be the Last Times, these peoples were not portrayed in the
homilies as quite so integral to apocalyptic drama as they were in the

---

[53] Gildas, *De excidio et conquestu*, cc. 21–2, pp. 36–8.

[54] Analysis of Jeremiah's influence on Gildas in K. George, *Gildas's 'De excidio Britonum'
and the Early British Church*, Studies in Celtic History, 26 (Woodbridge, 2009), pp. 20–5
and 29–47.

[55] Quodvultdeus, *Liber promissionum: Dimidium temporis*, vi. 8–12, ed. R. Braun, CCSL, 60
(Turnhout, 1976), pp. 195–8. For background: A. H. Merrills and R. Miles, *The Vandals*
(Chichester, 2010).

[56] Quodvultdeus, *Liber promissionum.*, xiii. 22, p. 207 – despite also quoting at iv. 6, p. 193
Augustine's non-historical interpretation of Gog and Magog, on which see below;
Landes, 'Lest the Millennium', p. 158, quoted approvingly in Markus, *The End*, p. 215.
D. van Slyke, *Quodvultdeus of Carthage: The Apocalyptic Theology of a Roman African in
Exile* (Strathfield, NSW, 2003), pp. 128–9 and 284.

[57] Quodvultdeus, *De cataclysmo*, i. 1, ed. Braun, p. 409: 'in proximo est dies redemptionis
nostrae'.

[58] On the circus: Quodvultdeus, *De tempore barbarico I*, ed. Braun, i. 11–19 p. 424. See also
Salvian, *De gubernatione Dei*, VI. 15. 85, p. 81.

Book of Promises, in which Quodvultdeus outlined those signs of the End. But how could a pupil of Augustine see the fulfilment of scripture in history? We need to step back to look at the development of the idea of Gog and Magog in more detail.

Legends about the peoples of Gog and Magog certainly lay at the heart of apocalyptic understandings of the Other. In Revelation, it was said that Satan would seduce the peoples once he had been released from his thousand-year bonds, and Gog and Magog would go into battle from the four corners of the world (20.7). In West and East this was thought to pick up on the prophecy from Ezekiel (38–9), in which Gog *of* the lands of Magog would lead his people against Israel from the North on account of its sins – itself a prophecy adapted in Jeremiah that 'from the North evil shall break forth upon all the inhabitants of the land' (Jer. 1.14; cf. Eze. 38.17).[59] The literal text establishes three themes: a people sent to scourge the lacklustre faithful, a geographical space from which they come (the North) and the reforming prophetic mode which warns that people will be punished for their sins if they do not correct themselves. Gog and Magog were damned peoples, yes, but they were also an instrument of God's wrath. It is precisely this mode of thought which framed the providential rhetoric of Salvian, Quodvultdeus and Gildas, even if they stopped short of pushing it too far in public.

Exegetical traditions naturally focused upon typological interpretations of Gog and Magog and Augustine's discussion of Revelation in *On the City of God* was again influential. The names, he argued, were not to be understood as referring to barbarians, neither to 'Getae' nor 'Massagetae' – i.e. the Goths – 'nor some other foreigners separated from Roman law'.[60] He offered etymologies which explained that Gog came from 'a roof' (*tectum*) and Magog from 'from a roof' (*de tecto*) or 'being revealed' (*detecto*), drawing on interpretations provided by Jerome in his book on Hebrew names (389–91) and commentary on Ezekiel (410–14).[61] The symbolic significance of the roof came from the association with Satan's imprisonment, as Augustine goes on to explain that they concealed him and that their assaults would represent the shift

[59] On the East see Brandes, "Anastasios ὁ Δίκορος", 24, and explicitly Ecumenius, *Commentary on Apocalypse*, 11th Discourse, p. 92 and Andrew of Caesarea, *Commentary on Apocalypse*, c. 63, p. 192.

[60] Augustine, *De civitate Dei*, XX.11, p. 720: 'siue aliquos alios alienigenas et a Romano iure seiunctos.'

[61] Jerome, *In Hezechielem*, XI. 38 ed. F. Glorie, CCSL, 75 (Turnhout, 1964), pp. 526–7; *Liber de nominibus Hebraicis*, ed. P. de Lagarde, CCSL, 72 (Turnhout, 1964), p. 68 (Gen), p. 131 (Eze.) and p. 160 (Rev.). Jerome also offers the Greek δῶμα (doma) as an interpretation and 'de domate' as a closer Latin equivalent.

from concealed to open hatred.[62] Moreover, this would not be a narrow moment of history, but the persecution of the Church as a whole, which is represented in Revelation here as 'the camp of the saints and the Beloved City'.[63] Quodvultdeus had read all of this – indeed even quoted it – but chose to reject it in the light of the evils of his own day.[64]

Earlier commentators discussed the North more squarely in relation to Ezekiel, with its relevance only consistently extended to interpretations of Revelation from the eighth century onwards (Chapter 4). The work of Jerome was seminal, not least for discussing and dismissing the Judaic identification of Gog and Magog with the Scythians, over the Caucasus and the Caspian Sea – although this view still circulated widely in the Latin Josephus.[65] Jerome's sense of urgency in addressing Ezekiel is revealed in a letter to Marcellinus and Anapsychia, in which he explains that his work was affected by, and then developed in response to, the sack of Rome in 410.[66] Like Augustine, he felt a clear need to challenge any effort to relate prophecy to recent history in a literal, historical manner. Interest in the genealogy of peoples meant that the association between Gog and Magog and the Scythians – and from them, the Goths – was preserved in interpretations of the Book of Generations in various forms, from Eucharius's *Instructions to Salonius* to Bede's *On Genesis*.[67]

The perceived relationship between Gog and Magog and historical, migrating peoples opened up a spectrum of interpretation rather than a strictly apocalyptic one. At one end Jordanes, a Goth in Constantinople, wrote in 550 to celebrate Emperor Justinian's peace with the Goths after over twenty years of war; in that context, however, his only use of 'Magog' was a passing reference to Josephus's history.[68] In the middle, Isidore of Seville wrote his *History of the Goths* (c. 624) for King Suintila, drawing attention to Ezekiel's prophecy but defusing it by actively celebrating how the Goths, even if Gog and Magog, were worthy to have taken over

---

[62] Augustine, *De civitate Dei*, XX. 11, pp. 720–1: 'et de tecto ipsae erunt, quando in apertum odium de operto erupturae sunt.'

[63] ibid., p. 721. Primasius, *Commentarius in apocalypsin*, V. 20, ed. A. W. Adams, CCSL, 92 (Turnhout, 1985), p. 279.

[64] van Slyke, *Quodvultdeus*, p. 284; Landes, 'Lest the Millennium', p. 158.

[65] Jerome, *In Hezechielem*, XI. 38, p. 525. This is also mentioned in Jerome, *In Esaiam*, XI, 27/29, ed. M. Adriaen, CCSL, 73 (Turnhout, 1963), p. 399. *The Latin Josephus*, I. 6. 1, ed. F. Blatt, Humanistik Serie 44 (Copenhagen, 1958), I. 139.

[66] Jerome, *Epistola*, 126. 2, p. 144.

[67] Eucharius, *Instructionum ad Salonium*, II. 221–2, ed. C. Mandolfo, CCSL, 66 (Turnhout, 2004), p. 199; Bede, *In Genesim*, III. 20, ed. C. W. Jones, CCSL, 118A (Turnhout, 1967), p. 142 (on Gen. 10.2).

[68] Jordanes, *Getica*, IV. 29, ed. T. Mommsen, MGH AA, 5. 1 (Berlin, 1882), p. 61. W. Goffart, *The Narrators of Barbarian History AD 550–800: Jordanes, Gregory of Tours, Bede and Paul the Deacon* (Princeton, NJ, 1988), ch. 1.

the dignity of Roman rule in Spain.[69] Political circumstance was neutralising the force of apocalyptic interpretations. Only in the East, for now, did people continue to report the historical appearance of an apocalyptic Gog and Magog, but in response to the presence of the Huns and Avars rather than the Goths.[70] Context was king.

Following Jerome, the real relevance of Gog and Magog as apocalyptic outsiders for the West lay in how they symbolised heretics – the 'secret' enemies within. As interpretations of scripture emphasised the allegorical over the literal, the struggles foretold in Revelation came to stand for the struggles of the Church at large, with heresy to the fore. There was, to be sure, no shortage of perceived heresies in this period, most prominently millenarianism (on which more shortly), Donatism in North Africa, the Arianism followed by most of the 'barbarian' groups except the Franks, and the 'Three Chapters' controversy started by Justinian.[71] And by the grandest of coincidences, each of these struggles led to the production of one of the earliest commentaries on Revelation: Jerome reworked Victorinus's millenarian commentary to make it more orthodox;[72] the rebel Donatist Tyconius wrote one of the most influential treatises on the subject;[73] Apringus of Beja and Caesarius of Arles (d. 542) each composed Catholic commentaries which dwelt on their persecution by Arians;[74] and Primasius of Hadrumentum (d. 565), author of a sixth commentary, was a prominent figure in the Three Chapters

---

[69] Isidore, *Historia Gothorum,Vandalorum et Suevorum*, cc. 1–2 (*De orgine Gothorum*), ed. C. Rodríguez Alonso (Léon, 1975), pp. 172–4; Palmer, 'Apocalyptic Outsiders'.

[70] Theodoret, *Historia ecclesiastica*,V. 36. 4, ed. L. Parmentier, Die griechischen christlichen Schriftsteller der Ersten Jahrhunderte, 4. 4 (2nd edn, Leipzig, 1954), p. 339; Andrew of Caesarea, *On Revelation*, c. 63, trans. W. C. Weinrich, *Greek Commentaries on Revelation* (Downers Grove, IL, 2001), p. 191.

[71] On the Donatists see B. Shaw, *Sacred Violence: African Christians and Sectarian Hatred in the Age of Augustine* (Cambridge, 2011). On Arianism there are many studies – e.g. M. R. Barnes and D. H. Williams (eds.), *Arianism after Arius* (Edinburgh, 1993) – but a new history is promised by Yitzhak Hen. On the Three Chapters see P. T. R. Gray, 'The Legacy of Chalcedon: Christological Problems and their Significance', in M. Maas (ed.), *The Cambridge Companion to the Age of Justinian* (Cambridge, 2005), pp. 215–38.

[72] Jerome, *Commentarius in Apocalypsin*, ed. J. Haussleiter, CSEL, 49 (Vienna and Leipzig, 1916); E. A. Matter, 'The Apocalypse in Early Medieval Exegesis', in R. Emmerson and B. McGinn (eds.), *The Apocalypse in the Middle Ages* (Ithaca, NY, 1992), pp. 38–41.

[73] Tyconius Afer, *Expositio Apocalypseos*, ed. R. Gryson, CCSL, 107A (Turnhout, 2011). The full text is lost and is reconstructed by Gryson on the basis of fragments and borrowings. See also K. B. Steinhauser, *The Apocalypse Commentary of Tyconius: A History of Its Reception and Influence* (Frankfurt-am-Main, 1987).

[74] Apringus, *Tractatus in Apocalypsin*, ed. R. Gryson, CCSL, 107 (Turnhout, 2003), pp. 33–97 (comments on Rev. 5.8–18.5 largely taken from Jerome's commentary); Caesarius of Arles, *Expositio de Apocalypsi sancti Iohannis*, ed. G. Morin, *Sancti Caesarii episcopi Arelatensis Opera Omnia*, 2 (Maredsous, 1942), pp. 209–77 with the attribution defended in G. Morin, 'Le commentaire homilétique de S. Césare sur l'Apocalypse', *Revue bénédictine*, 45 (1933), 43–61.

debate in Constantinople.[75] In this context, the ecclesiological interpretation of Revelation seems to be a little bit more than the anti-apocalyptic enterprise it has sometimes been portrayed as: it was a direct response to heresy itself and the struggles of the Church.[76]

Any effort to explain the internal logic of each text would quickly become rather repetitive given their similar conclusions so, given that their presence will be felt throughout much of the rest of this study, I will pick just Caesarius's to illustrate some key points because he is the best-documented figure in his struggles.[77] Caesarius's text is also both representative and not, because it follows Tyconius's interpretations closely but nominally casts his text as 'homilies' – that is to say that, if they were not for preaching to Caesarius's flock directly, they were to provide ammunition for preaching.[78] Any distinction between monastic exegesis and public discourse is hazy here and probably always was. Caesarius set out the two main positions at the beginning: that there were exegetes who thought Revelation described Judgement and the coming of Antichrist, but that the more diligent had recognised that much had been fulfilled in Christ's Passion and that therefore the Church would be in a continuous struggle until the End.[79] From that start point, earthquakes (Rev. 11.13) became a symbol of persecution, the tail of the dragon (Rev. 12.4) a sign for heretics, and the beast from the sea (Rev. 13.1–4) representative of the power of the Arians over the Catholics.[80] Non-Tyconian criticism of multiple baptisms is prominent, which is redolent of attacks on Arianism.[81] Caesarius attacked heretics in his writings in other ways too, which encourages us to see his treatment of Revelation as one part of his repertoire for dealing with conflict in the world.

The problem with apocalyptic outsiders was that focus on combating heretics could only be part of the story. Christ had told his disciples that 'this gospel of the kingdom shall be preached in the whole world, for a testimony to all nations: and then shall the consummation come' (Matt.

[75] Primasius, *Commentarius in Apocalypsin*. His presence at Constantinople is recorded in Victor of Tunnona, *Chronica*, ed. Mommsen, MGH AA, 11, p. 202, and he was the dedicatee of Junillus's *Instituta*, ed. and trans. M. Maas, in his *Exegesis and Empire in the Early Byzantine Mediterranean* (Tübingen, 2003).
[76] On the ecclesiological interpretation of Revelation see Matter, 'Exegesis'.
[77] W. Klingshirn, *Caesarius of Arles: The Making of a Christian Community in Late Antique Gaul* (Cambridge, 1994).
[78] A. Ferreiro, '*Frequenter legere*: The Propagation of Literacy, Education, and Divine Wisdom in Caesarius of Arles', *Journal of Ecclesiastical History*, 43.1 (1992), 5–15.
[79] Caesarius, *Expositio*, pref., p. 210 (found in C only).
[80] Ibid., IX, p. 240 and p. 242; X, p. 243. Compare the *falsi fratres* of Tyconius Afer, *Expositio Apocalypseos*, IV. 11, p. 176 and IV. 29, p. 182.
[81] Caesarius, *Expositio*, VI, p. 230; IX, p. 242. Compare XVIIII, p. 277 and Caesarius, *Breviarium adversus Haereticos*, ed. Morin, pp. 207–8.

24.14). The idea of universal mission to all peoples was slow to catch on in the Roman world, yet the conversion of pagans was an important landmark on the way to the coming End. In 398 Jerome thought that no one in the world, seriously, was ignorant of the name of Christ, so he believed that aspect of things was nearly complete.[82] Caesarius, just over a century later, seems to have subscribed to such a view when he said that heretics afflicted the Church where once it had been pagans who had done so.[83] On the other hand, when Hesychius expressed similar thoughts to Augustine, the bishop of Hippo wrote back that, on the contrary, there was still much work to be done in spreading the Gospel. It was one of many reasons why Augustine thought that the End could not really be as near as some people feared. Even so, while there were heretics in the world, any imperative to tackle the pagans beyond the imperial frontiers lacked bite. Eschatological missionary work would be left to later generations.

Millenarianism, AD 500, and the first 'crisis of the Year 6000'

Quietly, in the background, ran a different kind of apocalyptic anxiety. There were many mystical references to numbers and durations of time in scripture, and since the very first century of Christianity a number of writers had sought to use them to predict the end of time. One tradition, first evidenced by the critical *Letter of Barnabas*, added the Psalmist's association of thousands and days (Ps. 84.10; Ps. 90.4) to the six days of creation from Genesis to suggest that the world would endure for 6,000 years.[84] Two different traditions emerged over what would happen next: either, according to millenarians, there would be an earthly kingdom ruled by Christ and his saints or, according to mainstream Patristic thought, earthly things would be brought to a close. There were problems with both views because any speculation about timing clashed with warnings in scripture that the end of time was unknowable to anyone but God (Matt. 24.36; Mark 17.32; Acts 1.7). At the same time the use of linear reckonings of time was far from ubiquitous compared to the use

---

[82] Jerome, *Commentariorum in Mathaeum libri iv*, eds. D. Hurst and M. Adriaen, CCSL, 77 (Turnhout, 1969), p. 225.

[83] Caesarius, *Expositio*, X, p. 245. The statement is all the more intriguing because Caesarius criticised what seem to have been pagan practices carried over into his own day too: R. A. Markus, 'From Caesarius of Arles to Boniface: Christianity and Paganism in Gaul', in J. Fontaine and J. N. Hillgarth (eds.), *Le septième siècle, changements et continuités* (London, 1992), pp. 154–72.

[84] *Epistle of Barnabas*, 15. 4a–5a, ed. R. A. Kraft, trans. P. Prigent, Sources chrétiennes, 172 (Paris, 1971), p. 185; Landes, 'Lest the Millennium Be Fulfilled', pp. 141–3.

of AD-dating later in the Middle Ages – documents were dated according to the calendar, the fifteen-year tax cycle (called indictions), and/or in relation to the years of public officials, kings or emperors. There is little to suggest that most people were confronting repeated reminders that the clock was ticking towards that Year 6000. Nevertheless, it had its place, and often a prominent one, in the development of historical forms and chronological inquiry – and the first widely accepted date for the completion of six millennia was not far away, in 500.

The origins of attaching the date of the Incarnation to *circa* 5500 – to some projecting a potential end date into the middle of the first millennium – has two parts, one exegetical and the other chronological. Early in the third century, Hippolytus of Rome in his *On Daniel* argued that we could be certain that Christ had been born in AM 5500 because the dimensions of the tabernacle combined equalled 5½. At the same time, Hippolytus argued that one had to get from AM 5500 to 6000 'before the Sabbath' and the Judgement foretold by John, thus becoming one of the first Christian writers to deny an imminent Parousia.[85] From around the same time there was a Greek work of chronology by Julius Africanus, although this is alas now lost to us except through excerpts and fragments in a variety of different languages.[86] Africanus arrived at his conclusion drawing, he claimed, on a Jewish tradition which proposed 5,500 years from the Creation to the salvation of the world.[87] This number was then used as the central point around which a world chronology could be generated, synchronising information from biblical and profane histories.[88] Other justifications were tried. In the Latin West, the fourth-century 'Cologne Prologue' divided the duration of the world (6,000 years) into twelve hours, so that Christ's Incarnation in AM 5500 coincided with the last hour.[89] The author also adopted a brief chronological table, weakly paralleling the more detailed and popular *Book of Generations* – copied for centuries more – which affirmed the same date.[90]

[85] Hippolytus, *In Danielem*, IV. 23, ed. and trans. M. Lefèvre, Sources chrétiennes, 14 (Paris, 1947), pp. 308–10. See Landes, 'Lest the Millennium Be Fulfilled', p. 147.

[86] For a recent reconstruction: Julius Africanus, *Chronographia: The Extant Fragments*, ed. M. Wallraff, U. Roberto and K. Pinggéra, and trans. W. A. Adler (Berlin, 2007).

[87] Synkellos, *Ecloga chronographica*, c. 18, trans. W. Adler and P. Tuffin (Oxford, 2002), p. 24; A. Mosshammer, *The Easter Computus and the Origins of the Christian Era* (Oxford, 2008), p. 387.

[88] See the detailed account by Mosshammer, *The Easter Computus*, pp. 387–421.

[89] Cologne Prologue (= *Supputatio Romana*), c. 5, ed. B. Krusch, *Studien zur christlich-mittelalterlichen Chronologie. Der 84-Jährige Ostercyclus und seine Quellen* (Leipzig, 1880), p. 232.

[90] *Supputatio Romana*, c. 2, pp. 227–8; *Liber generationis II*, c. 334, ed. Mommsen, MGH AA, 9, p. 131. One important adaptation of the *Liber generationis* worth noting is its use in the Fredegar Chronicles: ed. B. Krusch, MGH SRM, 2 (Hanover, 1888), p. 40.

The authority of the tradition in the West remained murky: only one Western text, the mid-sixth-century *Paschale Campanum* from Vivarium, mentioned Africanus in relation to it, and indeed elsewhere his name was bracketed instead with the alternative reckoning of Eusebius-Jerome preferred in Vivarium.[91] Only in Byzantine circles did Africanus's reckoning or its variants enjoy prolonged use and authoritative status.

Millenarian hopes, meanwhile, were far more controversial.[92] Millenarians focused on a literal interpretation of Rev. 20.4 ('they lived and reigned with Christ for a thousand years'), which they could then associate with the seventh day of the Cosmic Week. An early millenarianism based on this had been taught by Papias of Hierapolis and Iranaeus of Lyon in the second century, and both believed that the binding of Antichrist would inaugurate Christ's earthly kingdom.[93] The 'seventh day' was to be real. Such views were later condemned by allegorists Origen of Alexandria (d. 253/4) and his pupil Dionysius (d. 265), who also had their own immediate millenarian opponent in Nepos of Arsinoe. But still millenarian beliefs were expounded by Lactantius and especially by the more moderate Victorinus of Pettau, whose work in general Jerome admired even if he felt compelled to rewrite his *Commentary on Revelation* to expunge its literalism and echoes of Papias and Nepos.[94] In the East, too, Ecumenios warned against the heresy early in the sixth century.[95] Having had a much contested history, literal millenarianism fell silent, but it remained part of the cultural baggage of early Christianity in the sense that it was something that many Church Fathers had explicitly argued against, and therefore their thoughts on the matter were transmitted throughout the Middle Ages.

[91] *Paschale Campanum*, ed. Mommsen, MGH AA, 9, p. 745. On the provenance see F. Troncarelli, 'Il consolato dell'Anticristo', *Studi Medievali*, 3rd series, 30.2 (1989), 567–92 at 569–80. Anastasius Bibliotecarius cited the calculation in the ninth century on the basis of George Synkellos and Nikephoros (*Chronographia tripertita*, ed. C. de Boor (Leipzig, 1885), ii. 41 and 61–2). For an eighth-century example of someone associating Julius Africanus with the Eusebian reckoning, see London, British Library, Cotton Nero A ii, 35v.

[92] J. Lössl, '"Apocalypse? No." – The Power of Millennialism and Its Transformation in Late Antique Christianity', in Cain and Lenski (eds.), *The Power of Religion*, pp. 31–44.

[93] Iranaeus, *Adversus Haereses*, V. 33. 2–4 and 35. 1–2, eds. A. Rousseau, L. Doutreleau C. Mercier, Sources chrétiennes, 153 (Paris, 1969), pp. 409–20 and 436–53.

[94] Victorinus, *Commentarius in Apocalypsin*, ed. Haussleiter, CSEL, 49. See also Jerome, *De viris illustribus*, c. 74, ed. E. C. Richardson, Texte und Untersuchungen zur Geschichte der altchristlichen Literatur, 14. 1 (Leipzig, 1896), p. 44. M. Dulaey, 'Jérôme, Victorin de Poetovio et le millénarisme', in Y.-M. Duval (ed.), *Jérôme entre l'occident et l'orient* (Paris, 1988), pp. 83–98, esp. pp. 95–8. Lössl, '"Apocalypse? No."', pp. 40–3.

[95] Ecumenius, 11th discourse, trans. Weinrich, p. 86. On Ecumenius as a Severian Monophysite see J. C. Lamoreaux, 'The Provenance of Ecumenius' Commentary on the Apocalypse', *Vigiliae Christianae*, 52.1 (1998), 88–108, esp. pp. 104–5 on the stance against Chialism.

With these points in mind we can begin to gauge the importance of the first 'fear of the Year 6000' around 500. The best evidence comes from North Africa, which Paula Fredriksen called 'the "bible belt" of the Mediterranean', and where existed a fundamentalism which embraced millenarianism.[96] In 397, the bishop Quintus Julius Hilarianus composed a short treaty on salvation history, in which he argued that the world would end 101 years after the time of writing with the completion of 6,000 years and the defeat of Satan and the Second Coming.[97] There would then be a thousand-year reign of the saints before one final battle. As with Hippolytus, the placing of the end of time at some distance meant that Hilarianus's treaty reads less like a comment on the instability of his own times and more like a statement about hope for life eternal in the future.[98] This sense of eternity was prefigured in the cyclical nature of the lunar calendar, and Hilarianus also composed a sermon on the keeping of the 'True Easter', emphasising the importance of liturgical regularity for salvation. Hilarianus was not just expressing anxiety about time, but using it to stir changes of practice. Nevertheless, he stands as an important figure because the reaction of his contemporaries to millenarian beliefs ensured that Hilarianus was one of the last vocal proponents of the heresy.

The North African assault on millenarianism hinged on scriptural interpretation. Tyconius, himself a non-orthodox figure on account of his Donatist beliefs, devised a strategy of biblical exegesis which prioritised typologies of meaning over literal readings of scripture.[99] As a result, the Cosmic Week symbolised a meaning about time, rather than a quantification. The number 1,000 signified perfection, but not a thousand years, and so it was really a 'part' standing for the 'whole'.[100] The strategy was embraced most enthusiastically by Augustine although, as Vercruysse has stressed, he used it to allegorise more than Tyconius would have done.[101] Regardless, inspired, Augustine set about challenging the millenarians

---

[96] Fredriksen, 'Apocalypse and Redemption', p. 157.

[97] Quintus Julius Hilarianus, *Libellus de mundi duratione*, cc. 17–18, PL, 13.1105–6; Daley, *The Hope*, p. 127.

[98] Quintus Julius Hilarianus, *Libellus de mundi duratione*, c. 19, 1106.

[99] Tyconius, *Liber regularum*, ed. F. C. Burkitt (Cambridge, 1894), with useful discussion in the translation by J.-M. Vercruysse, *Tyconius. Le livre des règles*, Sources chrétiennes, 488 (Paris, 2004). In addition to n. 73, see P. Fredriksen, 'Tyconius and the End of the World," *Revue des études augustiniennes*, 28 (1982), 59–75; eadem, 'Apocalypse and Redemption in Early Christianity: From John of Patmos to Augustine of Hippo', *Vigiliae Christianae*, 45.2 (1991), pp. 151–83; eadem, 'Tyconius and Augustine on the Apocalypse', in R. Emmerson and B. McGinn (eds.), *The Apocalypse in the Middle Ages* (Ithaca, NY, 1993), pp. 20–37; Daley, *The Hope*, pp. 127–31.

[100] Tyconius, *Expositio Apocalypseos*, VII. 15 and 20, pp. 218, 220.

[101] Vercruysse, *Tyconius*, pp. 387–9.

of the North African churches – of which he was once one – and pour-
ing scorn on those who claimed that one could calculate the date of
the End.[102] Augustine preferred to think of the 'Kingdom of Heaven'
(regnum caelorum) being inaugurated by the First Coming, and enduring
until its time was full as suggested by the reference to 1,000 (a line of
thinking ambiguous enough not to rule out an apocalyptic Y1K for some
readers).[103] In a separate passage, he argued the calculation of duration
was pointless because it was a divine mystery, citing Acts 1.7.[104] Here, in
part, Augustine was keen to draw attention to the embarrassing pagan
prophecy that Christianity would endure for only 365 years, which, if
taken from Christ's ministry, had already passed in 398 without incident
(perhaps providing a context for Hilarianus). Failed prophecy was being
condemned as guesswork.

Augustine's greater legacy here was to provide a new shape for history
which underscored a separation of chronology and eschatology: the six
world ages. Some Christians, it seems, believed that the 6,000 years of
the world was made up of six equal blocks of 1,000. Augustine, however, put it to them that history was really divided into six ages which
ran from Creation to the Flood (1), to Abraham (2), to David (3), to the
Babylonian captivity (4), to the birth of Christ (5), and then the rest of
history (6).[105] As none of the first five periods contained the same number of years as each other, the logic went, the significance of 6,000 years
was an illusion. Augustine muddied the water rather by explaining that
each age contained fourteen generations, but no one that we know of
attempted to calculate the length of generations until Joachim of Fiore in
the twelfth century. In the meantime, what happened was that Augustine's
model of history was taken up enthusiastically from the seventh century
onwards (see Chapter 3), ensuring that all history after the Incarnation
was explicitly set out as part of the last worldly age before the Sabbath
one could not predict. Augustinian historiography was written within the
shadow of the End.

[102] Augustine, De Genesi contra Manichaeos, I. 23. 35, ed. D. Weber, CSEL, 91 (Vienna,
1998), p. 104; De civitate Dei, XX. 7, p. 709: 'nam etiam nos hoc opinati fuimus
aliquando.'
[103] Augustine, De civitate Dei, XX. 9, p. 715; Daley, The Hope, p. 134. J. Fried, 'Die Endzeit
fest im Griff des Positivismus. Zur Auseinandersetzung mit Sylvain Gouguenheim',
Historische Zeitschrift, 275 (2002), 281–321 at p. 311.
[104] Augustine, De civitate Dei, XVIII. 53, pp. 652–3; Daley, The Hope, p. 135.
[105] Augustine, De civitate Dei, XXII. 30, pp. 865–6. See R. Schmidt, 'Aetates mundi. Die
Weltalter als Gliederungsprinzip der Geschichte', Zeitschrift für Kirchengeschichte, 67
(1956), 288–317. On the influence of the model see A.-D. von den Brincken, Studien
zur lateinischen Weltchronistik bis in das Zeitalter Ottos von Freising (Düsseldorf, 1957) and
J. T. Palmer, 'The Ordering of Time', in Wieser et al., Abendländische Apokalyptik, pp.
605–18 esp. at pp. 610–11.

What was less clear was whether it was possible to defuse speculation, as Landes has suggested, by suddenly abandoning the world age of
Hippolytus and Africanus for a lower one.[106] With 200 years left before
500, Bishop Eusebius of Caesarea recalibrated Christian history with
profane history in a series of parallel columns; with these, he pointed out
errors in Julius Africanus's calculations and redated the incarnation to
AM 5199/5200.[107] Eusebius did not intend to be too dogmatic about this
because he was not convinced historical time could be perfectly reconstructed before Abraham.[108] Eusebius was, however, another staunch
anti-millenarian and may well have sought to replace the tidy structures
of Africanus's history with something deliberately less orderly, something
which again spoke less readily of divine plans.[109] There were constraints.
Eusebius still had to work with the raw data of his columns and their
sources, which gave meat for his critics. Key to Eusebius's chronology
was moving the dates of Moses so that he became a contemporary of
Kekrops I, the founder of Athens, seizing on mistakes Africanus had
made in his synchronisation.[110] But, as George Synkellos wrote in the
early ninth century, even Eusebius contradicted himself here, as he had
assured his readers that Moses pre-dated the Trojan Wars and even the
gods, who clearly preceded Kekrops.[111] The critics played on Eusebius's
slips, and explored alternative synchronisations based on source criticism, even ultimately to defend (with significant caveats) Africanus's
original conclusions; the East was never swayed and instead entered a
seventh millennium of history. Never, perhaps tellingly, was Eusebius
attacked for undermining apocalyptic tradition by his enemies – because
he had not necessarily done so.[112]

---

[106] Landes, 'Lest the Millennium Be Fulfilled'; idem, 'Sur les traces du Millennium: la "via
negativa"', *Le Moyen Âge*, 99 (1993), 5–26 at pp. 7–9.

[107] On Eusebius's work see B. Croke, 'The Origins of the Christian World Chronicle', in
B. Croke and A. M. Emmett (eds.), *History and Historians of Late Antiquity* (Sydney,
1983), pp. 116–31, A. Mosshammer, *The Chronicle of Eusebius and Greek Chronographic
Tradition* (Lewisburg, PA, 1979) and R. W. Burgess, *Studies in Eusebian and Post-Eusebian
Chronography* (Stuttgart, 1999).

[108] Eusebius (-Jerome), *Canones*, pref., ed. R. Helm, Die Griechischen christlichen
Schriftsteller der ersten drei Jahrhunderte: Eusebius Werke, 7 (Berlin, 1956), pp.
10–12.

[109] Eusebius, *Historia ecclesiastica*, III. 28. 1–6 (I. 256–9) and IV. 14 (I. 332–5). The edition
contains a parallel edition of Rufinus's Latin translation, ed. T. Mommsen. Eusebius'
anti-millenarianism is highlighted in Podskalsky, *Byzantinische Reischseschatologie*,
pp. 82–3

[110] Eusebius, *Canones*, pref., pp. 10–12; pp. 40–1.

[111] Ibid., pref., p. 8–10; quoted at length and then dismissed in Synkellos, *Ecloga chronographica*, cc. 73–4, pp. 73–5.

[112] An important comparison can be made here with Bede: see Chapter 3, p. 95 and p. 99.

In the West, reactions to the passing of AM 6000 were muted.[113] Eschatological concerns can be found in sermons, treatises and histories from the fifth century in Europe, but they are rarely directly connected with the date. Sulpicius Severus (d. *c*. 425), for example, made numerous references to the imminence of the End, foreshadowed by the great evil in the world and the belief of his mentor, St Martin, in the proximity of Antichrist.[114] Closer to the year itself, on the other hand, there are a couple of historical notes in the *Paschale Campanum* of Vivarium which hint at adherents to Eusebian-Hieronymian chronology despairing at the more panicked followers of Africanus (indeed it is the only Latin source accurately to cite the two authorities side by side).[115] In 493, as Theoderic entered Ravenna, it was said that 'ignorant and reckless fellows said that Antichrist was about to be born', and then again in 496 'others deliriously said that Antichrist was about to be born' – both predicting, in effect, that Antichrist would come into his own sometime around 523–30.[116] The use of the future tense ('was about to be') in close proximity to 500 may hint at some genuine significance projected onto the date, even if the owlish author was unimpressed. It was certainly an unsettling time, and the chronicler mentions King Hunneric's persecution of Catholics in North Africa (for which Victor of Vita had called the king the 'beast [of the Apocalypse]'), the elevation of Anastasios I as emperor, Symmachus's synod of 502, an eclipse, and two eruptions of Mount Vesuvius (in 505 and 512).[117] Amidst political upheaval and signs in the natural world, the approach and passing of the year 500 alone was scarcely necessary to generate apocalyptic speculation. Nonetheless, some worried, some did not.

---

[113] Compare the response in the West to the East, esp. the overview of Brandes, 'Anastasios ὁ Δίκορος'.

[114] Sulpicius Severus, *Vita Martini*, 24. 1, ed. J. Fontaine, Sources chrétiennes, 133 (Paris, 1967), p. 306; *Chronica*, ed. G. de Senneville- Grave, Sources chrétiennes, 441 (Paris, 1999); II. 7. 3 Dan. (p. 238); II. 28. 1 persecution (p. 288); II. 33. 1 (pp. 300–2). See now V. Wieser, 'Die Weltchronik des Sulpicius Severus. Fragmente einer Sprache der Endzeit im ausgehenden 4. Jahrhundert', in Wieser *et al.*, *Abendländische Apokalyptik*, pp. 661–92.

[115] *Paschale Campanum*, ed. T. Mommsen, MGH AA, 9, p. 745.

[116] *Paschale Campanum*, pp. 746–7: 'ignari praesumptores ferunt Antechristum nasciturum' and 'alii delirantes ... dicunt Antecristum nasciturum'. See Troncarelli, 'Il consolato dell'Anticristo', pp. 585–92.

[117] Victor of Vita, *Historia persecutionis Africanae provinciae*, III. 21, ed. C. Halm, MGH AA, 3. 1 (Berlin, 1878), p. 45. Compare also the description of Hunneric's predecessor, King Genseric of the Vandals, in an interpolation to Jerome's edition of Victorinus, *Commentarius*, p. 127, which also affected the *Liber genealogus*, ed. Mommsen, MGH AA, 9, pp. 194–5, on which see Kitchen, 'Apocalyptic Perceptions', pp. 653–4.

A key difference between East and West now lay in their divergent chronological traditions because, thanks to Jerome, most of the Latin world followed Eusebius's reckoning in the fifth century. As Gregory of Tours (d. 594) noted, not only did Jerome's translation circulate, but its chronology was also taken up in the history of Orosius and the technical prologue to the Easter table of Victorius of Aquitaine (457).[118] Prosper of Aquitaine's (d. *c.* 455) epitome of Jerome – itself laced with principled Augustinian optimism – also became a vehicle for the reckoning, although inadvertently so as Prosper stripped away the multiple parallel columns of dating material and preferred to date events in Christian history to the year *ab anno passionis*, from the year of the Passion (= AD 28).[119] The oldest manuscript of Prosper's work, the same sixth-century Vivarium product which contained the *Paschale Campanum*, hinted at what was to come as the compiler brought more chronological material together to mark out the precise order of history running up to the present. The epitome chronicle became the foundation stone of a new historiography – the first link in 'chains of chronicles', which various anonymous historians and a few named individuals such as Victor of Tunnona (d. *c.* 570) could update, often with a final note on what the Eusebian year AM then was.[120] Pursued like this, chronography became something of a unified and ongoing project across the Latin-speaking world, with all participants happy to follow a different reckoning than was common in the East. Worrying about the approach of AM 6000 was for later generations (see Chapter 3).

Here, as Mischa Meier has observed, was one way in which Byzantine and Latin apocalyptic traditions parted ways with subtle but far-reaching results.[121] Quite simply, the logic of apocalyptic signs 'in time' functioned differently in the two broad culture zones. When Nicetius of Trier wrote to Emperor Justinian around 565, announcing that the end of the world was approaching, they were effectively in different time zones, with the West in a sixth millennium of world history and the East just starting out in a seventh because they had not changed chronological systems.

[118] Gregory of Tours, *Historiae*, I. pref., ed. B. Krusch and W. Levison, MGH SRM, 1.1 (Hanover, 1951), p. 5. Orosius, *Historiae adversus paganos*, I. 1. 5 (i. 10) and VII. 43. 19 (iii. 131, 133); Victorius of Aquitaine, prol., c. 7, ed. Krusch, Studien II, pp. 22–3. Victorius equates AP 430 (= AD 457) with AM 4658.

[119] Prosper, *Epistoma chronicon*, c. 386, ed. Mommsen, p. 409, gives the year AM of Christ's Passion as 5228, then begins a new running calculation after the Passion in c. 391, p. 410. On Prosper: A. Y. Hwang, *Intrepid Lover of Perfect Grace: The Life and Thought of Prosper of Aquitaine* (Washington, DC, 2009).

[120] Victor of Tunnona, *Chronica*, ed. Mommsen, MGH AA, 11, p. 206 (= AM 5766); John of Biclarum, *Chronica*, ed. Mommsen, MGH AA, 11, p. 220 (= AM 5791).

[121] Meier, 'Eschatologie und Kommunikation', pp. 50–2.

The resonance of Nicetius's words may consequently have been lost on Justinian, because acute expectation of the End had died away considerably in comparison to the West.[122] This would, of course, still be to prioritise a 'predictive' understanding of apocalypticism, which did little to constrain hopes or fears in the face of earthquakes, plague or invasion.

The coming Judgement

Our fourth necessary strand concerns the 'eschatology' of Judgement. Nobody was going to avoid being judged, whether they lived to see the Last Days or not. Death – itself scarcely predictable – simply meant that someone exited history to join up with things again later with the resurrection of the body. But exactly whether and how one's soul could be purified after death were very much up for debate. Modern historians sometimes argue that concern for such matters is somehow antithetical to apocalypticism because it is more 'everyday' and focuses on the individual soul rather than collective destruction. And yet, in practice, both 'eschatology' and 'apocalypse' were and remain expressly interested in how people get from their lived lives to the final evaluation of their efforts. A preacher reminding his audience of the need to correct sins in the face of 'the coming Judgement' worked with the same language of damnation and imminence as one might who spoke of the end of the world. At the same time there was an important aspect of *revelatio* in play, because people did have 'visions of the afterlife' just as they had 'visions of the End'. These vividly reminded people of the fate of their souls on death, and so underscored moral lessons through apocalypse. Apocalypse and eschatology were part of the spectrum of correction.

One of the most famous texts here was the *Vision of St Paul*, an apocryphal apocalyptic tour of hell which was likely composed in Greek *c.* 400 and translated with some changes into Latin by the end of the fifth century.[123] The extent of the text's influence is not everywhere so readily apparent: Carozzi, Moreira and others have been able to see its stamp on much late antique and early medieval thinking on the afterlife,[124] although the early Latin manuscript tradition is also remarkably

---

[122] Ibid., p. 69.

[123] C. Carozzi, *Eschatologie et au-delà. Recherches sur l'Apocalypse de Paul* (Aix-en-Provence, 1994); J. Bremmer, 'Christian Hell: From the *Apocalypse of Peter* to the *Apocalypse of Paul*', *Numen*, 56.2–3 (2009), 298–325 at 307. Various developments of the text are unravelled in L. Jiroušková, *Die Visio Pauli: Wege und Wandlungen einer orientalischen Apokryphe im lateinischen Mittelalter* (Leiden, 2006).

[124] C. Carozzi, *Le voyage de l'âme dans l'Au-delà, d'après la littérature latine (Ve–XIIIe siècle)* (Rome, 1994); I. Moreira, *Heaven's Purge: Purgatory in Late Antiquity* (Oxford, 2010), p. 52.

thin and its apocryphal status was well defined in the fifth century.[125] The images seen by Paul were deliberately shocking and encouraged those who read or heard them to reflect back on their behaviour. At one point, to give an example, Paul saw men and women suspended by their eyebrows and hair for joining with prostitutes, and then more on an obelisk of fire, torn at by beasts, for defiling the image of God through fornication.[126] Through such examples, which emphasised real and excruciating torture of the body as punishment, people were encouraged to repent of their sins before they lost the opportunity to do so in life.[127] Moreover, to achieve the desired effect, the descriptions of punishment resonated with cultures of law and punitive action one might actually encounter in the late antique world.[128] With the Last Judgement, however, the final verdict was to be one experienced eternally.

Eternal punishment was a powerful corrective threat, but it was hard for most people to live a life that was unambiguously pure. Indeed, it seems from Augustine's *Enchiridion for Laurentius*, written in 420, that many Christians were prepared to believe in a more merciful God who would eventually end sufferings.[129] Yet sins which were not repented remained a problem. From a pastoral perspective, the best strategy was to warn people of the terrors of Judgement in order to drive them to penitence, as the 'Eusebius Gallicanus' sermons illustrate repeatedly.[130] Augustine, followed by fellow North African Julianus Pomerius, argued nevertheless that the fate of the souls of the 'not-very-good' and 'not-very-bad' could be influenced by intercessionary prayer (although there was no fully developed model of Purgatory as a place yet).[131] Once Judgement had been made,

---

[125] *Decretum Gelasianum*, V. 5, ed. E. von Dobschütz (Leipzig, 1912), p. 53.

[126] *Visio Pauli* (L¹), c. 40, ed. M. R. James, *Apocrypha Anecdota* (Cambridge, 1893), pp. 32–3 (Paris version); ed. T. Silverstein, *Visio sancti Pauli* (London, 1935), p. 143 (St Gall version).

[127] Repeatedly *Visio Pauli* (L¹), c. 6–10, pp. 12–14 with the loss of time to repent emphasised in c. 16, p. 18 ('tu autem perdidisti tempus ponitenciae').

[128] Carozzi, *Le voyage*; Moreira, *Heaven's Purge*, pp. 51–2.

[129] P. Brown, 'The Decline of the Empire of God: Amnesty, Penance, and the Afterlife from Late Antiquity to the Middle Ages', in C. W. Bynum and P. Freedman (eds.), *Last Things: Death and the Apocalypse in the Middle Ages* (Philadelphia, PA, 2000), pp. 41–59 at pp. 40–6.

[130] L. Bailey, *Christianity's Quiet Success: The Eusebius Gallicanus Sermon Collection and the Power of the Church in Late Antique Gaul* (Notre Dame, IN, 2010), ch. 5. *Eusebius Gallicanus*, ed. F. Glorie, CCSL, 101 (3 vols, Turnhout, 1970). For background on the move to pastoral interest in death and penance, see E. Rébillard, *In hora mortis. Évolution de la pastorale chrétienne de la mort au IVe et Ve siècles dans l'occident latin* (Rome, 1994).

[131] Augustine, *Enchiridion*, 29. 109–10, ed. E. Evans, CCSL, 46 (Turnhout, 1969), pp. 108–9; Daley, *The Hope*, p. 141. Julianus Pomerius's work on Last Things is largely lost to us but his views on this subject were quoted by the seventh-century bishop Julian of Toledo, *Prognosticorum future saeculi*, II. 10, ed. J. N. Hillgarth, CCSL, 115 (Turnhout,

there was no doubt that there would be no going back for those who were to be saved and those who were to be cast into Hell.[132] And to be separated from the Eternal Kingdom forever, Augustine considered, would be a fate more unbearable than any punishment in Hell itself. Such rhetoric may have lent itself more plainly to 'power through persuasion' than 'power by coercion' – but it was a message that one could not ignore easily.

In further reflection and debate, Caesarius of Arles, a pupil of Pomerius, began to adapt aspects of Augustine's thinking for pastoral use as he built a new Christian community.[133] Fiery argument raged about Augustine's theology of grace and its effective antithesis in the teachings of Pelagius, the former position advocating grace as an essential precondition of a predestined salvation, and the latter asserting that grace must be secondary to one's ability to act morally so that one could earn salvation.[134] Caesarius held a moderate position which was eventually accepted at the Council of Orange in 529, but not before his teachings had first been condemned at the Council of Valence, convened by Bishop Julianus of Vienne who had a political axe to grind against his metropolitan neighbour.[135] The compromises reached at Orange essentially meant that Caesarius could preach to his flock that salvation was theirs to earn: 'observe, brothers, the mercy of our Lord!' he said in one sermon. 'He has placed in our power how we shall be judged on the day of Judgement.'[136] A 'fire-centred eschatology' had an important role to play here, as Caesarius told his audiences about how the 'not-very-good' would encounter purificatory fires on Judgement Day – something which stood as both a promise and a threat to those people who needed both encouragement and a degree of slack.

Eschatology was a powerful stick in this rhetoric as Caesarius sought to capture the attention of his audience and inspire their reform. A pupil later told the story of how once, when people started to walk out of church during one of his sermons, the bishop shouted at them that they would not be able to wander off on Judgement Day.[137] After that, he

---

1976), p. 49. A summary of the fragmentary evidence for Pomerius's career is provided in Klingshirn, *Caesarius*, pp. 73–4.

[132] See also Leo I, *Sermo*, 35. 4, PL, 54. 252; Julian of Toledo, *Prognosticorum future saeculi*, II. 14, p. 52.

[133] Klingshirn, *Caesarius*, esp. pp. 142–3. Brown, *Rise of Western Christendom*, pp. 150–4.

[134] R. A. Markus, 'The Legacy of Pelagius: Orthodoxy, Heresy and Conciliation', in R. Williams (ed.), *The Making of Orthodoxy: Essays in Honour of Henry Chadwick* (Cambridge, 1989), pp. 214–34.

[135] *Vita Caesarii*, I. 60, ed. B. Krusch, MGH SRM, 3, pp. 481–2; Klingshirn, *Caesarius of Arles*, p. 140.

[136] Caesarius, *Sermo*, 220. 3, p. 872: 'Videte, fratres, misericordiam domini nostri: in potestate nostra posuit, qualiter in die iudicii iudicemur.'

[137] *Vita Caesarii*, I. 27, p. 467.

often kept the doors shut until he had finished. The point, encountered repeatedly in the sermons themselves, was that the bishop's message could not be escaped: purity of life and penance for sins were the only strategies which would even give one hope for salvation and the eternal life. The alternative was damnation and fire, especially, as we saw earlier, for heretics. For a bishop defining his authority in the world there were clear practical ends to which he could channel 'renunciation of riches'.[138] After the struggles of war in 508, following the collapse of the Visigothic kingdom of Toulouse, he ransomed prisoners. He founded three 'ostentatiously' ascetic monasteries as moral beacons and a display of power in his city.[139] He directed attacks on the sex lives and standards of his community.[140] This was what Augustine's dissatisfaction with the world called for: leadership and agitation. And at its heart was the simple fact that everything ends and nothing escapes Judgement.

Conclusion

We leave this chapter at the doorstep of what Guy Halsall has called 'The transformation of the Year 600'. The Roman Empire had ceased to be a daily reality in the West but not in the East. The social and religious map of Europe had been fundamentally redrawn following mass migration, the emergence of smaller new polities, and the developing pastoral power of the Church. In the economy, modes of production and patterns of exchange were changing. As I suggested at the outset, apocalyptic thought might not explain all these processes, but we could see that the relationship between anagogy and lived experience was meaningful regardless. Crises such as the sack of Rome in 410 prompted soul-searching and polemics as people sought scapegoats and a better understanding of what their world meant, often channelling their anxiety through moral critiques. This was fundamentally grounded in existential investigation into identity and the way that God's world worked. Members of what perceived itself to be a united, orthodox-minded Church stood as a nonpolitical but proactive collective, pitched in battle against what it was not: heretics, the uncivilised and the sinful. Vigilance was paramount, not least because everything could be subverted by Antichrist and his pseudo-teachers claiming the definition of Christianity and its communities for their own perverted ends. Apocalypse framed the nature,

---

[138] Caesarius, *Sermo*, no. 178. 3–4, pp. 722–3.
[139] C. Leyser, *Authority and Asceticism from Augustine to Gregory the Great* (Oxford, 2000), pp. 89–92.
[140] See the lively account in L. Bailey, '"These Are Not Men": Sex and Drink in the Sermons of Caesarius of Arles', *Journal of Early Christian Studies*, 15.1 (2007), 23–43.

experience and direction of the Christian community. It was more than a matter of expecting the world to end.

Already we can see that the power of apocalypse worked at both a collective and individual level. While the Church was in perennial struggle, each member had to be mindful of his or her personal destiny. Letters and sermons served to remind people at all levels of society, religious and lay, what their personal duties were within the wider battle and the fate that would befall them if they succeeded or failed. Realistically, anyone was more likely to die at any moment from plague, war, feud or nature than to face the full terror of the End Times scenario. Sinners needed to undertake penance urgently and individual failure would result in eternal damnation. But collective failure was dangerous too: heretics and invaders existed in the world to challenge and to highlight the dangers of sin and as foreshadows of the reign of Antichrist. The Church's very existence was an apocalyptic struggle. With the fall of Rome we see how crisis could be met with varieties of apocalyptic thought, in order to change behaviour (the moral dimension), and to redefine political and religious ideals while conceptualising Others (especially heretics). In short, while the fall was a political event, it was also an apocalyptic discourse about the changing nature of power and identity. The Apocalypse had, for many, framed the changes of the Roman world.

A number of things had happened to apocalyptic theory in the process. Eastern and Western ideas – if they had ever been truly united – diverged over matters of chronology and the eschatology of empire. For the West, Jerome and Augustine had established crucial ways of interpreting apocalyptic scripture allegorically which robbed it of a certain literal potency. This did not mean that 'anti-apocalypticism' had won the day. The logical extension of Augustine's 'prohibition' of prediction was that the end could come at any time, so one needed to agitate, reform and be prepared. The same sense of 'unknowable imminence' in the face of certain judgement framed individual eschatology too. And, as we shall see in the next chapter, the next generation of post-Augustinian figures could see cause for alarm everywhere.

2   The new urgency (*c.* 550–*c.* 604)

As the first Year 6000 (= *c.* AD 500) passed further into the distance, apocalyptic tradition continued to evolve, but not always predictably. Augustine's prohibitions against predictive calculations and literalism had little of the calming effect he might have hoped for, even as his works became increasingly central to Western theology after the Council of Orange (529). The many and varied reasons reflect both the creativity of Christian culture and the shifting fates and fortunes of communities across Europe.[1] Few could face the ravages of the Justinianic plague, particularly strong between 542 and 590, without fear – and indeed it concentrated the minds of two key figures, Pope Gregory the Great (pope 590–604) and Bishop Gregory of Tours (bishop 573–94).[2] There were other revolutions taking place too which reorientated the relationships between Christendom, empire, identity and social structure, necessarily undermining the initial logic of Augustine's ideas in the process.[3] The distance between imperial and Christian identity in the West began to seem natural and therefore also somehow ambiguous and intangible, as the reality of *imperium* was increasingly less important than its imagined ideal. As the arguments of Augustine, Jerome and others were applied to changed times, the force and logic of their ideas changed.

The crucial writers in this period were often also significant political actors, directing the world around them in a pressing, apocalyptic drama. Gregory the Great wrote letters, sermons and treatises to rally the population of Rome in crisis, to sway the opinions of emperors, and to inspire

---

[1] For the early Middle Ages as a creative period of apocalyptic thought see B. McGinn, 'The End of the World and the Beginning of Christendom', in M. Bull (ed.), *Apocalypse Theory and the Ends of the World* (Oxford, 1995), pp. 58–89.

[2] Recent reassessment of the Justinianic plague in L. K. Little (ed.), *Plague and the End of Antiquity: The Pandemic of 541–750* (Cambridge, 2007). For bibliography on the two Gregorys see notes 4 and 5 below.

[3] At the forefront of recent scholarship on these developments stand C. Wickham, *Framing the Early Middle Ages: Europe and the Mediterranean, 400–800* (Oxford, 2005), J. M. H. Smith, *Europe after Rome: A New Cultural History, 500–1000* (Oxford, 2005), and the volumes of the Transformation of the Roman World series (14 vols, Leiden, 1997–2004).

change and reform amongst the English, Visigoths, Lombards and Franks.[4] His namesake in Tours was a constant and argumentative figure at Frankish royal courts, at least according to his own much-copied and much-edited *Histories*.[5] Each in their own way took Augustine's ideas and used them as part of a rhetoric agitating for change in a world unsettled. Gregory of Tours saw a world in which the Franks were locked in civil wars (*bella civilia*) while the Visigoths in Spain were mired in the Arian heresy.[6] The pope saw a world strained by Arian Lombard invasions and disunity in the Church. And in many ways this world was changing fast, and often decisively: in 589 King Reccared of Spain inaugurated a catholicisation of his kingdom; in 590 the Irishman St Columbanus began radicalising Frankish monasticism; in 597 Roman missionaries arrived in England (and St Columba of Iona had just died); and in the East the Byzantine Empire, overstretched since Justinian I's reign, was about to enter upon a period of prolonged and profound crisis.[7] To what extent these developments were interlocked is not always apparent but, as Guy Halsall has observed, one consequence was that the Bible itself became more essential as a common point of reference and comfort.[8] Here lay a central plank in the 'Transformation of the Year 600'.

This last point – the increased centrality of scripture to society in the post-Patristic era – is central to the argument of the present chapter. The achievement of the two Gregorys was the harnessing of an eschatological ecclesiology, projected through a rhetoric which sought to provoke action on account of the urgent need for change. Neither could have pursued their work in this way without common cultural points

---

[4] Key works on Gregory the Great include: S. Boesch Gajano, *Gregorio Magno: alle origini de medioevo* (Rome, 2004); C. Leyser, *Authority and Asceticism from Augustine to Gregory the Great* (Oxford, 2000); R. A. Markus, *Gregory the Great and His World* (Cambridge, 1997); and the essays in V. Grossi (ed.), *Gregorio Magno e il suo tempo* (2 vols, Rome, 1991) and J. Fontaine, R. Gillet and S. Pellistrandi (eds.), *Grégoire le Grand* (Paris, 1986).

[5] Key works on Gregory of Tours include: K. Mitchell and I. Wood (eds.), *The World of Gregory of Tours* (Leiden, 2002); M. Heinzelmann, *Gregory of Tours: History and Society in the Sixth Century*, trans. C. Carroll (Cambridge, 2001); N. Gauthier and H. Galinié (eds.), *Grégoire de Tours et l'espace gaulois* (Tours, 1997); W. Goffart, *The Narrators of Barbarian History AD 550–800: Jordanes, Gregory of Tours, Bede and Paul the Deacon* (Princeton, NJ, 1988), ch. 2; I. Wood, *Gregory of Tours* (Bangor, 1994).

[6] Note that Gregory often uses *bella civilia* in the sense of wars affecting or involving the *civitates*, not just in the modern sense of organised internal conflict.

[7] For the East, a useful overview can be found in A. Louth, 'Byzantium Transforming (600–700)', in J. Shepard (ed.), *The Cambridge History of the Byzantine Empire, c. 500–1492* (Cambridge, 2008), pp. 221–48. See also J. Howard-Johnston, *Witnesses to a World Crisis: Historians and Histories of the Middle East in the Seventh Century* (Oxford, 2010).

[8] 'Changing Minds around the Year 600': http://600transformer.blogspot.co.uk/2012/02/changing-minds-around-600.html. The importance of Gregory the Great's world of scripture is set out in Leyser, *Authority and Asceticism*, pp. 177–80.

of reference different from those in the mixed Christian–pagan–secular world of Augustine or Jerome. They may have needed to act as interpreters of scripture, for sure, but that was because meanings of individual passages in the Bible were often opaque and Christendom needed its experts. Indeed, the two Gregorys were significant and successful because they put forward clear and powerful ways for understanding the *mundus* in a breathlessly changing world. People could appropriate such ways of thinking. Their messages, however, were not exclusively eschatological or apocalyptic, and indeed were rather complex, so to explain those themes in relation to the totality of the Gregorys' outputs and world would be another study in itself. What needs to be done is to trace the contours of their eschatological thought and its situational logic, so as to understand how two exceptional figures injected imminence and urgency back into mainstream Latin apocalyptic.

New directions under Gregory the Great

Pope Gregory the Great bestrides modern scholarship as a pivotal figure, simultaneously the product of the late Roman world, and also someone whose way of thinking was consonant with the new political and intellectual landscapes which were emerging.[9] He was from a wealthy family in Rome and briefly served as prefect sometime between 573 and 575 before taking up a more contemplative life.[10] He was soon pulled from his retreat to serve the papacy, reluctantly pushed on by a sense of duty, and from there he found himself on business in Constantinople around 584, where he became part of a social network which included the future emperor Maurice and Bishop Leander of Seville, the brother of the famous polymath Isidore.[11] As pope, he maintained close ties with the East, nurtured his connection with Spain and sought new links with the Franks and the English (who needed converting first). Somehow his

---

[9] In addition to the literature in n. 4, see K. Greschat, *Die Moralia in Job Gregors des Großen. Ein christologisch-ekklesiologischer Kommentar* (Tübingen, 2005), pp. 1–3 and Leyser, *Authority and Asceticism*, pp. 132–3. On Gregory's eschatology here see also C. Dagens, 'La fin de temps et l'Église selon Saint Grégoire le Grand', *Recherches de science religieuse*, 58 (1970), 273–88; J. N. Hillgarth, 'Eschatological and Political Concepts in the Seventh Century', in J. Fontaine and J. N. Hillgarth (eds.), *Le septième siècle. Changements et continuités* (London, 1992), pp. 212–35; M. Meier, 'Eschatologie und Kommunikation im 6. Jahrhundert n. Chr. – oder: Wie osten und Westen beständig aneinander vorbei redeten', in W. Brandes and F. Schmieder (eds.), *Endzeiten. Eschatologie in den monotheistischen Weltreligionen* (Berlin and New York, 2008), pp. 41–73.

[10] Gregory the Great, *Registrum*, IV. 2, ed. D. Norberg, CCSL, 140 (2 vols, Turnhout, 1982), I. 218.

[11] A summary of networks and relevant letters is provided by Markus, *Gregory the Great*, pp. 11–12.

sense of Christian universality began to shift paradigms, so that in the imagination Constantinople and the Mediterranean became less central to contemporary imaginations than they had been, as the world to the north became more vibrant and valued.[12]

What Gregory achieved and what he set out to do are not quite the same thing. The pope was largely conservative in the sense that what he was striving for was peace and order, both at a secular and an ecclesiastical level. He still referred to the empire in secular terms as *rei publicae*, and he could imagine it co-existing with Christendom (*imperium Christianum*).[13] The *ecclesia* and the empire could be partners – indeed were institutionally bound together – but there was no real question in Gregory's mind of their being the same thing in a post-Augustinian world.[14] Even so, the real and tangible sufferings of the city of Rome seemed pregnant with meaning. As Lombards besieged the city in 593 Gregory drew on Ezekiel's boiling pot metaphor (Ezek. 24.3–5) to preach that Rome's fate was fulfilling the prophecies made about Samaria and Nineveh, and on Micah's balding eagle (Micah 1.16) to comment on Rome and the world's old age.[15] Yet the way in which Gregory sought to co-ordinate emperors, kings, bishops, abbots, or anyone in the face of crisis, 'unwittingly created … a Europe-wide language of power', as Peter Brown put it.[16] In terms of both rhetoric and vision, Gregory's actions had set in motion new currents which would help to define the Latin West.[17] In no small way, as Greschat has shown, this was embodied in his *Moralia in Job*, which established an ecclesiological reading of Job's sufferings to bind together the *vita contemplativa* and the *vita activa* for preachers.[18]

---

[12] Markus, *Gregory the Great*, pp. 203–5.

[13] Gregory the Great, *Registrum*, VII. 5, ed. Norberg, I. 452. See also I. 16a (ed. P. Ewald and L. Hartmann, MGH, Epp., 1 [Berlin, 1891], pp. 18 and 20) and VI. 64, ed. Norberg, I. 439.

[14] P. Magdalino, 'Church, Empire and Christendom in *c.* 600 and *c.* 1075: The View from the Registers of Popes Gregory I and Gregory VII', *Settimane di studio del Centro Italiano di studi sull'Alto Medioevo*, 51 (2004), 1–30 at p. 12; R. A. Markus, 'Gregory the Great's Europe', *TRHS*, 5th series, 31 (1981), 21–36 at p. 22.

[15] *Homilia in Hiezechihelem prophetam*, II. 6. 22–3, ed. M. Adriaen, CCSL 142 (Turnhout, 1971), p. 311–12 (Samaria and Nineveh); II. 6. 24. Dagens, 'La fin du temps', pp. 280–2.

[16] P. Brown, *The Rise of Western Christendom: Triumph and Diversity AD 200–1000* (2nd edn, Oxford, 2003), p. 211, deriving the idea of a 'language of power' from the important analysis of Gregory's rhetoric in Leyser, *Authority and Asceticism*, pp. 160–87 and the comment on p. 134 'For better or worse, the Gregorian sense of the moral possibility attendant on the exercise of power has proved unforgettable.'

[17] Markus, 'Gregory the Great's Europe'; Dagens, 'La fin du temps', p. 288.

[18] Gregory the Great, *Moralia in Job*, ed. M. Adriaen, CCSL, 143 (3 vols, Turnhout, 1979–85). Greschat, *Die Moralia in Job*, especially pp. 200–5. The importance of Greschat's contribution here lies in the establishment of coherent purpose in the *Moralia* and,

By seeking order, Gregory spearheaded a theology and politics of action which reminded people to take responsibility for the fate of their souls.

The power of Gregory's message came from its capacity to make sense of evil and suffering in a way which felt empowering. As Claude Dagens observed, Gregory's eschatology was at once shaped by his gloomy assessment of the world around him and his triumphant vision for the Church.[19] Order and disorder were in constant competition. When he addressed Leander at the beginning of the *Moralia*, Gregory wailed about the tempests of the world and about how he had been pulled from the 'quiet of the monastery' (*quies monasterii*) and 'plunged on a sudden in a sea of secular matters'.[20] But he did not retreat and instead taught patience and perseverance in the face of tribulation. Later in the *Moralia* he argued that 'from her adversaries Ecclesia suffers persecution in two ways, namely either by words or by swords. When she bears persecution by words, her wisdom is put to the test, when by swords, her patience.'[21] The highest threat, naturally, would come from Antichrist as a symbol of collective evil which would have to be endured, but also challenged. Gregory was explicit that preaching in the countdown to the End of Days was essential as a rebuke to Antichrist and in order to bring fruit to the faithful.[22] Passivity, retreat or fear were not options for Gregory nor, he hoped, for those he addressed. Anyone could be a *praedictor* – living by example and word – in the Last Days.[23]

In this context, an important legacy was the sense of urgency with which Gregory pursued his goals. The world, he was convinced, no longer hinted at its End – it showed it forth.[24] Gregory was no intellectual opponent of Augustine and indeed was deeply influenced by his writings.[25] His sense

---

through that, the happier coincidence of the active and contemplative. See also Markus, *Gregory the Great*, ch. 2, who was less impressed by the 'impenetrable jungle' of Gregory's text (p. 21).

[19] Dagens, 'La fin du temps', p. 274.

[20] Gregory the Great, *Moralia in Job*, Epistola, pp. 2–3: 'in causarum saecularium pelago reperi.' On the rhetorical edge to this, see Leyser, *Authority and Asceticism*, p. 161.

[21] Gregory the Great, *Moralia in Job*, XIX. 9. 16, ed. Adriaen, II. 968: 'ab adversariis namque suis duobus modis Ecclesia persecutionem patitur, scilicet, aut verbis aut gladiis. Sed cum verbis persecutionem sustinent, exercetur eius spaientia; cum vero gladiis, exercetur eius patientia.'

[22] Ibid., IX. 11. 15, ed. Adriaen, I. 467; XV. 57. 68, ed. Adriaen, II. 792–3.

[23] Leyser, *Authority and Asceticism*, p. 157. A more institutional take is given in Greschat, *Die Moralia*, pp. 79–139.

[24] Gregory the Great, *Dialogi*, III. 38. 3, SC 260 (Paris, 1979), ed. A. de Vogüé, II. 430: 'nam hac in terra, in qua vivimus, finem suum mundus non iam nuntiat, sed ostendit.' G. R. Evans, *The Thought of Gregory the Great* (Cambridge, 1988), p. 43; Greschat, *Die Moralia in Job*, p. 8.

[25] Leyser, *Authority and Asceticism, passim*; Evans, *The Thought*, p. 15 (Gregory diminished Augustine by making his thought popular).

of apocalyptic imminence came from a logical extension of Augustine's agnosticism on the subject, particularly the sense that the unknowable nature of the End meant that it could come at any moment. But this meant action was needed: there was to be no reward or excuse for being unprepared.[26] Gregory was, in this, still more convinced by the proximity of the End, because his world was uncertain.[27] As Markus characterised it, 'Gregory's sense of his own time [was] poised between experience of disaster and a hope born of his awareness of real possibilities. Both were articulated in the language of eschatology.'[28]

The greatest difference between Augustine and Gregory lay in their attitude towards signs.[29] A typical Gregorian moment came near the beginning of a sermon on Luke (21.9–12; cf Matt. 24.6–8) given in St Peter's in 591:

For with people rising against people, and their pressure on the land, we discern more now in our own tribulations than we read in books. That earthquakes undermine many cities, you know from other parts of the world, as we frequently hear. We suffer pestilence without end. Truly we used to see openly only a few signs in the Sun and moon and stars, but because there is not long left, we now keep track of change in the air. And although in earlier times Italy was given over to the blows of the swords of Gentiles, we see battle lines of fire in the sky, and afterwards the blood of the human race will be shed. A confusion of the sea and tides has not yet brought up anything new. But with much prophesied now fulfilled, it is not doubtful how little there remains to come, because the certainty of things to come is shown in things past.[30]

[26] C. Straw, *Gregory the Great: Perfection in Imperfection* (Berkeley, CA, 1988), pp. 14–15; Martyn, *The Letters of Gregory the Great*, Medieval Sources in Translation, 40 (Toronto, 2004), I. 17.

[27] Martyn, *The Letters of Gregory the Great*, I. 17–18.

[28] Markus, *Gregory the Great*, p. 54, seconded in Meier, 'Eschatologie und Kommunikation', pp. 62–3.

[29] On Gregory's miraculous, see R. A. Markus, *Signs and Meanings: World and Text in Ancient Christianity* (Liverpool, 1996); W. D. McCready, *Signs of Sanctity: Miracles in the Thought of Gregory the Great* (Toronto, 1989). Much here rests on the authenticity of Gregory's *Dialogi*, which remains contested. The modern case against is set out in F. Clark, *The Pseudo-Gregorian 'Dialogues'* (2 vols, Leiden, 1987). Responses include A. de Vogüé, 'Les Dialogues, oeuvre authentique et publiée par Grégoire lui-même', in *Gregorio Magno*, II. pp. 27–40, P. Meyvaert, 'The Enigma of Gregory the Great's *Dialogues*: A Response to Francis Clark', *JEH*, 39.3 (1988), 335–81 and most recently M. Dal Santo, 'The Shadow of Doubt? A Note on the *Dialogues* and *Registrum Epistolarum* of Pope Gregory the Great (590–604)', *JEH*, 61.1 (2010), 3–17.

[30] Gregory the Great, *Homiliae in Evangelia*, I. 1. 1, ed. R. Étaix, CCSL, 141 (Turnhout, 1999), p. 6: 'Nam gentem super gentem exsurgere earumque pressuram terris insistere plus iam in nostris tribulationibus quam in codicibus legimus. Quod terraemotus urbes innumeras subruat, ex aliis mundi partibus scitis quam frequenter audimus. Pestilentias sine cessatione patimur. Signa vero in sole et luna et stellis adhuc aperte minime vidimus, sed quia et haec non longe sint ex ipsa iam aeris immutatione colligimus. Quamvis priusquam Italia gentili gladio ferienda traderetur, igneas in caelo acies vidimus, et ipsum qui

War and the natural world proved the truth of what was happening, revealing the truth in Luke's apocalypse. The End was no abstract, distant concern. In unsettled times, this kind of language had the potential to channel anxiety and action.[31] These were dangerous times for all. Such rhetorical flourishes might hint at Gregory's own thought-world or a more widespread one, highlighting a heightening of the eschatological mood. Yet, as we shall see, Gregory did not compose unreflexively, but rather as a deliberate attempt to engage his audience, to get them to reflect on Judgement and to behave accordingly. Gregory was both reflecting inner angst and deliberately using it as a catalyst.

The apocalyptic mode was, for Gregory, an important weapon he could use in a variety of contexts. In another sermon, this time delivered in the basilica of St Felix, Gregory told his audience: 'Our Lord ... wants the final hour to be unknown to us – so that it can always be suspected, so that while we cannot foresee it, we might be prepared for it without pause. Therefore, my brothers, fix your mind's eye on the mortal condition, prepare yourselves for the coming Judgement with daily tears and laments!'[32] It provided agitation – an urgency to engage in good works. It also created an imaginative context in which to promote order and obedience. Writing a letter to the exiled clergy of Milan, he encouraged them to support their new bishop-elect Constantius in a manner befitting people who could see for themselves that 'the destruction of the world has come to look like the pages of our Scriptures' and who therefore needed to prepare for Judgement.[33] Moral apocalypse concerned him no less and he urged the empress's attendant (*cubicularia*) Gregoria to remain fearful of sin in life so that she could reap the rewards forever thereafter.[34] Uncertainty and anticipation were the root of action.

From Gaul, we have one account of how people might have reacted to Gregory's rhetoric. The story, told by Gregory of Tours, concerns his

postea humani generis fusus est sanguinem coruscantem. Confusio autem maris et fluctuum necdum nova exorta est. Sed cum multa iam praenuntiata completa sint, dubium non est quod sequantur etiam pauca quae restant, quia sequentium rerum certitudo est praeteritarum exhibitio.' The sermon is highlighted by Dagens, 'La fin du temps', p. 275; Markus, *Gregory the Great*, p. 51; Meier, 'Eschatologie und Kommunikation', pp. 59–62.

[31] Meier, 'Eschatologie und Kommunikation', p. 62.

[32] Gregory the Great, *Homilia in Evangelia*, I. 13. 6, ed. Étaix, p. 94: 'Horam vero ultimam Dominus noster ... nobis voluit esse incognitam, ut semper possit esse suspecta, ut dum illam praevidere non possumus, ad illam sine intermissione praeparemur. Proinde, fratres mei, in conditione mortalitatis vestrae mentis oculos figite, venienti vos iudici per fletus cotidie et lamenta praeparate.'

[33] Gregory the Great, *Registrum*, III. 29, ed. Norbert, II. 175: 'quasi paginae nobis codicum factae sunt ipsae iam plagae terrarum' (trans. Martyn, II. 255).

[34] Gregory the Great, *Registrum*, VII. 22, ed. Norbert, I. 474.

deacon Agiulf, who visited Rome to procure relics in 590 and arrived to find the city in chaos and Gregory not yet elected.[35] The bishop of Tours was no less prone than his namesake to a touch of artifice and drama, as is betrayed by his scene-setting story of how Rome flooded and sea-snakes and a log-like dragon (a crocodile?) were seen to swim down the Tiber and drown. The floods were followed by an outbreak of plague, which killed Pope Pelagius II. Gregory the Great was called upon to take his place but sought to refuse. Instead, he preached an eschatologically toned sermon to the people of the city, exhorting them to enjoin penance.[36] They did, and for three days they sang psalms – a notably monastic response to crisis – even as eighty people fell dead from plague at the start. And when they had finished, and their sins had been cleansed (for now), Gregory was seized and enthroned as the new pope on Maurice's orders. Even though the rhetorical voice was very much Gregory of Tours's, the representation of Gregory the Great seems in keeping with the pope's own writings and we need not doubt the underlying realities. He was introduced as 'so well-versed in grammar, dialectic and rhetoric that he was held second to none in the city'.[37] He knew how to capture the mood and to direct the anxiety caused by flood and plague, and did so with aplomb. By giving eschatological voice to the people's fears, Gregory could provide compelling leadership – and the citizens of Rome followed him.

There is another case which takes us to the heart of Gregory's strategies of persuasion. When John of Constantinople upset Gregory by claiming the title *patriarches oikoumenikos*, the bishop of Rome wrote to Emperor Maurice to lament how sad it was to see priests engaging in vanity when the world was in turmoil:

I am compelled to exclaim and say: 'What times! What immorality!' Look, in parts of Europe everything has been handed over to the control of barbarians, and cities have been destroyed, army camps overwhelmed, provinces depopulated, and no farmer inhabits the land. Worshippers of idols run riot and daily

---

[35] Gregory of Tours, *Historiae*, X. 1, ed. B. Krusch and W. Levison, MGH SRM, 1 (Hanover, 1951), pp. 477–81. It has been argued that this entire section is a later interpolation (O. Chadwick, 'Gregory of Tours and Gregory the Great', *Journal of Theological Studies*, 50 (1949), 38–40) but support for its authenticity is provided by Heinzelmann, *Gregory of Tours*, p. 76 n. 76 and p. 80 n. 83. The section was certainly part of the text in the earliest manuscripts for Book X.

[36] The sermon is reproduced in full by Gregory of Tours (*Historiae*, X. 1, pp. 479–81). It did not form part of either of Gregory's homily collections but the first part was added to a copy of the *Homiliae in Evangelia* in Paris, Bibliothèque nationale, lat. 12255, f. 190v (Tours, s. ix).

[37] Gregory of Tours, *Historiae*, X. 1, p. 478: 'litteris grammaticis dialecticisque ac rethoricis ita est institutus ut nulli in Urbe ipsa putaretur esse secundus.'

oversee the deaths of the faithful, and yet priests, who should have lain on the pavement and in the ashes with tears in their eyes, seek out names for themselves full of vanity, and boast of new and profane titles.[38]

While Jeffrey Richards considered this flamboyant rhetoric, Hervé Savon thought instead that it revealed 'the fundamental categories with which Gregory instinctively perceived and transfigured the event'.[39] But even Savon's argument, with its appeal to Gregory writing 'instinctively', would render Gregory's prose a relatively unreflexive by-product of the author's subconscious.[40] It underplays the strategic force of carefully chosen words with which the pope sought to colour events for the benefit of Maurice – the audience who needed to be convinced of John's 'evil' and to act. Gregory cast himself as a new Elijah warning against the worshippers of Baal (1 Kings 18). The rhetorical games extended to including an exclamation from Cicero's *Orationes in Verrem*, from when the then-consul of Rome lambasted the sacrilegious Verres. Gregory also made separate arguments in the letter which appeal to scripture, canon law, friendship and the authority of the emperor himself. He did not even characterise the Lombards quite so darkly in a letter written the same day to Maurice encouraging action against them.[41] The style of his prose in each section was carefully considered as a means to an end.

The sense of strategy was underlined further by the accompanying two letters which Gregory addressed to Maurice's wife, Constantina, on the same day. Gregory not only liked to write separately to male and female figures of authority about specific issues to capture the court, but in this case he knew Maurice and Constantina well from his time in Constantinople. He could make social connections work for him. And again the representation of the Lombards is subtly different. In the first letter, he wrote about the problems in Corsica and Sicily posed by the

---

[38] Gregory the Great, *Registrum*, ed. Norberg, V. 37, I. 309: 'Exclamare compellor ac dicere: O tempora, o mores! Ecce cuncta in Europae partibus barbarorum iuri sunt tradita, destructae urbes, euersa castra, depopulatae prouinciae; nullus terram cultor inhabitat; saeuiunt et dominantur cotidie ut nece fidelium cultores idolorum: et tamen sacerdotes, qui in pauimento et cinere flentes iacere debuerunt, uanitatis sibi nomina expetunt et nouis ac profanis uocabulis gloriantur'. H. Savon, 'L'Antéchrist dan l'oeuvre de Grégoire le Grand', in J. Fontaine (ed.), *Grégoire le Grand* (Paris, 1986), pp. 389–404, at pp. 398–90; Markus, *Gregory the Great*, p. 94.

[39] Savon, 'L'Antéchrist chez Grégoire, p. 399: 'catégories fondamentales à travers lesquelles Grégoire perçoit et transfigure instinctivement l'événement'. J. Richards, *Consul of God: The Life and Times of Gregory the Great* (London, 1981), p. 219: 'It is splendid hellfire and damnation rhetoric'.

[40] Note also the influence of Savon on Markus, who also wrote of Gregory's 'instinctive' eschatological tone ('Living within Sight of the End', in C. Humphrey and M. Ormrod (eds.), *Time in the Medieval World* (York, 2001), p. 32).

[41] *Registrum*, V. 36, ed. Norberg, II. 304–7.

'most nefarious' Lombards so that she might consider instigating some kind of response, and in the second letter the Lombards were redeployed amongst other problems to make the patriarch's actions seem all the more careless. 'In his arrogance, what is revealed other than that the time of Antichrist is already near?'[42] Gregory was wont to talk about Antichrist as an internal enemy in his theological works, and yet here he cast him as a near-historical figure to fear and oppose.[43] In this, we glimpse what Gregory believed would move Constantina and, in the process, what he held back from Maurice.

Gregory's laments about barbarians to Maurice and Constantina, even if rhetorical, were symptomatic of a strong current in the pope's thought-world. After the collapse of Gothic power in the Italian peninsula, Lombard groups had travelled across the Alps and set up new duchies in the north, causing havoc in the process. On the one hand, of course, there was nothing new in such actions, not even in the invaders' persistence in observing Arianism.[44] But they were aggressive and ambitious, which meant that popes from Pelagius II to Hadrian I fretted about the threat posed to the security of Rome. Indeed, the language of 'calamities and tribulations' was one Pelagius used when writing to Gregory in his Constantinople days.[45] Many of Gregory's eschatological flourishes employed the Lombards – often *gentiles* – as a symptom of a world in disarray.[46] Gregory did not, however, see them as Gog and Magog or indeed any other singular fulfilment of prophecy, even when preaching about Ezekiel during the Lombard siege of 593, perhaps because they were still an instance of a type of evil rather than the one historical enemy of the End Times. Moreover, as his pontificate proceeded, Gregory treated with the Lombards, urged their conversion to Catholicism, sought peace treaties with them and used different rhetorical strategies in dealing with

---

[42] *Registrum*, V. 39, ed. Norberg, II. 316: 'Sed in hac eius superbia quid aliud nisi propinqua iam Antichristi esse tempora designantur?'

[43] Gregory's idea of Antichrist is also covered in B. McGinn, *Antichrist: Two Thousand Years of the Human Fascination with Evil* (New York, 1994), pp. 80–2 and K. L. Hughes, *Constructing Antichrist: Paul, Biblical Commentary, and the Development of Doctrine in the Early Middle Ages* (Washington, DC, 2005), pp. 108–14 (in which he treats Gregory as an 'aside' because he does not engage in any systematic exegesis concerning Antichrist other than as a symbol of the Church's struggles).

[44] There could have been greater pagan survival than some sources suggest: S. Fanning, 'Lombard Arianism Reconsidered', *Speculum*, 56.2 (1981), 241–58; W. Pohl, 'Deliberate Ambiguity: The Lombards and Christianity', in G. Armstrong and I. N. Wood (eds.), *Christianizing Peoples and Converting Individuals* (Turnhout, 2002), 47–58.

[45] See Pelagius, *Epistola ad Gregorio*, ed. L. Hartmann, MGH Epp., 2 (Hanover, 1899), pp. 440–1 at p. 440. See also *Liber pontificalis*, 64–5, ed. L. Duchesne (Paris, 1884), pp. 308–9, which tersely paints a bleak picture.

[46] See again *Dialogi*, III. 38. 3, ed. de Vogüé, II. 430; *Homiliae in Evangelia*, I. 1. 1, p. 6, and the letters in nn. 41–2.

them.[47] To Gregory, they were clearly not a literal fulfilment of Revelation (20.7).

Other 'barbarians' fitted into a different eschatological niche because they were pagans. The Gospel was unambiguous: there was a duty to preach unto all nations, and Judgement would not come until that had been fulfilled. (As we shall see in Chapter 6, 'preaching' did not have to be successful). Gregory's most famous success on this score was the conversion of the English, to whom he sent missionaries in 596 – possibly at the request of Bertha, the Christian Frankish wife of the pagan King Æthelberht of Kent, but in Bede's popular story the pope sent them because he had encountered some English slaveboys in a market and thought they looked like angels (a play on the Latin *Angli* ('English') and *angeli* ('angels')).[48] The legend is perhaps less irrelevant than it might look. When Michael Richter assessed the plausibility of Gregory having made such a pun, one of the pope's letters that struck him included a comment to Eulogios of Alexandria that the converting English lived in the 'corner of the world' (*angulus mundi*).[49] Layers of wordplay aside, this points to a geographical sense of the English being off in the far corner, as if on the edge of a map – literally at the end of the world. To preach to them fulfilled Christ's instruction in Matthew (24.14). Eulogios, living so far away, needed to know that this was going on.

In most respects, the story of the conversion can be told without any obvious appeal to apocalyptic tradition – except that, after King Æthelberht of Kent converted to become the first Christian English king, Gregory wrote to him in 601 warning him about the world's old age.[50] One wonders what the neophyte king would have made of such news put so bluntly, but Gregory may have had a more subtle purpose in mind.[51] The letter opened with a call for Æthelberht to be proactive

---

[47] E.g. *Registrum*, IX. 66, ed. Norberg, II. 621–2 (Gregory to King Agilulf, backed up in Gregorian style with a letter to Queen Theudelinda: *Registrum*, IX. 68, ed. Norberg, II. 624).

[48] Bede, *Historia ecclesiastica*, II. 1. 11, ed. M. Lapidge (Rome, 2008–10), I. 178; *Vita Gregorii papae*, c. 9, ed. and trans. B. Colgrave, *The Earliest Life of Gregory the Great* (Cambridge, 1986), pp. 90–1 (where the pun works better because *Angli* is spelt *Anguli*).

[49] M. Richter, 'Bede's *Angli*: Angles or English?', *Peritia*, 3 (1984), 99–114 at 103; Gregory the Great, *Registrum*, VIII. 29, ed. Norberg, II. 551–2. Compare Gregory the Great, *Moralia in Job*, 27. 11. 19–21, ed. Adriaen, pp. 1344–6.

[50] Gregory the Great, *Registrum*, XI. 37, ed. Norberg, II. 931–2. The letter is quoted in full in Bede, *Historia ecclesiastica*, I. 32, ed. Lapidge, pp. 148–52. Gregory had already articulated the importance of preaching right up until the end of time: *Homilia in Evangelia*, I. 19. 1, ed. Étaix, pp. 143–4. But note also its irrelevance as a theme in Gregory's letter of support for Augustine (*Registrum*, VI. 55, ed. Norberg, I. 426) or any other correspondence concerning the mission.

[51] Dagens, 'La fin du temps', 277. Compare the interpretation of Markus ('Gregory the Great's Europe', 25) that the pope was 'disappointed' with the king, prompting him to

in converting his people, 'by encouraging the morality of your subjects with your great purity of life, by terrifying them, by flattering them, [and] by correcting them'.[52] The unfolding of Gregory's prose thereafter was a lesson in how to do this: Æthelberht was flattered by comparison to Emperor Constantine, encouraged to follow the correcting advice of pious Augustine of Canterbury, terrified with news of the imminent apocalypse and then offered gifts. The actual content of the 'apocalyptic section' barely departed from the language and tone of the homily Gregory had preached in St Peter's a decade earlier, illustrating not only consistency of theme in his work but consistency of manipulative strategy. Gregory hoped not only that Æthelberht would be stirred into action but also that he would appreciate how the pope had achieved this effect in him.[53] The king had been taught how to use the apocalyptic to his advantage.

In context, Gregory's attitude to mission was very much of its day. A few generations earlier there were few notions within the Christian Roman world that barbarians counted as targets for mission. This had changed with the conversion of Ireland – it was never part of the empire, and St Patrick himself cited the apocalyptic imperative to preach unto the ends of the earth as part of the rationale for his work (see Chapter 3). By coincidence, the year that Gregory became pope, an Irish monastic reformer and missionary called Columbanus arrived in Gaul, eager to draw on the support of Gregory, and no less slow to see that the necessity to act promptly was revealed by the old age of the world. It was in many ways the influence of Columbanian monasticism and the universality of papal authority in the West that laid the foundations of universal mission for the next two centuries.[54] That there were apocalyptic undercurrents is important to the way Christian culture unfolded as it moved north and east, as we shall see. In England, an eighth-century biographer of

---

write, echoed in J. M. Wallace-Hadrill, *Bede's Ecclesiastical History of the English People: An Historical Commentary* (Oxford, 1988), pp. 47–8. See also G. Demacopoulos, 'Gregory the Great and the Pagan Shrines of Kent', *Journal of Late Antiquity*, 1.2 (2008), 353–69 at pp. 358–66 on the rhetorical context for this letter and a detailed study of its contents, and I. N. Wood, 'The Mission of Augustine of Canterbury to the English', *Speculum*, 69.1 (1994), 1–17 at pp. 11–12.

[52] Gregory the Great, *Registrum*, XI. 37, ed. Norberg, II, 930: 'subditorum mores in magna vitae munditia exhortando, terrendo, blandiendo, corrigendo'.

[53] See Demacopoulos, 'Gregory the Great', p. 363: 'Gregory employed the apocalyptic card not only because it was part of his theological vision but also because it offered clear missionary objectives.' A 'weak' indication of Gregory's success here is that Æthelberht did continue the work of spreading Christianity amongst the English.

[54] W. Fritze, '*Universalis gentium confessio*: Formeln, Träger und Wege universalmissionarischen Denkens im 7. Jahrhundert', *Frühmittelalterliche Studien*, 3 (1969), 78–130, esp. pp. 109–13 on Gregory but more generally for the importance of Columbanian networks.

Gregory even wrote that it would be the pope who represented all the English on Judgement Day.[55]

A shared concern of Columbanian and Gregorian circles was personal eschatology and the immediate judgement of the soul on death, which of course lay at the heart of missionary work too. The Gregorian high-point of this idea comes in a discussion of purgatory in Book of IV of the *Dialogues*. Unfortunately, it is precisely Book IV which seems stylistically and thematically out of place in the *Dialogues*, which otherwise focuses on the deeds of saints.[56] Was it a forgery? In many ways, however, the authenticity does not matter: wherever it came from, the text was in circulation by about 678/9 and communities across the West believed it was real and copied it.[57] Its success promoted the idea that penance could be undertaken in the afterlife, with some imperfect souls held up outside Heaven until Judgement Day, and some forced to endure purgation – all in stark contrast to the immediacy of Judgement set out by Augustine, Pomerius and Caesarius (see Chapter 1).[58] It formed part of a surge in the production of texts which detailed visions of the afterlife, to which we shall return in the next chapter. Here, what we need to emphasise is simply how Gregory's calls for people to take greater moral responsibility had shaped both the way in which he was perceived and the terms of debate for the nature of 'moral apocalypse'.

While remaining uncertain about when the End would come, Gregory had developed an active and enduring eschatology which he wove into his wider work as pope. He had deployed motifs in sermons and letters to rally people in trouble times and to promote a particular sense of order and right. A neophyte king had not only been warned but taught how to warn his people about the troubles leading up to Judgement in order to establish a healthier Christian community. A new theology of struggle and suffering had been opened, drawing on Job and Ezekiel. As much as

---

[55] *Vita Gregorii papae*, c. 30, pp. 132–3.

[56] Book IV is not about saints in the same way as I–III, and it is not promised in the prologue (*Dialogi*, I. prol. 7–10, ed. de Vogüé, II. 14–18). M. Dunn, 'Gregory the Great, the Vision of Fursey and the Origins of Purgatory', *Peritia*, 14 (2000), 238–54. The most recent defence of the authenticity of the *Dialogi* (Dal Santo, 'The Shadow of Doubt?') sidesteps this issue, as convincing as it is on its own terms, by focusing on whether Gregory would have been interested in saints' cults.

[57] Summarised in Clark, *The Pseudo-Gregorian 'Dialogues'*, pp. 179–81, although it is difficult to prove much on the basis of there being relatively few extant manuscripts. The oldest fragment is written in a Luxeuil minuscule of the late seventh century (Trier, Stadtbibliothek, fragm. s. n. = *CLA*, 1808), and another early manuscript, Autun, Bibliothèque municipale, 20 = *CLA*, 719 is also from Luxeuil, so if we were to look for a possible centre for fabrication on that basis it is there. But that is a big 'if'.

[58] *Dialogi*, IV. 29, ed. de Vogüé, III. 98 (stopping outside Heaven); IV. 42, ed. de Vogüé, III. 150–5 (further purgation).

he sought to direct what was going on in his day, the success of Gregory's vision also lay in the way his works were copied again and again across the Latin West, which meant that many of his eschatological ideas were accessible in libraries where they could then inspire new works. Gregory of Tours and Bede, amongst others, embraced the pope's interest in Last Things. The widespread reception of Gregory's thought meant that the urgency that he had injected into Augustine's basic agnosticism would endure, even as it faded in and out of prominence.

Gregory of Tours's *ecclesia Dei*

As Gregory the Great took on the world, Gregory of Tours, a bishop from a powerful Gallo-Roman family, looked on in admiration. This Gregory's world was rather different from the pope's, as he had ringside seats for Frankish court intrigue and farce, as well as his own cults of saints to promote. He came from a family which had produced its own holy bishops, who had controlled a number of bishoprics in and around the Auvergne, and who could now be written up as shining beacons of behaviour in a world fallen into chaos – a world which was definitely fast approaching its End. Yet Gregory and the scholarship about him pose some intriguing challenges, not least because there is rarely ever agreement about what Gregory's intentions were, and again there is only very limited scope for comparing his worldview to any of his contemporaries in Gaul. At the least we have a different eschatological take on the world Gregory the Great inhabited, one often injected with a dark humour.

Most of Gregory's eschatology is embedded in his most famous work, the ten-book *Histories*.[59] Indeed it is notably less prominent in his hagiographical works, but then the *Histories* were designed to put forward a view on the totality of history.[60] How Gregory structured the text is key

[59] On the history of the title and the fate of Gregory's work, see W. Goffart, 'From *Historiae* to *Historia Francorum* and Back Again: Aspects of the Textual History of Gregory of Tours', in his *Rome's Fall and After* (London, 1989), pp. 255–74, and his *The Narrators of Barbarian History*, pp. 119–27, with significant refinement in Heinzelmann, *Gregory of Tours* and H. Reimitz, 'Social Networks and Identities in Frankish Historiography: New Aspects of the Textual History of Gregory of Tours' *Historiae*', in R. Corradini, M. Diesenberger and H. Reimitz (eds.), *The Construction of Communities in the Early Middle Ages: Texts, Resources and Artefacts* (Leiden, 2003), pp. 229–68. G. Halsall, 'Nero and Herod? The Death of Chilperic and Gregory of Tours' Writing of History', in Mitchell and Wood (eds.), *The World of Gregory of Tours*, pp. 337–50 and A. Breukelaar, *Historiography and Episcopal Authority in Sixth-Century Gaul: The Histories of Gregory of Tours Interpreted in their Historical Context* (Göttingen, 1994).

[60] An essential starting point for Gregory's view of saints' cults and hagiography remains R. Van Dam, *Saints and Their Miracles in Late Antique Gaul* (Princeton, NJ, 1993), esp. pp. 110–13 on the saints and the Last Judgement.

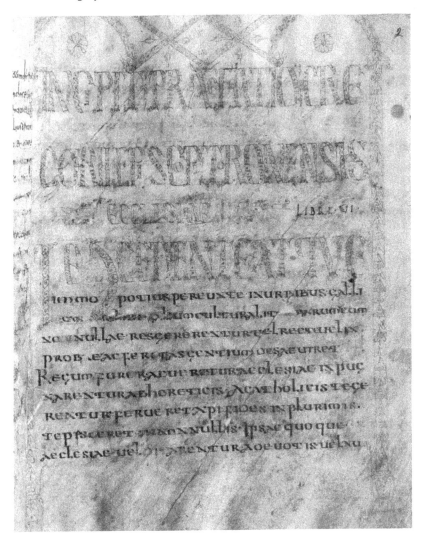

Figure 1 The opening of Gregory of Tours's *Histories* in a seventh-century Corbie manuscript.

to understanding how this worked. Like many other late antique and early medieval chronicles, it starts with Creation – although for narrative purposes it really begins with Cain's murder of Abel – and moves in a largely linear fashion towards a future End that is both distant and yet somehow tangible. His was not a triumphant narrative, and it began 'not

a few things have occurred, both proper and shameless'.[61] Developing
this theme through his history, Gregory placed 'good' stories antithet-
ically against no less instructive 'bad' ones, as he did for instance in his
comparison of how the sisters Brunhild and Galswinth were treated in
Gaul.[62] Alongside such structural devices, there seems to be a crescendo
of apocalyptic mood as the work unfolds. Nevertheless, we should resist
de Nie's conclusion that Gregory grew unhappier as he grew older.[63]
Guy Halsall, for instance, has shown that Gregory's apocalyptic laments
about civil wars were evident from the preface of Book V, based on a
sermon delivered in 576 after the assassination of King Sigibert I the
year before.[64] It may well be, then, that this represents the earliest part
of *Histories* that Gregory composed, which means that eschatology was
a central concern to the bishop from the very beginning all the way
through to their completion in 593 (and probably then his death a year
later). We need, then, to consider elements in Gregory's work as parts of
a whole.[65]

Let's begin by considering the eschatological scheme of the *Histories*
implied by its linear history. In many respects Gregory was entirely
orthodox here, having looked explicitly to Eusebius, Jerome, Orosius and
Victorius of Aquitaine for his basic framework.[66] Yet he noted: 'indeed,
it seems appropriate on account of those who despair at the approaching end of the world that it is explained openly [*aperte*] how many years
have passed since the beginning of the world – the collected sum of years

[61] Gregory of Tours, *Historiae*, Prefatio prima, ed. Krusch, p. 1: 'nonnullae res gererentur vel rectae vel inprobae.' I reject the standard English translation 'some of them good, some of them bad' (L. Thorpe, *The History of the Franks* [London, 1974], p. 63), as the Latin implies a more expanded moral sense of right and wrong rather than *bonum/malum*. Compare Bede's juxtaposition in *Historia Ecclesiastica*, pref., ed. Lapidge, p. 6.
[62] Gregory of Tours, *Historiae*, IV. 27–8, pp. 160–1. For two contrasting spins on this theme in Gregory's *Histories*, see Goffart, *The Narrators*, pp. 174–83 and Heinzelmann, *Gregory of Tours*, pp. 146–52.
[63] G. de Nie, *Views from a Many-Windowed Tower: Studies of Imagination in the Works of Gregory of Tours* (Amsterdam, 1987), p. 56: 'his view of the events of his own time was at first relatively optimistic but became increasingly grim as misfortunes continued to accumulate'. See Goffart, *The Narrators*, p. 187 n. 324: 'I disagree with [de] Nie ... as with other readings of the *Hist[oriae]* that presuppose a development in Gregory's outlook.'
[64] G. Halsall, 'The Preface to Book V of Gregory of Tours' *Histories*: Its Form, Context and Significance', *English Historical Review*, 122.496 (2007), 297–317, esp. pp. 301–2.
[65] This is the only strong objection to R. Landes, '*Millenarismus absconditus*: L'historiographie augustinienne et l'An Mil', *Le Moyen Age*, 98 (1992), 355–77, at p. 377, who suggested a small window of eschatological crisis in *c.* 590–2. Heinzelmann, *Gregory*, p. 84 n. 91: 'The danger of considering a single chapter in isolation is apparent here.' Aside from that point, the rest of Landes's analysis is not necessarily undermined.
[66] Gregory of Tours, *Historiae*, I. pref, p. 5.

passed from chronicles or histories.'[67] Solace in chronology is, however, provided only bluntly. At the end of Book IV – namely at the end of his prequels to Book V – he added up the total of years from Creation up to the death of Sigibert, giving a total of 5,774, but said nothing more about why this might be relevant to anybody.[68] The subject was then revisited at the end of the work, where Gregory updated the total to 5,792 (= AD 591). The comfort of this Eusebian chronology was that the Year 6000 still lay 208 years away – not that Gregory was remotely explicit about that, and indeed he maintained an Augustinian ambivalence by quoting the Gospel of Mark (13.32) on the matter.[69] 'Of the end of the world', he wrote, 'I believe that which was understood by people in the past – that first, Antichrist will come.'[70] And he had not. Yet it is an indication that, for Gregory, it was not merely time or sequence which indicated an ending, but sin and prodigies.

The prodigies which run through Gregory's *Histories* could be, by themselves, quite disconcerting. More often than not, as de Nie noted, their meaning was left unresolved, as if the reader were supposed to make the final interpretative leap without the author's strong guiding hand.[71] Maybe the overtones of divine punishment were obvious or worried Gregory. In the fifth year of Childebert (= 580), for instance, floods destroyed crops and cattle and damaged the walls of Lyon, an earthquake shook the walls of Bordeaux, there was an avalanche in the Pyrenees, villages near Bordeaux were burned by fires from heaven, Orléans burned too (impoverishing even the rich!); in Chartres, blood flowed from a loaf of bread, and Bourges was struck by a hailstorm.[72] As if these afflictions of the *civitates* (and elsewhere) were not enough, and as the kings

---

[67] I. pref, p. 3: 'Illud etiam placuit eos, qui adpropinquantem finem mundi disperant, ut, collectam per chronicas vel historias anteriorum annorum summam, explanitur aperte, quanti ab exordio mundi sint anni.'

[68] IV. 51, p. 190. The equation of AM 5774 with AD 575 is in keeping with Merovingian AM synchronisations of the two schemes –see below p. 91. The passage was repeated in Fredegar's epitome of Gregory (= III. 73, pp. 112–13), and a corrupted version appeared in the *Computus Bobiensis*, c. 78, PL, 129. 1312–13.

[69] X. 31, p. 537; I. pref., p. 5. Cf. Breukelaar, *Historiography and Episcopal Authority*, p. 53 (apocalypticism as the 'exclusive motive for the computation') and R. Landes, 'Lest the Millennium Be Fulfilled: Apocalyptic Expectations and the Pattern of Western Chronography 100–800 CE', in W. Verbeke, D. Verhelst and A. Welkenhuysen (eds.), *The Use and Abuse of Eschatology in the Middle Ages* (Leuven, 1988), pp. 137–211 at p. 166.

[70] I. pref., p. 4: 'De fine vero mundi ea sentio quae a prioribus didici, Antechristum prius esse venturo.' Antichrist will introduce circumcision and set himself up in the Temple of Jerusalem. Given that Gregory had just denounced the Arian heresy in the preface, the passage reads as if he was associating heresy with the opponents of Christ of the Last Times.

[71] de Nie, *Views*, pp. 49–50.

[72] Gregory of Tours, *Historiae*, V. 33, pp. 237–8.

prepared another civil war (*bellum civile*), a plague broke out and many died.[73] Gregory cried and quoted Job. But as the story unfolded, Gregory moved attention from the condition of the world to detail the vices and virtues of a succession of individuals who died of the plague, establishing a sustained mood of 'moral apocalypse', highlighting the importance of individual eschatologies within society as a whole. On the darker side, we have Queen Austrechild, wife of King Guntram, condemned for ordering the murder of her doctors on her death bed; on the other, Martin of Braga was mourned because he was well read and venerated St Martin. Both good and bad, the rightful and the shameless, would be judged. Prodigies in many ways only set the tone for God's Judgement.

The focus on individual eschatologies within a collective history was used elsewhere to pass powerful comment on the political sphere. A central moment in Gregory's narrative comes with King Guntram's visit to Orléans in 585 as the king of Burgundy extended his power to the west – including over Tours – in the wake of the murder of his brother Chilperic. The story played out to create the impression of a wise king and prophet pair such as David and Nathan, with Gregory clearly recommending himself for prominence.[74] At one point, at dinner, Guntram and Gregory each related a vision of the 'wicked' king Chilperic.[75] Gregory's played on an inversion of the *ecclesia Dei*, with the king 'tonsured as if he were ordained bishop, then carried on a plain seat covered only by a black cloth'.[76] Guntram replied with his own vision about the fate of such a sinner, in which three bishops – two, tellingly, related to Gregory – argued about Chilperic's fate. 'He should be consumed by fire for his sins', argued one, before Guntram realised he could see a cauldron boiling away, and into the fire the broken body of the king was cast to liquefy, leaving no trace.[77] This visionary moment reinforced the new unity of royal and episcopal authority at a crucial moment in Merovingian polit-

---

[73] V. 34, pp. 238–9.

[74] VIII. 1–7, pp. 370–6. Interpretation: Heinzelmann, *Gregory of Tours*, pp. 61–2. Useful additional reflection on Gregory's development of authority in I. Moreira, *Dreams, Visions and Spiritual Authority in Merovingian Gaul* (Ithaca, NY, and London, 2000), pp. 95–9.

[75] Gregory of Tours, *Historiae*, VIII. 5, p. 374. W. Levison, 'Die Politik in den Jenseitsvisionen des frühen Mittelalters', in his *Aus rheinischer und fränkischer Frühzeit* (Düsseldorf, 1948), pp. 229–46 at p. 231. Although Chilperic is often characterised as 'wicked' there might have been more ambiguity in Gregory's constructions: see Halsall, 'Nero or Herod?' and his addendum at http://600transformer.blogspot.co.uk/2011/12/good-king-chilperic-again.html.

[76] VIII. 5, p. 374: 'ante tonsorato capite, quasi episcopum ordinari; deinde super cathedram puram, sola fuligine tectam, inpositum ferri.'

[77] VIII. 5, p. 374: 'igni concremabitur pro sceleribus suis.'

ics, and did so by creating distance from a former king now characterised as a member of Antichrist's church and a sinner destroyed.

In the last books of the *Histories*, such stories are interwoven with more explicit apocalyptic framings of the *ecclesia Dei* in action. A letter sent by seven bishops to St Radegund, the founder of the nunnery whose funeral Gregory attended, proclaimed that 'as the world declines in its old age, faith bursts into flower through the contest of your sense'.[78] The old age of the world could be refreshed by good works and spirituality. Radegund's own perception of her work unsurprisingly incorporated the same theme:

> on account of the uncertainty of the human condition, moments and times – with, of course, the world running to an end – when some would rather observe their own rather than divine will, while I am still alive, and in full devotion, in Christ's name and with God to guide me, I send you this document in which I have set out all my plans [for the nunnery].[79]

These are, for sure, just two sentences in two long letters which Gregory copied out. They must have had immediate and localisable rhetorical use but, at the same time, they did not overwhelm the mood of the writings. Nevertheless, even in their wider context the sentences hint at the importance of proactively challenging laxity in the face of time running short.

Laxity, however, was the tip of the iceberg: there were charismatics putting themselves forwards as real alternatives to the piety and salvation offered by the episcopate.[80] Gregory tells the stories of three but also remarked that 'there are many who, exercising seductions, do not cease to put the rustic population in error – and of these people, so I imagine, the Lord said in his Gospel, in the last times pseudo-Christs and pseudo-prophets rise up and, making signs and prodigies, they lead the Elect into error'.[81] In modern historiography, different interpretations

---

[78] Gregory of Tours, *Historiae*, IX. 39, p. 461: 'nam, declinante tempore saeculi vetustate, vestri sensus certamine fides revirescit in flore.' On Radegund's spirituality, see J. Smith, 'Radegund Peccatrix: Authorizations of Virginity in Late Antique Gaul', in P. Rousseau and M. Papoutsakis (eds.), *Transformations of Late Antiquity: Essays for Peter Brown* (Aldershot, 2009), pp. 303–26.

[79] IX. 42, p. 471: 'Sed quoniam incerta sunt humanae conditionis momenta vel tempora, quippe undo in fine currente, cum aliqui magis propriae quam divinae cupiant voluntate servire, zelo ducta Dei, hanc suggestionis meae paginam mereto apostulatus vestry in Christi nomen supraestis porrego vel devota.'

[80] Discussed in M. Rouche, *L'Aquitaine des Wisigoths aux Arabes, 418–781* (Paris, 1979), pp. 409–14. The importance of these figures on Gregory's interpretation of history is stressed in Breukelaar, *Historiography and Episcopal Authority*, pp. 52–3.

[81] Gregory of Tours, *Historiae*, IX. 6, p. 420: 'Multi enim sunt, qui, has seductiones exercentes, populum rusticum in errore ponere non desistunt, de quibus, ut opinor,

have emerged concerning these stories. Rouche and Landes, as we shall see below, interpreted these people as popular messianic figures, stirred by apocalyptic fervour at odds with the mainstream. Both Goffart and Heinzelmann felt that such analysis neglected the role of the stories in the *Histories* as a whole, but while Goffart argued that Gregory was undermining such figures, Heinzelmann saw further evidence for the eschatology which permeates the text.[82] There is perhaps evidence both ways in the way the bishop stressed their apocalyptic resonance but, in the very next sentence, wrote 'that's enough about that – we'd better get back on track'.[83] Even when dealing with matters of the utmost importance, Gregory could be a slippery writer, so we need to take care not to misunderstand these stories.[84]

Gregory's three charismatics are treated with some disdain, all might agree. The first story concerned a man named Desiderius, who visited Tours in 587. He gained fame for seeming to heal people; this was, however, soon denounced as necromancy, and he was chased out of town after people became suspicious of how he knew secrets and of how much he ate. As a particular 'type' of character, to Gregory, he was clearly the kind of man who would pretend to be Christ in the Last Times.[85] (If Desiderius himself believed he was Christ, of course, then he was enacting the Second Coming and it was the End, but Gregory did not comment on Desiderius's thoughts on the matter.) This first story led Gregory to jump back seven years in his narrative to relate the story of the second charismatic. This man was unnamed and had caused trouble in Tours and Paris – largely, it seems, for wearing strange clothes, being uneducated and disruptive, and for trying to lead the 'multitude' into sacred places. He had, in other words, assumed religious leadership without authority. Nevertheless, he was eventually found drunk in church in Paris, where Bishop Ragnemod recognised him as one of his servants and took him away hastily. These two stories are told combined and straight after the account of more prodigies, achieving a tone which both vulgarised the behaviour of the unlegislated pseudo-holy men while affirming their relevance to an impending End-Times narrative.

---

et Dominus in euangelio ait, consurgere in novissimis temporibus pseudo-christus et pseudoprophetas, qui, dantes signa et prodigia, etiam electos in errore inducant.'

[82] Heinzelmann, *Gregory of Tours*, p. 83; Goffart, *The Narrators*, p. 187 (where in n. 323 he dismisses at least some as 'literary color rather than seriously meant').

[83] Gregory of Tours, *Historiae*, IX. 6, p. 420: 'De his ista sufficiant; nos potius ad propositium rediamus.'

[84] Useful comparison can be made with Ashley and Sheingorn's analysis of Bernard of Angers (eleventh century) as a 'trickster': K. Ashley and P. Sheingorn, *Writing Faith: Text, Sign, and History in the Miracles of Ste Foy* (Chicago, 1999), ch. 2.

[85] IX. 6, p. 417.

The third case Gregory related in Book X and was deployed between a story about the salvation of a good Syrian and the report of Ragnemod's death in 591.[86] Again, far from downplaying the significance of what happened, Gregory reintroduced his earlier theme by quoting from the Gospels: 'there will be pestilence and famine and earthquakes throughout the land; and pseudo-Christs and pseudo-prophets will rise up and they will make signs and prodigies in the heavens, so that they can hurl the Elect into error' (Mark 13.22). Indeed, plague returned to Marseilles and famine to the north-west, establishing, as Heinzelmann noted, the 'social circumstances' for anxiety.[87] At the time a man near Bourges was chopping wood and was attacked by flies (*muscae*) and was inspired to become a holy man in the Javols in the south, calling himself Christ and his wife 'Mary'. The False Christ's assumed identity implied that he believed he was overseeing the Last Days, that he was the Second Coming. He made prophecies, led prayers, and later on led an army of 3,000 – 'not just rustics, but also church priests' (*non solum rusticiores, verum etiam sacerdotes eclesiastici*) – who would rob the rich to feed the poor. Eventually, they made as if to attack Le Puy but then sent naked, dancing messengers, and the bishop's men sent in return simply killed 'this Christ, who ought better be named Antichrist' (*Christus ille, qui magis Antechristus nominare debet*). Once compared to Gregory's earlier account of *the* Antichrist in Jerusalem, the description is clearly meant typologically, conveying both opposition to the Church and the serious apocalyptic disorder such things posed. As Gregory lamented: still more tricksters came to lead the people (*populus*) astray.

Gregory's three charismatics are quite different despite fulfilling similar typological roles: one necromancer-trickster (a glutton), one low-born usurper of mainstream devotional practice (a drunk), and one proper, but anti-social, pseudo-Christ. The first two at least were not as openly anti-institutional or anti-clerical, but by promoting behaviour and assuming ideas which fell outside Gregory's sense of good order, they unsettled the *ecclesia Dei* and the authority of its own charismatics, the bishops. Gregory fretted about both *rustici* and the *populus*, as he indicated that the charismatics appealed to a wide cross-section of society but especially the undereducated. The salvation of the members of the *ecclesia* was at stake. There are also hints of different apocalypticisms at play. Gregory fully embraced the same sense of indefinite imminence as Gregory the Great, and wrote about the challenge from his three 'pseudo-Christs and pseudo-prophets' in as plainly apocalyptic terms as one could imagine,

---

[86] X. 25, pp. 517–19.
[87] Heinzelmann, *Gregory of Tours*, p. 83.

just as the pope had done in his letters to Constantinople.[88] The follow-ers of these charismatics, on the other hand, would have been partici-pating in a different kind of apocalyptic scenario more akin to popular millenarian movements, which is to say that they had features of ecstasy, active female involvement, a charismatic leader, popularity and oppos-ition to hierarchy.[89] The two did not sit easily together.

The triggers for these different apocalypticisms might not have been so different. Michel Rouche, citing Laplantine, analysed these cases on the basis that there are two causes of messianic movements: the destabilisa-tion of society or overwhelming frustration.[90] To this we should probably add the preaching of eschatological themes and Christian education in general, given that the logic and the form of these movements draw on a theological repertoire, shared with spiritual authorities in the community such as Gregory himself, but embraced differently. There was certainly enough in terms of plague, 'civil war' and general destabilisation to cause an 'eschatological crisis' in the last years of the sixth century. Bourges, home of the False Christ, had been the scene of great devastation and the death of 7,000 soldiers – an eschatologically significant number! – during fighting between Chilperic's and Guntram's supporters in 583.[91] Such miseries may well explain the False Christ and his popularity. The combination of destabilised social circumstances and utopian hopes – indeed, promises – should provoke response and attempts by people to take control. It is essential, therefore, to recognise that Gregory was also one of the people caught up in the apocalyptic agitation of events beyond his control, to which his solution was the unity of royal and episcopal authority to lead people to salvation.[92] Gregory, in other words, needs to be understood both on similar terms to the charismatics, and as an opponent to them.

The apocalyptic theme of Gregory's history was underscored by some of his closing statements. John of Patmos himself had ended Revelation

[88] This has rarely been acknowledged, despite the emphasis of N. Cohn, *The Pursuit of the Millennium: Revolutionary Millenarians and Mystical Anarchists of the Middle Ages* (2nd edn, London, 1970), p. 42. R. Landes, *Heaven on Earth: The Varieties of Millennial Experience* (Oxford, 2011), pp. 63–4 does note Gregory's apocalyptic voice, but never-theless insists on seeing the bishop primarily as a suppressor of popular, charismatic, millenarianism.

[89] Landes, '*Millenarismus absconditus*', 376–7, adding nuance to the definition by Cohn, *The Pursuit of the Millennium*, p. 13, which centres on movements which are collective, terrestrial, imminent, total and miraculous. See Introduction, pp. 12–13.

[90] Rouche, *L'Aquitaine*, p. 412.

[91] Gregory of Tours, *Historiae*, VI. 31, pp. 299–300.

[92] Note that Gregory was not against popular revolt per se, as is shown by the story in *Historiae* VI. 31, pp. 301–2, which ends with the army of King Childebert and Bishop Egidius rising up for not stopping Chilperic's destruction around Bourges.

with warnings against editing his words, threatening anyone who thought either to add or omit things (Rev. 22.18–19). Gregory followed a similar line but laid it on even more heavily, urging his successors in Tours not to rewrite or edit or destroy his work in any way at all, but to keep it all exactly as he had left it, lest they find themselves damned on Judgement Day.[93] (They were, however, given permission to put the work into verse.) For Landes this was really an appeal to preserve the 'anti-apocalyptic' Eusebian chronology which followed.[94] But really it underscored Gregory's own sense in which he was fighting for his version of events against the opinions of many around him.[95] Indeed, one of the first things which demonstrably happened to Gregory's text was that it was heavily edited to play down the bishop's role in the recent past.

Gregory's work, and its apocalyptic currents, ultimately needed prompt reassessment in light of political change. The oldest manuscripts bear testament to a version which omitted the last four books – a trimming down which, according to Helmut Reimitz, helped to downplay Gregory's attacks on the descendants of Chilperic, who dominated Frankish politics after King Chlotar II's victories in 613.[96] In the process of this political reworking of the text, Eusebian chronology was no longer the grand punchline of the work, and, since the period from late 584 was omitted, so too was the crescendo of prodigies and pseudo-Christs leading into Gregory's 'present'. Nevertheless, earlier material in Gregory's first six books could still be edited to unsettling effect. The epitome used in the Austrasian 'Fredegar Chronicles' of *c.* 660 condensed the signs, 'civil war' and death of Austrechild in 580 down into a chapter which maintained all the terror and none of the political commentary.[97] Meanwhile the material omitted from the six-book version was far from suppressed, and in at least three early copies, material from Books VII–X was restored by *c.* 800.[98] Editors and copyists were busy indeed, but it was the politics which triggered editorial sensitivity, not Gregory's apocalypticism. As

---

[93] X. 31, p. 536. Compare Irenaeus's words recorded in Eusebius-Rufinus, *Historia ecclesiastica*, V. 20, ed. T. Mommsen, Die Griechischen christlichen Schriftsteller der ersten drei Jahrhunderte: Eusebius Werke, 2 (2 vols., Leipzig, 1903), I. 483. Heinzelmann, *Gregory of Tours*, p. 94 and n. 3.

[94] Landes, 'Lest the Millennium Be Fulfilled', p. 167.

[95] In addition to the literature in nn. 62–4 on this subject see I. Wood, 'The Secret Histories of Gregory of Tours', *Revue Belge de philologie et d'histoire*, 71 (1993), 253–70.

[96] Reimitz, 'Social Networks', pp. 257–9. Compare Heinzelmann, *Gregory of Tours*, pp. 192–201.

[97] Fredegar, *Chronicae*, ed. B. Krusch, MGH SRM, 2 (Hanover, 1888), III. 82, p. 115.

[98] Cambrai, Bibliothèque municipale, MS 684 (624) (= *CLA*, no. 742a and 742b); Brussels, Koninklijke Bibliotheek van België, MS 9403 (= *CLA*, no. 1544); Heidelberg, Universitätsbibliothek, Cod. Pal. lat. 864 (a copy which also includes material from the Continuation of Fredegar).

Gregory's work was received and adapted by subsequent generations, his black humour may not have inspired imitation, but it was quite in keeping with later sensibilities.

Conclusion

The world as seen by the two Gregorys, then, was a dark and dangerous place. Civil war, 'barbarian' conquest, ecclesiastical disputes and missionary activity all played out under the shadows of the End – shadows which both figures created as much as lived through. The Augustinian suspicion about prediction remained strong, however, and there is no evidence that people were anticipating the Last Days to begin at a particular moment. Judgement was nevertheless close, and this was far from inconvenient. As Rome descended into chaos, Pope Gregory encouraged his people not to be passive, but to be restless, and to work hard both for individual and collective salvation. The very shape of Western Christendom changed, embracing the north more than ever before. Here Gregory of Tours articulated a vision of a world in conflict, which found leadership and direction in the union of royal and ecclesiastical authority. As the Bible had become more established as *the* common point of reference for Latin Christendom, ecclesiological and eschatological interpretations now generated a 'language of power' and action. This was not how Augustine or Jerome had been able to argue about the world (see Chapter 1). The historical reality of apocalypse, or at least its potentiality, helped to move society, from its emperors down. But there were competing visions in play. Gregory of Tours's messianic outsiders and his colouring of them attest to competing apocalyptic moods. Meanwhile, the two Gregorys articulated and disseminated their ideas specifically to engage audiences, who either had alternative views or else were there to be persuaded of a course of future action. As so often with the early Middle Ages, it is difficult to gauge the full extent to which there was a shared language or ongoing debate – but these voices survived, inspired and were adapted for generations. In embracing apocalyptic rhetoric and ideas, the Gregorys had begun to reform their world grown old and provide inspiration for many in the years to come.

3 The ends of time and space (*c. 600–c. 735*)

After the ravages of plague, the long seventh century witnessed a period of great creativity.[1] Many historians have considered this a proper 'Dark Age', of chaotic politics and of learning in decline, and yet this was also a time of innovation in law and monastic organisation, when missionaries proactively sought to expand Christendom north and east, and the Irish and Isidore of Seville transformed the frameworks for knowledge. While the power of Merovingian kings might have declined over time, this was in many respects a time of strength and vitality for Frankish, Visigothic, English and Irish political orders compared to the sixth century.[2] As so often, the colour of history depends on which hues one prefers. Eschatology and apocalypticism were, regardless, rarely divorced from the cultural intersections which shaped change. At times they lurked, unsettlingly, on the peripheries of 'corporate' ideas, particularly following Isidore's reformulation of the Hieronymian-Prosperian chronicle. At other times, they stood centre stage as a major element in ascetic renunciation and attempts to improve morality throughout society. No less than under Gregory the Great and Gregory of Tours, Augustinian sensibilities were adapted, adopted and reshaped to meet new needs – and not silently, or hidden away in impenetrable intellectual tomes, but for a range of publics and situations.

Fundamentally, the major developments in apocalyptic thought responded to the need to orientate personal eschatologies within time. Christianity was a religion with a 'complete' narrative, contained between a firm beginning and ending which projected meaning, if not onto everything that happened, then at least onto the temporal space

---

[1] J. Fontaine and J. N. Hillgarth (eds.), *Le septième siècle, changements et continuités* (London, 1992), esp. the essay by Hillgarth himself, 'Eschatological and Political Concepts in the Seventh Century', pp. 212–35.

[2] As the chapter covers significant ground, readers in need of orientation could consult the following: I. N. Wood, *The Merovingian Kingdoms 450–750* (Harlow, 1994); R. Collins, *Visigothic Spain 409–711* (Oxford, 2004); C. Wickham, *The Inheritance of Rome: A History of Europe from 400 to 1000* (London, 2009).

in which it occurred. History was salvation history. At a practical level, envisaging the totality of history was only so useful as a tool of moral correction because it was meditative rather than exhortative, and many historians signalled their lessons rather than explaining them directly. One read not only the story but, as with Roman historiography, also the form and the anti-language.[3] Sermons and the rapidly developing tales of the afterworld complemented the big picture by drawing attention to the fate of the individual's soul more directly.[4] Together, these worlds of moral reflection addressed two different sides of the same issue, drawing on a broad repertoire from the apocalyptic–eschatological spectrum. Judgement concerned everyone, regardless of the proximity of the end of the world, because everyone would die at some point and, one way or another, be catapulted towards that last day. The fate of the individual of the soul had to be adequately theorised, particularly for anyone who would not witness the Last Times themselves, and so who needed to know how they fitted into things at a universal level.

Scholars have often treated the fate of the individual soul and the world-in-collective separately, and sometimes for good reasons. Nevertheless, in this chapter I want to process issues of eschatology and apocalypse alongside each other because they were related bodies of thought and the same people tended to develop both, notably Julian of Toledo (d. 690) and the Venerable Bede (d. 735) in Northumbria. Indeed, this multi-fronted pursuit to understand the End from both personal and collective perspectives is arguably the most radical contribution to apocalyptic thought in the period from the Gregorys and Bede.[5] So many sources reveal that the shadow of the End continued to weigh heavily upon the imagination as a spur to action, and even millenarianism was not banished as comprehensively as some have believed. Now, it may dampen things to note that the wealth of liturgical material produced in the period contains little to no reference to the End Times, even where Revelation was used – unglossed! – in readings.[6] Nevertheless, as we shall see, the *battle* for universal liturgical rhythms actively ensured

[3] J. Henderson, *Fighting for Rome: Poets and Caesars, History and Civil War* (Cambridge, 1998).
[4] Important on the development of visions of the afterlife is C. Carozzi, *Le voyage de l'âme dans l'Au-delà, d'après la littérature latine (Ve–XIIIe siècle)* (Rome, 1994). For an attempt to see early purgatorial thought detached from its later baggage, see I. Moreira, *Heaven's Purge: Purgatory in Late Antiquity* (Oxford, 2010), although possibly too much is placed on idiosyncratic Bede.
[5] Cf. C. Carozzi, *Apocalypse et salut dans le christianisme ancien et médiéval* (Paris, 1999), pp. 62–7.
[6] *The Bobbio Missal*, cc. 262 and 271, ed. E. A. Lowe, Henry Bradshaw Society, 58 (London, 1920), pp. 78–9, 81–2 (readings from Rev. 1 and 4 at Easter).

that millenarian and apocalyptic thought remained on the agenda. The seventh century witnessed not the triumph of a non-apocalyptic eschatology, but the development of a wider reconceptualisation of humanity's endings and its duties to act.

Columbanus and the ends of the earth

As we left Gregory the Great in the last chapter, his work and worldview were being amplified by the similar ideas of the Irishman St Columbanus (d. 615). He had been a teacher at Bangor in County Down before travelling to the Frankish kingdoms in 590 and embarking on a cantankerous career as monastic founder, missionary and critic of kings. Christianity in Ireland was founded strongly upon eschatological traditions.[7] St Patrick, the apostle of the Irish, had seen his missionary work in the late fifth century squarely as fulfilment of Christ's missionary imperative (Matt. 24.14) in an apocalyptic framework:

However ignorant I am, he has heard me, so that in these last days I can dare to undertake such a holy and wonderful work. In this way I can imitate somewhat those whom the Lord foretold would announce his gospel in witness to all nations before the end of the world. This is what we see has been fulfilled. Look at us: we are witnesses that the gospel has been preached right out to where there is nobody else![8]

Patrick's apocalypticism was attractive. Muirchú, in renarrativising the story of Patrick, made the saint's recitation of Revelation central to his assiduity in prayer.[9] Patrick was also to judge the Irish on Judgement Day, in a nice twist on Gregory representing the English.[10] A different tradition, set down by Tírechán around the same time, had Patrick request that the Irish be spared the floods seven years before Judgement.[11] The

---

[7] There is no reliable overview of Irish eschatology in this period but many useful things can be found through the *De finibus* project website: http://definibus.ucc.ie/.

[8] Patrick, *Confessio*, c. 34, ed. L. Bieler, *Libri epistolarum sancti Patricii episcopi* (Dublin, 1993), I. 76: 'qui me audieret ut ego inscius et *in nouissimis diebus* hoc opus tam pium et tam mirificum auderem adgredere, ita ut imitarem quippiam illos quos ante Dominus iam olim praedixerat praenuntiaturos euangelium suum *in testimonium omnibus gentibus ante finem mundi*, quod ita ergo uidimus itaque suppletum est: ecce testes sumus quia euangelium praedicatum est usque ubi nemo ultra est.' See also Patrick, *Epistola ad milites Corotici*, c. 40, ed. Bieler, I. 80–1.

[9] Muirchú, *Vita Patricii*, II. 1, ed. L. Bieler, *The Patrician Texts in the Book of Armagh* (Dublin, 1979), p. 114.

[10] Ibid., II. 6 (5), p. 116.

[11] Tírechán, *Collectanea de sancto Patricio*, ed. Bieler, *Patrician Texts*, p. 164. See also the *Cáin Fhuithirbe*, written shortly after 680 (L. Breatnach, 'The Ecclesiastical Element in the Old Irish Legal Tract *Cáin Fhuithirbe*', *Peritia*, 5 (1986), 36–52 at pp. 50–1).

End Times played an important role in early Irish Christian identity with consequences for later developments on the continent.

Elements of Irish eschatology flicker in Columbanus's own career on the continent. In a letter to Pope Boniface IV (608–15), he argued that although the Irish lived in the farthest parts of the world they were orthodox (and, in Gregorian spirit, despite being in a world of stormy seas).[12] He did not shy away from the urgency of their shared situation: 'the world already declines, the prince of shepherds draws near.'[13] There was even a little linguistic play here, as Columbanus had added 'draws near' (*appropinquat*) in place of Peter's original 'when [he] appears' (*cum apparuit* – 1 Peter 5.4). This is another good example of apocalyptic intensification, turning the indefinite into something more pressing. What alarmed Columbanus was the prominence of heresy in Lombardy, both with Arianism – although he made some headway at the Lombard court – and the Three Chapters controversy, neither of which the pope seemed to have in hand.[14] Peace was needed and soon. Pope Boniface could, perhaps, have pointed to his more immediate problems with famine, plague and floods as an excuse for his inactivity.[15] But Columbanus was struck by the fleeting nature of the mortal life, and the need to keep one's mind on higher things.[16]

The transitory nature of earthly things was a major theme in Columbanus's monastic sermons.[17] These the saint composed as a series, in which he explored a number of themes relating to internal discipline and the fate of the soul. 'The world will pass and passes daily, and revolves towards its end (for what does it have that it does not assign an ending?)' he argued, 'and in a manner it is propped up upon the pillars of vanity.'[18] The only way to embrace the eternal was to reject possession and home.

---

[12] Columbanus, *Epistola*, 5. 3, ed. G. S. M. Walker, Scriptores Latini Hiberniae, 2 (Dublin, 1970), p. 38 Compare of course Gregory's letter to Leander: Gregory the Great, *Moralia in Job*, Epistola, ed. M. Adriaen, CCSL, 143 (3 vols, Turnhout, 1979–85), I. 2–3.

[13] Columbanus, *Epistola*, 5. 4, ed. Walker, p. 40. See also 5. 15, p. 54, on Judgement and non-Christians.

[14] See Columbanus, 5. 15, p. 54. On Columbanus and the Three Chapters, see P. Gray and M. Herren, 'Columbanus and the Three Chapters Controversy – A New Approach', *Journal of Theological Studies*, n.s., 45 (1994), 160–70.

[15] *Liber pontificalis*, 69, ed. L. Duchesne (Paris, 1886), p. 317.

[16] Columbanus, *De mundi transitu*, ed. and trans. Walker, pp. 182–5. The attribution to Columbanus is defended in D. Schaller, '"De mundi transitu": A Rhythmical Poem by Columbanus', in M. Lapidge (ed.), *Columbanus: Studies on the Latin Writings* (Woodbridge, 1997), pp. 240–54.

[17] The authenticity of the sermons is defended in C. Stancliffe, 'The Thirteen Sermons Attributed to Columbanus', in Lapidge, *Columbanus*, pp. 93–199.

[18] Columbanus, *Instructiones*, 3. 1, ed. Walker, p. 72: 'Mundus enim transibit et cottidie transit et rotatur ad finem (quid enim habet quod fini non assignet?) et quodammodo vanitatis columnis fulcitur.'

It was for that reason, it seemed, that Columbanus left Ireland in the first place, providing a mode of permanent exilic existence which he hoped others could embrace.[19] This seems to have extended to engaging in missionary work as he spent a while as a missionary in Alemannia in *c.* 610, although there is no extant evidence that this was a deliberate attempt to fulfil prophecy in the way that Patrick or Gregory might have imagined.[20] The power of an eschatologically inspired lifestyle nevertheless ran deep and Columbanus's own sadness, when King Theuderic of Burgundy tried to have him exiled a year earlier, was palpable.[21] It was felt, too, by Columbanus's hagiographer, Jonas of Susa, who was afflicted by fever upon visiting his childhood home until he returned to his monastery.[22] Jonas also turned his hand to writing a series of stories about people threatened by visions of Judgement or by demons, all of which served to rephrase Columbanus's argument against worldly things (and, in reality, to encourage those in Columbanian houses to submit to Columbanian discipline).[23]

Jonas's repackaging of Columbanus's eschatological piety raises important issues about the direction of Western (continental) monasticism. As Albrecht Diem has argued, there was a point at which Jonas's hagiographical project and the quest for discipline within Columbanian houses cohered to institutionalise the saint's charisma and spirituality.[24] For the 'holy man', this meant less opportunity to wander about exploring asceticism in an unregulated manner. It also therefore meant that the ideas of a popular apocalypse-preaching charismatic had been channelled into a monastic setting rather than into excitable public devotion. Columbanus's work can hardly be said to have unfolded without opposition, thanks to his commitment to an Easter reckoning unpopular on the continent, and his harsh asceticism.[25] But his eschatological vision

---

[19] Columbanus, *Instructiones*, 8, ed. Walker, pp. 94–7.

[20] Jonas, *Vita Columbani*, ed. B. Krusch, MGH SRG, 37 (Hanover, 1905), I. 27, pp. 213–14. On Columbanian influence on developing ideas of universal mission see W. H. Fritze, 'Universalis gentium confessio: Formeln, Träger und Wege universalmissionarischen Denkens im 7. Jahrhundert', *Frühmittelalterliche Studien*, 3 (1969), 78–130 at pp. 84–8.

[21] Columbanus, *Epistola*. 4. 8, ed. Walker, pp. 34–5; Jonas, *Vita Columbani*, I. 20 and 23, ed. Krusch, pp. 193–4 and pp. 205–6.

[22] Jonas, *Vita Columbani*, ed. Krusch, II. 5, pp. 237–8.

[23] See A. O'Hara, 'Death and the Afterlife in Jonas of Bobbio's *Vita Columbani*', *Studies in Church History*, 45 (2009), 64–73. Dr O'Hara argues that Jonas's stories are 'not eschatological' (p. 72), but I would suggest that the eschatological function supports the institutional one he identifies.

[24] A. Diem, 'Monks, Kings, and the Transformation of Sanctity: Jonas of Bobbio and the End of the Holy Man', *Speculum*, 82.3 (2007), 521–59.

[25] See especially C. Stancliffe, 'Columbanus and the Gallic Bishops', in G. Constable and M. Rouche (eds.), *Auctoritas: Mélanges offerts au Professeur Olivier Guillot* (Paris, 2006), pp. 205–15.

proved less controversial, even inspiring in the case of Jonas. The institutional context successfully framed Columbanus's spirituality and, with
some modifications, took it forward into the next generation of thinkers.
Eschatological renunciation was mainstream.

One of the best known facets of Columbanian monasticism was the
way it was supported enthusiastically by the Frankish nobility in the
seventh century. There were, at times, hints of abuse, of *Klosterpolitik*,
with the powerful playing monasteries against ecclesiastical authority by
supporting their rights to 'immunities'.[26] But there was also a spiritual
agenda, stimulated by Columbanus's insistence on divorcing monastic
life from things secular, including the Church. Even here, secular leaders
stood to the fore where they could. We can see this, for instance, in Clovis
II's privileges for Saint-Denis in 654 which talked at length about the
intercession of saints and seeking eternal life.[27] Political action was being
driven by concerns about Judgement. Indeed, it is then doubly striking
that Clovis's wife Balthild (d. 680), who sought to use monastic patronage and episcopal appointments politically, was also considered by her
hagiographer-apologist to have begun an almost millenarian era of peace
through her work.[28] The better defined the lines between spiritual and
secular, the easier it was to appropriate each side to buttress power.

Lay enthusiasm for Columbanian monasticism paved the way for
embracing other eschatologically minded wanderers. The most prominent was St Fursey, an Irishman famed for his visions, who was warmly
received by the courts of Sigibert in East Anglia and Clovis II in
Neustria.[29] The *Journey of Blessed Fursey*, probably written in Péronne
late in the seventh century, is an account of Fursey's life which incor-
porates a number of visions, which mark a turning point in the literary
representation of Purgatory and the fate of the soul before Judgement.[30]

---

[26] E. Ewig, 'Das Privileg des Bischofs Berthefrid von Amiens für Corbie von 664 und die
Klosterpolitik der Königin Balthild,' *Francia*, 1 (1973), 62–114. The best treatment of
monastic immunities is B. Rosenwein, *Negotiating Space: Power, Restraint, and Privileges
of Immunity in Early Medieval Europe* (Manchester, 1999).

[27] *Diplomata*, no. 85, ed. T. Kölzer, MGH Diplomata regum Francorum e stirpe
Merovingica (Hanover, 2001), I. 218; *Chartae latinae antiquiores*, 13 (Zürich, 1981),
pp. 40–1 (= no. 558).

[28] *Vita Balthildae*, c. 5, ed. B. Krusch, MGH SRM, 2 (Hanover, 1888), pp. 487–8 (both
versions). J. L. Nelson, 'Queens as Jezebels: Brunhild and Balthild in Merovingian
History', in her *Politics and Ritual in Early Medieval Europe* (London, 1986), pp. 1–48 at
pp. 21–2.

[29] Bede, *Historia ecclesiastica*, III. 19, ed. M. Lapidge (2 vols, Rome, 2010), II. 82–94. On
Fursey's career see M. Brown, *The Life of Fursey: What We Know, Why It Matters*, Fursey
Occasional Paper 1 (Norwich, 2001).

[30] Carozzi, *Le voyage*, pp. 99–138 but with caution urged fairly by Moreira, *Heaven's Purge*,
pp. 127–9. The text is edited by Carozzi at pp. 679–92.

The first was triggered by a near-death experience, with the highlight being a vision of demons defeated by angels.[31] A sense of personal apocalypse was reinforced by the concern, again, for punishment by fire, meted out according to the severity of sin, with four different stations seen by Fursey as a lesson for the laity.[32] It is unlikely this gave hope that penance could be enjoined after death, but rather stood as a warning for the living.[33] More striking still was a vision in which he met two holy men (*viri venerabiles*), who commanded him to return to earth 'and preach to all that Judgement is near'.[34] Asking them about the end of the world, however, Fursey was told that it was not near, but that the human race would be vexed by famine and plague – interpreted allegorically as struggles and punishment. Judgement was ever-present.

While Fursey's visions represented one of the first medieval tours of the afterlife, the first politicised one followed only shortly afterwards in the *Vision of Barontus*, written sometime after 678/9.[35] The text was one of the 'bestsellers' of the early Middle Ages, and even generated an illustrated version for the library of King Charles the Bald, all no doubt for its clear moral lessons.[36] Barontus was a nobleman and a recent convert to the monastic life in Lonrey, near Bourges, when he fell ill and had a vision of heaven and hell. Much more than Fursey's, this vision was directly inspired by the Gregorian *Dialogues* and the pope's eschatological *Homilies on the Gospels*, which meant that there was an emphasis on the living's intercessions for the dead and penance.[37] Barontus himself, when seized by demons for his sins as a layman which included having three

[31] *Transitus beati Fursei*, cc. 6–8, ed. Carozzi, pp. 681–3. The most recent assessment, in relation to 'Irish' tariffed penance, is M. Dunn, *The Vision of St Fursey and the Development of Purgatory*, Fursey Occasional Paper 2 (Norwich, 2007) but see Moreira, *Heaven's Purge*, pp. 116–17 and pp. 125–9.

[32] *Transitus beati Fursei*, c. 8, ed. Carozzi, pp. 682–3. The description of the fires seen by Fursey was the section of the text which most impressed Bede. Carozzi, *Le voyage*, pp. 132–7 on the instructive penitential mode of the account.

[33] Moreira, *Heaven's Purge*, pp, 115–25.

[34] *Transitus beati Fursei*, c. 12, ed. Carozzi, p. 687: 'ergo omnibus adnuntia quia in proximo est vindicata'.

[35] *Visio Baronti*, ed. W. Levison, MGH SRG, 5 (Hanover, 1910), pp. 377–94. The date is indicated at the end with a mark of almost legal authenticity: 'acta sunt haec omnia viii. kal. April. in sexto anno regnanate Theoderico regem Francorum.' On the text: J. Contreni, '"Building Mansions in Heaven": The *Visio Baronti*, Archangel Raphael, and a Carolingian King', *Speculum*, 78.3 (2003), 673–706 and Y. Hen, 'The Structure and Aims of the *Visio Baronti*', *Journal of Theological Studies*, n.s. 47 (1996), 477–97.

[36] Now St Petersburg, Publichnaja Biblioteka, O. v. I. 5 On the manuscript see, Contreni, 'Building Mansions', and on the library see R. McKitterick, 'Charles the Bald (823–877) and His Library: The Patronage of Learning', *EHR*, 95.374 (1980), 28–47.

[37] The author of the *Visio Baronti* differed from Gregory in his promotion of almsgiving and good works: Contreni, 'Building Mansions', pp. 687–90; Hen, 'Structure and Aims', pp. 491–3.

wives, was saved by St Peter because he had given up everything upon
his conversion – or at least, what little he had kept for himself, he agreed
to release upon his return to the living. This was but one piece in an
extended lesson about the communal responsibility for individual eschatologies, with the living and dead bound together to work for individual
souls.[38] What made the *Vision of Barontus* so political was that it identified
recently deceased figures from the monastery in heaven, and named the
recently deceased diocesan bishop Vulfoleodus of Bourges and his neighbour Dido of Poitiers in hell.[39]

The political circumstances of the vision provide some indication of
how we should understand all this. Claude Carozzi suggested that there
was some regional partisanship involved because the author curiously
omitted mention of the monastery's founder, Sigiramnus, in heaven,
and because of the hostility towards Vulfoleodus and Dido.[40] Yet, as
Hen pointed out, no one from the distant past is mentioned in heaven,
and it is hard to see the condemnation of the bishops as anything other
than a political reaction against episcopal involvement in opposition to
kings Sigibert III and Dagobert II.[41] Whether this is sufficient, as Hen
also suggests, to make the *Vision* a 'declaration [of] affiliation with the
Merovingian court', is not clear, especially given the monastic homiletic
mood of the text. We could look to a slightly different political context,
for 678/9 was the same time that Dido's nephew, Bishop Leudegar of
Autun, was captured and murdered by the men of Ebroin and King
Theuderic III for taking a leading role in the coup of Childeric II in 673–
5, the end of which caused so much distress that 'it was believed that
manifestly the coming of Antichrist was at hand'.[42] Rivalries involved
here are well known to have driven the production of competitive hagi-
ographies.[43] What better an environment in which to write a lament in

[38] A similar point is made by Carozzi, *Le voyage*, p. 173.
[39] *Visio Baronti*, c. 8 (heaven) and c. 17 (hell). W. Levison, 'Die Politik in den Jenseitsvisionen des frühen Mittelalter', in his *Aus rheinischer und fränkischer Frühzeit* (Düsseldorf, 1948), p. 234.
[40] Carozzi, *Le voyage*, pp. 140–4.
[41] Hen, 'Structure and Aims', 494–7. Dido's role in the 'Grimoald coup': *Liber historiae Francorum*, c. 43, ed. B. Krusch, MGH SRM, 2 (Hanover, 1888), p. 316. Vulfoleodus holding a synod without Sigibert's permission: Sigibert, *Epistolae Desiderii*, II. 17, ed. W. Arndt, MGH Epp., 2 (Berlin, 1892), p. 212.
[42] *Passio Leudegarii*, c. 15, ed. Krusch, MGH SRM, 5 (Hanover and Leipzig, 1890), p. 296: 'ut manifeste crederetur adventum imminere Antichristi.' *Liber historiae Francorum*, c. 45, ed. Krusch, p. 317 Context in Wood, *The Merovingian Kingdoms*, pp. 224–38; R. Gerberding, *The Rise of the Carolingians and the Liber Historiae Francorum* (Oxford, 1987), ch. 5; P. Fouracre and R. Gerberding, *Late Merovingian France: History and Hagiography, 640–720* (Manchester, 1996), pp. 198–200.
[43] P. Fouracre, 'Merovingian History and Merovingian Hagiography', *P&P*, 127 (1990), 3–38 at pp. 13–26.

a sermonic tone in which bishops could be condemned in hell for their worldliness– 'the proud with the proud, the self-indulgent with the self-indulgent, liars with liars, murderers with murderers, the jealous with the jealous, detractors with detractors, deceivers with deceivers'?[44] The politics would be about defending a rightful order of things as much as promoting any pro-Merovingian sentiments.

With the Gregorian *Dialogues*, *Journey of Blessed Fursey* and *Vision of Barontus*, a new idea of 'moral and personal apocalypse' had been articulated which emphasised personal responsibility for salvation within a collective framework more than ever before. Seeing action in the world as a tension between sin and penance coloured the world in a way which meant that God's mercy on Judgement Day could not be relied on as the ultimate 'get-out clause'. Peter Brown has argued that this is one of the defining features of a distinctly Western early medieval Christian worldview, which had no direct parallels in Byzantine Christianity or Islam where God's final call remained all important.[45] How souls got from death to the Last Judgement could be visualised and the necessary action by the living for both themselves and the departed could be called for, because all debts had to be paid. In apocalyptic terms, this was literally revelatory but also important for the 'codification' of the relationship between the living and the dead and, therefore, a crucial part of how people understood their own place in the totality of salvation history.[46] Augustine's 'seventh world age', which runs in parallel to the sixth but which is not earthly, is perhaps a helpful way of thinking about this, because people belonged not to one progression of time but two: one in the world and one outside. If it were otherwise, the apocalypse would only affect the last people, whereas in theological terms it was a matter for everyone regardless of when they lived or died.

Isidore's final countdown and the way back to millenarianism

Developments in the Iberian peninsula brought unintended consequences for apocalyptic thought elsewhere. Gregory's tense sense of imminence

---

[44] *Visio Baronti*, c. 17, ed. Levison, p. 391: 'superbi cum superbis, luxoriosi cum luxoriosis, periuri cum periuris, homicidi cum homicidis, invidi cum invidis, detractores cum detractoribus, fallaces cum fallacibus.'

[45] P. Brown, 'The Decline of the Empire of God: Amnesty, Penance, and the Afterlife from Late Antiquity to the Middle Ages', in C. W. Bynum and P. Freedman (eds.), *Last Things: Death and the Apocalypse in the Middle Ages* (Philadelphia, PA, 2000), pp. 41–59 at pp. 58–9.

[46] 'Codification' suggested in Carozzi, *Le voyage*, p. 639.

had little place under the Visigoths, despite a strong interest in the pope's works.[47] There was a healthy concern for Judgement, as Julian of Toledo's popular and influential *Prognosticum futuri saeculi* shows.[48] In 633, at the Fourth Council of Toledo led by the powerful bishop and influential intellectual Isidore of Seville (d. 636) alongside King Sisenand (r. 661–36), bishops not only affirmed the authority of Revelation but ordered that it be used in preaching at Easter and Pentecost.[49] Isidore also wrote about Antichrist as a future enemy who would bring persecutions, pretend to be Christ and rebuild the temple in Jerusalem.[50] Few writers used any of this lighter eschatological mood to motor reform or to criticise current affairs, with Braulio of Zaragossa's hopeful grumbling about King Chindesuinth's violence around 642 almost all there is.[51] This impression maybe distorted, however, by the fact that we have a wealth of legal material but little of the rich chronicle or hagiographical material found elsewhere.[52] We cannot expect the 'logic of apocalypse' to look the same. Nevertheless, the way in which time was conceptualised by Isidore in particular would have far-reaching effects.

The crucial issues emerged out of Isidore's chronographical writings, as Landes pointed out. At one level Isidore followed in the footsteps of other continuators of Jerome's Eusebian canons, with AM[II] a defining feature of his two chronicles (and the Spanish 'era' date the basic measure

[47] Hillgarth, 'Eschatological and Political Concepts', p. 225; T. Stancati, *Julian of Toledo: Prognosticum futuri saeculi* (New York, 2010), p. 248. For a survey of eschatological thought in Visigothic Spain see L. A. García Moreno, 'Expectatives milenaristas y escatolólogicas en la España tardoantigua (ss. V–VIII)', in *Spania. Estudis d'Antiguitat Tardana oferts en homenatge al professor Pere de Palol I Salellas* (Barcelona, 1996), pp. 103–9.

[48] Julian of Toledo, *Prognosticum futuri saeculi*, ed. J. N. Hillgarth, CCSL, 115 (Turnhout, 1976), pp. 1–126 on which, alongside the commentary by Stancati, see J. Wood, 'Individual and Collective Salvation in Late Visigothic Spain', *Studies in Church History*, 45 (2009), 74–86 at pp. 81–5. See also Fructuosus, *Epistolae Braulii*, no. 43, PL, 80. 691; Ildefonsus of Toledo, *Epistola ad Quirico*, PL, 96. 194; Taio of Zaragossa, *Sententiae*, pref., c. 4, PL, 80. 729–30; Ervig, *Forum Iudicum*, XII. 14, ed. K. Zeumer, MGH LL nationum Germanicarum, 1 (Hanover, 1902), p. 442.

[49] Toledo IV, c. 17, ed. G. Martinínez Diez and F. Rodríguez, *La colección hispania* (6 vols., Madrid and Barcelona, 1966–2002), V. 205–6. On Isidore see J. Fontaine, *Isidore de Séville: genèse et originalité de la culture hispanique au temps des Wisigoths* (Turnhout, 2000) and P. Cazier, *Isidore de Séville et la naissance de l'Espagne catholique* (Paris, 1994).

[50] Isidore, *Etymologiae*, VIII. 11. 20–2, ed. W. Lindsay (Oxford, 1911) [unpaginated]; *Sententiae*, I. 25, ed. P. Cazier, CCSL, 111 (Turnhout, 1998), pp. 79–80. Important given the unification of Spain, conversion of the Jews and the building of the new church in Toledo, while things were going less well in the East: García Moreno, 'Expectativas milenaristas', pp. 106–7.

[51] Braulio of Zaragossa, *Epistolae Braulii*, no. 24, PL, 80. 673. *Chronicle of 754*, c. 29, ed. J. Gil, in *Corpus scriptorum Muzarabicorum* (Madrid, 1974), p. 22.

[52] Wickham, *The Inheritance of Rome*, pp. 130–1.

of time's passing in his *History of the Goths, Vandals and Suebi*.[53] Prosper, Victor of Tunnuna and John of Biclarum had each arranged chronological material relative to reigns of emperors or to consuls, with AM dates only in summaries at the end.[54] Isidore, on the other hand, added AM numbers for the emperors' deaths, so, for example, the sack of Rome was now filed under 'Honorius with his younger brother Theodosius, reigned 15 years, AM 5621'.[55] He had injected a sense of the universal into local date-markers and in the process started to make time more abstract and linear. More problematic still, Isidore accidentally gave rise to a new way to think about apocalyptic time because he was the first person to apply the six world ages as an organisational category within a universal history.[56] His chronicles divided history accordingly, and therefore served to emphasise that all the history that had happened since the Incarnation had belonged to the Sixth Age and so had unfolded in the shadow of the End. Isidore scarcely acknowledged this in his preface, as he explained time as a relentless 'succession' and pointed out his simple debt to earlier chronographers. At the end of the *Chronica maiora*, he moved to control his readers' understanding of his calculations by citing the usual statements about how the End could not be known. The abstract structures of the work, however, encouraged readers to pay closer attention to the clock ticking down to the Year 6000.

Countdowns, or *summae annorum*, became a common feature of Isidorian chronicles as they entered Irish computistics and Frankish historiography. Isidore had a deep interest in structure, hence etymologies and investigations into temporality and nature – all of which appealed greatly to readers in Ireland who were already working through similar

---

[53] The different extant endings give AM^II 5813 (Herakleios 5), AM^II 5821 (Herakleios 16) and AM 5831 (Herakleios 21). One explanation for the Era date – that it is based on backprojecting Easter tables – is given by O. Neugebauer, 'On the Spanish Era', *Chiron*, 11 (1981), 371–80 and the texts of the *Historia Gothorum, Vandalorum et Suevorum*, ed. C. Rodríguez Alonso (Léon, 1975).

[54] Victor of Tunnona, *Chronica*, ed. T. Mommsen, MGH AA, 9 (Berlin, 1892), p. 206 (AM 5766); John of Biclarum, *Chronica*, ed. Mommsen, MGH AA, 9, p. 220 (AM 5791).

[55] Isidore, *Chronica maiora*, cc. 371–2, ed. J. C. Martín, CCSL, 112 (Turnhout, 2003), pp. 206–9.

[56] R. Landes, 'Lest the Millennium Be Fulfilled: Apocalyptic Expectations and the Pattern of Western Chronography, 100–800 CE', in W. Verbeke, D. Verhelst, and A. Welkenhuysen (eds.), *The Use and Abuse of Eschatology in the Middle Ages* (Leuven, 1988), pp. 137–211 at pp. 165–6. The scheme is not always consistently applied in manuscripts of the *Chronica maiora* – I note in Paris, Bibliothèque nationale, lat. 10910 (before 715, possibly Lyon) only the third and sixth ages are labelled (f. 172v and f. 177v) and in Albi, Bibliothèque municipale, MS 29 (= *CLA*, no. 705, Spain or Septimannia, mid-eighth-century) only the fourth age is not labelled but the sixth age starts with Octavian rather than Tiberius (f. 28v). The scheme is more consistently applied in the *Chronica minora*: Isidore, *Etymologiae*, V. 39. 2–25.

issues when Isidore's work appeared there within his lifetime.[57] The greatest consequence of this Hiberno-Hispanic learning was that time was no longer an Augustinian 'mystery', but a collection of artificial structures superimposed on a natural world full of laws and rhythms, which were often cyclical yet were so only within a rigid linear timeline.[58] Once combined with eschatological reflection the conclusion was straightforward: 'time is the space which extends from the beginning up until the end.'[59] It was finite, enclosed and measureable. It was, therefore, a natural extension of counting the years up to the present to then count up to the next big millennial marker, the Year 6000. Of course, as far as we can tell from the calculations, people may have hoped that time continued after that. Regardless, they made the calculation.

Those who did so had to keep in mind that the date was arbitrary. In 686 Bishop Julian of Toledo launched an attack on Jews who had made a two-part argument against the structure of Christian history: first, they had pointed out that, if one compared the Hebrew Pentateuch to the later Greek Septuagint, the age of the world was significantly lower than Christians had calculated; and second, that if there were to be six world ages, each a thousand years in length, with Christ inaugurating the seventh, then clearly Jesus was not the prophesied Christ because he had been born too early in history.[60] The danger, Julian warned King Ervig in his prefatory letter, was that such thinking could corrupt Christian thought and stimulate false expectations. (Indeed, as we shall see shortly, in England this is exactly what happened.) The bishop could readily appeal to Augustine against the 6 × 1,000 structure of history and millenarian hopes – it was generations, not years, which mattered.[61] More unusually, his sifting of the difficult Old Testament dating material led him proclaim that the Year 6000 had passed eleven years previously with

[57] On the dissemination of Isidore's work see B. Bischoff, 'Die europäische Verbreitung der Werke Isidors von Sevilla', in his *Mittelalterliche Studien* (3 vols, Stuttgart, 1966), I. 171–94 (esp. here pp. 180–2 on Ireland), with corrections and elaborations in M. Herren, 'On the Earliest Irish Acquaintance with Isidore of Seville', in E. James (ed.), *Visigothic Spain: New Approaches* (Oxford, 1980), pp. 243–50. Important remarks on Isidore's influence on computus can be found throughout I. Warntjes, *The Munich Computus: Text and Translation. Irish Computistics between Isidore of Seville and the Venerable Bede and Its Reception in Carolingian Times* (Stuttgart, 2010).
[58] J. T. Palmer, 'The Ordering of Time', in V. Wieser, C. Zolles, C. Feik, M. Zolles and L. Schlondorff (eds.), *Abendländische Apokalyptik. Kompendium zur Genealogie der Endzeit* (Berlin, 2013), pp. 603–18 at pp. 616–18.
[59] So *The Munich Computus*, c. 1, ed. Warntjes, p. 1.
[60] García Moreno, 'Expectativas milenaristas', p. 109.
[61] Julian of Toledo, *Prognosticum*, esp. I. 3–5, pp. 150–2. See Chapter 1, p. 46. The emphasis on generations was a cornerstone of Joachim of Fiore's efforts to understand the structures of history in the twelfth century.

no problem, so that was irrelevant too. It is perhaps therefore unsurprising, rather than deeply suspicious, that Julian made nothing of these arguments in his popular handbook on Christian eschatology, *Prognosticum
futuri saeculi*.[62] This book detailed many issues, such as Gregory's purgatorial fires and the fate of the soul, and when Julian turned to the issue
of the Last Judgement at length he began by asserting the standard position on how the timing of the End could not be known.[63] It may be too
much to describe Julian's eschatology as 'anti-apocalyptic' on account of
this emphasis, because he drew his argument directly from the Bible. At
the same time, in the work as a whole, he had chosen to emphasise the
practical side of individual salvation over the catastrophism of uncertain
collective doom.[64]

In the Frankish kingdoms, fascination with numbers grew despite such
warnings. The added ingredient here was the use of the cyclical 532-year
Easter tables of Victorius of Aquitaine as a point of historical reference,
much as people would soon use Dionysiac tables and their lists of years
ab incarnatione (AD dates), as I shall explain below. One *summa annorum*
from 672, set down in a copy of Isidore's *Etymologiae*, is typical.[65] It starts
with an AM date from the end of Isidore's chronicle (AM 5812), notes
another sixty up to the fifteenth year of Chlothar III, a year when there
was a battle against the Danes. The note then states it is twenty-six years
since the death of St Sulpicius of Bourges and that it is the 113th year
of the Easter table of Victorius of Aquitaine. Finally the author records
that 5,873 years have passed since Creation and that there are 127 years
left until the Year 6000. The reader is left with multiple points of reference with which to orientate themselves in time, linking politics, saints'
cults and liturgical cycles. Moreover, at the end, an apocalyptic tradition had become a useful part of this practice of memory and temporal
orientation.[66]

The tradition of countdowns seems to have had some kind of distinct
but elusive trigger. Of the fifteen known to us, four date to the years 672–
5, which coincide with the height of the conflict between Childeric II,
Leudegar of Autun and Ebroin, the mayor of the palace, although these
events are otherwise not clearly related to the computations themselves.[67]

---

[62] Suspicions cast in Landes, 'Lest the Millennium', pp. 173–4, where Julian's work is
presented as being 'swallowed up by the opposition'.
[63] Julian of Toledo, *Prognosticum*, III. 1, p. 182. Hillgarth, 'Eschatological and Political
Concepts', pp. 226–7.
[64] Stancati, *Julian*, pp. 252–5.
[65] Biblioteca Apostolica Vaticana, Reg. lat. 294 (*c.* 1100), printed in Mommsen, MGH AA,
11 (Berlin, 1894), pp. 505–6.
[66] Palmer, 'Ordering of Time', p. 617.
[67] See above p. 86 and n. 42.

Another two date to 727, the same year that Charles Martel first sub-jugated Burgundy and the *Liber historiae Francorum* was completed, a text which stands as our only sustained Frankish narrative source for the period from 643.[68] A third of our evidence, then, comes from two narrow windows of time – and both comfortably remote from AM 6000 itself, although that could be read as silent proof that people worried too much about such things thereafter to say anything. The rest of our examples seem rather diffuse. The earliest by some margin was composed in 643;[69] one in 736 was written in a Burgundian continuation of a chronicle;[70] an Irish or Lombard computist in 747, and another in 767, added to the tradition;[71] and Beatus of Liébana in 784/5 and John of Modena in 800 itself also played along.[72] With the possible exception of the first example, what they all had in common was the influence of Isidore of Seville.

The new anxiety about historical time and its structures deeply shaped the chronicles of 'so-called Fredegar', and the later extension and revi-sion, the *Historia vel gesta Francorum*.[73] Fredegar consciously placed him-self as an heir to Gregory of Tours's historical enterprise, albeit with some differences in approach.[74] Most of his work was a compilation, drawing on *The Book of Generations*, a hybrid version of Jerome-Hydatius, and the six-book version of Gregory's *Histories*, to which he added his own com-posite chronicle up to 643, but with allusions to events as late as 659. There is little of Gregory's fascination with signs and heretics, and there was only so much editing for the sake of consistency between chronicles. The compilation includes, for instance, the Incarnation dated both to

---

[68] *Dialogus de computo Burgundiae*, c. 17C, ed. A. Borst, *Schriften zur Komputistik im Frankenreich von 721 bis 818*, MGH QQ zur Geistesgesch., 21 (3 vols, Hanover, 2006), I. 374; London, British Library, Cotton Nero A ii, f. 35v. *Liber historiae Francorum*, ending at c. 53, p. 328 with a reference to the sixth year of Theuderic III. Dates for this period are not entirely certain but see B. Krusch, 'Chronologica regum Francorum stirpis Merowingicae', MGH SRM, 7 (Hanover and Leipzig, 1920), pp. 468–516 (pp. 505–7 on Theuderic).

[69] A note (printed in Krusch, 'Chronologica', p. 493) in Würzburg, Universitätsbibliothek, Mp. th. f. 28, ff. 67v–68r, an eighth-century copy of Caesarius's homilies with the note copied directly before a homily on Judgement Day.

[70] *Historia vel gesta Francorum*, III. 109 = *Chronicon Fredegarii – Continuationes*, c. 16, ed. B. Krusch, MGH SRM, 2 (Hanover, 1888), p. 176.

[71] Florence, Biblioteca Medici Laurenziana, Conv. Soppr. 364, f. 117v; London, British Library, Cotton Nero A ii, 35v (thirty-two years remaining, but the source material had originally said seventy-two years).

[72] Beatus, *Tractus in Apocalipsin*, IV. 16a–18, ed. R. Gryson, CCSL, 107A (2 vols., Turnhout, 2012), I. 518–519; John of Modena in MGH AA, 11, p. 505.

[73] On the text see R. Collins, *Die Fredegar-Chroniken*, MGH Studien und Texte, 44 (Hanover, 2007). A still-useful account of the problems posed by manuscripts and con-tent is provided by W. Goffart, 'The Fredegar Problem Reconsidered', *Speculum*, 38.2 (1963), 206–41.

[74] Fredegar, *Chronicae*, IV, prol., p. 123.

AM 5500 in the *Book of Generations*, and AM 5199, if only by implication, through Gregory and Isidore.[75] Because the chronicles circulated
anonymously, they never achieved the reputation of other early works of
history, but they were nevertheless read widely throughout the Frankish
world and were adapted and edited wherever they went.[76] They were, if
nothing else, useful as a chain of chronicles to continue.[77]

It is in the eighth-century reception of the compilation that it became
a marker of apocalyptic time. In a space at the end of the oldest extant
manuscript, after Isidore's chronicle, the priest Lucerius noted that in
the fourth year of Dagobert III's reign – namely, to us, in 715 – there
were eighty-four years left until the completion of the sixth millennium.[78]
Again, there was the instinct to take a historical composition and work
out at the end where one stood in relation to it ('through this chronicle
and through the other chronicles', Lucerius wrote).[79] Twenty-one years
later an extension of some version of the chronicle added similar detail,
this time adding a reference to Victorius and announcing sixty-three years
left to complete 'this millennium'.[80] By themselves these notes attest to
a persistent interest in the approach of the Year 6000. The dynamic was,
however, surely only intensified by the next significant editorial development: the integration of Hilarianus's millenarian *On the Duration of the
World* into the corpus of the Fredegar chronicles.

Interest in Hilarianus's unorthodox work at this juncture provides a
significant challenge to the notion that Augustinian dogma was absolutely
dominant and suppressive. As we saw in Chapter 1, Hilarianus taught
that there would be 6,000 years of history, to be followed by a 1,000-year

[75] Fredegar, *Chronicae*, I, ed. Krusch, p. 40 (AM^I), II. 34, p. 58 (building blocks for AM^{II}),
III. 73, p. 113 (Gregory's dating of Sigibert I's death to AM 5774). There are also mistakes, for instance equating AD 641 with AM 5149 (p. 42) and AD 378 with AM 5588
(p. 69).

[76] H. Reimitz, 'Der Weg zum Königtum in historiographischen Kompendien der
Karolingerzeit', in M. Becher and J. Jarnut (eds.), *Der Dynastiewechsel von 751.
Vorgeschichte, Legitimationsstrategien und Erinnerung* (Münster 2004), pp. 283–326.

[77] On a related chronicle chain see I. Wood, 'Chains of Chronicles: The Example of
London, British Library, Ms. Add. 16974', in R. Corradini and M. Niederkorn-Bruck
(eds.), *Zwischen Niederschrift und Wiederschrift* (Vienna, 2010), pp. 67–78.

[78] Ed. Krusch, MGH SRM, 2, pp. 9–10, reconstructed from Paris, Bibliothèque nationale,
lat. 10910, f. 184r, the end of which is now barely visible on account of the deterioration
of the parchment. Lucerius's date is often taken to date the manuscript itself but readers
should be aware that, on inspection, it is in a different hand to the body text, so the note
provides only a *terminus ante quem*.

[79] 'Per ista croneca et per alia cronesu' (*sic*).

[80] *Historia vel gesta Francorum*, III. 109, ed. Krusch, p. 176. On the implications of the passage compare Collins, *Die Fredegar-Chroniken*, p. 88 and J. T. Palmer, 'Computus after
the Paschal Controversy of AD 740', in D. Ó Cróinín and I. Warntjes (eds.), *The Easter
Controversy of Late Antiquity and the Early Middle Ages* (Turnhout, 2011), pp. 213–41 at
pp. 238–40.

earthly reign of Christ and his saints, and Hilarianus did this with his own countdown, asserting that there were 101 years left. There is no way to ascertain whether the first person to copy it did so because of their own millenarian interests, or because Hilarianus's text was useful as chronography and the millenarianism did not really matter. Either way it was not silenced. Hilarianus's work was first adopted into the corpus in the Lake Constance region in the 'Class 3' of Fredegar manuscripts, in which it is added at the end of Fredegar's Book I, *The Book of Generations*.[81] On the face of it, the move repeated a significant amount of historical information from *The Book of Generations*, with lists of patriarchs and emperors ultimately anchoring the Incarnation in AM 5500. *On the Duration of the World* offered two things: first, it was shorter than *The Book of Generations* (although this was largely redundant where both were copied together); and second, it provided a theological conception of time which tied the 6,000 years of the world to millenarian expectation. At the very least, it demonstrates the scribal impulse to accumulate more material about time and history from the eighth century onwards.[82]

No efforts at suppression were in evidence as the chronicle was developed. *On the Duration of the World* attracted the author behind the *Historia vel gesta Francorum*, who copied it across from a 'Class 3' manuscript in *c*. 787 for his new work.[83] The decision again raises the question of why a millenarian text was actively preserved in allegedly 'Augustinian' Frankish historiographical circles. Hilarianus's work, in Collins's reconstruction, was now placed alongside the Jerome-Hydatius epitome to form a new Book I, with the Gregory epitome as Book II and Fredegar plus continuations up to 768 as Book III.[84] If a colophon in one manuscript of *c*. 900 is to be believed, the composition was commissioned by the father and son Childebrand (up to 751) and Nibelung, dukes of Burgundy and close relatives of the Pippinids who seized the Frankish throne in 751. The *Historia* and its 'heretical' first section emerged, then, in a politically central context – not on the peripheries, and not in a 'semi-detached' intellectual environment. It was widely copied and had influence, giving rise to two more compositions – expanded versions of

---

[81] Leiden, Universitatsbibliothek, Voss. lat. Q. 5 (continued in Biblioteca Apostolica Vaticana, Reg. lat. 713 and, combined, likely the manuscript in the St Gall library catalogue described as 'Chronicae diversorum temporum libri v. Et gesta Franocorum in volumine i': St Gall, Stiftsbibliothek, Cod. Sang. 728, p. 12). This was the only manuscript used by Frick for his edition in *Chronica minora*, 1 (Leipzig, 1892), pp. 155–74.

[82] See in particular R. McKitterick, *History and Memory in the Carolingian World* (Cambridge, 2004); Reimitz, 'Der Weg zum Königtum'.

[83] The date is suggested by Collins, *Die Fredegar-Chroniken*, p. 92.

[84] Collins, *Die Fredegar-Chroniken*, p. 89. Note, however, that no manuscript treats Hilarianus and the Jerome-Hydatius epitome as a single book.

Gregory's *Histories* and the *Liber historiae Francorum* of 727 – by the early ninth century. Admittedly *On the Duration of the World* neither played a role in the *Historia*'s popularity, nor gained any popularity outside that work. Presumably what mattered to later copyists and readers was the usefulness of the chronological material rather than the controversial but disproved millenarian prophecy they failed to censor. There is something of an indifference to the heretical at play here.

The heretical Bede

All these different strands – the visions, the calculations of time, the shifting status of millenarianism – crashed together in assorted contexts, but rarely as memorably as in the work of the Northumbrian priest Bede (d. 735).[85] Bede is famous as the 'Father of English History' and a prolific author of biblical commentaries, textbooks on science and chronology, homilies and poetry. His position in English history is especially marked because he flourished only one eventful century after the Gregorian mission had first set out to convert the English. As unique and special as he may seem, two generations of modern historians have increasingly understood Bede best as someone very much engaged with debates and controversies in Northumbria, Ireland and the continent, rather than a genius out of step with his own time.[86] That the debates were often hostile, Bede did little to hide. His famous *Ecclesiastical History of the English People* (completed 731–4) detailed conflicts over culture, practice and politics, not least where the use of different Easter tables threatened to pull entire kingdoms apart through the disunity of liturgical rhythms. Even then, his *Letter to Plegwine* (708) and *On the Reckoning of Time* (725) reveal further battle lines concerning chronography, computus and eschatology scarcely hinted at in his later work. Indeed, in the *Letter to Plegwine*, Bede's defence of a position which was for all intents and purposes 'Augustinian' got him branded a heretic at a heated dinner debate. Bede takes us to the heart of controversy about apocalypse and salvation only hinted at elsewhere.

---

[85] P. Darby, *Bede and the End of Time* (Farnham, 2012). For context see S. DeGregorio (ed.), *The Cambridge Companion to Bede* (Cambridge, 2010) and S. Foot, *Monastic Life in Anglo-Saxon England, c. 600–900* (Cambridge, 2005).

[86] W. Goffart, *The Narrators of Barbarian History AD 550–800: Jordanes, Gregory of Tours, Bede and Paul the Deacon* (Princeton, NJ, 1988) and A. Thacker, 'Bede and the Irish', in L. A. J. R. Houwen and A. A. MacDonald (eds.), *Beda Venerabilis* (Groningen, 1996), pp. 31–59; Warntjes, *The Munich Computus*; D. Ó Cróinín, 'The Irish Provenance of Bede's Computus', *Peritia*, 2 (1983), 229–47, F. Wallis, *Bede: The Reckoning of Time* (Liverpool, 1999).

Bede was scarcely apocalyptic in his outlook but made good use of eschatological themes in his works. In his homilies on the Gospels, Bede was notably cagey about Judgement except in the vaguest terms, and he avoided commenting on the passages from which his hero Gregory the Great had got so much rhetorical apocalyptic mileage (Chapter 2).[87] The Last Judgement was important as the point towards which all human existence migrated. As such, it stood as something which people should keep in mind so that they could reflect on their sins and correct their behaviour. Bede wrote a poem on precisely this subject, *On Judgement Day*, to console and encourage Bishop Acca of Hexham when he was chased into exile in 731 when King Ceolwulf – to whom the *Ecclesiastical History* was dedicated – was 'captured, tonsured and restored to his kingdom'.[88] Art played a pastoral role in Bede's world here, and he noted that his one-time abbot Benedict Biscop, in 676, had brought back amongst other things wall-paintings depicting scenes from Revelation, which were then hung in the church at Jarrow so that those ignorant of letters could consider the fate of their souls when they entered.[89] Curiously, given anxiety about how people might interpret scripture, all early visual schemes for Revelation are exclusively literal which suggests faith in the power of the text's imagery to move, even if the words themselves were difficult. Revelation was useful for encouraging reform. What people should believe about how their souls reached Judgement was an issue that would prove more contentious.

At the safer end of things, Bede was able to use visions of the afterlife for political ends, much as had happened in Merovingian Gaul. The 'revelatory' content of the *Ecclesiastical History* – aimed, remember, at Ceolwulf's troubled court – is best represented by a Gregory-of-Tours-

---

[87] Bede, *Homilies*, I. 24, ed. D. Hurst, CCSL, 122 (Turnhout, 1955), pp. 170–1 (extract from Gregory's *Moralia* on salvation and damnation at the Last Judgement, on Luke 21.27) and II. 2, pp. 198–9 (reference to Christ's return at the consummation of the world, after Matt. 28.20). This might of course indicate that Bede sought not to overlap with Gregory's work but Markus in general found little of the sense of imminence until Bede's later writings: R. A Markus, 'Gregory and Bede: The Making of the Western Apocalyptic Tradition', in *Gregorio Magno nel XIV centenario della morte* (Rome, 2004), pp. 247–55, esp. p. 250.

[88] *Baedae continuatio*, s.a. 731, ed. C. Plummer, *Bedae Opera Historica* (Oxford, 1898), p. 361: 'Ceoluulf rex captus, et adtonsus et remissus in regnum; Acca episcopus de su sede fugatus.' See J. Story, 'After Bede: Continuing the *Ecclesiastical History*', in S. Baxter, C. Karkov, J. L. Nelson and D. Pelteret (eds.), *Early Medieval Studies in Memory of Patrick Wormald* (Aldershot, 2009), pp. 165–84 at pp. 172–3; Darby, *Bede and the End of Time*, p. 103.

[89] Bede, *Historia abbatum*, I. 6, ed. Plummer, *Bedae Opera Historica*, p. 370; P. Klein, 'The Apocalypse in Medieval Art', in R. Emmerson and B. McGinn (eds.), *The Apocalypse in the Middle Ages* (Ithaca, NY, 1992), pp. 177–9; P. Meyvaert, 'Bede and the Church Paintings at Wearmouth-Jarrow', *Anglo-Saxon England*, 8 (1979), 63–77.

style antithetical pairing of stories which detailed the experiences of two such visionaries. In the first story, a former laymen named Dryhthelm from Melrose saw the locations where the saved and damned resided, as well as where the 'not very good' and 'not very bad' were stationed for purgation in between.[90] Bede's unusual four-point geography for the afterlife has attracted much attention but, within our theme, the key function lies in what followed: Dryhthelm was inspired to retire to a monastery to live a purer, austere life on earth, which in turn inspired many people including King Aldfrid (d. 705), who would visit him to discuss his experiences.[91] The genre of revelation worked to correct behaviour and attracted the interests of the highest secular powers. The political dynamic is underlined in the second story, in which a doomed sinner warned King Coenred of Mercia about the importance of penance after he had seen two youths with a small book of his good deeds and a horde of demons coming for him with a large book of his bad deeds and thoughts. The man, unlike Dryhthelm, had left it too late to save himself, but not so late that he could not warn others, who could then hasten to penance.[92] There is a sequel to this in the *Vision of the Monk of Much Wenlock*, which contains another vision of purgatory in which Coelred, Coenred's successor, had angelic protection taken away from him, after demons asked them to on account of his catalogue of sins.[93] Warnings for kings and others to reform their ways abounded.

We might see that Bede's visionary material in the *Ecclesiastical History* represented the 'acceptable face' of the eschatological–apocalyptic spectrum. There was little of the gloom or the ominous signs of Gregory of Tours's *Histories*, which Bede almost certainly knew, and no repeat of Gregory's attempts to integrate AM dates and warnings about the End into his narratives. Indeed, in terms of the ticking clock of apocalypse, Bede notably became the first historian to adopt AD dates for his work which at least had the accidental consequence of side-stepping the Y6K problem. Landes has seen this as a deliberate anti-apocalyptic or anti-millenarian decision by Bede, but it is necessary to ask why this must be the case.[94] Bede could have been imitating Isidore's 'national' *History of*

---

[90] Bede, *Historia ecclesiastica*, V. 12, ed. Lapidge, pp. 372–86. Carozzi, *Le voyage*, pp. 226–53

[91] H. Foxhall Forbes, '*Diuiduntur in quattuor*: The Interim and Judgement in Anglo-Saxon England', *Journal of Theological Studies*, 61.2 (2010), 659–84; S. Foot, 'Anglo-Saxon Purgatory', *Studies in Church History*, 45 (2009), 87–98.

[92] Bede, *Historia ecclesiastica*, V. 13, ed. Lapidge, pp. 386–92.

[93] *Bonifatii et Lulli Epistolae*, no. 10, ed. M. Tangl, MGH Epp. Sel., 1 (Berlin, 1916), p. 14. Carozzi, *Le voyage*, pp. 194–226; P. Sims-Williams, *Religion and Literature in Western England, 600–800* (Cambridge, 1990), pp. 243–72.

[94] Landes, 'Lest the Millennium Be Fulfilled', p. 178.

the Goths, Vandals and Suebi with its Spanish Era in place of AM dating, although that text did not enjoy wide circulation and Bede may not have known it. Alternatively, it is notable that in *On the Reckoning of Time*, Bede had advocated using Easter tables as a tool for clarifying dates because of their rich, linear framework for tracking time which included since at least 525 a column for AD dates.[95] Bede had not added AD dates to his chronographical chronicles in any systematic way, including just a couple of isolated references notably when he dated the conversion of the Ionan monks to Bede's preferred Easter table in 716.[96] He had, however, begun to compile a significant amount of relative dating material on the basis of letters and other material, so that at least a number of events in English history could be cited under the reign of an emperor (the Gregorian mission under Emperor Maurice, for instance). The extensive use of AD dating in the *Ecclesiastical History* might therefore reflect the maturing of Bede's idea for history, perhaps even taking his cue from notes in some Easter table.[97] The key point from the perspective of apocalyptic tradition is that the focus seems very much on attention to historical dates and scientific chronology. Nowhere did Bede tie his use of AD dating to concerns about apocalyptic time – a silence more telling because he did address the problems themselves directly.[98]

When it came to how he conceptualised time, the extent to which Bede was a polemicist in the middle of heated fights is often underappreciated.[99] At the heart of the problem was a battle over Easter tables and for liturgical unity – a point which itself complicates Claude Carozzi's view that focus on the liturgy obscured apocalyptic thought. Different Easter tables in use in the British Isles meant that communities were divided over when to observe the most central feast of the Christian calendar. At the Synod of Whitby in 664 King Oswiu of Northumbria had attempted to heal the rift – and his marriage – by announcing a preference for 'Roman' reckonings over an 'Irish' one, the two reckonings sometimes

---

[95] Bede, *De temporum ratione*, c. 65, ed. C.W. Jones, CCSL 123B (Turnhout, 1980), p. 460.
[96] Ibid., c. 66, pp. 521, 532.
[97] J. Story, 'The Frankish Annals of Lindisfarne and Kent', *Anglo-Saxon England*, 34 (2005), 59–109, esp. at p. 73.
[98] Compare Dionysius's own suggestion that people use AD dates instead of years from the Diocletian persecution to purify time: Dionysius Exiguus, *Libellus de cyclo magno paschae*, ed. B. Krusch, in *Studien zur christlich-mittelalterlichen Chronologie [II]: Die Entstehung unserer heutigen Zeitrechnung*, Abhandlungen der Preußischen Akademie der Wissenschaften, Jahrgang 1937, Phil.-hist. Klasse, 8 (Berlin, 1938), p. 64.
[99] J. T. Palmer, 'The Ends and Futures of Bede's *De temporum ratione*', in P. Darby and F. Wallis (eds.), *Bede and the Future* (Farnham, 2014); Darby, *Bede and the End, passim*.

giving Easter dates up to a month apart.[100] Adherents to the Irish table in Dál Riata and Pictland remained unmoved until 716. But more significantly for our concerns, there remained two 'Roman' Easter tables in play: the 532-year table of Victorius of Aquitaine (455) and the translation of the 'Greek' reckoning by Dionysius Exiguus (525). Now, Easter is calculated by identifying the first Sunday after the first full moon after the vernal equinox. The problem was that the tables of Victorius and Dionysius used different sub-tables to calculate the age of the moon so they were never quite synchronised, and they had different attitudes to what 'lunar limits' were acceptable for Easter.[101] Although they disagreed only occasionally, and only by a week, it was enough to be unacceptable. Bede's works on time, culminating in *On the Reckoning of Time*, were designed as a point-by-point defence of the Dionysiac table, and a subtle attack on the 'lovers of Victorius' (*amatores Victorini*). This was, however, only half the battle, as Victorian tables supported the Eusebian age of the world – but Bede most certainly did not, and this was why he was accused of heresy in 708.

The root of the problem was that Bede had come across a revised age of the world, possibly calculated in Ireland, and based on the very Hebrew reckoning we saw earlier attacked by Julian of Toledo.[102] Bede and other critics going back to Augustine had scholarly reasons for doubting the accuracy of AM[II] because, when they compared biblical time-spans in the *Chronological Canons* of Eusebius-Jerome to those in the Vulgate or Hebrew Bible, they discovered that the translators of the Greek Bible used by Eusebius had often added hundreds to ages early on, with serious implications.[103] Even at the beginning, when Adam is said in the Greek

---

[100] Bede, *Historia ecclesiastica gentis Anglorum*, III. 25, ed. Lapidge, II. 118–34; Stephanus, *Vita Wilfridi*, c. 10, ed. and trans. B. Colgrave (Cambridge, 1927), pp. 20–3. Such has been the advance in knowledge concerning the technical side of this debate one is now advised to begin with Warntjes, *The Munich Computus*, xxxviii–xli and L. Holford-Strevens, 'Marital Discord in Northumbria: Lent and Easter, His and Hers', in D. Ó Cróinín and I. Warntjes (eds.), *Computus and Its Cultural Context in the Latin West, AD 300–1200* (Turnhout, 2010), pp. 143–58.

[101] Where the full moon is *luna xiv*, the 'Greek' attitude was that one could celebrate Easter as early as the next day, *luna xv* (and no later than *luna xxi*), if it was a Sunday, to coincide with the Passion. With the Victorian table, the earliest one could celebrate Easter was two days later, *luna xvi* (and no later than *luna xxii*).

[102] D. Mac Carthy, 'Bede's Primary Source for the Vulgate Chronology in His Chronicles in *De temporibus* and *De temporum ratione*', in Ó Cróinín and Warntjes (eds.), *Computus and Its Cultural Context*, pp. 159–89; *Laterculus Malalianus*, c. 4, ed. J. Stevenson (Cambridge, 1995), p. 124.

[103] Augustine, *De civitate Dei*, XV.13, 470–2 (but complicated by XVIII.43, 638–40). Bede, *Epistola ad Pleguinam*, c. 3, ed. C.W. Jones, CCSL, 123C (Turnhout, 1980), pp. 617–18; Bede, *De temporibus*, cc. 16–17, ed. Jones, CCSL, 123C, pp. 600–11 (implied); Bede, *De temporum ratione*, c. 66, ed. Jones, pp. 463–534.

to have fathered Seth when he was 230, the Hebrew and Jerome's Vulgate stated instead that Adam was 130. Pursuing such threads further, Bede and his contemporaries found that one could deduct 1,258 years from AM[II] and place the Incarnation in AM 3941 instead of AM 5199. This reckoning was then known as the 'Hebrew Truth' because it was based on the original text. Bede's *Letter to Plegwine* (708), in which the scholar first explained this, is a revealing and honest letter. He was acutely aware that he was challenging orthodoxy and that he would receive criticisms, so he followed Jerome in urging his audience simply not to read anything he wrote which might offend them.[104] If Bede's motivation was simply to rejuvenate the age of the world, as Landes supposed,[105] then it is an attempt soaked in scholarly enquiry and self-consciousness rather than an exercise in the suppression of a dangerous date. He could have relied on the Augustinian assertion that prediction was pointless, as he had done in his exegesis when he scolded those who made literal interpretations of 1,000 years.[106] Moreover, the argumentative form of Bede's work openly used critiques of opposing points of view to justify his position, so no 'suppression by silence' was involved. Unfortunately for Bede, when he invited his opponents to ignore him if they felt that he was wrong, most did – only on the continent did his revised world chronology obtain any popularity.[107] But the crucial thing for Bede, anyway, was that people should concentrate on the fate of their souls rather than speculation about the end of the world, lest they get caught out by Judgement Day.

Bede's new AM date in fact had opponents on two fronts, as Peter Darby has demonstrated most clearly.[108] The Greek-influenced school of Theodore at Canterbury had already produced one text which poured scorn on the 'Irish' early dating of the Incarnation, and followed Byzantine tradition to defend the passing of the Year 6000 sometime previously.[109] The spirit of Julian of Toledo was at work. Elsewhere, others defended versions of Eusebian orthodoxy against Bede, most famously leading to the accusations against Bede at the dinner table of St Wilfrid, when

---

[104] Bede, *Epistola ad Pleguinam*, c. 12, ed. Jones pp. 622–3.

[105] Landes, 'Lest the Millennium Be Fulfilled', p. 178.

[106] Bede, *Expositio Apocalypseos*, III. 35. 17–19 and 81–4, ed. R. Gryson, CCSL, 121A (Turnhout, 2001), pp. 503/5 and p. 509; Bede, *In epistolas septem catholicas*, ed. D. Hurst, CCSL, 121 (Turnhout, 1983), pp. 277–8 (on 2 Peter 3.8).

[107] London, British Library, Harley 3017, f. 66r (Fleury, 862–4); London, British Library, Harley 3091, f. 4r (Nevers, *c.* 850); Oxford, Bodleian Library, Digby 63, f. 26r (Northumbria, 867, but primarily copied from a manuscript from St Bertin).

[108] Darby, *Bede and the End*, ch. 2. See also his 'Bede's Time Shift of 703 in Context', in Wieser *et al.*, *Abendländische Apokalyptik*, pp. 619–40.

[109] *Laterculus Malalianus*, cc. 3–4, ed. Stevenson, pp. 122–4; c. 24, p. 154.

an unnamed priest seems to have said that a fourth millennium date 'denied' that Christ was born in the sixth age.[110] Here the argument, like the one Julian had countered, conflated millennia and world ages so that only dates for the Incarnation after AM 5000, such as those put forward by Julius Africanus and Eusebius, counted as being 'in the sixth age'.[111] The only proponent of such a position cited by Bede in his account is the fourth-century author of the *Cologne Prologue* (see Chapter 1), who had followed the older tradition and who Bede himself labels a heretic to discredit his opponents.[112] The letter also explicitly scolded those who expected the world to endure for only 6,000 years and those trained in Canterbury who believed it would last 7,000, confirming the presence of the ongoing three-way argument perhaps even just in Bede's monastery at Jarrow.[113] Bede's key point, reiterated in *On the Reckoning of Time*, was that no form of prediction was acceptable. What they needed to do was prepare their souls.

Bede's thought about the Apocalypse was more thoroughly grounded in the Augustinian-Gregorian matrix than it was the debate about numbers. He quoted Gregory the Great's apocalyptic warnings to Æthelberht of Kent in full and unedited in *Ecclesiastical History*.[114] In *On the Reckoning of Time* he quoted Augustine's *Letter to Hesychius* at length, where the bishop had warned that predictions were liable to place the End too soon or too late and so would lead to disappointment. Only vigilance would do, he stressed in his commentary on Acts, using the words of Jerome: 'being always uncertain about the coming of the Judge, they should live every day as if the next day they were to be judged.'[115] The only two 'certain signs' of the End, thought Bede, would be the conversion of the Jews (which he believed to be nearly complete!) and the coming of Antichrist himself for his reign of three and a half years.[116] Yet more certainly, he

[110] Bede, *Epistola ad Pleguinam*, c. 1, ed. Jones, p. 617.
[111] Landes, 'Lest the Millennium Be Fulfilled', p. 175.
[112] Bede, *Epistola ad Pleguinam*, c. 14, ed. Jones, p. 624.
[113] Ibid., c. 15, pp. 624–5. For a list of the exclusively continental manuscripts see Jones, CCSL, 123C, p. 616.
[114] Bede, *Historia ecclesiastica*, I. 32. 5, ed. Lapidge, pp. 150–2.
[115] Bede, *Expositio Actuum Apostolorum*, I. 7, ed. M. Laistner, CCSL, 121, p. 8 (on Acts 1.7): 'Et quando dicit, non est uestrum scire, ostendit quod et ipse sciat, cuius omnia sunt quae patris sunt, sed non expediat nosse, mortalibus; ut semper incerti de aduentu iudicis sic cotidie uiuant, quasi die alia iudicandi sint.' See also Bede, *In Marci evangelium exposition*, 4, ed. D. Hurst, CCSL, 120 (Turnhout, 1960), p. 590.
[116] Described thoroughly in Darby, *Bede and the End of Time*, pp. 95–124. For Bede's views that the Jews had almost converted see Darby, pp. 201–4 drawing on: Bede, *De tabernaculo*, 2, ed. D. Hurst, CCSL, 119A (Turnhout, 1969), p. 65; Bede, *De templo*, 1, ed. D. Hurst, CCSL, 119A, p. 182; Bede, *In Tobiam*, X. 1–3, ed. D. Hurst, CCSL, 119B (Turnhout, 1983), p. 14, and *In regum librum xxx quaestiones*, c. 1, ed. D. Hurst, CCSL, 119 (Turnhout, 1962), p. 297.

warned Archbishop Ecgbertht of York and others, the date of Judgement was unknown.[117] Again, we are left in a position where imminence was not being denied, but rather left hanging. Bede's sense of urgency might have been stoked by the accusations of heresy in 708 or the disturbances which saw his friend Bishop Acca of Hexham chased into exile in 731. Nevertheless, he refrained from making anything portentous out of signs he catalogued, and used apocalyptic rhetoric sparingly against his enemies, and even avoided comment on King Ceolwulf's troubles. Bede's was a different kind of battle, and one which points towards the direction of early medieval apocalyptic thought to come.

Where Bede's thoughts on individual judgement, correct liturgical observance and orthodox beliefs come together is in his vision of a church in struggle. It focused on the way in which people took responsibility for action rather than the way that they might fit into salvation history. This is clearest in his *Commentary on Revelation* (*c.* 703), one of his earliest works and his third-best attested work in the century after his death, after *On the Reckoning of Time* and *On the Nature of Things*.[118] In many respects, Bede was not much of an innovator in interpretation but, rather subtly, he refined the line-by-line analysis begun by Tyconius – openly recognised by Bede as a heretic – and developed by Primasius to establish an allegorical reading of the text.[119] Still, he saw that John's vision revealed 'by words and figures the wars and internecine tumults of the Church'. Using a model based on the seven movements of Revelation, he identified seven *periochae* or themes to show the Church moving through its 'wars and fires' (*bella et incendia*) towards the Heavenly Jerusalem.[120] These were (to emphasise the sense of repetition):

1 general conflicts and victories of the Church
2 future conflicts and triumphs of the Church

[117] Bede, *Epistola ad Ecgberhtum*, ed. C. Plummer, *Bedae Opera Historica* (Oxford, 1898), I. 406. See also *In Lucam evangelium expositio*, 5 ed. D. Hurst, CCSL, 120 (Turnhout, 1960), p. 316 (Luke 17.23); Bede, *In Marci evangelium exposition*, 4, ed. Hurst, CCSL, 120, p. 603 (Mark 13.32), following Jerome's commentary on Matt. 24.36).
[118] See the table in J. Westgard, 'Bede in the Carolingian Age and Beyond', in DeGregorio, *Companion*, pp. 201–15 at p. 211. On the work see G. Bonner, 'Saint Bede in the Tradition of Western Apocalypse Commentary', Jarrow Lecture (Jarrow, 1966) and F. Wallis, *Bede: Commentary on Revelation* (Liverpool, 2013).
[119] Bede, *Expositio Apocalypseos*, pref., ed. Gryson, pp. 223–31. On Bede's use of Tyconius and Primasius, see pp. 28–31.
[120] On the *periochae* see now C. Carozzi, 'Apocalypse et temps de l'église selon Bède le vénérable', in R. E. Guglielmetti (ed.), *L'apocalisse nel medioevo* (Florence, 2011), pp. 115–32. The symbolic value of patterns of seven is a notable feature of Visigothic and Spanish liturgy and exegesis (E. A. Matter, 'The Pseudo-Alcuinian *De septem sigillis*: An Early Latin Apocalypse Exegesis', *Traditio*, 36 (1980), 111–37), although did not influence Bede directly here.

3 various events of the Church
4 toils and victories of the Church
5 the last seven plagues
6 the condemnation of the whore, the Ungodly City
7 the descent of the Heavenly Jerusalem.

As is evident, these were loose ecclesiological themes rather than World
Ages, although he came close to pointing out parallels in his later recap-
itulation because the sixth and seventh *periochae* were descriptions of the
End Times.[121] They were also historical in the sense that they applied
to analysis of the real world rather than to spiritual truths, just not in
sequence.

Once the Church is viewed as being in a universal, but not quite
'timeless', struggle, various matters began to build up resonance. In the
Commentary on Revelation, two of the four horsemen plus Gog and Magog
readily lent themselves to interpretation as false brothers and heretics, as
we might expect.[122] It took little after the accusations of heresy in 708
to dismiss his enemies as heretics and antichrists when commenting on
Luke: 'they are not to be followed.'[123] Again, commenting on the Catholic
Epistles, John's antichrists who would come at the last hour were the
heretics – and there would be many of them until the Last Judgement.[124]
The mood hardly dictated his rhetorical modes, as is shown in *On the
Reckoning of Time* where he preferred to chastise his opponents for being
un(der)-schooled. But heresy and error were part of a greater struggle.
And although Peter Darby has characterised Bede's earlier exegesis as
lacking a sense of imminence, we have already seen plenty of evidence to
support McGinn's assertion that a radically unpredictable End brought
its own fears, little distinct from the fear of dying at any moment which
underpinned the second vision in *Ecclesiastical History*.[125] Indeed, as with
Gregory, this seems to have fed into the way that Bede understood missionary work in his own day, as he described St Wilfrid preaching in
Frisia in the same terms that he described preachers in the End Times

[121] Bede, *Expositio Apocalypseos*, II. 11. 1–14, ed. Gryson, p. 333 (Rev. 8.1). Carozzi,
'Apocalypse et temps', p. 124; Wallis, *Bede: Commentary on Revelation*, pp. 59–61.
Cf. Bonner, *Saint Bede*, pp. 14–15 and E. A. Matter, 'Exegesis of the Apocalypse', in
Frassetto (ed.), *The Year 1000*, pp. 34–5 who do draw connections between the *periochae*
and world ages.
[122] Bede, *Expositio Apocalypseos*, III. 35. 92–102, ed. Gryson, p. 511 (Gog and Magog).
[123] Bede, *In Lucae evangelium expositio*, 5, ed. D. Hurst, CCSL, 120 (Turnhout, 1960), p.
316 (Luke, 17.23).
[124] Bede, *In epistolas septem catholicas*, ed. Hurst, p. 295 (on 1 John 2.18). See also pp. 281–2
on 2 Peter, 3.16.
[125] See also here Wallis, *Bede: Commentary on Revelation*, pp. 51–6 on Bede's variable – even
situational – apocalyptic thought.

who would convert Israel and the gentiles.[126] As an integral part of scripture, apocalyptic text was not suppressed but was deliberately employed to conceptualise and encourage action.

An easily overlooked aspect of Bede's thought here is that, however innovative it was in places, in spirit it often reflected the worldviews of many other, less studied contemporaries. Bernhard Bischoff long ago identified a rich seam of Hiberno-Latin exegesis in Western libraries in the eighth and ninth centuries, much of which is little studied despite providing ready analogues for Bede's ideas.[127] Struggle against heretics features, for example, in interpretations of the horsemen and Gog and Magog in the mammoth *Pauca problesmata*.[128] The earlier *Commemoratorium* proclaims a Tyconian-Augustinian stance against the heretics' literal interpretations of the Devil's binding and Christ's millennial kingdom.[129] There are differences of emphasis, such as the *Commemoratorium*'s focus on the Trinity as unifying motif where Bede had his sevens, but it cannot cover up that in the Hiberno-Irish world – and there alone – there were suddenly multiple efforts to follow the lead of Primasius to provide line-by-line interpretations of Revelation and other books. Whether this was simply because of strong schooling or because of conflicts similar to or related to the ones Bede was engaged in is not so clear. What is clear is that Bede's vision was a widespread one: the many Irish and English religious who travelled to the continent in the seventh and eighth century understood Revelation as a particular story of struggle, and they took many of their commentaries with them to stock libraries in their new

---

[126] Bede, *Historia ecclesiastica*, V. 19. 8, ed. Lapidge, II. 418; Bede, *Expositio Actuum Apostolorum*, III. 1, p. 23. See J. T. Palmer, 'Wilfrid and the Frisians', in R. Higham (ed.), *Wilfrid: Abbot, Bishop, Saint* (Donington, 2013), pp. 231–42 at p. 236.

[127] B. Bischoff, 'Wendepunkte in der Geschichte der lateinischen Exegese in Frühmittalter', in his *Mittelalterliche Studien*, I. 205–73. Bischoff's conclusions were challenged in M. Gorman, 'A Critique of Bischoff's Theory of Irish Exegesis: The Commentary on Genesis in Munich Clm 6302 (Wendepunkte 2)', *Journal of Medieval Latin* 7 (1997), 178–233 and 'The Myth of Hiberno'Latin Exegesis', *Revue bénédictine*, 110.1–2 (2000), 42–85, but this met with strong defences from G. Silagi, 'Notwendige Bemerkungen zu Gormans 'Critique of Bischoff's Theory of Irish Exegesis', *Peritia*, 12 (1998), 87–94 and D. Ó Cróinín, 'Bischoff's Wendepunkte Fifty Years On', *Revue bénédictine*, 110.3–4 (2000), 204–37. On influence on Bede see J. Kelly, 'Bede and the Irish Exegetical Tradition on the Apocalypse', *Revue Bénédictine*, 92 (1982), 393–406.

[128] *Commemoratorium*, ed. R. Gryson, CCSL 107 (Turnhout, 2003), p. 208 (horsemen) [Wendepunkte, no. 37]. The section of *Pauca problesmata* concerning Revelation is edited as *De enigmatibus*, ed. Gryson, CCSL 107, pp. 257–8 (horsemen), and p. 290 (Gog and Magog) [Wendepunkte, no. 1]. See also on heresy: *In epistolas septem catholicas*, ed. R. E. McNally, CCSL, 108B (Turnhout, 1973), p. 112 (on 1 John 2.18) [Wendepunkte, no. 35], *Liber questionum in evangeliis*, ed. J. Rittmueller, CCSL, 108F (Turnhout, 2004), pp. 374–5 [Wendepunkte, no. 16] and various parts of *Expositio evangelii secundum Marcum*, ed. M. Cahill, CCSL, 82 (Turnhout, 1997) [Wendepunkte, no. 28].

[129] *Commemoratorium*, p. 224. See also *In epistolas septem catholicas*, ed. McNally, p. 106 (on 2 Peter, 3.8).

homes. Apocalyptic discourse across the West could now be grounded in a new, codified interpretation of scripture, which encouraged focus on Judgement and strength in the face of adversity.

Conclusion

'Apocalypse' had continued to develop in a number of different guises as the West's micro-Christendoms sought to define themselves. The Hiberno-Latin projects to process and interpret scripture more systematically than ever before reframed and refocused the logic of apocalypse for a start. Commentators did not just accept Tyconian-Augustinian exegesis – they engaged with it and made it integral to their Christianity, which embraced the idea of a Church in struggle. From that starting point it did not matter if the end was imminent or not, as the action required remained the same, just as the Church's enemies were typologically the same either way. In some ways this is not so far from the ideas set out by Augustine and Jerome (Chapter 1) and the two Gregorys (Chapter 2), but the intellectual resources for expressing and understanding such matters had been radically expanded. This fed into a continued politicisation of apocalyptic discourse in which reform and the combating of heresy grew as a responsibility for everyone in society, from kings downward. Revelatory material concerning the afterlife and salvation was part and parcel of this way of thinking, rather than something antithetical to apocalyptic discourse. The inevitability of Judgement for all meant that the difference in projected response to eschatology and to apocalypse was minimal.

There were intended and unintentional consequences to the ways in which these things developed in new ways in Spain, Ireland and the English and Frankish kingdoms. The processing of scripture helped to support orthodox stands against predictive apocalyptic beliefs and millenarianism through the authority of accumulated tradition. Calls for reform did inspire secular leaders to engage in change, and maybe the growth in visionary literature played a part too. The broader quest for orthodoxy affected apocalyptic tradition, changed its meaning and even confused it. Arguments to ensure liturgical unity through Easter tables combined with scholarly enquiry into chronology provoked new arguments and the production of new texts in Ireland and England whereas they had not caused so much fuss in, say, Spain. But then one suspects that Isidore would not have predicted that his dismissal of apocalyptic chronologies would have provided fuel for apocalyptic speculation in Gaul, nor that Julian of Toledo's attack on Jewish chronology had been enacted just as that very chronology was being enthusiastically adopted in Ireland. Nothing ever quite works as it should do.

Figure 2 Tomb of Mellebaudus of Poitiers. Inscription in the Dunes
Hypogeum, Poitiers: 'all things become every day worse and worse,
for the end is drawing near.'

Whatever kind of Dark Age modern historians might imagine existed
in the seventh and early eighth centuries, many of the intellectual and
political foundations for centuries of Christendom were being established. Members of 'micro-Christendoms' fought the battles they faced
and doctrine and practice evolved in response. The spectre of heresy
remained strong but at least political fragmentation and plague were
less pronounced as universal anxieties. And yet, as one stone-carver in
Poitiers observed gloomily sometime around 700, 'all things become
every day worse and worse, for the end is drawing near'.[130] Indeed, while
all these things had been debated in the West, renewed crisis in the East
meant that the Augustinian-Gregorian paradigm was about to be presented with its greatest challenge.

[130] Crypt of Mellebaudus of Poitiers: ed. E. le Blant, *Nouveau recueil des inscriptions chrétiennes de la Gaule* (Paris, 1892), p. 260: 'Quoniam quidquid quotidie pejus et pejus, quia
jam finis adpropinquat.'

4   Pseudo-Methodius and the problem of evil (c. 680–c. 800)

While arguments about time persisted, renewed concerns about evil and authority in the world stimulated developments in the West's apocalyptic repertoire. Few people had fretted about Gog and Magog since Augustine and Jerome's non-historical interpretation back in the fifth century, even when Gregory the Great had been anxious about the implications of Lombard attacks. Isidore's celebration of the Goths as heroic descendants of Gog and Magog seemed to complete the Augustinian anti-apocalyptic project on that front. Over the course of the seventh century, however, the Arab conquests of the Middle East and North Africa changed the religious and political map of the Mediterranean, unsurprisingly leading some shocked and disillusioned Christians in the East towards eschatological reflection.[1] What was needed was a strong response from the Byzantine emperor and, as polemics were launched, soon the idea spread that the empire would play a much larger part in End Times narratives than had previously been considered acceptable. The new reflections on evil and authority, pitched in battle against each other, were given popular form in a prophetic sermon by the Syriac Pseudo-Methodius – a work so powerful and adaptable that it was available in Greek and Latin versions across Europe within half a century.[2] Apocalypticism had a new voice and one which would deeply influence medieval traditions.[3]

---

[1] On Western reactions to the Arab conquests see R. Hoyland, *Seeing Islam as Others Saw It: A Survey and Evaluation of Christian, Jewish and Zoroastrian Writings on Early Islam* (New York, 1997) and J. Tolan, *Saracens: Islam in the Medieval European Imagination* (New York, 2002).

[2] The reconstructed original Syriac version is G. J. Reinink (ed.), *Die syrische Apokalypse des Pseudo-Methodius* (Leuven, 1993). A parallel edition of the Greek and first Latin translations is provided in W. J. Aerts and G. A. A. Kortekaas (eds.), *Die Apokalypse des Pseudo-Methodius. Die ältesten Griechischen und Lateinischen Übersetzungen* (2 vols., Leuven, 1998), which forms the basis for the texts and translations in B. Garstad's *Apocalypse of Pseudo-Methodius*, Dumbarton Oaks Medieval Library, 14 (Cambridge, MA, 2012).

[3] A. R. Anderson, *Alexander's Gate, Gog and Magog, and the Inclosed Nations* (Cambridge, MA, 1932), p. 49. On Pseudo-Methodius: G. J. Reinink, 'Pseudo-Methodius und die Legende vom römischen Endkaiser', in W. Verbeke, D. Verhelst and A. Welkenhuysen

107

The problem of evil was that it existed at all and at times triumphed over good. Such challenges undermined confidence in the rewards of faithfulness until the logic of the threat was understood. But then a theology of suffering and being tested was built into Christian tradition. The Old Testament prophets had announced precisely that sinners would be punished unless they corrected themselves (Elijah, Ezekiel, Jeremiah), while numerous passages throughout the Bible alluded to or foretold challenges in the End Times (Daniel, Matthew, Luke, Revelation). Augustine's applications of Tyconian exegesis reinforced the notion that the enemies of the faithful could be internal enemies such as heretics or bad Christians maybe even more so than external ones. There was no hint in Bede's conservative *Commentary on Revelation* that anything had changed by the eighth century as he explained that Gog and Magog were secret enemies and heretics.[4] Contemporaries agreed.[5] Yet it was external enemies who had seemed more worrying to Quodvultdeus, Gregory the Great and others, looking at the crumbling world around them. Otherness and invasion provided a more tangible expression of evil than technical (if hardly insignificant) variants in Christology and liturgical rite. Pseudo-Methodius's sermon, in its angry response to Arab invasions, captured the attraction of real evil well. Even so, as we shall see, the translation and circulation of the text prompted a range of positive and negative responses.

Pseudo-Methodius was as important for influencing the ways in which apocalyptic 'authority' was understood in the West as it was in the East. Following visions of the afterlife, such as the *Journey of Blessed Fursey* and the *Vision of Barontus*, this was the first text popular in the medieval West in which an author had claimed immediate and definite knowledge about earthly things to come. The authority of the text was derived

(eds.), *The Use and Abuse of Eschatology in the Middle Ages* (Leuven, 1988), pp. 82–111; G. J. Reinink, 'Pseudo-Methodius: A Concept of History in Response to the Rise of Islam', in A. Cameron and L. I. Conrad (eds.), *The Byzantine and Early Islamic East: Problems in the Literary Source Material* (Princeton, NJ, 1992), pp. 149–87; H. Möhring, *Der Weltkaiser der Endzeit. Entstehung, Wandel und Wirkung einer tausandjährigen Weissagung* (Stuttgart, 2000), pp. 54–103. On influence in the West see P. J. Alexander, 'Byzantium and the Migration of Literary Works and Motifs: The Legend of the Last Roman Emperor', *Medievalia et Humanistica*, n.s. 2 (1971), 47–68; H. Möhring, 'Karl der Große und die Endkaiser-Weissagung: Der Sieger über den Islam kommt aus dem Westen', in B. Z. Kedar, J. Riley-Smith and R. Hiestand (eds.), *Montjoie: Studies in Crusade History in Honour of Hans Eberhard Mayer* (Aldershot, 1997), pp. 1–20, elaborated in Möhring's, *Der Weltkaiser*, pp. 136–43.
4 Bede, *Expositio Apocalypseos*, XXXV, 100–2, ed. R. Gryson, CCSL, 121A (Turnhout, 2001), p. 511.
5 *Pauca Problesmata* (Munich, Bayerische Staatsbibliothek, Clm 14277, f. 339v) = *De enigmatibus*, c. 97, ed. R. Gryson, CCSL, 107 (Turnhout, 2003), p. 290.

from its association with the fourth-century St Methodius of Olympus, a relatively obscure writer but known for his dialogues in praise of virginity and his anti-Origenist views on the resurrection of the body on Judgement Day. But authority was also projected through a prophetic language which was strikingly impersonal and free from first-hand revelation – there was no *ego*, no Danielian interpreter at work, no Ezekiel channelling mysteries through visions, just a straightforward recitation of things past and future. This pushed at the boundaries of Sibylline traditions by exchanging mystic visions for concrete historical expectation. And through its historical mode of narration, Pseudo-Methodius asserted a non-allegorical new role for the (Roman) Byzantine Empire as a source of Christian authority in the Last Days, capable of leading a decisive assault against the enemies of Christendom in order to establish one last earthly peace. The eschatology of empire had, of course, scarcely retreated in Byzantine thought the way it had in the West, but it took the transmission of Pseudo-Methodius to challenge seriously Augustine's separation of Church and worldly polity. Authority of prophetic voice and political authority, here, began to mutually support each other as a stimulus for change. As will be shown in this chapter, the relationship between message and form was important to how Pseudo-Methodius was understood.

Before proceeding, it should also be noted that Pseudo-Methodius has enjoyed only uneven scholarly interest, at least with regards to its Latin history. The most important studies of the work, most recently by Reinink and Möhring, have focused on the Syriac original and the context of its composition. Pseudo-Methodius's influence on Byzantine tradition is also reasonably well synthesised in a study by Paul Alexander.[6] The Latin Pseudo-Methodius, however, remains more enigmatic despite two fine modern editions of the text.[7] Since the work is not so different from its Eastern siblings, scholars have taken most interest in it as a text marking a stage either in the development of traditions about Antichrist en route to other popular works such as Adso's *On Antichrist* (*c.* 950), or in the spread of the Last World Emperor legends over the centuries.[8] What is

[6] P. J. Alexander, *The Byzantine Apocalyptic Tradition*, ed. D. Abrahamse (Berkeley, CA, 1985).
[7] The predecessor to Aerts and Kortekaas's edition is E. Sackur, *Sibyllinische Texte und Forschungen* (Halle, 1898).
[8] Alongside the works cited in n. 2 see D. Verhelst, 'La préhistoire des conceptions d'Adson concernant l'Antichrist', *Recherches de théologie ancienne et médiévale*, 40 (1973), 52–103 at 95–8 (advising caution about the connection at pp. 100–1); B. McGinn, *Antichrist: Two Thousand Years of the Human Fascination with Evil* (New York, 1994), pp. 89–92; M. Gabriele, *An Empire of Memory: The Legend of Charlemagne, the Franks, and Jerusalem before the First Crusade* (Oxford, 2011), variously across pp. 107–17.

not yet quite so fully worked through is the Latin Pseudo-Methodius – in all three of its early recensions – in its eighth-century contexts.[9] The present chapter consequently seeks to place Pseudo-Methodius's discussion of evil and authority, and the debates it provoked, within the intellectual networks which first supported the popularity of what was, for the West, a rather unorthodox apocalypse.

A world crisis and Pseudo-Methodius

Deep crisis beset the Byzantine Empire in the early seventh century. Under Herakleios, Constantinople lost control of Syria, Jerusalem and Egypt, not once, but twice in quick succession – first to the Persians and then, despite a comprehensive fightback, to the Arabs.[10] The first had a crucial impact upon apocalyptic tradition, as the siege of Constantinople in 626 led Theodoros Syncellos to compose a homily identifying the city's enemies as the peoples of Gog, here understood as 'an assembly of the people' united against 'this Israel'.[11] Ezekiel's prophecy helped to conceptualise Byzantine struggles. The second collapse represented something new again, and only partly because the Arabs had been energised by the recent emergence of Islam. From almost nowhere, tribal groups considered peripheral and uncultured took hold of the Middle East and North Africa, even seizing Iberia in 711 and besieging Constantinople by 717. The coherence of the old Roman world, one way or another, had been shattered.[12] Syrian sources in particular painted a bleak picture of

[9] Important groundwork is nevertheless provided by O. Prinz, 'Eine frühe abendländische Aktualisierung der lateinischen Übersetzung des Pseudo-Methodius', *DA*, 41 (1985), 1–23, Möhring's 'Karl der Große' and *Der Weltkaiser*; R. M. Pollard, 'One Other on Another: Petrus Monachus' *Revelationes* and Islam', in M. Cohen and J. Firnhaber-Baker (eds.), *Difference and Identity in Francia and Medieval France* (Farnham, 2010), pp. 25–42; and C. Gantner, 'Hoffnung in der Apokalypse? Die *Ismaeliten* in den älteren lateinischen Fassungen der *Revelationes* des Pseudo-Methodius', in V. Wieser, C. Zolles, C. Feik, M. Zolles and L. Schlondorff (eds.), *Abendländische Apokalyptik. Kompendium zur Genealogie der Endzeit* (Berlin, 2013), pp. 521–48.
[10] See most recently J. Howard-Johnston, *Witnesses to a World Crisis: Historians and Histories of the Middle East in the Seventh Century* (Oxford, 2010). Particularly relevant in terms of apocalyptic tradition is J. Flori, *L'Islam et la fin des temps. L'interprétation prophétique des invasions musulmanes dans la chrétienté médiévale* (Paris, 2007), ch. 7.
[11] Theodoros Syncellos, *Homily on the Siege of Constantinople*, esp. c. 40, ed. L. Sternbach, *Analecta Avarica*, (Krakow, 1900), p. 316; W. Brandes, 'Anastasios ὁ Δίκορος. Endzeiterwartung und Kaiserkritik in Byzanz um 500 n.Chr.', *Byzantinische Zeitschrift*, 90 (1997), 24–63 at p. 38.
[12] This was a central point in H. Pirenne, *Mohammed and Charlemagne* (London, 1939), defended with revisions in R. Hodges and D. Whitehouse, *Mohammed, Charlemagne and the Origins of Europe: Archaeology and the Pirenne Thesis* (London, 1983).

a world in chaos.[13] Christians could live under and work with Muslims without problem, but the challenges that this posed to people's understanding of the *mundus* were profound. If the Roman Empire was supposed to have endured until the end of time, then what had happened? Many early Latin commentators saw either providential history at work or else just another military threat amongst many. (Islam itself, note, barely registered as a factor here.) In Austrasia, the chronicler Fredegar looked back on Herakleios's failures as punishment for the emperor sponsoring the Monothelitist heresy and marrying his own niece.[14] Many years later in Germany, St Boniface wrote a letter to King Æthelbald of Mercia in *c.* 746 to point out to him that the fate of Iberia at the hands of the Saracens was a warning about sexual excess.[15] But by then, Charles Martel's victories against the Saracens near Poitiers in 732/3 and in the years afterwards had encouraged a certain confidence in the West, at least outside Iberia.[16] Chroniclers on the whole saw the whole affair as Charles establishing his political authority to the south.[17] Bede commented only that the Saracens deserved to lose for their slaughter.[18] Compared to the Goths and Huns in the fifth century and the Vikings in the ninth, the Arab conquests were less unsettling for the West and generated less apocalyptic or moral reflection.[19] This is not to say that they were not a threat, and indeed King Liudprand of the Lombards acted quickly – and

---

[13] See for instance book 15 of John bar Penkaye, translated in S. Brock, 'North Mesopotamia in the Late Seventh Century: Book XV of John bar Penkaye's *Riš Melle*', *Jerusalem Studies in Arablic and Islam*, 9 (1989), 51–75. See also the sources translated in A. Palmer, *The Seventh Century in the West-Syrian Chronicles* (Liverpool, 1993).

[14] Fredegar, *Chronicae*, IV. 66, ed. B. Krusch, MGH SRM, 2 (Hanover, 1888), p. 154.

[15] Boniface, *Bonifatii et Lulli Epistolae*, no. 73, ed. M. Tangl, MGH Epp. Sel., 1 (Berlin, 1916), p. 151.

[16] In addition to the literature in n. 1, see M. Frassetto and D. R. Blanks (eds.), *Western Views of Islam in Medieval and Early Modern Europe* (New York, 1999) and on English views more specifically see K. Scarfe Becket, *Anglo-Saxon Perceptions of the Islamic World* (Cambridge, 2003). On the date of Poitiers see R. Collins, *The Arab Conquest of Spain 710–797* (Oxford, 1989), pp. 90–1 (preference for 733) and P. Fouracre, *The Age of Charles Martel* (Harlow, 2000), pp. 87–8.

[17] Mozarabic Chronicle of 754, ed. T. Mommsen, MGH AA, 11 (Berlin, 1894), pp. 361–2, is a touch more dramatic – see Flori, *L'Islam*, pp. 156–7. *Historia vel gesta Francorum*, III. 108 = Fredegar, *Chronicae – Continuationes*, c. 13, ed. B. Krusch, MGH SRM, 2 (Hanover, 1888), p. 175; *Annales Laureshamenses*, s.a. 732, ed. E. Katz (St Paul, MN, 1889), p. 29; *Chronicon Moissiacense*, s.a. 732, ed. G. H. Pertz, MGH SS, 1 (Hanover, 1826), p. 291. See also the *Vita Pardulfi*, c. 15, ed. W. Levison, MGH SRM, 7 (Hanover, 1920), pp. 33–4, in which the 'belligerent' people of Ishmaelites were barred from entering the monastery during conflict, and the *Liber pontificalis*, 91. 11, ed. L. Duchesne (Paris, 1886), on Eudo of Aquitaine's massacre of 375,000 Saracens in 721.

[18] Bede, *Historia Ecclesiastica*, V. 23. 2, ed. M. Lapidge (2 vols., Rome, 2010), II. 466–8.

[19] I would qualify this statement by noting that we know too little about how contemporaries in Spain reacted to the events of 711, which could have been quite different to how commentators in Britain, Gaul or Italy responded.

apparently at great expense – to rescue the relics of St Augustine from Sardinia after it was conquered.[20] Christendom and its polities in the West, though, were not under quite the same threat as in the East.

Anxiety in the East could nevertheless be felt in the Latin world. As early as 660, hints of the apocalyptic resonance of the Arab conquests for Byzantium appeared in Fredegar's version of events. Herakleios, so it was said, had been frustrated by Saracen raids and had opened the Caspian Gates built by Alexander the Great to seek mercenaries from amongst the hordes enclosed there. The chronicler may well have been drawing on accounts transmitted at least indirectly from the East, so relatively well informed he seems to have been – although at least one Byzantine chronicler associated the Gates with the Khazars assaults on Persia in 625.[21] This is notable because in Syria and Byzantium, before the Arab conquests had even begun, the story of Alexander and the Caspian Gates was being used to establish the idea that the hordes of Gog and Magog had been unleashed from the North in fulfilment of Ezekiel and that the End was near.[22] The Alexander legend by Pseudo-Callisthenes was coupled with prophecies about the Huns, Arabs and destruction of empires in a Syriac version of c. 629/30, then in another linked to the prophecy of Jeremiah, and then in a *Vaticinium* written to celebrate Constans II (d. 668).[23] The most enduring expression of this interest in Alexander and Gog and Magog came in Pseudo-Methodius's *Revelation*, written according to Möhring between 685 and 690 in Mesopotamia, when there were hopes that Justinian II would defeat the Arabs before Gog and Magog

---

[20] Bede, *De temporum ratione*, c. 66, ed. C. W. Jones, CCSL 123B (Turnhout, 1977), p. 535 – a story repeated in Paul the Deacon, *Historia Langobardorum*, VI. 48, ed. L. Bethmann and G. Waitz, MGH SS rer. Lang. (Hanover, 1878), p. 181 and *Gesta episcoporum Neapolitanorum*, I. 36, ed. G. Waitz, MGH SS rer. Lang., p. 422.

[21] Theophanes, *Chronographia*, AM 6117, ed. C. de Boor, p. 316; trans. C. Mango and R. Scott (Oxford, 1997), p. 447. Note also the possible influence on his use of the word *uxus* (sword) in Fredegar, *Chronicon*, IV. 64, ed. Krusch, p. 152 (discussion in J. M. Wallace-Hadrill, *The Fourth Book of the Chronicle of Fredegar* (London, 1960), p. 53 n. 1). Gantner, 'Hoffnung in der Apokalypse?', pp. 538–41 points out the geographical problems with Fredegar's account.

[22] The classic study of the legends in the East remains Anderson, *Alexander's Gate*, esp. ch. 2. See also A. B. Schmidt, 'Die "Brüste des Norden" und Alexanders Mauer gegen Gog und Magog', in W. Brandes and F. Schmieder (eds.), *Endzeiten. Eschatologie in den monotheistischen Weltreligionen* (Berlin and New York, 2008), pp. 89–99. The connection to Ezekiel is made explicit in Pseudo-Methodius, *Sermo*, [8], 10, p. 117.

[23] *A Christian Legend concerning Alexander*, trans. E. A. W. Budge (Cambridge, 1889), p. 155; *Discourse of Jacob of Serūgh*, trans. Budge, p. 167. See Reinink, 'Ps.-Methodius: A Concept of History', pp. 166–7 and n. 73. The *Vaticinium of Constans* is extant only as a layer in the eleventh-century *Oracula Tiburtina*, ed. Sackur, *Sibyllinische Texte*, pp. 177–87, recently associated with Constans II in G. L. Potestà, 'The *Vaticinium of Constans*. Genesis and Original Purposes of the Last World Emperor', *Millennium: Jahrbuch zu Kultur und Geschichte des Jahrtausends n. Chr.*, 8 (2011), 271–89.

came.[24] Fredegar seems to bear witness to an intermediate stage of development in the Alexander legend, with the Saracens only slowly taking up a role in the drama of the End Times.

Pseudo-Methodius's *Revelation* was soon to head west to make a significant impact upon apocalyptic tradition and to become one of the most copied texts of the early Middle Ages.[25] Although the original had been written in Syriac, it was quickly translated into Greek and then, not long afterwards, from the Greek into Latin by a figure who identified himself as Petrus Monachus.[26] Little is known about Petrus beyond what can be ascertained from analysis of his translation. He wrote what his modern editors call a typically 'Merovingian' Latin (i.e. heavy with non-classical grammar and spelling), possibly with some features common to south of the Alps.[27] He was relatively unusual in his day for understanding Greek and may therefore have been one of the many Greek monks living in Rome at the time.[28] Richard Pollard has shown that Petrus betrayed a hatred of the Arabs a touch more heated than many of his contemporaries.[29] Indeed, with this last point, it is worth noting that Petrus was no passive translator – if such a thing ever exists – because he still had to choose the colour of his Latin and because he took time to embellish some parts of the text, even though he promised he had not done so.[30] An early date for the translation is suggested by the oldest extant manuscript, which was written in a centre whose script was deeply influenced

[24] Möhring, *Der Weltkaiser*, pp. 78–82 (the *terminus ante quem* derived from the prophecy of the seventy-year rule of the Muslims, which would be 691 if it began with the *hijra* in 622). Cf. Reinink, 'Ps.-Methodius: A Concept of History', pp. 180–6, where the case is set out for 690–1. If, however, one took Arab dominance to begin with the Battle of Yarmuk in 635, then the seventy years would end in 704/5. On the relevance to Justinian II see also P. Magdalino, 'The History of the Future and Its Uses: Prophecy, Policy and Propaganda', in R. Beaton and C. Roueché (eds.), *The Making of Byzantine History* (Aldershot, 1993), pp. 3–34 at pp. 19–20.
[25] For a full list of the Latin manuscripts, divided into their four recensions, see M. Laureys and D. Verhelst, 'Pseudo-Methodius, *Revelationes*: Textgeschichte und kritische Edition. Ein Leuven-Groninger Forschungsprojekt', in Verbeke *et al.*, *The Use and Abuse*, pp. 112–36.
[26] A useful summary of the scholarship building up to this chronology of translations is provided by Alexander, *The Byzantine Apocalyptic Tradition*, pp. 13–16.
[27] Aerts and Kortekaas, *Die Apokalypse des Pseudo-Methodius*, pp. 20–5, but on his likely Italian location preferred in Möhring, *Der Weltkaiser*, p. 104 and Gantner, 'Hoffnung in der Apokalypse?', p. 525.
[28] On knowledge of Greek see W. Berschin, *Greek Letters and the Latin Middle Ages: From Jerome to Nicholas of Cusa* (Washington, DC, 1988). Having mentioned Fredegar in the context of Petrus Monachus, it is worth noting that the scribe of the oldest extant manuscript and at least one early reader practised Greek: Paris, Bibliothèque nationale, lat. 10910, 23v and 170r for Greek titles, and 63v, 79r, 132r for Greek marginalia.
[29] Pollard, 'One Other on Another', pp. 31–2.
[30] Petrus, *Sermo*, pref., p. 65.

by Luxeuil, and which contains a computus from 727 (with a countdown to AM 6000), although palaeographically the manuscript could be a decade or two later.[31] Möhring has suggested that Petrus wrote before the conquest of Spain in 711 because no allowance is made for that event,[32] although this also assumes that an Eastern translator in Italy or Gaul would have adapted the text accordingly. It was, anyway, known in the West by at least 767 at the latest when Ambrosius Autpertus – a Gallic monk writing in Italy – referred to it in his commentary on Revelation.

The text Petrus translated is an unusual combination of world chronicle and prophetic vision – a combination which, as Paul Alexander noted, was mutually reinforcing because it grounded expectation in what was known to have already occurred.[33] This was where the text, devoid of its *ego*, gained its authority. In that sense Pseudo-Methodius was scarcely more radical than Gregory the Great, who had similarly read the world around him gloomily; it was just that Pseudo-Methodius had more to say about what was to come than had the pope. He was also as polemical as Gregory and, in the Latin, his text was cast as a *sermo* or *dicta*, which implies potential use in preaching.[34] The historical form is straightforward, structuring time from the expulsion from Paradise to the Last Judgement, and using the passing of millennia as a supplementary device for orientation. The content, however, has been described as being 'full of the most extraordinary distortions and misrepresentations'.[35] For a text composed with a sense of Christian history, it is striking that there is no mention of Christ until the end, nor much early Roman or Christian history.[36] On the other hand, Alexander the Great is rather prominent. After the inauguration of the seventh millennium – being a text rooted in Eastern chronology – there is little history given except the prolonged crisis of empire against the Saracens and its eventual, prophesied resolution. Indeed, in practice, everything coalesces around three prophecies: (1) that Saracen dominance will last seventy years, (2) that afterwards twenty-two unclean nations will defile the earth and (3) that the Roman (or Byzantine) Empire will endure for eternity (following Ps. 68.31).[37] Pseudo-Methodius's past and future, then, were clearly defined as a

[31] Bern, Burgerbibliothek, 611, ff. 94–115. Elias Lowe accepted the date of 727 based on the date of the computus (*CLA*, no. 604c).
[32] Möhring, *Der Weltkaiser*, p. 102.
[33] E.g. P. Alexander, 'Medieval Apocalypses as Historical Sources', *AHR*, 73.4 (1968), 997–1018 at p. 1009.
[34] Alexander, *The Byzantine Apocalyptic Tradition*, pp. 22–3.
[35] Ibid., p. 14, drawing on the analysis in M. Kmosko, 'Das Rätsel des Pseudo-Methodius', *Byzantion*, 6 (1931), 273–97
[36] Möhring, *Der Weltkaiser*, p. 63.
[37] Alexander, *The Byzantine Apocalyptic Tradition*, pp. 18–19.

response to the Arab presence in Syria, wrapped up in a historical form which could be used for preaching.

Let's proceed by considering in more detail the nature of the Arab threat in Pseudo-Methodius and its relevance for Petrus. The Arabs were introduced by Pseudo-Methodius as 'the sons of Ishmael, the son of Hagar the Egyptian slave girl of Sara, wife of Abraham'.[38] The genealogical tradition we encountered in Chapter 1 was here used to identify the Arabs as a people whose line had deviated from salvation – something reinforced in a spurious account of how they inflicted destruction and chaos upon the world until they were subjected to the Romans at the end of the fourth millennium.[39] Later in the seventh millennium, Pseudo-Methodius prophesied, 'the Lord will give them the power to conquer the lands of the Christians, not because he loves them, but because of the sin and iniquity committed by the Christians' – introducing an aggressive take on recent history which guarded against any suggestion that the Muslims triumphed because they were right.[40] Indeed, in the passages amplified from the Greek by Petrus, the Arabs were too full of pride, too quick to commit atrocity, the very antithesis of civility.[41] Even so, Christians would find accommodation by paying tax (jizya, paid to secure protected dhimmi status). Compromised, their sins would increase for seventy years, until the Last World Emperor came to defeat the sons of Ishmael and restore peace for a time (with echoes of Matt. 24.38). The Arab conquests represented a providential scourge on the earth prior to the events of the End Times but one which ultimately preserved the superiority of Christianity. In Italy or Gaul, where the Saracens were not remotely dominant, Petrus could still have seen the power in the universality of such conclusions.

Importantly, in the above scenario, the Saracens were distinct from the threat of Gog and Magog and the final persecutions, which would follow only after the brief respite.[42] This meant that, as with Gregory's Lombards, the Arabs could be treated with due concern as part of a realised apocalyptic narrative without them being a direct fulfilment of scripture. Pseudo-Methodius thought that after the Saracens' defeat, the Caspian Gates would be opened and the 'peoples from the North' (gentes

[38] Pseudo-Methodius, Sermo, [5], 2, p. 93.
[39] Ibid., [5], 4–9, pp. 95–101.
[40] Ibid., [11], 5, pp. 138–41: 'Sic etenim filios Ishmael, non quod eos diligat dominus Deus, dabit eis potentiam hanc, ut obteneant terram christianorum, sed propter peccatum et iniquitatem, quae ab eis committitur.'
[41] Pollard, 'One Other on Another', pp. 30–1.
[42] The identification of Gog and Magog with the Ishmaelites proposed in Anderson, Alexander's Gate, p. 45 works better typologically than it does as a reflection of Pseudo-Methodius's own words.

ab Aquilone) imprisoned by Alexander would come down to purge society once more, forcing people to hide in mountains and secret places. The Northerners included Gog and Magog, but only amongst other tribes such as the Dog-Heads. The reference to the persecutors' northernness, significantly, ties the prophecy to Ezekiel, rather than Revelation in which the final assault would be worldwide rather than from a single direction.[43] Compared to even the dark representations of the Saracen attacks, meanwhile, the otherness of the persecutors was marked by particularly monstrous behaviour: 'they will eat unclean serpents, scorpions, and every kind of filthy and abominable beast and reptile which crawls the earth. They will consume the dead bodies of beasts of burden and even women's abortions. They will slay the young and take them away from their mothers and eat them.'[44] This was a bodily sinfulness which eroded the very fabric of society. Their reign of terror would last 'a week of times' (*ebdomada temporis* – an allusion to Dan. 9.24), but eventually one of the king's generals (*princeps*) would strike them down. Gog and Magog, like the Saracens, could not prevail in the End because their otherness marked them out as being beyond salvation.

The role of the Last World Emperor in this part of the drama provided a particular political framework for understanding the End Times. The figure of the emperor – more accurately *rex* ('king') – is set up across the second half of the text, with a typological association between Alexander, the first conquering Greek king, and the last to come.[45] In doing so, as Reinink observed, Pseudo-Methodius argued for the endurance of the 'Greek/Roman/Byzantine kingdom' as the fourth and last prophesied by Daniel, at a time when some Syrians had begun to wonder if that role was to be fulfilled by the Ishmaelites.[46] Pseudo-Methodius's *rex* was a

---

[43] See also Jeremiah 1.14 and Joel 2.20 on dangers from the North, the latter of which Jerome had taken to be symbolic of anyone opposing the righteous: Jerome, *Commentarorium in Joelem*, PL, 25. 970–1. The connection with Gog and Magog in the texts suggests Ezekiel was the first line was influence.

[44] Pseudo-Methodius, *Sermo*, [13], 20, pp. 183–5: 'commedent inmunda[s], serpentes et scurpionis et omnem sord<i>dissimum et abomniabilem genus bestiarum et reptilia, que repunt super terram, iumentorum autem et corpora mortua et abortitia mulierum. Etiam occidnunt parvulum et cedunt eos suis matribus <...> et edunt eos.' See also *Sermo*, [11], 17, p. 155, where the Saracens impale women and smash babies for fodder for their beasts – a possible reference to Hosea 13.16.

[45] Pseudo-Methodius, *Sermo*, [9], 1–[10], 6, pp. 119–35 and [13], 11–18, pp. 175–83; Reinink, 'Ps.-Methodius: A Concept of History', pp. 165–8.

[46] Reinink, 'Ps.-Methodius: A Concept of History', pp. 157–8. The contemporary source which makes the Ishmaelites the fourth kingdom is *The Armenian History Attributed to Sebeos*, trans. R. W. Thomson (Liverpool, 1999), pp. 105–6, where a geographical interpretation is followed rather than a chronological one. See T. Greenwood, 'Sasanian Echoes and Apocalyptic Expectations: A Re-Evaluation of the Armenian History Attributed to Sebeos', *Le Muséon*, 115.3–4 (2002), 323–97, esp. pp. 376–8.

good emperor with messianic resonance who, after waking 'as if from a drunken stupor', would cross the sea to restore Christian peace and order.[47] If one took the seventy years of Ishmaelite dominance to start with the Battle of Yarmuk in 635, this imperial prophecy would resonate particularly well with Justinian II, who was exiled from 695 until his restoration as emperor in 703.[48] Nevertheless, the prophecy ended on a strange note because, ten and a half years after rising up, the *rex* himself would do little to resist Gog and Magog or the Son of Perdition, instead retiring to Jerusalem to ascend Golgotha and lay down his crown on the Cross.[49] The prophecy established a narrative which explains the circumstances in which the fourth kingdom would be handed over to the people of God (Ps. 68.31; Dan. 2.44; 7.27). It redefined the character of the 'king of kings, lord of lords' from Revelation (19.16), as an earthly ruler, and in a way which resonated with Justinian II's *rex regnatium* coinage.[50] So much would, no doubt, have been lost on Western audiences half a century later, but the clear flow of history from the past, through the present, into a predictable future provided a concrete and worldly framework for apocalyptic expectations attached to the fate of political figures.

Perhaps an accidental but crucial defining note was the emperor's ambiguous 'Roman/Greek' identity. Of course in many respects this reflected various levels of ideological reality: a Byzantine emperor, 'emperor of the Hellenes', was the heir to the unbroken Roman imperial tradition, even in Western eyes.[51] In Syria, it was also entirely understandable that someone might hope that a powerful Christian figure might come to restore order – from where else would such a figure come, even if Justinian II turned out to be a hopeless saviour?[52] The nature of prophecy, however, meant that there was only the shape of a story and the most

---

[47] Reinink, 'Pseudo-Methodius und die Legende vom römischen Endkaiser', argued against P. A. Alexander, 'The Medieval Legend of the Last Roman Emperor and Its Messianic Origin', *Journal of the Warburg and Courtauld Institutes*, 41 (1978), 1–15 esp. at p. 8, that the emperor figure was derived from Jewish messianic tradition. Even so, there is a quasi-messianic quality to his role as saviour of the Christians before Judgement.

[48] Theophanes, *Chronographia*, AM 6196, ed. de Boor, pp. 372–4; trans. Mango and Scott, pp. 520–1.

[49] Pseudo-Methodius, *Sermo*, [13], 19–21, pp. 183–5. This is different from the prophecy in the *Oracula Tiburtina*, although Pseudo-Methodius may still have had some version of this legend in mind: Möhring, *Der Weltkaiser*, pp. 68–9.

[50] Möhring, *Der Weltkaiser*, p. 87; J. D. Breckenridge, *The Numismatic Iconography of Justinian II (685–695, 705–711 AD)* (New York, 1959), pp. 51–2. See Magdalino, 'History of the Future', p. 20.

[51] Pseudo-Methodius, *Sermo*, [13], 11, p. 174 (Greek) and p. 175 (Latin).

[52] Theophanes, *Chronographia*, ed. de Boor, p. 366; trans. Mango and Scott, p. 511. Möhring, *Der Weltkaiser*, p. 87.

basic sketch of who the *rex Romanorum* might be. Indeed, apart from his title, there was little about the emperor which limited identification, meaning that any *rex Romanorum* or *rex Gregorum* could in principle seek to assume an apocalyptic role for themselves by intervening in the affairs of the East. As we shall see, this was particularly portentous where, say, we have the proposed reunion of East and West through Charlemagne and Irene (Chapter 5) or the half-German, half-Greek emperor Otto III (Chapter 7).

The third part of Pseudo-Methodius's End Times drama concerned the actions of the Son of Perdition – not quite Antichrist – in the End Times.[53] Again this was something which was far from clear in scripture and which did not figure explicitly in Revelation. Scholars turned to Paul's Second Epistle to the Thessalonians which, in an allusion to Daniel's prophecy, stated that the End could not come until there had been a 'falling away' (*discessio*) from imperial authority and the Son of Perdition had revealed himself (2 Thess. 2.3).[54] Even here Petrus's choice of words was significant because the idea of a 'falling away' was not quite the same in the Greek (ἀποστασία, 'rebellion') or Syriac (*mardūtā*, 'chastisement'), which suggested that the train of translation had amplified the sense of Rome's collapse.[55] But the action attributed to the Son of Perdition was that he would pretend to be God, oppose Christian things, and sit in the temple in Jerusalem. Pseudo-Methodius brought together a variety of additional motifs to show that the Son of Perdition would be descended from the tribe of Dan, announce himself and sit in the temple after the *rex Romanorum* had relinquished his power, kill the prophets Enoch and Elijah who had been sent against him – adding identities for the two anonymous witnesses in Revelation (11.3–7) – and by this point it would be time for the Parousia. It was not necessarily original, but the key elements of the story of Antichrist, later more famously fleshed out by Adso in *c.* 950, were in place (see Chapter 7); and more than this, they had been set out in a narrative form which lent themselves to further historical interpretations of the End.

What remains uncertain is what relevance the Pseudo-Methodian tradition had for Petrus. Only at the most impressionistic levels could the ideas and motifs have been applied to events or figures in Gaul or

---

[53] The difference between the Son of Perdition and Antichrist in this context is discussed in Potestà, 'The *Vaticinium of Constans*', 288–9.
[54] Pseudo-Methodius, *Sermo*, [10], 1–2, pp. 127–9 and [11], 17, p. 153. McGinn, *Antichrist*, 62–3, 74; Alexander, *The Byzantine Apocalyptic Tradition*, pp. 32–3.
[55] In contrast Petrus's translation of παιδεία as *disciplina* in Pseudo-Methodius's gloss of the 'falling away' seems more literal: Pseudo-Methodius, *Sermo*, [11], 17, p. 152 (Greek) and p. 153 (Latin).

Lombardy, where Christian–Arab relations were quite different from those in the East, and the need for a saviour king could have seemed exaggerated.[56] Of course the translation suggests that Petrus was an Easterner – displaced or emigrated – with universal concerns triggered by distant events.[57] And there would have been potential audiences with Byzantine points of reference in Rome or in the Byzantine-dominated south or east of the Italian peninsula. In terms of the logic of Petrus's interest in translation, we can rely on only two indicators: his preface and his work's reception. The first of these suggests the need to inspire a group, an audience, to which Petrus belonged – hence his repeated use of the first person plural rather than a direct second-person address. The second, which links Luxeuil, Corbie and, as we shall see, Bobbio and St Gall, basically attests to Petrus's work circulating quickly and widely in Columbanian circles. Given the eschatological Franco-Columbanian culture sketched out in Chapter 3, the early popularity of Petrus's translation starts to make sense as another apocalyptic text to inspire reform, this time adding a political dimension which was relevant at a universal level. In its Latin third home, Pseudo-Methodius's sermon became important more for its big themes than for its power to offer a close reading of recent history. But that did not mean that it passed uncritically into mainstream traditions, as we shall now see.

The early reception of Petrus Monachus's translation

The early transmission and use of Petrus's translation presents a range of problems for understanding eighth-century apocalyptic tradition. Compared to the large number of manuscript copies from the eleventh century onwards, the survival of eighth- or ninth-century manuscripts is underwhelming: four of the first recension, two of the second, two of the third.[58] One can at least make local observations about how Pseudo-Methodius was archived and where, which will provide some indications of the appeal or use of the text in those instances, even if global conclusions are impossible. Moreover, the fact that there are two further early recensions – unrelated but both derived from the first – reveals some of the 'editorial' interests of at least two of Petrus's early readers. To those,

---

[56] Compare the arguments of Gantner, 'Hoffnung in der Apokalypse?', esp. p. 547 that the medium of apocalypse here offered hope for a Christian victory against the Muslims.
[57] A context for Petrus travelling west could be provided by M. McCormick, *Origins of the European Economy: Communication and Commerce AD 300–900* (Cambridge, 2001), esp. Part II on the movement of peoples.
[58] Laureys and Verhelst, 'Pseudo-Methodius, *Revelationes*'; Verhelst, 'La préhistoire', 95. On the manuscript of Recension 3 missed by Verhelst see below pp. 123–4.

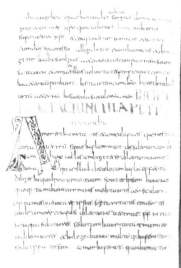

Figure 3 Petrus Monachus's Preface to Pseudo-Methodius in an eighth-century Corbie manuscript.

we can add two further responses to the work in the *Cosmography of Aethicus Ister* and Ambrosius Autpertus's commentary on Revelation, both written in Italy in the middle of the eighth century. This level of 'chatter' about a text may not seem like much compared to later centuries, but in the context of the eighth century it amounts to a surprisingly lively reception history. And all this for a very different kind of text for the West: it predicted a narrative of the future – without an end date, true – when most writers preferred biblical exegesis; it predicted a real Gog and Magog, out of step with Augustinian sensibilities; and it asserted a greater role for empire in the apocalyptic drama than Western commentators had entertained for a while. In form and content Pseudo-Methodius presented challenges.

The second oldest extant manuscript alone provides a varied context for the reception of Petrus's translation. The manuscript was written in northern France, most in a distinctive script known as the 'en-type', which immediately locates it to the middle of the eighth century.[59] For

[59] Paris, Bibliothèque nationale, lat. 13348. See D. Ganz, *Corbie in the Carolingian Renaissance* (Sigmaringen, 1990), p. 131, with further discussion on p. 42, and G. Kortekaas, 'The Transmission of the Text of Pseudo-Methodius in Cod. Paris. Lat.

a long time the manuscript was kept in Corbie, an important monastery that had maintained close ties to royal courts since its foundation by Queen Balthild.[60] In the manuscript – the only one to contain a full text with Petrus's own preface – the copy of Pseudo-Methodius forms a discrete codicological unit with another prophetic sermon, the *Scarpsum* of Pseudo-Ephraim.[61] The binding together of these two distinctive apocalyptic texts might suggest a common purpose, but we shall return to that. At an early date the two sermons were added to a collection of texts in Corbie, mostly by Jerome and Eucherius, such as *On Hebrew Names* and *On the Holy Places* – in other words, exactly the kinds of treatise which underpinned the genealogical and geographical interpretations of peoples in relation to the biblical past.[62] For some reason, a part of Pseudo-Methodius missing in the initial copy – the fictional account of the first time the sons of Ishmael had conquered most of the world – was added into this part, intertwining the two sections.[63] The two-part manuscript, then, suggests an interest in eastern prophecy juxtaposed with a desire to understand the geography of the East.

Like Pseudo-Methodius, Pseudo-Ephraim was striking for ideas about political apocalyptic and imminence. The sermon declared at the outset that the End was near and went on to state that all the signs from scripture had been fulfilled except for the completion of the Roman kingdom, uniquely for this time making the state of the empire the sole indicator of the fulfilment of prophecy. The preacher was not optimistic about the chances of his audience turning things around: 'we neither become very much afraid of the report nor of the appearance [of barbarian assaults], in order that we might do penance; because they instil fear in us, and we do

13348', *Revue d'histoire des textes*, 18 (1988), 63–79. The exemplar also gave rise to the eighth-century manuscripts Biblioteca Apostolica Vaticana, Barb. lat. 671, ff. 167v–174v and Karlsruhe, Badische Landesbibliothek, Aug. perg. 196, ff. 29v–30r. Mid-eighth-century date given by Elias Lowe: *CLA*, no. 656 (with other examples of EN listed in *CLA* vi, xxiv–xxv). Note that this Pseudo-Ephraim sermon is not the same as the Syriac Pseudo-Ephraim sermon on the apocalypse.
[60] *Diplomata*, no. 86, ed. T. Kölzer, MGH Diplomata regum Francourm e stirpe Merovingica (Hanover, 2001), I. 222–4 (but 'unecht'); *Vita domnae Balthildis*, c. 7, ed. B. Krusch, MGH SRM 2 (Hanover, 1888), p. 490.
[61] Paris, Bibliothèque nationale, lat. 13348, ff. 89r–111v. Pseudo-Ephraim, *Scarpsum*, ed. D. Verhelst, in R. Lievens, E. van Mingroot and W. Verbeke (eds.), *Pascua Mediaevalia*, Historica Lovaniensia, 155 (Leuven, 1983), pp. 518–28, with discussion in Verhelst, 'La préhistoire', pp. 97–8.
[62] Note here Lowe's comment: 'It is a curious coincidence that this manuscript contains the same text as Lat. 13347 of the same school, only in an abridged version' (*CLA*, no. 656).
[63] Paris, Bibliothèque nationale, lat. 13348, ff. 81r–82v = Pseudo-Methodius, [4], 3–2–[5], 5–9, pp. 89–99, from 'Cumque igitur' to 'usque ad numerum temporum'. (Aerts and Kortekaas, *Die Apokalypse* p. 49).

not wish to be changed, even though we need penance for our actions.'[64] People did not fully recognise what was going on and therefore did not act appropriately. But, as Pseudo-Ephraim made the Roman Empire central to the future, the sermon lacked many of Pseudo-Methodius's key motifs. Even its 'warlike peoples' (*gentes bellicae*) – the closest we get to the *gentes ab Aquilone* – are only implicitly Gog and Magog. There was no Alexander, no interest in the North, no Arab conquests, not even a *rex Romanorum* – just war and the decline of the Roman Empire as it fought the Persian Empire until both were overrun by tribes. Despite their differences, the two sermons attest to a different way of dealing with apocalypse, with a focus on future things rather than the evaluation of present things which concerned the Gregorys.

More direct adaptations of Petrus's work soon followed in the late eighth century in Alemannia, and they changed few of the key ingredients. The second recension, edited by Otto Prinz in 1985, is the better studied of the two.[65] References to Spain, Gaul, Germany(!) and Aquitaine as victims of the Arabs show an updating of the prophecy to include Western problems, now explicitly *Saraceni* in keeping with Western nomenclature.[66] For Prinz this was in response to the Arab attacks of 732/3, but Hannes Möhring has suggested equally plausibly that it might have been composed in relation to Charlemagne's ill-fated campaign in northern Spain in 778, just after the king had begun flirting with imperial imagery and founded his own *Urbs Karoli* (modern Paderborn).[67] Certainly these were the two main negative encounters between the Latin West and Islam, but either association stands ill at ease with Pollard's observation that the author of the second recension deliberately toned down Petrus's negative portrayal of the Saracens.[68] There were other concerns more closely related to orthodoxy: Alexander and the Caspian Gates were struck out, perhaps, as we shall see, for being too historical, while the *gentes ab Aquilone* were identified as Gog and Magog, and the Son of Perdition was now firmly named as Antichrist,

---

[64] Pseudo-Ephraim, ed. Verhelst, p. 524: 'nos nec auditu nec aspectu pertimescimus, ut paenetentiam utique agamus; etiam nobis metum incutiunt, et nec sic converti volumus, cum indigeamus paenitentiam pro nostris facinoribus.'

[65] Prinz, 'Eine frühe abendländische Aktualisierung', with full list of manuscripts listed in Laureys and Verhelst, 'Pseudo-Methodius', pp. 119–29. See Möhring, 'Karl der Große', pp. 6–16 and *Der Weltkaiser*, pp. 136–43, and Pollard, 'One Other on Another', pp. 33–5.

[66] Pseudo-Methodius II, ed. Prinz, p. 12 (commentary p. 20). On the sources naming the Arabs 'Saraceni', see Scarfe Becket, *Anglo-Saxon Perceptions*, pp. 90–115.

[67] Prinz, 'Eine frühe abendländische Aktualisierung', pp. 20–2; Möhring, *Der Weltkaiser*, pp. 142–3.

[68] Pollard, 'One Other on Another', pp. 33–5.

all bringing things in line with Western ideas.[69] Most tellingly of all, the redactor moved the events of recent history out of the seventh millennium and into the sixth, to keep it within the chronological system of Eusebius-Jerome.[70] However Pseudo-Methodius may have pushed at the sensibilities of Latin audiences, it remained useful enough for someone to adapt.

The third recension, meanwhile, has not been factored into any understandings of Pseudo-Methodius's treatment in the West.[71] Nevertheless, like the second recension, it illustrates that people in the West were interested in repurposing Petrus's original. The text survives in only two manuscripts – the earliest from Reichenau, not so far away from the likely origin of the second recension.[72] This witness was written in a late eighth-century minuscule most readily comparable to a north Italian manuscript now in Novara.[73] There are fewer of the novelties found in the second recension, like the list of Western regions affected by Arab conquests; and some of the elements rejected there, such as the role of Alexander the Great, are maintained in this one.[74] But there are significant editorial tweaks so, for instance, the fictional first Arab conquest was 'corrected' to become a prophecy about the later one.[75] The text also shares with the second recension the clarifications that the Son of Perdition is Antichrist and that the 'northern peoples' at the End Times are Gog and Magog, although here the editor dropped references to the North in order to emphasise the general assault prophesied in Rev. 20.7.[76] The sermon was also drastically shortened and copied alongside a number of homilies – including two on the Day of Judgement – providing

---

[69] Pseudo-Methodius II, ed. Prinz, p. 15. Prinz, 'Eine frühe abendländische Aktualisierung', p. 18 on the omissions.
[70] Möhring, Der Weltkaiser, pp. 136–7
[71] Verhelst's comment that 'un autre manuscript, datant due VIIIe–IXe siècle, présente une nouvelle version, dans laquelle plusieurs passages manquent' ('La préhistoire', 96) is as much as anyone has written on the matter. I am preparing a more detailed study to supplement what is said here.
[72] Karlsruhe, Badische Landesbibliothek, Aug. perg. 254 (= CLA, no. 1110). Laureys and Verhelst, 'Pseudo-Methodius', p. 129. The second manuscript is the late ninth-century Cologne, Dombibliothek, MS 15, ff. 84v–86r – a witness missed by Laureys and Verhelst. My thanks to Stephan Pelle for bringing it to my attention.
[73] B. Bischoff, Katalog der festländischen Handschriften des neunten Jahrhunderts (Wiesbaden, 1998), I. 364 (no. 1735). The Novaran manuscript is Novara, Biblioteca Capitolare, 2 (LXXXIV) (= CLA, no. 406 – where the first example printed is significantly closer).
[74] The Alexander legend is repeated on ff. 206r–208r, taking up a significant proportion of the overall text.
[75] f. 205v.
[76] Universal assault is emphasised on f. 208r: 'tunc faciunt universa mala in toto orbem terrarum' and f. 209r 'et faciunt universa mala vastantes terram' (explaining the actions of 'Gog et Amagog et ceteri'). The filius perditionis is glossed as Antichristus on f. 208v and f. 209r. The editor retained the reference to the ubera aquilonis (f. 207r).

one of our strongest indications that this new tradition was being studied (at least here) in the context of arming priests with material for preaching.[77] This in itself reminds us that Pseudo-Methodius could have been adapted for practical reasons, such as its length, as well as for its apocalyptic content. Moreover, its undifferentiated treatment alongside homilies and other material dealing with sin and penance – all with one eye on Judgement – makes Pseudo-Methodius part of a continuum of correction, rather than an apocalyptic aberration.

There were still plenty of critics alongside those who made use of Pseudo-Methodius. In Bobbio – a northern Italian monastery with more Columbanian connections – one creative mind made good use of some key motifs he found in Petrus's work in the course of writing a satirical geography, composed fraudulently as a 'translation' by Jerome of a *Cosmographia* by 'Aethicus Ister'.[78] Just like Petrus, the author may well have been a well-travelled and displaced individual with a heightened dislike of those who lived on the edges of the old Roman world (especially northerners), accounting for his sharp commentary.[79] He was, however, less interested in prophecy about the End Times and more on creating a geography in which Gog, Magog and the other enclosed nations of the North – especially the savage Turks – could burst forth from Alexander's Gate to join with Antichrist.[80] The process of 'borealisation' was perversely pursued with little concern for precise geography, sidestepping the awkwardness of having the gates to the North and many of Gog and Magog's descendants in the East.[81] What had begun to matter was the association between the North and evil.[82] In this imaginative space, at least a generation before the First Viking Age, peoples who lived beyond the frontiers of civilised society such as the island-bound Dog-Heads were the vile, monstrous antitheses of good – and it was hoped that they

---

[77] ff. 161r–165v (to my knowledge unedited); ff. 180r–181r (PL, 39. 2210). On preaching see n. 91 below.

[78] *The Cosmography of Aethicus Ister*, ed. and trans. M. Herren, Publications of the Journal of Medieval Latin, 8 (Turnhout, 2011).

[79] M. Herren, 'The *Cosmography of Aethicus Ister* and Ancient Travel Literature', in K. Dekkers, K. Olsen and T. Hofstra (eds.), *The World of Travellers: Exploration and Imagination*, Germania Latina, 7 (Leuven, 2009), pp. 5–30; Pollard, 'One Other on Another', pp. 40–1.

[80] Aethicus Ister, *Cosmographia*, c. 32 and cc. 39–41, ed. and trans. Herren, pp. 32–3 and pp. 48–53. Cf Pollard, 'One Other on Another', pp. 35–8, where it is argued that Aethicus Ister's focus on the Turks at the expense of the Arabs, along with other features, represent a learned mocking of Petrus Monachus's work.

[81] Cf Anderson, *Alexander's Gate*, p. 51

[82] See also here J. R. Berg, '"Breasts of the North" and Other Apocalyptic Imagery in the *Cosmographia* of Aethicus Ister', in V. Wieser, C. Zolles, C. Feik, M. Zolles and L. Schlondorff (eds.), *Abendländische Apokalyptik. Kompendium zur Genealogie der Endzeit* (Berlin, 2013), pp. 563–76 esp. 574–6.

would stay away from the riches of the south.[83] The author was not the only person thinking in exaggerated terms about north/south divides at this time but, inspired by Petrus, he was the first to bind them so closely to apocalyptic expectations.[84]

Only once did a proponent of an Augustinian approach to the apocalyptic offer clear criticism of Pseudo-Methodius's work. Ambrosius Autpertus further south, in San Vincenzo al Volturno, had clearly come across Pseudo-Methodius and made a critical note in his influential commentary on Revelation written for Pope Paul I (d. 767).[85] Like other exegetes, his interpretation of Revelation was more strictly spiritual and ecclesiological, and bedded down in the writings of previous authorities. On the issue of time, for instance, he commented: 'how long remains in length until the end of this time, we do not know.'[86] When discussing the 'king of kings, lord of lords' (Rev. 19.11–16) he saw only metaphors for Ecclesia and the ministry of Christ, and no hints of future historical conflicts.[87] In such a context it is unsurprising to find, in his thoughts on Rev. 20.7, a lack of appreciation for Pseudo-Methodius's historical outlook. For a start, he argued, Alexander's enclosure of Gog and Magog belonged to human history, not divine truths.[88] That it was Pseudo-Methodius that irked him is suggested by his reference to the enclosed 'twenty-four kingdoms', which can only be a misunderstanding of Petrus's twenty-two.[89] Gog and Magog in Revelation, however, were to rise up in all four corners of the world, which suggested to Ambrosius that they were not one specific people coming from a single location, so they could not be these kingdoms. Perhaps here we find an explanation

---

[83] Dog-Heads: *Cosmographia*, c. 28, ed. and trans. Herren, pp. 26–9 and see I. Wood, 'Aethicus Ister: An Exercise in Difference', in W. Pohl and H. Reimitz (eds.), *Grenze und Differenz im frühen Mittelalter* (Vienna, 2000), pp. 197–208 and his 'Categorising the cynocephali', in R. Corradini, M. Gillis, R. McKitterick and I. van Renswoude (eds.), *Ego Trouble: Authors and their Identities in the Early Middle Ages* (Vienna, 2010), pp. 125–36. Fear of northerners attacking the south: *Cosmographia*, c. 33, ed. and trans. Herrren, pp. 34–5.

[84] Compare Daniel of Winchester's letter to Boniface: *Bonifatii et Lulli Epistolae*, no. 23, ed. Tangl, p. 40.

[85] On San Vincenzo al Volturno see R. Hodges, *Light in the Dark Ages: The Rise and Fall of San Vincenzo al Volturno* (London, 1997), but bearing in mind the criticisms of R. Balzaretti, 'San Vincenzo al Volturno: History Rewritten?', *EME*, 8.3 (1999), 387–99.

[86] Ambrosius Autpertus, *Expositio in Apocalypsin*, 6. 13, ed. R. Weber, CCSM 27 (Turnhout, 1975), p. 107. E. A. Matter, 'The Apocalypse in Early Medieval Exegesis', in R. Emmerson and B. McGinn (eds.), *The Apocalypse in the Middle Ages* (Ithaca, NY, 1993), pp. 38–50 at pp. 47–8.

[87] Ambrosius Autpertus, *In apocalypsin*, IX, pp. 722–31.

[88] Ibid., IX, p. 758 – repeated with a little elaboration in Haimo, *In apocalypsin*, PL, 117. 1187.

[89] Pseudo-Methodius, *Sermo*, [8], 10, pp.117–19; *Cosmographia*, c. 39, pp. 48–9. Anderson compares this to Syrian tradition in *Alexander's Gate*, p. 54.

for the third Pseudo-Methodius's omission of the North: it was too specific. Ambrosius was naturally advocating an Tyconian-Augustinian reading of Rev. 20.7, yet there is more at work here. The original translation
of Pseudo-Methodius talked of Gog and Magog only when referring to
their enclosure by Alexander, so Ambrosius's comments reveal that readers had been making the connection with the later *gentes ab Aquilone* for
themselves. The mid-eighth century was witnessing a small interpretative
crisis about the reality of evil.

The moral use of Apocalypse

The reception of Pseudo-Methodius in the early eighth century – and
indeed beyond – exposes the extent to which the text's popularity relied
on matters other than those which inspired the writer himself. While
people in Spain would have been unsettled by conquest, and in Gaul
by attacks, debate seems to have been most lively in centres some distance away and in no obvious danger. Refugees and travellers may have
stimulated anxiety; news of a global crisis could have triggered all manner of speculation; and yet chronicles barely mention it, while only few
letters and only one carefully written saintly biography provide any indication that it was even going on, let alone that it all might have been
part of an eschatological drama. And no other enemies – not even the
perfidious, bellicose and pagan Saxons, as obvious a *gens ab Aquilone* as
any – inspired such fears either; or at least, not until the Vikings. Writers
preferred to imagine that true evil lay beyond the frontiers of everyday
experience. Of course speculation about the apocalyptic significance of
Gog and Magog, combined with the fate of an eschatological empire,
could have been suppressed, and we would never know. Yet there, somewhere, were Petrus and his copyists and redactors and critics, all engaged
in a game of scholarly interpretation. What was it all about if it was not a
response to perilous times?

   In some respects we could perhaps treat Pseudo-Methodius as the kind
of moralising yelp produced by Salvian and Gildas in the last days of the
Roman Empire (Chapter 1). Superficially, for instance, it is striking that
both Salvian and Pseudo-Methodius seized on the same Pauline comments on unnatural sex acts when deploring the standards of decency.
Romans and Syrians both deserved the chastisement of being conquered
for their 'effeminate' ways.[90] It is these kinds of comments which defined
the mood of Pseudo-Methodius, more so than did the Arabs or the *gentes*

---

[90] Salvian, *De gubernatione Dei*, VII. 76, ed. C. Halm, MGH AA, 1 (Berlin, 1877), p. 97;
Pseudo-Methodius, *Sermo*, [11], 6–7, pp. 141–3.

ab Aquilone. The problem was the escalation of sin in the world and a failure of people to be corrected, and that was what the author dwelt on longest. The Arabs, for all their viciousness, were the rod of God's wrath rather than the army of the Devil. Pseudo-Methodius's appeal to an impressionistic providential history, meanwhile, was no less part of the rhetorical art than it was when Gildas launched his assault on his peers in the mid-sixth century. The universality of persecution, however, meant that the faithful were being punished too; as Pseudo-Methodius emphasised, however, it was necessary for their faith and proscribed in scripture (e.g. Luke 6, 22–3). This was why the *rex Romanorum* was a necessary figure in the claim that the Roman Empire would endure: tests could be overcome, and therefore there was hope.

What mattered was how Latin audiences were going to encounter such ideas, and on the whole Petrus's translation appeared in miscellanies for private study.[91] In the oldest manuscript, from somewhere within the circles of Luxeuil, it is accompanied by material on grammar, canon law and computus, and a letter of Gregory the Great to Brunhild.[92] An early copy from St Gall is not so different, placing Petrus alongside Eucherius's *Instructions to Salonius*, excerpts of Isidoriana and more computus.[93] These were not, then, apocalyptic compendia. Some elements, most notably the computistical material, could have fed into wider investigations into apocalyptic time; and indeed the oldest manuscript's computus of 727 contains one of the countdowns to AM 6000 discussed at the end of the previous chapter.[94] Nevertheless, this was mostly introductory-level material, chosen for scholarly reference either for students or their

---

[91] There is disagreement about how clear the distinction between sermons for preaching and those used for study was. A sharp one is suggested by R. McKitterick, *The Frankish Church and the Carolingian Reforms, 789–895* (London, 1977), pp. 165–6 and M. McC. Gatch, *Preaching and Theology in Anglo-Saxon England: Aelfric and Wulfstan* (Toronto, 1977), pp. 28–9; T. L. Amos, 'Preaching and the Sermon in the Carolingian World', in T. L. Amos, E. A. Green and B. M. Kienzle (eds.), *De ore domini: Preacher and Word in the Middle Ages* (Kalamazoo, MI, 1989), pp. 41–60 at p. 47, suspected otherwise. R. Meens, 'Christianization and the Spoken Word: The Sermons Attributed to St Boniface', in R. Corradini, M. Diesenberger, and M. Niederkorn-Bruck (eds.), *Zwischen Niederschrift und Wiederschrift* (Vienna, 2011), pp. 211–22 at pp. 212–13 accepts the mixed situation.
[92] H. Hagen, *Catalogus codicum Bernensium* (Bern, 1875), pp. 479–83.
[93] G. Scherrer, *Verzeichniss der Handschriften der Stiftsbibliothek von St Gallen* (Halle, 1875), pp. 80–1. One could compare here also the use in the same monastery of the second recension, in Trier, Stadtbibliothek, 564/806 (M. Keuffer, *Die ascetische Handschriften der Stadtbibliothek zu Trier* (Trier, 1900), p. 27) and St Gall, Stiftsbibliothek, Cod. Sang. 569 (s. x), pp. 252–7, alongside notes on medicine, virtues and Seneca's *Apocolocyntosis* ('Pumpkinification').
[94] For one context see J. T. Palmer, 'Computus after the Paschal Controversy of AD 740', in D. Ó Cróinín and I. Warntjes (eds.), *The Easter Controversy of Late Antiquity and the Early Middle Ages: Manuscripts, Texts and Tables* (Turnhout, 2011), pp. 213–41 at pp. 228–9.

teachers in monasteries or, as Charlemagne's reforms took hold, cathedral schools, where aristocrats and future priests were educated as well as monks. The potential was there for its ideas to spread outside libraries through a variety of people in society. As such, it shows that Pseudo-Methodius was considered instructive rather than controversial.

The use of the text in study by monks, rather than in preaching, makes sense when considering its long and eccentric structure. From here it was a short distance to use in monastic readings. The Corbie manuscript with Pseudo-Ephraim – with its monastic address 'Most beloved brothers!' – could well be for use in such a context, perhaps as a reading at meal times. This is also likely with the Alemannic second recension, which quickly gained the new opening 'Let it be known to *us*, most beloved brothers' – which suggests it might have been intended for collective reflection.[95] In one early copy, the second recension was copied alongside other sermons which emphasise this point further, but also alongside Defensor of Ligugé's *Book of Sparks*, and a version of the Visigothic *On the Seven Seals* which would have been for study.[96] Such 'mixed use' compilations also include the earliest manuscript of the third recension from north Italy and then Reichenau, with its combination of brief annals, the Pseudo-Gregorian *Commentary on the Evangelists*, Isidore's *On Ecclesiastical Offices*, various homilies on correction, a litany of pre-Carolingian saints and prayers for Emperor Louis the Pious.[97] It is difficult to characterise interest in Pseudo-Methodius simply in such varied company except that, in general, copies tended to be in collections which pertained to the inner life of monasteries. It was in this intellectual environment, away from 'frontline' defence of society or political counsel, that Pseudo-Methodius throve for a time.

The proper contextualisation of the Pseudo-Methodian tradition helps to elucidate how it fitted into the dynamics of eighth-century apocalypticism, because it seems so locked into monastic reflection rather than class warfare or high politics. It seems inappropriate to see Pseudo-

---

[95] Prinz, following the reading in Zürich, Zentralbibliothek, C 65, f. 80v, gives *vobis* rather than *nobis* ('Eine frühe abendländische Aktualisierung', p. 6). The text was changed in Trier, Stadtbibliothek, 564/806, f. 35r (c. viii¹) and Stiftsbibliothek, Cod. Sang. 569, pp. 252 (s. x).

[96] For the contents of Zürich, Zentralbibliothek, C 65 see C. Mohlberg, *Mittelalteriche Handschriften* (Zürich, 1951), p. 38. On *De septem sigillis*, but not in reference to this manuscript, see E. A. Matter, 'The Pseudo-Alcuinian *De septem sigillis*: An Early Latin Apocalypse Exegesis', *Traditio*, 36 (1980), 111–37, in which Professor Matter demonstrates a likely Visigothic origin for the text.

[97] Karlsruhe, Badische Landesbibliothek, Aug. Perg. 254, described in A. Holder, *Die Pergamenthandschriften*, Die Handschriften der Badischen Landesbibliothek in Karlsruhe, 5. 1 (Wiesbaden, 1970), 573–9. See also n. 73. The first and last parts of the manuscript post-date the homilies and Pseudo-Methodius and were added north of the Alps.

Methodius as a reflection of popular or widespread anxiety at particular events (Arab attacks or the approach of the Year 6000) which may have necessitated some kind of ecclesiastical censure to suppress things. There was no ecclesiastical 'consensus of silence' pitched against inconvenient ideas outside the mainstream, at least not as such, because here was an 'unorthodox' text being read, copied and adapted in major centres. From San Vincenzo al Volturno to northern France, there was engagement with the apocalyptic in all its forms. Sometimes this was 'situational' and to do with immediate evil (e.g. whatever prompted Petrus into action); sometimes this was to do with texts and interpretation (e.g. how the Alemannic editor of the second recension Westernised the text); and sometimes this was to do with daily eschatological reflection in monasteries (e.g. with the 'preaching' of the sermon in Reichenau or wherever). Pseudo-Methodian tradition was not part of visionary or revelatory literature as such – it was more another imaginative space in which sin, evil and conflict could be considered in reference to one possible interpretative framework.

Considering the powerful influence of Pseudo-Methodius in later centuries, from Adso's *On Antichrist* to the Oxford *Song of Roland*, such conclusions for the text in the eighth century seem muted. But then here was a text which only really found the heights of its popularity from the eleventh century onwards. In the meantime, we do not find the Last Emperor legend feeding into discussions of empire or politics, nor do we find Western audiences following Petrus's lead in demonising the Arabs. For now, issues of evil and authority had their bite in other ways. Conflict in the world was a reminder of conflict in the soul. Pseudo-Methodius's sermon in the Latin world may have been something to be read or read out, but primarily it was to be reflected upon for its warnings about the difficult relationship between suffering and salvation. New ideas about political apocalypse here perhaps gained a hold on Latin apocalyptic traditions because they had appealed to people interested in moral apocalypse and the relationship between personal and collective eschatologies. In the process any Augustinian anti-apocalypticism in mainstream Christian culture was diluted further, because a prophesied future with real implications for empire, Ecclesia and outsiders had begun to affect expectations.

5 Charlemagne, *pater Europae* (c. 750–c. 820)

The world grew old. The Year 6000 approached. And yet the last decades of the eighth and the beginning of the ninth century have often been considered a Golden Age. The increased competition for power in the last days of the Merovingian kingdoms eventually gave rise to a new political order under the Pippinids (later Carolingians) which, even if prone to posturing and great acts of self-legitimisation, believed in the centrality of the sacred. More plainly than before – or at least for a while – political activity in the West was conducted with a consciousness of apocalyptic tradition as part of the mix of ideas which inspired, shaped and drove people onwards. This was possible in no small part because of the actions of Charlemagne (r. 768–814) – one of the most famous figures of early medieval history and 'Father of Europe' (*pater Europae*) in his own lifetime.[1] He forged the widest sense of political and intellectual hegemony since the Roman Empire, engaging in conquest, mission, reform and cultural production.[2] And on Christmas Day 800, as the world did not breathe its last in its 6,000th year, he was crowned emperor in Rome, recreating the empire that was to endure in the West until the *discessio* predicted by Paul and reinterpreted by Pseudo-Methodius.

Judging the power of the apocalyptic in Charlemagne's empire is no easy task. The last sentence of the above paragraph describes a view of events that emerges only *ex silentio*. Richard Landes, one of the first historians to explore Carolingian apocalyptic, argued that the silence spoke volumes

---

[1] *Karolus magnus et Leo papa*, ed. E. Dümmler, MGH Poetae, 1 (Berlin, 1881), p. 379, line 504. Charlemagne remains a key figure in European Union identity, with a number of prizes associated with him and a Charlemagne Building in Brussels.

[2] The literature on Charlemagne is vast. Good recent starting points include: W. Hartmann, *Karl der Große* (Stuttgart, 2010); R. McKitterick, *Charlemagne: The Formation of a European Identity* (Cambridge, 2008); M. Becher, *Karl der Große* (2nd edn, Munich, 2007), revised 1st edn trans. D. S. Bachrach (New Haven, CT, 2003); J. Story (ed.), *Charlemagne: Empire and Society* (Manchester, 2005); R. Collins, *Charlemagne* (London, 1998); D. Bullough, *The Age of Charlemagne* (2nd edn, London, 1972). A wider perspective is provided in M. Costambeys, M. Innes and S. MacLean, *The Carolingian World* (Cambridge, 2011).

about the anti-apocalyptic majority, probably led by Charlemagne, who wished to avoid the uncomfortable non-Augustinian significance of the completion of 6,000 years and who successfully reached a quiet 'consensus' to say nothing.[3] The silent anxiety, then, would be the defining dynamic at work. Few Carolingianists have been interested in following up Landes's thesis, some uneasy at the 'silence', some left cold by a theme which seems peripheral to both their research and their sources.[4] Wolfram Brandes once had an important study of Carolingian apocalypticism rejected for publication because an editor could not 'believe that Charlemagne had anything whatsoever to do with eschatological thinking'.[5] This is more than a little regrettable because there is a rich source-base which rather indicates that there were vigorous mainstream apocalypticisms. These encouraged a range of actions, often with explicit deference to apocalyptic tradition, motivating the possible conclusion that Charlemagne's empire was more apocalyptically minded than it is often considered, but also differently so than Landes has argued.

The argument about Charlemagne's empire needs to be this: because of the way he blended political and religious authority, power was eschatologically framed, and the threat of heresy became an apocalyptic-charged issue.[6] The first part of this – the intimate relationship between Church and polity – is scarcely controversial, and indeed, Charlemagne's kingdom has been described by Mayke de Jong as one 'defined by prayer'.[7]

[3] R. Landes, 'Lest the Millennium Be Fulfilled: Apocalyptic Expectations and the Pattern of Western Chronography 100–800CE', in W. Verbeke, D. Verhelst and A. Welkenhuysen (Leuven, 1988), pp. 137–211 at pp. 178–203. See also W. Brandes, '"Tempora periculosa sunt". Eschatologisches im Vorfeld der Kaiserkrönung Karls des Großen', in R. Berndt (ed.), *Das Frankfurter Konzil von 794. Kristallisationspunkt karolingischer Kultur* (Mainz, 1997), I. 49–79, and P. Dutton, *Charlemagne's Mustache and other Cultural Clusters of a Dark Age* (London, 2005), pp. 153–4.
[4] Exceptions include M. Alberi, 'The Evolution of Alcuin's Concept of the *Imperium Christianum*', in J. Hill and M. Swan (eds.), *The Community, the Family and the Saint: Patterns of Power in Early Medieval Europe* (Turnhout, 1998), pp. 3–18; M. Alberi, '"Like the Army of God's Camp": Political Theology and Apocalyptic Warfare at Charlemagne's Court', *Viator*, 41.2 (2010), 1–20; J. Heil, '"Nos nescientes de hoc velle manere" – "We Wish to Remain Ignorant About This": Timeless End, or: Approaches to Reconceptualising Eschatology after 800 (AM 6000)', *Traditio*, 55 (2000), 73–103; J. T. Palmer, 'Calculating Time and the End of Time in the Carolingian World, c. 740–820', *EHR*, 126.523 (2011), 1307–31.
[5] 'Ich kann nicht glauben dass Karl der Grosse irgend etwas mit eschatologische Dingen zu tun hatte' – reported in R. Landes, *Heaven on Earth: The Varieties of Millennial Experience* (Oxford, 2011), p. 71 and n. 28, via Johannes Fried.
[6] The importance of heresy as an apocalyptic issue is emphasised also in J. Fried, *Karl der Große: Gewalt und Glaube. Eine Biographie* (Munich, 2013), pp. 435–9.
[7] M. de Jong, 'Charlemagne's Church', in Story, *Charlemagne*, pp. 103–35 and 'Carolingian Monasticism: The Power of Prayer', in R. McKitterick (ed.), *The New Cambridge Medieval History*, II (Cambridge, 1995), pp. 622–53. See also H. Arquillière, *L'Augustinisme politique: Essai sur la formation des théories politiques du moyen-âge* (Paris, 1934); N. Staubach,

Liturgical unity was important, even if diverse practice was permitted.[8] Famously, Paulinus of Aquileia poetically called Charlemagne 'king and priest' (*rex et sacerdos*) as a nod to the nickname of 'David' given to him by Alcuin, and Charlemagne presented himself as a new King Josiah as he took a personal lead in the reform of the Church.[9] The political world was increasingly 'textualised' in relation to scripture.[10] Since none of our sources makes anything of the passing of the Year 6000, it is impossible to understand precisely what kind of influence this had on affairs. It might be, as I suggest here, that an overlooked paradigm shift under the Carolingians in the way that Easter was calculated – more reform and perfection! – accidentally confused experts keeping track of the age of the world. The Y6K problem lost its bite. The struggle against heresy, however, ensured that apocalypse was a live issue, as a renewed quest for reform and unity was undertaken. The prevailing ecclesiological interpretation of Revelation (see Chapters 1 and 3) had, after all, provided a powerful framework for understanding the Church in its struggles.

The rebirth of empire

So why was imperial authority reborn in the West on Christmas Day 800, over three centuries after it had quietly come to an end? On that day Pope Leo III, having received help from the Franks in restoring order in Rome, crowned Charlemagne emperor. The closest extant chronicle account of this event reflected that:

Because then the name of emperor had ceased in the regions of the Greeks, and they placed a feminine imperium over themselves. Then it seemed to the apostolic Leo and all the holy fathers, who came together in council, as well as to the rest of the Christian people, that Charles, king of the Franks, ought to be named emperor. He held Rome, where the caesars were always accustomed to sit, as well as other seats, which he held throughout Italy, Gaul and indeed Germany, because the Omnipotent God had given to him all those seats in his power.[11]

'"Cultus divinus" und karolingische Reform', *Frühmittelalterliche Studien*, 18 (1984), 546–581 and McKitterick, *Charlemagne*, ch. 5.

[8] R. McKitterick, *The Frankish Church and the Carolingian Reforms, 789–895* (London, 1977) and her 'Unity and Diversity in the Carolingian Church', *Studies in Church History*, 32 (1996), 59–83; Y. Hen, 'Unity in Diversity: The Liturgy of Frankish Gaul before the Carolingians', *Studies in Church History*, 32 (1996), 19–30.

[9] Paulinus, *Libellus sacrosyllabus episcoporum Italiae*, ed. A. Werminghoff, MGH Conc., 2. 1 (Hanover, 1906), p. 142 (PL, 99.166); *Admonitio generalis*, pref., ed. A. Boretius, MGH Cap., 1 (Hanover, 1883), p. 54.

[10] This is particularly apparent in the reigns of Charlemagne's successors: M. de Jong, *The Penitential State: Authority and Atonement in the Age of Louis the Pious, 814–840* (Cambridge, 2009).

[11] *Annales Laureshamenses*, s.a. 801, ed. E. Katz (St Paul im Lavanttal, 1889), pp. 44–5: 'Et quia iam tunc cessabat a parta Grecorum nomen imperatoris et femineum imperium

This reported what was probably the contemporary public justifications, given to explain why the Franks – still in some eyes barbarous and uncouth – had effectively refounded the Western Roman empire.[12] The situation in the East seemed unsettling, as Irene, widow of Emperor Leo IV and mother and one-time regent of Constantine VI, had had her son deposed and blinded in 797 so that she could reclaim the power from which she had been excluded by her son.[13] In Constantinople there were questions about her competence to rule, but these were far from restricted to objections to feminine rule from an empress (basilissa, augusta), and there is no indication that people considered there to be even a theoretical power vacuum. Theophanes, our principal Eastern narrative source for the period, was even broadly sympathetic to 'pious' Irene, and wrote with as much sadness and outrage about her deposition by Nikophoros in 802 as he had about Irene's earlier vicious treatment of Constantine.[14] In that context, the chronicler portrayed Charlemagne not as a usurper of imperial authority in the West, but as a king who restored order to Rome and then sought Irene as his bride so that the empire could be reunited.[15] The real threat lay in the destabilising actions first of rivals Staurakios and then Nikephoros. In Byzantium, as in the West, Charlemagne's rise seemed to be a good thing – he was a figure who brought with him strength, justice and a sense of unity. One opaque historical note written in Cologne in 798 even stated that a Greek embassy had come 'to hand imperial authority over to him'.[16]

apud se habebant: tunc visum est et ipsum apostolico Leoni et universis sanctis patribus, qui in ipso concilio aderant, seu religuo christiano populo, ut ipsum Carolum, regem Francorum, imperatorem nominare debuissent, qui ipsum Romam tenebat, ubi semper Cesaras sedere soliti errant, seu reliquas sedes, quas ipse per Italiam seu Galliam nec non et Germaniam tenebat, quia deus omnipotens has omnes sedes in potestate eius concessit.'

12 R. Collins, 'Charlemagne's Imperial Coronation and the Annals of Lorsch', in Story, *Charlemagne*, pp. 52–71 at p. 68.

13 On Irene's reign see R.-J. Lilie, *Byzanz unter Eirene und Konstantin VI. (780–802)* (Frankfurt-am-Main, 1996).

14 Compare Theophanes, *Chronographia*, s.a. AM 6289, ed. C. de Boor, pp. 471–3 (trans. C. Mango and R. Scott [Oxford, 1997], pp. 648–9) and s.a. AM 6295, ed. de Boor, pp. 476–9 (Mango and Scott, pp. 655–6).

15 Theophanes, *Chronographia*: restoration of Rome, s.a. AM 6289, ed. de Boor, pp. 472–3 (Mango and Scott, p. 649); proposed marriage to Irene, s.a. 6293–3, ed. de Boor, p. 475 (Mango and Scott, pp. 653–4).

16 *Additamenta Coloniensia ad Chronica*, II. 3, ed. A. Borst, *Schriften zur Komputistik im Frankenreich von 721 bis 818*, QQ zur Geistesgeschichte, 21 (3 vols, Hanover, 2006), II. 793: '[quando missi venerunt de Graecia] ut traderent ei imperium.' Compare *Annales regni Francorum*, s.a. 798, ed. F. Kurze, MGH SRG, 6 (Hanover, 1895), p. 104. What to make of this is difficult to say: R. Schieffer, 'Karl der Große, Eirene und der Ursprung des westlichen Kaisertums', in W. Pohl (ed.), *Die Suche nach den Ursprüngen: Von der Bedeutung des frühen Mittelalters* (Vienna, 2004), pp. 151–8 and his 'Neues von der

This was a remarkable position for Charlemagne to have found himself in. It was only fifty years since his father, Pippin III (r. 751–68), had brought 300 years of Merovingian kingship to an end by deposing Childerich III with the pope's permission and the support of the bishops in order to seize the throne for himself.[17] Pippin and then Charlemagne – briefly alongside his brother Carloman (d. 771) – campaigned vigorously to expand their authority in Aquitaine, Frisia, Saxony, Lombardy and eventually as far afield as Spain and Bohemia, while also promoting church reform and a cultural renaissance. The vitality of the regime in this period saw the Franks become the papacy's 'special people' (*populus peculiaris* [Deut. 7.6]) and sometime protectors.[18] When Pope Leo III travelled to Paderborn in Saxony to meet Charlemagne in 799 and requested his help in restoring order to Rome, this came out of a long history of good Franco-papal relations.[19] The king's standing in the East was impressive for a barbarian usurper too, with the Patriarch of Jerusalem sending him relics from the Holy Sepulchre and Caliph Harun al-Rashid an elephant called Abul Abaz ('elephant').[20] Einhard suggested that Charlemagne was surprised when Leo placed the crown on his head, but few historians have believed him – the new emperor fitted the part.

There were plenty of non-apocalyptic ideological cues at work in the background to the imperial coronation. The Frankish monarchy had for a long time exercised degrees of overlordship and hegemony over

Kaiserkrönung Karls der Großen', *Bayerische Akademie der Wissenschaften, Philosophisch-historische Klasse, Jahrgang 2004*, Heft 2 (Munich, 2004), p. 14, is cautious in contrast to J. Fried, 'Papst Leo III. besucht Karl den Großen in Paderborn oder Einhards Schweigen', *Historische Zeitschrift*, 272 (2001), 281–326. General context in P. Classen, 'Karl der Große, das Papsttum und Byzanz. Die Begründung des karolingischen Kaisertums', in H. Beumann (ed.), *Karl der Große. Lebenswerk und Nachleben, I: Persönlichkeit und Geschichte* (Düsseldorf, 1965), pp. 537–608. Also Costambeys *et al.*, *The Carolingian World*, pp. 166–9.

[17] A good starting point is provided by M. Becher and J. Jarnut (eds.), *Der Dynastiewechsel von 751. Vorgeschichte, Legitimiationsstrategien und Erinnerung* (Münster, 2004)

[18] M. Garrison, 'The Franks as the New Israel? Education for an Identity from Pippin to Charlemagne', in Y. Hen and M. Innes (eds.), *The Uses of the Past in the Early Middle Ages* (Cambridge, 2000), pp. 114–61.

[19] *Annales regni Francorum*, s.a. 799, p. 106; C. Stiegemann and M. Wemhoff (eds.), *799: Kunst und Kultur der Karolingerzeit. Karl der Grosse und Papst Leo III. in Paderborn*, Mainz, 1999); P. Godman, J. Jarnut and P. Johanek (eds.), *Am Vorabend der Kaiserkrönung. Das Epos 'Karolus Magnus et Leo Papa' und der Papstbesuch in Paderborn 799* (Berlin, 2002).

[20] *Annales regni Francorum*, s.a. 799, p. 108; s.a. 800, p. 112; s.a. 801, pp. 114–16. On the elephant's name see Dutton, *Charlemagne's Mustache*, p. 190. Hartmann, *Karl der Große*, p. 217 connects Charlemagne's Eastern connections here loosely to Pseudo-Methodius but otherwise follows the doubts of Schieffer (as n. 15). On Charlemagne and Jerusalem see M. McCormick, *Charlemagne's Survey of the Holy Land: Wealth, Personnel, and Buildings of the Mediterranean Church between Antiquity and the Middle Ages* (Cambridge, MA, 2011) and for the development of later legends M. Gabriele, *An Empire of Memory:*

Britons, Bretons, Bavarians, Saxons, Frisians, Lombards, Catalans, Aquitainians, English and more, with an informal sense of imperial authority (*imperium*) already in currency to describe such authority in the eighth century.[21] Indeed, annals and chronicles of the early Carolingian world often read like campaign journals, as successive Frankish kings and mayors of the palace campaigned against their neighbours to maintain this. Charlemagne's one-time advisor Alcuin of York could readily refer to Charlemagne's 'empire [or authority] of the Franks' (*imperium Francorum*) in c. 796, well in advance of his coronation.[22] There was also a sense that this was a 'kingdom of Europe' (*regnum Europae*), as the English courtier Cathwulf described it in a letter of advice to Charlemagne two decades earlier.[23] Some parallels could be made with Bede's comment in 731 – known to Alcuin and Charlemagne – that there had been a number of English kings who had held *imperium* in Britain, exerting influence over neighbouring kings.[24] There were, at least, informal concepts of empire in currency which enabled people dealing with the Frankish court to express ideas of political overlordship without appeal to a formal, institutionalised political framework. Conferring the title of *imperator* onto Charlemagne in a move sanctioned by the pope potentially legitimised realities of power, particularly in the wake of those prolonged military campaigns; and Henry Mayr-Harting has argued that, although no source says as much,

The Legend of Charlemagne, the Franks and Jerusalem before the First Crusade (Oxford, 2011).

21 R. Folz, *L'idée d'empire en occident du Ve au XIVe siècle* (Paris, 1953), chs. 1–2; D. Bullough, 'Empire and Emperordom from Late Antiquity to 799', *EME*, 12.4 (2003), 377–87; I. Wood, 'Frankish Hegemony in England', in M. Carver (ed.), *The Age of Sutton Hoo: The Seventh Century in North-Western Europe* (Woodbridge, 1992), pp. 235–42. An interesting back-projection is also evident in *Annales Mettenses priores*, s.a. 691, ed. B. von Simson, MGH SRG, 10 (Hanover, 1905), pp. 12–13, where Pippin II reasserts dominion over Saxons, Frisians, Alemans, Bavarians, Aquitanians, Basques and Bretons. On the text see Y. Hen, 'The Annals of Metz and the Merovingian Past', in Hen and Innes, *The Uses of the Past*, pp. 175–91. Note also Willibald, *Vita Bonifatii*, c. 7, ed. W. Levison, MGH SRG, 57 (Hanover, 1905), pp. 39–40, written around 760.

22 Alcuin, *Vita Willibrordi*, c. 23, ed. W. Levison, MGH SRM, 7 (Hanover and Leipzig, 1920), p. 133; J. T. Palmer, *Anglo-Saxons in a Frankish World 690–900* (Turnhout, 2009), pp. 81–3.

23 Cathwulf, *Epistola ad Carolo*, ed. E. Dümmler, MGH Epp., 4 (Berlin, 1895), p. 503. See M. Garrison, 'Letters to a King and Biblical Exempla: The Examples of Cathuulf and Clemens Peregrinus', *EME*, 7.3 (1998), 305–28; J. Story, 'Cathwulf, Kingship, and the Royal Abbey of Saint-Denis', *Speculum*, 74 (1999), 1–20.

24 Bede, *Historia ecclesiastica*, II. 5. 1, ed. M. Lapidge (2 vols., Rome, 2010), I. 196–8. Alberi, 'The Evolution', pp. 4–6. On Bede here see: S. Fanning, 'Bede, *Imperium*, and the Bretwaldas', *Speculum*, 66.1 (1991), 1–26; B. Yorke, 'The Bretwaldas and the Origins of Overlordship in Anglo-Saxon England', in S. Baxter, C. E. Karkov, J. L. Nelson and D. Pelteret (eds.), *Early Medieval Studies in Honour of Patrick Wormald* (Farnham, 2009), pp. 81–95.

Charlemagne was seeking to justify a century of conquest and the sub-jugation of the Saxons in particular.[25]

On the edges of these 'imperial' ideas was the same eschatological concern for missionary work that we saw develop under Gregory the Great and Columbanus. In 796 Alcuin wrote to advise his king to soften his policy of forced conversions and the impositions of tithes in the Saxon mission-field, but in doing so he opened optimistically by praising Charlemagne for his efforts in expanding the *regnum Christianitatis*.[26] Imagining a corporate identity like this, freed from the earthly constraints of ethnicity, had clear ideological overtones which pointed towards future unity and peace. The rewards for Charlemagne were also end-focused: 'What glory will be yours, O most blessed king, on the day of eternal judgement?'[27] But, despite Mary Alberi's vivid portrayal of Alcuin's thought on these fronts, it is difficult to see any widespread interest in Christ's statement that, once the Gospel had been preached as a 'testimony to all nations' (*in testimonium omnibus gentibus*), the End would come (Matt. 24.14; see also Matt. 28.19–20). No active missionary around the time spoke of this urgency, and Charlemagne even retreated from supporting missions after his imperial coronation. Other ideals and practicalities dominated the reality of empire.

One of these alternative models came with a heightened concern for the age-old ideal of *romanitas*.[28] Charlemagne had already claimed the title of *patricius Romanorum*, 'patrician of the Romans', for defending Rome and the papacy from the Lombards, much as his father Pippin III had done in 753–4, and his grandfather Charles Martel had nearly done in 739.[29] After 800, the title *imperator Romanorum* was often used in charters alongside royal titles, although many of the charters themselves are spurious, and in capitularies – decrees of canon and secular law – Charlemagne was often 'just' called *imperator*. Sometimes there

[25] H. Mayr-Harting, 'Charlemagne, the Saxons, and the Imperial Coronation of 800', *EHR*, 111.444 (1996), 1113–33.
[26] I. Wood, *The Missionary Life: Saints and the Evangelization of Europe 400–1050* (Harlow, 2001), pp. 85–6 and 89–90; L. von Padberg, 'Die Diskussion missionarischer Programme zur Zeit Karls des Großen', in P. Godman, J. Jarnut and P. Johanek (eds.), *Am Vorabend der Kaiserkrönung. Das Epos 'Karolus Magnus et Leo papa' und der Papstbesuch in Paderborn 799* (Berlin, 2002), pp. 125–43. A provocative view of Charlemagne's Saxon policy is put forward in Y. Hen, 'Charlemagne's *Jihad*', *Viator*, 37 (2006), 33–51.
[27] Alcuin, *Epistola*, no. 110, ed. E. Dümmler, MGH Epp., 4, (Berlin, 1895), p. 157: 'Qualis erit tibi gloria, o beatissime rex, in die aeternae retributionis?' Alberi, 'The Evolution', p. 12.
[28] On representations of the Franks and *romanitas* see McKitterick, *Charlemagne*, pp. 370–2 and her *Perceptions of the Past in the Early Middle Ages* (Notre Dame, IN, 2006), ch. 2.
[29] Charlemagne was acutely aware of this history: *Divisio regnorum*, c. 15, ed. A. Boretius, MGH Cap., 1, p. 129. Pope Gregory III's appeal to Charles Martel is, symbolically, *Codex Carolinus*, no. 1, ed. W. Gundlach, MGH Epp., 3 (Berlin, 1892), pp. 476–7.

were rhetorical flourishes, such as when, in the prefatory statement to the 'division of the kingdom' in 806, setting out his heirs' future kingdoms, he was called 'Charles, the most serene Augustus, crowned by God the great peace-making emperor, governing the Roman Empire, and by the mercy of God king of the Franks and of the Lombards'.[30] In this case, Charlemagne announced his legislation at a grand assembly of *optimates* at the centrally placed palace of Thionville before sending it to the pope to sign, so there was a sense in which he was playing to his audiences at their greatest.[31] And yet, twenty or so years later, it suited the purposes of his courtier Einhard – who had carried that very document to the pope – to inject more ambiguity into Charlemagne's relationship with things Roman. The coronation, it was now alleged, was an unwelcome surprise and he refused to dress in Roman styles.[32] But this was a learned literary game, in which Einhard parodied Suetonius's representation of Augustus for the education of the young Charles (II) the Bald.[33] The Franks wanted to play with Latin imperial culture, as much as they wanted to wear it as a badge of authority.

Such secular political posturing could not stay detached from apocalyptic tradition. Embracing Roman imperial ideas brought confrontation with Daniel's prophecy about the role of empire in the End Times, and Charlemagne demonstrated interest in it, even while it seems doubtful that he knew Pseudo-Methodius or the Last Emperor legend.[34] In his considerable library, there was already a copy of Peter of Pisa's *Questions on Daniel* (written before 799), and in the only extant manuscript it is clearly stated that Charlemagne ordered its copying.[35] Peter's heavy dependence

---

[30] *Divisio regnorum*, pref., p. 126: 'Karolus serenissimus augustus, a Deo coronatus magnus pacificus imperator, Romanum gubernans imperium, qui et per misericordiam Dei rex Francorum atque Langobardorum.'
[31] McKitterick, *Charlemagne*, pp. 96–8.
[32] Einhard, *Vita Karoli*, c. 23, p. 28 (dislikes foreign dress), c. 28, p. 32 (imperial coronation).
[33] The use is suggested by D. Ganz in his preface to *Two Lives of Charlemagne* (London, 2008), p. 10. On the Suetonian connection see M. Innes, 'The Classical Tradition in the Carolingian Renaissance: Ninth-Century Encounters with Suetonius', *International Journal of the Classical Tradition*, 3.3 (1997), 265–82. M. Tischler, *Einharts Vita Karoli: Studien zur Entstehung, Überlieferung und Rezeption*, MGH Schriften, 48 (2 vols, Hanover, 2001).
[34] Brandes, 'Tempora periculosa sunt', p. 61; S. Gouguenheim, *Les fausses terreurs de l'an mil: Attente de la fin des temps ou approfondissement de la foi* (Paris, 1999), pp. 207–8. See n. 120.
[35] Brussels, Koninklijke Bibliotheek van België, MS II 2572, f. 1r, all in capitals (*CLA* 10.1553). Bischoff strongly doubted that this manuscript was the original, pre-800 copy ordered by Charlemagne, insisting rather that it must have been an early copy: B. Bischoff, 'The Court Library of Charlemagne', in M. Gorman (ed.), *Manuscripts and Libraries in the Age of Charlemagne* (Cambridge, 1994), pp. 56–75 at p. 61 n. 24 and p. 65 n. 45. Edition: PL, 96.1347–62.

on Jerome has ensured that his text has scarcely received much attention in modern scholarship, because it simply says little that is new. It was, nevertheless, a careful and selective enterprise on Peter's part, as he tailored his material in order to answer sixty-eight questions about the text. Given his patron, it is no doubt significant that he began by answering the question 'what are the kingdoms which King Nebuchodonosor saw in his vision?' (Dan. 2) even though most of the text is taken in order. The assessment of Rome remained Jerome's bleak one: 'just as there was at first nothing stronger or hardier than the Roman Empire, so in the end there is nothing weaker.'[36] On this reading, Charlemagne was almost better pursuing the strong *imperium Christianum* than the failing *imperium Romanorum* which preceded it.

Nevertheless, the defining feature of Peter's *Questions* is the way that the author retreated from Jerome's full eschatological vision. Jerome had been fascinated with the implications of Daniel's prophecies for the legend of Antichrist and wrote about it at length, whereas Peter restricted himself to discussing the blasphemy of Antichrist destroying the Roman Empire and the Jews handing over the saints to Antichrist's power at the end.[37] There is also something coy about Peter's trimming of Jerome's interpretation of Little Horn (Dan. 7.7): he deleted the direct identification with the Son of Perdition but maintained Jerome's words about Little Horn being the man filled with Satan who would dare to sit in the temple, so it was difficult to imagine anything else.[38] Peter's questions ended before he had even reached Jerome's thoughts on the 1,290 days of suffering, which he had equated to the three and a half years of Antichrist's reign (Dan. 12.12–13).[39] Links between other prophecies and history remained from Jerome's work, for instance how the seventy weeks prophesied by the angel to Daniel represented weeks of years up to the Incarnation (i.e. 490 years). Peter had edited his work so that Charlemagne was presented with a text on prophecy in Old Testament history rather than a treatise on Antichrist and the dangers of empire in the future.

Yet Charlemagne was still confronted with arguments about the eschatological urgency of providing leadership. In 799, Alcuin of York,

---

[36] 'Sicut enim in principio nihil Romano imperio fortius et durius fuit, ita in fine rerum nihil imbecillius': PL, 96.1347, taken from Jerome, *In Danielem*, ed. F. Glorie, CCSL, 75A (Turnhout, 1964), pp. 794–5. The interpretation of the fourth kingdom is repeated for Dan. 7.7 and 2.33 at PL, 96.1353.

[37] PL, 96.1354. taken from Jerome, *In Danielem*, p. 847 and p. 851.

[38] PL, 96. 1353–4, edited from Jerome, *In Danielem*, p. 845.

[39] Jerome, *In Danielem*, p. 944. It does not appear that there is any text missing as the text in the manuscripts concludes with a firm EXPLICIT before a grammatical treatise begins: Brussels, Koninklijke Bibliotheek van België, MS II 2572, 17v.

then abbot of Tours, wrote to his king about the importance of the popes, emperors and Frankish kings to the world, concluding that:

On you alone the whole safety of the churches of Christ depends. You punish wrong-doers, guide the straying, console the sorrowing and advance the good. Has not the worst impiety been committed in Rome, where the greatest piety was once to be seen? ... These are the perilous times foretold in Scripture (2 Tim. 3.1), for the love of many grows cold (Matt. 24.12).[40]

Such certainty that trouble in the world was the fulfilment of prophecy had come only slowly to Alcuin particularly, according to Mary Garrison, after the shock of regicide in his native Northumbria in 796.[41] The quotation from 2 Timothy – squarely apocalyptic in full – became a favourite refrain for Alcuin, and he used it twice more to explain the importance of Charlemagne as a defender of Christians in the End Times.[42] This may be evidence of an apocalyptic standpoint, as Brandes has argued, or a more moderate eschatology as Gouguenheim suggests.[43] Either way, it is carefully crafted rhetoric designed to impress upon people responsibility and the urgency of action, not cheap noise. Apocalyptic expectations did not cast much of a shadow over Alcuin's work as a whole, even in his aborted, conservatively ecclesiological commentary on Revelation, and his *Questions on Revelation*, with its Job-inspired digressions on sin and purgation.[44] This suggests that we should pay attention to Alcuin's use of apocalyptic motifs in his prose as part of his attempts to mobilise

---

[40] Alcuin, *Epistola*, no. 174, p. 288: 'Ecce in te solo salus Christi inclinata recumbit. Tu vindex scelerum, tu rector errantium, tu conolator maerentium, tu exaltation bonorum. Nonne Romana in sede, ubi relegio maxime pietatis quondam claruerat, ibi extrema impietatis exempla emerseunt? ... Tempora periculosa sunt olim ab ipsa veritate praedicta, qui refrigescit caritas multorum.' Compare also the lament to Arno of Salzburg: Alcuin, *Epistola*, no. 193, pp. 320.

[41] Alcuin, *Epistola*, no. 116, p. 171. M. Garrison, 'The Bible and Alcuin's Interpretation of Current Events', *Peritia*, 16 (2002), 68–84 at p. 78; Brandes, 'Tempora periculosa sunt', p. 68.

[42] Alcuin, *Epistola*, nos. 111, p. 161 and 121, p. 176.

[43] Brandes, 'Tempora periculosa sunt', p. 70. Gouguenheim, *Les fausses terreurs*, pp. 212–13 (but Professor Gouguenheim requires a very narrow reading of the sources to maintain that Alcuin's words have nothing to do with apocalyptic thought). Support for Brandes in J. L. Nelson, 'Why Are There So Many Different Accounts of Charlemagne's Imperial Coronation?' in her *Courts, Elites and Gendered Power in the Early Middle Ages* (Aldershot, 2007), p. xii; and M. Garrison, 'Quid Hinieldus cum Christo?', in K. O'Brien O'Keeffe and A. Orchard (eds.), *Latin Learning and English Lore: Studies in Anglo-Saxon Literature for Michael Lapidge* (Toronto, 2005), I. 240.

[44] Alcuin, *Expositio Apocalypsin*, PL, 100. 1055–1156; Alcuin, *Interrogationes*, unpublished, in Munich, Bayerische Staatsbibliothek, Clm 13581 (Regensburg, s. ix¹), ff. 3r–31r, alongside his *Interrogationes in Genesin* and Julian of Toledo's *Antikeimenon*. T. Mackay, 'Apocalypse Commentary by Primasius, Bede and Alcuin: Interrelationship, Dependency and Individuality', *Studia Patristica*, 36 (2001), 28–34.

people around him. We will see this further below when we get to the Carolingian fight against heresy. For now, we can at least see that one voice was prepared to offer Charlemagne justifications for taking a lead in world affairs in the context of an imagined apocalyptic scenario – and one which only at best complemented Daniel's kingdoms, Pseudo-Methodius or the ticking clock of the Y6K problem.

There was, then, the potential for some kind of apocalyptic interests in some 'cultural clusters' at Charlemagne's court, associated with encouraging reform. Political action could be framed by Daniel's sequence of kingdoms, and by a sense of spiritual duty in which the secular world had a role to play in the Church and as an opponent of evil. Advisors were armed with apocalyptic and prophetic ideas, and some were willing to argue them. It is unfortunate that we do not know more about the counsel supplied by people closer to Charlemagne, such as his palace chaplain Archbishop Hildebold of Cologne, on whom more below. Whatever the counsel, it is still difficult to align these things with Charlemagne's actions, particularly as emperor, because the 'public' face of the Carolingian regime in historiography and capitularies made little to no use of them. No one would read the *Annales regni Francorum* or Einhard's *Vita Karoli* alone and think an eschatological drama was being played out.[45] After Christmas Day 800, various measures were pursued, with new oaths sworn, and the different law codes governing different peoples within the empire investigated and corrected.[46] Coins were minted to portray Charlemagne as a Roman emperor. Emissaries were sent to Constantinople to clear the air. New rounds of force and diplomacy were pursued in Spain and the far north.[47] Many of these actions were the pragmatic responses of someone taking their new imperial reality seriously – empire had a biblical and historical pedigree which needed to be defended, and the emperor's subjects needed to be encouraged to buy into the new reality. What role the Y6K problem played in contextualising action, therefore, is clearly a matter we need to attend to next.

Counting to 6,000 again

To recap: it has been argued by some historians that holding Charlemagne's coronation on Christmas Day AM 6000 must have

---

[45] This is precisely the view of one of Charlemagne's recent biographers: Hartmann, *Karl der Große*, p. 217.

[46] *Capitulare missorum generale* (802), ed. Boretius, MGH Cap., 1, pp. 91–9; *Annales Laureshamenses*, s.a. 802, pp. 45–6.

[47] *Annales regni Francorum*, end of s.a. 801 (p. 106) and all of s.a. 802 (p. 117).

been a provocative act relative to apocalyptic tradition.[48] And yet our sources say nothing about this – perhaps a surprising discovery when we consider the Merovingian countdowns to Y6K we encountered in Chapter 3.[49] Richard Landes argued that this was exactly what we might expect as the Frankish clergy studiously ignored the Y6K problem, or else sidestepped the issue by enthusiastically adopting Bede's younger age for the world or AD dates. Indeed, the adoption of AM[III] over AM[II] after a council in 809 could be read as a delayed response to the world not having ended in AM[II] 6000 – a process similar to cognitive dissonance could have meant that, rather than accepting that the Y6K prophecy had failed, Frankish bishops preferred to adopt the new reckoning to preserve it.[50] But we also saw in Chapter 3 that the roots of changes in chronological systems lay not in an aversion or attachment to their apocalyptic implications, but rather in debates about computistical orthodoxy. Charlemagne's decision to establish schools to impose higher standards of learning on his kingdom, supported by scholars such as Peter and Alcuin, ensured that these issues were discussed across Europe. The results, I will argue, muddied the water for understanding the passing of the world's 6,000th year considerably, which makes it harder to determine if the silence of the sources is quite as deliberate as it might at first sight seem.[51]

Part of the problem was simply that the tradition of counting down to Y6K seems to have petered out in the key decades.[52] The last prominent example came in an apocalypse commentary written by the Asturian monk Beatus, whose work was virtually unknown outside north-west Spain until the eleventh century. Beatus wrote apocalyptically, and clearly without millenarian hopes:

And so compute from the first man Adam up to the present Era 822 [= 784], and you will find one under 5,984. And so there are sixteen years left of the sixth millennium, and the sixth age will end in Era 838. The time remaining in the world

[48] J. Gil, 'Los terrores del ano 6000', in *Actas del simposio para el estudio de los codices del 'Comentario al apocalypsis' de Beato de Liebana* (Madrid, 1978), pp. 217–47, at pp. 217–18 and 245–6; Landes, 'Lest the Millennium Be Fulfilled', pp. 196–201; Brandes, 'Tempora periculosa sunt', esp. pp. 74–9.

[49] Gouguenheim, *Les fausses terreurs*, pp. 205–6 tries to make too much of this absence because he believes the evidence is too scant for interest in the Eusebian reckoning (AM[II]). The evidence cited in Palmer, 'Calculating Time', counts against this. The important thing is really that few people made anything *of* the date.

[50] Heil, 'Timeless End', pp. 75–7.

[51] This is a central strand in Palmer, 'Calculating Time'.

[52] Karlsruhe, Badische Landesbibliothek, Aug. perg. 167, f. 15r ('ab initio mundi'). Compare Landes, 'Lest the Millennium Be Fulfilled', p. 198 and n. 235 and Palmer, J. T. Palmer, 'The Ends and Futures of Bede's *De temporum ratione*', in P. Darby and F. Wallis (eds.), *Bede and the Future* (Farnham, 2014).

is uncertain to human investigation … You should know in truth the world will end in its 6,000th year; whether they will be lengthened or shortened is known to God alone.[53]

The closest such statement we find at the heart of the Carolingian world was a scribe at Hildebold's Cologne, who noted in 798 in an appendix to Isidore's agnostic chronicle that anyone who was unhappy with the date should 'sweat, read and count better', without ever clarifying why.[54] But even then, the writer seemed confused about something. He introduced the year AM as 5998, but called it the 'Hebrew Truth' – the name Bede had given to his younger world age based on the Vulgate over the Greek Septuagint. The writer also gave a year 'according to the Septuagint' of AM 6268 when of course it should have been 5998. Landes sees here a deliberate effort at confuscation on the grounds that no educated person would have made such a mistake. And yet educated people are perfectly capable of such slips. In 809 a meeting of 'computists' (*computistes*) at Aachen was recorded at which it was readily agreed what the year *ab incarnatione* was, but on the matter of the years *ab exordio mundi* they professed confusion 'on account of the different authorities' before asserting a preference for the 'Hebrew Truth'.[55] Why were people now confused when things had seemed so clear a couple of generations previously?

The simplest answer to this question is that Frankish computistical thought was undergoing its own paradigm shift, much as Britain had experienced a century earlier. In Gaul, bishops had preferred the Easter tables of Victorius of Aquitaine, with their avowed preference for the Eusebian age of the world, since the early sixth century.[56] It was enshrined

---

[53] Beatus, *Tractus in Apocalipsin*, IV. 16a–18, ed. R. Gryson, CCSL, 107A (Turnhout, 2012), I. 518–519: 'Conputa ergo a primo homine Adam usque in presentem eram DCCCXXII, et invenies annos sub uno DCCCCLXXXIIII. Supersunt ergo anni de sexto miliario XVI; finiebit quoque sexta etas in era DCCCXXXVIII. (17) Residuum seculi tempus humanae investigationis incertum est … (18) [S]ciatis in veritate sexto millesimo anno finiendus erit mundus.'

[54] *Additamenta Coloniensia ad Chronica*, ed. Borst, *Schriften*, II, p. 794 (Cologne, Dombibliothek, MS 83ii, f. 14v): 'Cui vero sic non placet, sudet et legat et melius numeret.' Apocalyptic interests at Cologne are difficult to pin down. Cologne, Dombibliothek, MS 92, f. 136r reveals an interest in Gregory's apocalyptic warnings to Æthelbert of Kent (see Chapter 2). Cologne, Dombibliothek, MS 63 shows a striking interest in sin and penance: see H. Mayr-Harting, 'Augustine of Hippo, Chelles, and the Carolingian Renaissance: Cologne Cathedral Manuscript 63', *Frühmittelalterliche Studien*, 45 (2011), 51–75. There is a *Glossae in Apocalypsin* in Cologne, Dombibliothek, MS 416, but it represents only a fragment which was used in the binding of another manuscript.

[55] *Capitula, de quibus compotiste convocati interrogati fuerunt*, c. 2, ed. Borst, *Schriften*, III. 1041.

[56] Victorius's preference for Eusebius is stated in *Prologus ad Hilarum* c. 7, ed. B. Krusch, *Studien zur christlich-mittelalterlichen Chronologie. Die Entstehung unserer heutigen Zeitrechnung* (Berlin, 1939), pp. 22–3.

in canon law.[57] The situation was challenged by Irish and Anglo-Saxon monks entering the sphere of influence of the Pippinids in particular between 690 and 754, because they took first 'Greek' Dionysiac Easter tables, and later the works of Bede, to places such as Echternach and Fulda which were effectively the properties of the Frankish mayors.[58] It is unimaginable that the nobility and their priests would have been celebrating Easter at different times of year, as would have happened if the Franks persisted in using Victorius while the 'foreign monks' (*monachi peregrini*) followed Dionysius. Because the lunar calendars used were not in sync, there were times such as in 740 when, because the Victorian Easter was a week earlier than the 'Greek' one, followers of Dionysius would have considered the rival Easter Sunday to have fallen on the fourteenthth day of the lunar month – which was a widely condemned Judaizing heresy.[59] No one was going to let that stand. The details, as is quite obvious, were very complicated, and that is before use of Dionysiac Easter tables became associated with the Iro-Bedan world age, and before anyone confronted any of the many ancient treatises in circulation which dealt with Easters other than the Victorian or Dionysiac ones.[60] The paradigm shifts involved required considerable intellectual effort and a significant increase in the resource base of the Frankish monasteries.

It was, then, in this context that in 789 Charlemagne ordered that computus – the science and theory behind Easter reckonings – be taught in schools as part of a package to ensure liturgical unity which also included lessons on the psalms, musical notation, singing and grammar.[61] The schools took this seriously. Most libraries had one compendium, if not several, with information on Easter calculations and chronology, often with Bede's *On the Reckoning of Time* at the centre, but mostly full of apparently random assortments of *argumenta* on any and every relevant subject from leap years to astronomy, and from Greek letters to weights

---

[57] *Concilium Aurelianense* (541), c. 1, ed. C. de Clercq, CCSL, 148A (Turnhout, 1963), p. 132.

[58] On this, and what follows, see J. T. Palmer, 'Computus after the Paschal Controversy of 740', in D. Ó Cróinín and I. Warntjes (eds.), *The Easter Controversy of Late Antiquity and the Early Middle Ages* (Turnhout, 2011), pp. 213–41.

[59] 17 April (Victorius) compared to 24 April (Dionysius): see Palmer, 'Computus', p. 214. For the 'heresy' and its controversy in the seventh century, see C. Stancliffe, *Bede, Wilfrid, and the Irish* (Jarrow, 2003) and her 'Columbanus and the Gallic Bishops', in G. Constable and M. Rouche (eds.), *Auctoritas: Mélanges offerts á Olivier Guillot* (Paris, 2006), pp. 205–15.

[60] A sense of the older reckonings is given in G. Declercq, *Anno Domini: The Origins of the Christian Era* (Turnhout, 2000). See also the essays in Ó Cróinín and Warntjes, *The Easter Controversy*.

[61] *Admonitio generalis*, c. 72, p. 60. Liturgical unity here: R. McKitterick, *History and Memory in the Carolingian World* (Cambridge, 2004), p. 99.

and measures.[62] In the most developed modern narrative of what happened, by Arno Borst, Charlemagne and his court were so frustrated at the sheer confusion that the material caused – even once liturgical unity was virtually assured in practice – that they made a series of interventions and commissions to ensure that new coherent 'encyclopaedias' were produced.[63] Centrepieces of reform included a new 'prototype' calendar in 789 and a magisterial seven-book encyclopaedia on natural science produced in 809 which sponsored the Iro-Bedan AM[III] reckoning and labelled it 'ours'.[64] If Charlemagne had ever ordered these things – which is doubtful on the evidence – and done so to create unity, he would have been disappointed, because his new materials only added to the sourcebase which scribes filleted when compiling new, less coherent notebooks, many of which preserved AM[II] alongside AD dates and AM[III].[65] On the other hand, at least the empire now *had* the materials to develop sophisticated understandings of time.

All this is to say that, on Christmas Day in 800, the date represented something of a problem. Most people could probably have agreed that it was 800 – or that it had just turned to 801 – because nearly everybody by then was using Dionysiac Easter tables on which the first column was the year *ab incarnatione*. Liturgical conformity for the most important festival of the year determined this collective innovation, rather than (*contra* Landes) an attempt to ignore the year *ab exordio mundi*. Indeed, few people were entirely sure how old the world was, or at least they would not necessarily have been able to settle on a single number. Communities in the Rhineland flirted with the Greek world age, in which Y6K had long since passed. At St Gall in 810 they used both Bede's date and a Eusebian date synchronised so that AM 6000 would have been in 801.[66] Some people using seventh-century texts would have considered 801 to have been AM 6002. Many people just stuck with the old dating system into the new

[62] A flavour of the number and variety of manuscripts relevant to this study is given by the conspectus in Borst, *Schriften*, I. 205–317. There were at least fifty-seven ninth-century manuscripts of Bede's *De temporum ratione* alone: J. Westgard, 'Bede and the Continent in the Carolingian Age and Beyond', in S. DeGregorio (ed.), *The Cambridge Companion to Bede* (Cambridge, 2010), pp. 201–15 at p. 211.
[63] A. Borst, 'Alkuin und die Enzyklopädia von 809', in P. L. Butzer and D. Lohrmann, (eds.), *Science in Western and Eastern Civilization in Carolingian Times* (Basel, 1993), pp. 53–78; Borst, *Computus. Zeit und Zahl in der Geschichte Europas* (3rd edn, Berlin, 2004), pp. 53–4; idem, *Die karolingische Kalenderreform* (Hanover, 1998); idem, *Der karolingische Reichskalender und seine Überlieferung bis ins 12. Jahrhundert*, MGH Libri mem., 2 (3 vols, Hanover, 2001); Borst, *Schriften, passim*.
[64] *Libri computi*, 1.7C, ed. Borst, *Schriften*, III. 1122.
[65] Palmer, 'Calculating Time', pp. 1320–1.
[66] St Gall, Stiftsbibliothek, Cod. Sang. 902, 153–79 (St Gall, s. ix³). A copy can also be found in St Gall, Stiftsbibliothek, Cod. Sang. 251, 1–25 (St Gall, s. ix³).

millennium.[67] (One might also note that while the Year AD could change at Christmas in line with the Incarnation, the Year AM might not have changed until Easter because the world was created on 18 March, confusing matters further.) In the middle of all this, only four Easter tables are known to have been composed which sought to synchronise AM and AD dates.[68] The silence of our sources on the Y6K problem might simply reflect the unexciting fact that calculating AM dates had become less reliable compared to AD dates. Times had changed.

We should not be caught out here: the evidence of Beatus and Hildebold's scribe alone should remind us that people still wondered about the proximity of the End. Yet we should be cautious when proceeding, if we are tempted to ascribe all evident apocalyptic anxieties and excitement to the proximity of Y6K. It has been popular to cite the evidence of terrible signs in 786: battle arrays in the sky, blood rain, great mortality and crosses appearing on clothes.[69] This could be understood as notable, maybe even worrying or the cause of hope, because there were only fourteen years left of the millennium, as Gil and Landes seem to suggest.[70] A number of matters cast doubt on this association. Isolated instances of dramatic weather, for a start, stand capable of being portentous regardless of the date, so we might seek strong evidence linking the two events. In that context, we should also take note of anything else unusual ongoing which might unsettle an annalist – and indeed their principal other concerns that year were clearly Charlemagne's conquest of Bavaria and a Thuringian uprising against the king, two events which forced Charlemagne to re-evaluate the direction of his reign.[71] After that

[67] Biblioteca Apostolica Vaticana, Pal. lat. 1448, f. 19r (Trier, 810). Borst notes eight other manuscripts of this 'protest' text: Borst, *Schriften*, II. 1014; London, British Library, Harley 3091, f. 4r; Oxford, Bodleian Library, Digby 63, ff. 26r–27r.

[68] These are Cologne, Dombibliothek, MS 83ii, 76v–79r (compares AD, AM[II] and Spanish Era years); Leiden, Universitatsbibliothek, Scaliger 28, 2r–21v (compares AP and AM[II], and AD and AM[III] years); Bremen, Staats- und Universitätsbibliothek, msc 0046 (compares AD and AM[II] years – I. Warntjes, 'A Newly Discovered Prologue of AD 699 to the Easter Table of Victorius of Aquitaine in an Unknown Sirmond Manuscript', *Peritia*, 21 (2010), 255–84); and a lost Reichenau manuscript from St Paul im Lavanttal which used the Greek AM, possibly because that would be appropriate to a 'Greek' Dionysiac table (described in Katz, *Annales Laureshamenses*, pp. 13 and 47).

[69] *Annales Laureshamenses*, s.a. 786, p. 35. See also *Annales Petaviani*, ed. G. H. Pertz, MGH SS, 1 (Hanover, 1826), p. 17, the Chesne Fragment, ed. Pertz, MGH SS, 1, p. 33, *Annales Iuvavenses minores*, s.a. 786, ed. Pertz, MGH SS, 1, p. 88, and *Annales sancti Emmerammi maiores*, ed. Pertz, MGH SS, 1, p. 92.

[70] Gil, 'Los terrores', p. 238; Landes, 'Lest the Millennium Be Fulfilled', pp. 191–2.

[71] *Annales Nazariani*. s.a. 786, ed. Pertz, MGH SS, 1, pp. 41–3 (written in Lorsch – Biblioteca Apostolica Vaticana, Pal. lat. 966, ff. 57r–58r) and see again *Annales Iuvavenses minores*, s.a. 786, ed. Pertz, MGH SS, 1, p. 88, which juxtaposes the signs and the revolt. On the revolt see J. L. Nelson, 'Opposition to Charlemagne', German Historical Institute Lecture (2009).

we might look for further reports of the unusual over the next decade and a half, but there are virtually none, so it is hard to see this a part of an escalating pattern of apocalyptic signs related to a countdown. Even if we cannot find good reason to see it as part of a pattern, however, we can still at least see it as a good instance of portentous things turned towards political commentary in relation to Bavaria or Thuringia. Eschatology and apocalypticism thrived on immediate personal experience more than the date in abstract.

Finally, in that context, one must consider the ways in which the Carolingian court must have failed to control the narrative if it was motivated by the date. Charlemagne had encouraged people in his schools to study computus and yet seems to have done little to stamp down on diversity of practice concerning the date except, on Borst's generous reading of the evidence, late in the day in 809 when a preference for the Iro-Bedan AM[III] was declared. Obscuring the significance of the date by providing precious little guidance would have been a dangerous strategy. Obscuring the significance of the date and then bringing attention to it again by relaunching an eschatologically charged concept of empire at the crucial moment would have been self-defeating. The association between the date and the coronation may look pregnant with meaning, but it also looks a high-risk strategy not to tell anyone what that 'real' meaning was. This gives credence to the explicit reports in the sources, which give the impression that 800 just happens to have been when Leo III's problems and the unpopularity of Irene gave rise to the opportunity to crown Charlemagne. In the face of predictive apocalyptic beliefs, Charlemagne's decisions and leadership come across as incoherent, while the trust they placed in the 'readers' of unfolding events seems very great indeed. In Carolingian eschatological imaginations, authority and heresy were more important in the struggle to be prepared for Judgement than was the date, and it is to this that we should turn to get a better sense of early Carolingian eschatology.

Heresy and the 'precursors of Antichrist'

There was a spiritual agenda to be upheld. As we have already seen, Charlemagne's *regnum Francorum* was easily framed by Alcuin as a *regnum Christianum*, with duties for salvation and peace. Drawing on biblical motifs for political theology, this was the *castra Dei* ('camp of God' [Gen. 32.2]), to be defended vigorously from its enemies, who typologically (rather than literally) appeared as the enemies of the Last Times.[72]

[72] M. Alberi, '"Like the Army of God's Camp": Political Theology and Apocalyptic Warfare at Charlemagne's Court', *Viator*, 41.2 (2010), 1–20, esp. 3–5.

'O, O, the days are close', Cathwulf had warned a young Charlemagne. 'Who now holds, let him hold, until he be taken out the way. Read and understand carefully!'[73] Roman heritage and papal authority abounded in culture north of the Alps: Roman histories and books were copied in Frankish monasteries, including an autograph of the *Rule of Benedict* and a monumental collection of canon law; the relics of Roman martyrs were translated to new homes from 760 onwards; and devotion to St Peter was reinforced at Church councils. When reports reached Charlemagne that the Byzantine Empire was, yet again, mired in controversy surrounding the veneration of icons, he helped to compile a dossier attacking their 'heresy'. The Franks were the new champions of orthodoxy.

Intensifying political anxiety, the eighth century had witnessed a robust approach to ecclesiastical and monastic regulation. The self-professed instigator of this new mood was another Englishman abroad, St Boniface, the peripatetic 'bishop of the Germans', archbishop of Mainz, and later enthusiastic martyr in 754.[74] His single-minded and occasionally hypocritical pursuit of canonical order shook the establishment as he challenged the secularised living of churchmen and the power of engrained nobilities in towns, including Mainz. He even tested the patience of Pope Zacharias, both with questions about minutiae such as whether it was legitimate to eat birds, and complaints about New Year celebrations in Rome and accusations of simony.[75] Boniface's humourless love of orderliness gelled with the piety of the brothers Pippin III and Carloman – the first, Charlemagne's father and a man capable of writing to popes himself about canon law; and the second, a man who eventually turned his back on a moderately successful political career to become a monk in Monte Cassino. Having such characters at the forefront of Frankish politics just at the point when Merovingian authority completely collapsed naturally only helped to build the harmony between Frankish polities and Christendom. As a consequence, those who threatened the project appeared to be particularly dangerous, prompting the Frankish Church to engage in what Matthew Innes has called a 'hereticification' of perceived enemies.[76]

[73] Cathwulf, *Epistola ad Carolo*, p. 505: 'O, o, dies prope sunt. Qui tenet tenat, donec dimidium fiat. Lege et intellege diligenter.'

[74] T. Schieffer, *Winfrid-Bonifatius und die christliche Grundelgung Europas* (2nd edn, Darmstadt, 1972); L. von Padberg, *Bonifatius: Missionar und Reformer* (Munich, 2003). See also now J. Palmer, *Anglo-Saxons in a Frankish World, 690–900* (Turnhout, 2009) and the different approach in J.-H. Clay, *In the Shadow of Death: St Boniface and the Conversion of Hessia, 723–754* (Turnhout, 2010).

[75] Boniface, *Bonifatii et Lulli Epistolae*, no. 58, ed. M. Tangl, MGH Epp. Sel., 1 (Berlin, 1916), p. 107.

[76] M. Innes, 'Immune from Heresy: Defining the Boundaries of Carolingian Christianity', in P. Fouracre and D. Ganz (eds.), *Frankland: The Franks and the World of the Early Middle Ages* (Manchester, 2008), pp. 101–25, esp. pp. 111 and 117–18.

The first infamous challenge came from a wandering holy man called Aldebert, active near Soissons in the early 740s – someone perhaps with a whiff of the 'millenarian' about him. Charismatic Aldebert whipped up popular enthusiasm for reformist practices, much as Gregory's pseudo-prophets had 150 years earlier, so he has been seen squarely in that kind of End Times drama.[77] His crimes, as listed by Boniface and upheld by both Pippin III at Soissons in 744[78] and Zacharias in Rome in 745, included denouncing pilgrimage to Rome, setting up shrines in fields, taking confession without imposing penance, and presenting himself as a saint with his own self-penned hagiography and his own ready supply of 'relics' (hair and nail clippings).[79] Moreover, he claimed to have a letter sent to him by Christ, which simultaneously served to 'legitimise' Aldebert's non-institutional holiness while making him appear even more like a heretic to his opponents. Loose-living kings or priests and disagreeable backsliders Boniface had faced with displeasure.[80] Confronted with someone actively subverting his institutional take on order, looking and sounding like the real thing while leading souls astray, the archbishop went further and denounced Aldebert and another heretic named Clemens to Zacharias as 'precursors of Antichrist'.[81] The co-ordination of action supports the severity of Boniface's words, with the two councils in different kingdoms summoned to denounce the heretic. This was anxiety about unregulated popular piety projected outwards as a warning, enshrined and circulated in canon law, at least in the reformist circles of St Boniface.[82]

Aldebert hints at exactly the kind of charismatic and populist piety which goes hand-in-hand with millenarianism, but this is much less evident in practice than it was in the case of Gregory of Tours's enemies. Apart from Boniface's comment about Antichrist, no explicit apocalyptic dynamic is apparent, and if Aldebert had been preaching an apocalyptic

---

[77] N. Cohn, *In Pursuit of the Millennium: Revolutionary Millenarians and Mystical Anarchists of the Middle Ages* (2nd edn, 1970), pp. 42–4.

[78] *Concilium Suessionense*, c. 2, ed. Werminghoff, MGH Conc., 2. 1 p. 34. Intention to condemn Aldebert and Clemens is also evident from the 'conferenda' for Soissons, edited in M. Glatthaar, *Bonifatius und das Sakrileg. Zur politischen Dimension eines Rechtsbegriffs* (Frankfurt-am-Main, 2004), pp. 117–18 (no. 21, p. 117).

[79] *Bonifatii et Lulli Epistolae*, no. 59, pp. 109–18.

[80] *Bonifatii et Lulli Epistolae*, no. 73, pp. 148–55 (rebukes to King Æthelbald of Mercia); no. 87, p. 198 (complaints about bishops); E. Ewig, 'Milo et eiusmodi similes', in *Sankt Bonifatius* (Fulda, 1954), pp. 412–40; von Padberg, *Bonifatius: Missionar und Reformer*, ch. 6 (on reform) and pp. 90–4 (on Æthelbald).

[81] *Bonifatii et Lulli Epistolae*, no. 59, pp. 110 and 113.

[82] Innes, 'Immune from Heresy'. For a useful view see N. Zeddies, 'Bonifatius und zwei nützliche Rebellen: die Häretiker Aldebert und Clemens', in M. T. Fögen (ed.), *Ordnung und Aufruhr im Mittelalter: historische und juristische Studien zur Rebellion* (Frankfurt-am-Main, 1995), pp. 217–64.

message, it did not offend Boniface, Pippin or the pope as much as the
other things he was doing. Matthew Innes has even interpreted Aldebert
as acting, on the whole, like a Merovingian bishop. It is no less likely that,
if people were supporting under-regulated holy men such as Aldebert,
it was because they spoke of simple, direct, tangible holiness in a way
which the institutional Church of the mid-eighth century did not.[83]
There was a long-running battle over access to relics and holy places.
Hardliners such as Boniface sought control to ensure both correct practice and the unity of the Church. The whole project of reforming society
for its own salvation could be seriously undermined if an Aldebert went
off-message and inspired the general population with ideas which would
only lead to damnation, as we saw with Gregory of Tours' opposition to
charismatics (Chapter 2). A list of 'superstitions' thought to have been
discussed at one of Boniface's councils emphasises this anxiety in a different way: there is no sense of 'heresy' or apocalypticism as a danger,
but rather pagan observances and syncretic practices such as sacrifices
made to saints.[84] If anything it remained Boniface who had the vision of
peace and order, his frustration a symptom of his own difficulties in real-
ising his dreams rather than a desire to stamp out millenarian hopes. The
Antichrist comment shows that this was Boniface's apocalyptic fight, not
Aldebert's.

Canon law was, after all, promulgated to ensure unity and peace. So
much was explicitly announced in chapter 60 of Charlemagne's grand
plan for correction, *Admonitio generalis*, issued 'publicly' in the palace
of Aachen in March 789.[85] Thereafter, the king had capitularies drawn
up on a regular basis after councils, giving guidance and judgement on
a range of secular and religious matters, taking up the spiritual (and
eschatological) fight against the Church's enemies.[86] Often, Charlemagne
and his bishops faced exactly the same kinds of challenges as Boniface –
or at least they had read enough Boniface and, probably, Gregory of
Tours to have a ready-formed vision of the problems. In *Admonitio generalis*, there was felt to be a need to condemn 'pseudografia and dubious
tales ... which are all against the Catholic faith, and the most wicked
and most false letters ... which fall from heaven' after an incident in

[83] P. Brown, *The Rise of Western Christendom* (2nd edn, Oxford, 2003), p. 422.
[84] *Indiculus superstitionum et paganiarum*, ed. G. H. Pertz, MGH LL, 1 (Hanover, 1835),
pp. 19–20.
[85] *Admonitio generalis*, c. 60, p. 57.
[86] Alberi, 'Like the Army of God's Camp', 10–12. On Carolingian capitularies and government see J. Davis, 'A Pattern for Power: Charlemagne's Delegation of Judicial
Responsibilities', in J. Davis and M. McCormick (eds.), *The Long Morning of Medieval
Europe: New Directions in Medieval Studies* (Aldershot, 2008), pp. 235–46 and M. Innes,
'Charlemagne's Government', in Story, *Charlemagne*, pp. 71–89.

788.[87] The shadow of Aldebert remained. There was also a clampdown on veneration of angels other than Michael, Gabriel and Rafael, implying novelties were being introduced by popular proclamation. In 794 at the Council of Frankfurt, it was decreed that no new saints ought to be cultivated except those venerated properly and with the authority of a *passio* or *vita*, addressing the long-standing problem of how to keep check on new cults springing up without some kind of control.[88] Popular aspects of religion could cause problems through 'excessive' religiosity as well as through deficiency.

A key issue Charlemagne's legislation presents again is whether 'popular religion' was inherently apocalyptic, stirred against more conservative secular and ecclesiastical authorities. This is the kind of problem we encountered looking at Gregory of Tours's stories, and which we might expect if we projected some of Norman Cohn's ideas about later millenarianism back onto our sources.[89] Without better evidence it may be impossible to pass judgement. The capitularies are often rather vague when it comes to things like letters from heaven, novelty angels and spurious saints – these are not the kinds of problems which crop up in histories, saints' Lives or letters. Perhaps, like the 'imagined paganisms' of the period, which were portrayed more according to old books than experience, there was a significant amount of worrying about what might be, as much as there was combating difficulties on the ground.[90] The more compelling aspects of the drama come to light in comments such as Boniface's condemnation of Aldebert as a 'precursor of Antichrist'. The final statement of *Admonitio generalis*, for instance, rallied preachers to take care 'because we know that in the last times pseudo-teachers will come, just as the Lord preached in his Gospel, and the apostle Paul testified to Timothy (1 Tim. 4.1)'.[91] The *correctio* of the Carolingian realm did not challenge apocalypticism – it harnessed such ideas to lend urgency to its fight.

[87] *Admonitio generalis*, c. 78, p. 60: 'pseudografia et dubiae narrationes, vel quae omnino contra fidem catholicam sunt et epistola pessima et falsissima … quod de celo cecidisset.'
[88] *Concilium Francofurtensis*, c. 42, ed. Boretius, MGH Cap., 1, p. 77. P. Fouracre, 'The Origins of the Carolingian Attempt to Regulate the Cult of Saints', in P. A. Hayward and J. Howard-Johnston (eds.), *The Cult of Saints in Late Antiquity and the Middle Ages: Essays on the Contribution of Peter Brown* (Oxford, 1999), pp. 143–65.
[89] Cohn, *In Pursuit of the Millennium*. For the wider critique, see Introduction, pp. 12–13.
[90] J. T. Palmer, 'Defining Paganism in the Carolingian World', *EME*, 15.4 (2007), 402–25.
[91] *Admonitio generalis*, c. 82, p. 62: 'quia scimus temporibus novissimis pseudodoctores esse ventuos, sicut ipse Dominus in evangelio praedixit, et apostolus Paulus ad Timotheum testatur.'

The clearest cases of 'reform as apocalyptic drama' revolved around
a series of disputes in Spain and Bishop Elipandus of Toledo. The first
of these was triggered by a fight with another charismatic, Migetius –
'also known as Satan' and a man incomparable to other heretics and
paving the way for Antichrist, as he was described in 785.[92] According
to Elipandus's list of Migetius's crimes we find – aside from a famous
dispute over Trinitarian doctrine – suggestions of a rigorist movement,
which included Migetius promoting the higher holiness of himself and
priests, and arguing against eating with 'the infidel' (i.e., Muslims).[93]
Elipandus in no uncertain terms condemned such ideas as presump-
tuous and excessive, as he sought to assert his authority in his see and
maintain a level of moderation in religious practice alien to his sense
of rhetoric. For Migetius there is a stronger case for seeing something
of a millennarian outlook, because his final sin in Elipandus's eyes was
to proclaim that in Rome alone resided the power of God – and that it
was 'the New Jerusalem, which John saw descending from Heaven [=
Rev. 3.12]'.[94] Here was a prophesied centre for peace on earth. Except,
as Elipandus was quick to point out, Rome could not hold this position because 'Peter's Church' stood as a symbol of the universal Church,
and the city of Rome itself was 'Babylon'. It was, of course, also not *de
rigueur* to interpret Revelation so literally, and no less so in Spain: the
New Jerusalem was a vision of peace.[95]

Elipandus's argument escalated on two fronts. First, Migetius's millenarian sect attracted and converted the preacher Egila, who had been sent
to the Iberian peninsula by Archbishop Wilcharius of Sens (d. 786/7)
with licence confirmed by Pope Hadrian (772–95). Hadrian, unsurprisingly, was shocked to hear that one of his own representatives had begun
to teach heresies 'against the Roman and orthodox faith', and wrote to

[92] Elipandus, *Epistula ad Migetium*, c. 2, c. 5, ed. J. Gil, in *Corpus scriptorum Muzarabicorum* (Madrid, 1974), p. 69 and p. 73. On the whole debate see W. Heil, 'Der Adoptionismus, Alkuin und Spanien', in B. Bischoff (ed.), *Karl der Große. Lebenswerk und Nachleben II: Das Geistige Leben* (Düsseldorf, 1965), pp. 95–155 at pp. 108–12; K. Schäferdiek, 'Der adoptianische Streit im Rahmen der spanischen Kirchengeschichte I', *Zeitschrift für Kirchengeschichte*, 80 (1969), 291–311, continued in 81 (1970), 1–16; R. Collins, *The Arab Conquest of Spain 710–797* (Oxford, 1989), pp. 220–2; J. Cavadini, The *Last Christology of the West: Adoptionism in Spain and Gaul, 785–820* (Philadelphia, 1993).
[93] Elipandus, *Epistula ad Migetium*, c. 10–11, pp. 75–7.
[94] Elipandus, *Epistula ad Migetium*, c. 12, p. 77:' ipsa est Iherusalem noba, quem vidit Ioannes descendentem de celo.'
[95] Compare also Beatus, *Tractatus de Apocalipsin*, II. 102, ed. R. Gryson, CCSL, 107B–C (Turnhout, 2012), I. 349 (New Jerusalem as a vision of peace (*visio pacis*), just as it is in Elipandus's letter) and the Visigoth Theodulf, *Commemoratorium*, ed. Gryson, CCSL, 107, pp. 310–1 (New Jerusalem as an image of the Church inaugurated through baptism).

the other bishops of Spain.[96] Charlemagne was already involved somehow, being instrumental in requesting that the pope write to the errant
bishop, which meant that the heresies of Migetius were becoming international news.[97] As Cavadini pointed out, the irony was that those arguing for the eschatological significance of Rome were now condemned by
its bishop.[98] The turn of events did not, however, offer Elipandus support either, and here we encounter the second point of escalation. In the
course of his attacks on Migetius, the primate of Toledo had commented
on the 'adopted persona' of Christ, which had then led to a dispute with
the monk Beatus of Liébana over whether Elipandus was denying the
divinity of Christ. The clash between the two was particularly fiery, as
Beatus wrote at length associating Elipandus with the antichrists of the
last hour (1 John 2.18), which prompted Elipandus later to snort that
Beatus himself was a 'disciple of Antichrist' (*discipulus Antichristi*) for
his stubborn opposition and rebukes.[99] But Pope Hadrian sided against
Elipandus and, in the same letter in which he condemned Egila and
Migetius, he denounced the Toledan's 'Nestorianism'.[100] This was the
beginning of a conflict which was going to make full use of apocalyptic
drama in its rhetoric.

Beatus, at the forefront of the debate, cuts a rather peculiar figure
as the point man for the 'anti-apocalyptic' Carolingian regime. Indeed,
one of the accusations Elipandus levelled against his Asturian opponent was that, in 793, Beatus preached that the world would end on an
Easter Sunday, which drove his flock into a frenzy saying – in Elipandus's
words – 'let's feast and drink now, and if we die, we shall die sated'.[101] This
was no doubt a rhetorical flourish designed to condemn Beatus given
that it does not fit well with Beatus's belief that the world would end after
6,000 years. Nevertheless, it reveals interesting things about Elipandus's
expectations about an apocalyptic sect. Beatus's followers did not fear

[96] *Codex Carolinus*, no. 95, p. 637. For the chronology of the letters and further details on
Wilcharius, see D. Bullough, 'The Dating of Codex Carolinus Nos. 95, 96, 97, Wilchar,
and the Beginnings of the Archbishopric of Sens', *DA*, 18 (1962), 223–30.
[97] *Codex Carolinus*, no. 97, p. 648.
[98] Cavadini, *The Last Christology*, p. 12.
[99] Beatus of Liébana and Eterius of Osma, *Adversus Elipandum libri duo*, II. 13–17, ed. B.
Löfstedt, CCCM, 59 (Turnhout, 1984), pp. 113–16; Elipandus, *Epistula ad Albinum*, c.
3, p. 96.
[100] *Codex Carolinus*, no. 95, p. 637. Nestorius of Constantinople had asserted that Christ
had distinct human and divine natures.
[101] *Epistula episcoporum Hispaniae*, c. 5, ed. Gil, p. 92: 'Commedamus et bibamus, et si
fuerimus mortui, saltim uel satiati.' J. Williams, 'Purpose and Imagery in the Apocalypse
Commentary of Beatus of Liébana', in R. Emmerson and B. McGinn (eds.), *The
Apocalypse in the Middle Ages* (Ithaca, NY, 1993), pp. 217–33 at pp. 222–3 reasonably
doubts this is anything other than Elipandus making noise. See also D. C. van Meter,

the end – they celebrated its possible imminence in an earth(l)y manner, and were happy to accept that this was only *potential*, this was not a hard-and-fast prophecy (note that crucial 'if' hanging over the direct speech).[102] Not for the first time, we see also apocalypticism having a different kind of cachet to the Christological heresies or disputes about the liturgy. It was almost acceptable as long as it was not too predictive – and Beatus, in Elipandus's eyes, had crossed the line.

It was also at the time that the arguments were starting up in Spain, in 784, that Beatus produced a second edition of his classic Iberian commentary on Revelation, famous from the tenth century for the vivid illustrations added to it.[103] Little about the commentary is particularly innovative compared to other Tyconian commentaries, and Umberto Eco once decried it as 'unbearable'.[104] Yet by incorporating large passages from Isidore on ecclesiastical office, Beatus succeeded in amplifying the ecclesiological interpretations so beloved of his intellectual predecessors, and in doing so seems to have set out to create a basis for articulating the importance of the unity of the Church. In that context, vigilance against Satan and the Antichrist was paramount.[105] As Williams pointed out, Beatus began writing in at least 776, so before Elipandus had even arrived at Toledo, but that does not mean that Beatus was not responding to pre-existing anxiety about orthodoxy in the Iberian peninsula.[106] He was one of few commentators to follow Jerome over Augustine when he interpreted Magog as *de dogmate* (Rev. 20.7), and he clearly signalled his view of the Church in struggle in Book II by using John's seven churches as a vehicle for discussing the universal Church's battle against heretics, schismatics and hypocrites.[107] The clash with Elipandus may still have

---

'Christian of Stavelot on Matthew 24:42 and the Tradition that the World Will End on a March 25th', *Recherches de théologie ancienne et médiévale*, 63 (1996), 68–92 at pp. 73–4.

[102] For a useful survey of attitudes towards prophecy, although with a rather limited view of apocalypse, see R. Southern, 'Aspects of the European Tradition of Historical Writing: 3. History as Prophecy', *TRHS*, 5th series, 22 (1972), 159–80.

[103] Williams, 'Purpose and Imagery', esp. pp. 220–1 on the date; Williams, *The Illustrated Beatus: A Corpus of the Illustrations of the Commentary on the Apocalypse* (5 vols, London, 1994–2003).

[104] U. Eco, 'Waiting for the Millennium', in A. Gow, R. Landes and D. van Meter (eds.), *The Apocalyptic Year 1000: Religious Expectation and Social Change, 950–1050* (Oxford, 2003), pp. 121–35 at pp. 121–2. E. A. Matter, 'The Apocalypse in Early Medieval Exegesis', in Emmerson and McGinn, *The Apocalypse in the Middle Ages*, pp. 38–50 at pp. 45–6 points out that the density of the text has discouraged detailed analysis.

[105] Gryson, CCSL, 107B, cxlvi–cxvliii.

[106] Williams, 'Purpose and Imagery', pp. 221–2. Also Heil, 'Der Adoptionismus', p. 101

[107] Beatus, *Tractatus*, XI. 11, ed. Gryson, II. 881. Book II, 'de ecclesia et sinagoga', starts strongly on the theme of struggle (II. 1.2, ed. Gryson, I. 141) and continues at length, e.g. II. 6, ed. Gryson, pp. 177–90.

been the trigger for any final changes in 784–5, when he wrote about the world ending after 6,000 years. His ecclesiological understanding of Revelation combined with a sense of time running short began to encourage action, whether it was directed specifically at the Adoptionists or to more systemic problems in Christian Spain.[108] The commentary might not have been a response to Elipandus, but it is little surprise to have found its author challenging someone he perceived to be a heretic. The apocalyptic battle came to a head in the last decade of the eighth century. In 792 Elipandus's supporter, Felix of Urgell, was condemned at a council at Regensburg, and then fled, to be addressed in a letter by Alcuin about peace and concord in the universal Church. 'With the love of many growing cold [Matt 24.12], what are little men like us at the end of the world able to devise better, than to follow ... the teaching of the Apostles and the Gospels with all faith, firmness, and truth?'[109] Further condemnation at Frankfurt in 794 led to the drafting of further letters and treatises in response, with Alcuin and Paulinus of Aquileia each contributing dossiers of counterarguments.[110] Alcuin also sought contact with Beatus as an ally.[111] The rhetoric focused on the 'hereticification' of the enemy, as Adoptionism was denounced as evil, the unity and catholicism of the Church of God were defended, and the court's representatives articulated their fighting spirit as soldiers of Christ (*milites Christi*).[112] So much here resonated with the ecclesiological understanding of Revelation and the struggles of the Church. The language was harsh even if it lacked some of the explicit apocalyptic register of Elipandus's assaults. Argumentative strategy was no doubt important when they decided to avoid such excesses, because certainly Alcuin, quoting 2 Timothy again, considered the Adoptionists to be the anticipated pseudo-prophets of the End Times and that therefore the Church was in need of many defenders.[113] This was precisely the kind of struggle Charlemagne had warned about in the *Admonitio generalis*.

[108] Gil, 'Los terrores', pp. 222–4; Williams, 'Purpose and Imagery', pp. 222–5.
[109] Alcuin, *Epistola*, no. 23, p. 61: 'Quid nos homunculi in fine seculi, refrigescente caritate multorum, melius excogitare poterimus, quam ut ... apostolicam et evangelicam omni fidei firmitate et veritate sequamur doctrinam?' Alberi, 'Like the Army of God's Camp', p. 17.
[110] Alcuin, *Liber Alcuini contra haeresim Felicis*, ed. G. B. Blumenshine (Vatican City, 1980); Paulinus of Aquileia, *Contra Felicem libri tres*, ed. D. Norberg, CCCM, 95 (Turnhout, 1990). A collection of materials from Frankfurt is ed. A. Werminghoff, MGH Conc., 2. 1, pp. 110–71.
[111] W. Levison, 'A Letter of Alcuin to Beatus of Liébana', in *England and the Continent in the Eighth Century* (Oxford, 1946), pp. 314–23.
[112] Alberi, 'Like the Army of God's Camp', p. 19.
[113] Alcuin, *Vita Vedasti*, c. 3, PL, 101.666; Palmer, 'Calculating Time', p. 1317. Relevant observations on Alcuin's ideals in hagiography in C. Veyard-Cosme, *L'œuvre*

The Adoptionist debate did prompt new proclamations about the unknowable timing of the End, which may have influenced caginess about the Y6K problem. In the course of debates, Felix had made much of Mark's comment that 'but of that day or hour no man knows, neither the angels in heaven, *nor the Son*, but the Father' (Mark 13.32), where Matthew had said nothing about the Son. Did Christ's ignorance about a Day of Judgement he himself was prophesying prove his adopted nature (if not an out-and-out paradox)? Alcuin, Paulinus and later Agobard of Lyon could find plenty of support from Augustine, Jerome and Bede to say that Christ's lack of omniscience proved nothing.[114] This had come up in Christological debates before and was prominent in Gregory of Tours's preface to his *Histories*, when he had criticised Arian 'heretics' for similar misuse of Mark while arguing that the only sure sign of the end was the coming of Antichrist.[115] Of course, for Gregory there was a jibe here as heretics and pseudo-prophets were antichrists. And indeed at Hildebold's Cologne the resonance of Gregory's preface for Carolingian struggles was not lost as it was included in that bullish but agnostic appendix to Isidore's chronicle in which diligent reading as well as counting were encouraged.[116] As Borst thought, something about the rephrasing strongly suggests that the Adoptionist controversy was on the writer's mind.[117] Heresy reminded people that the struggle with Antichrist was more important in confronting apocalyptic scenarios than the date alone.

Nevertheless, two decades of moderately successful reform and a solid record in combating heresy did not leave the Carolingian regime with the self-confidence one might imagine. As Paul Dutton argued, the world had begun to feel old, precisely because the leading figures from Charlemagne's court were then genuinely old, if they even lived into the last years of the reign.[118] Charlemagne himself was probably fifty-seven or fifty-eight when he became emperor, Alcuin was into his sixties and gloomy when he left court in 796, and many of the court's old guard – including Paulinus of Aquileia, Peter of Pisa and Paul the Deacon – had gone home, leaving intellectual life in new hands. In 809, the *Annales*

hagiographique en prose d'Alcuin. Vitae Willibrordi, Vedasti, Richarii. Edition, traduction, études narratologiques (Florence, 2003), pp. 258–61.

[114] Cavadini, *The Last Christology*, p. 113; Alcuin, *Contra Felicem Urgellitanum libri septem*, V. 9, PL, 101. 195–6; Paulinus, *Contra Felicem*, I. 12, pp. 17–18; Agobard, *Adversum dogma Felicis*, c. 5 and c. 25, ed. L. van Acker, CCCM, 52 (Turnhout, 1981), pp. 76–7 and 92–3.

[115] Gregory of Tours, *Historiae*, pref., p. 5.

[116] *Additamenta*, I. 2, ed. Borst, *Schriften*, II. 781–2; Cologne, Dombibliothek, 83ii, 12v–13r.

[117] Borst, *Schriften*, II. 774–7.   [118] Dutton, *Charlemagne's Mustache*, pp. 153–8.

regni Francorum announced the growing sense of anxiety. At Aachen, that November, a Church council was held which was characterised as deciding nothing 'on account of the magnitude of things'.[119] Twenty years on from *Admonitio generalis*, this was a bleak assessment. Two years further on still Charlemagne even wondered out loud at a council whether he and his followers were truly Christians.[120] True, luck had started to desert the emperor. Famine and plague in 805–7 had ripped the heart out of the empire. The emperor's sons and heirs, Pippin and Charles, died in 806 and 810 respectively. Danes and Transalbingians contrived to embarrass Frankish armies in the field, although at least King Godefrid's boasts that he could beat Charlemagne seem to have led to nervous followers prematurely ending his reign before he got into more serious trouble. Charlemagne, nevertheless, forbade missions to the north, at least for now.[121] There was, anyway, more important business to which to attend.

Charlemagne's final year, from 813 to 814, witnessed no less dedication to leaving a harmonised and well-equipped empire as he entered his mid-sixties with failing health.[122] He began by seeking peace with Emperor Michael in Constantinople and by having Louis, his only surviving son, crowned co-emperor in Aachen. The centrepiece was a series of councils attended by the emperor, held in Arles, Rheims, Mainz, Chalon-sur-Saône and Tours – all as remarkable for their different preoccupations as their common thrust, but collectively a grand response to the anxiety expressed in 809 and 811. Diversity within unity remained the *modus operandi*, with the emperor evidently content to let his archbishops and bishops identify their own concerns and then to submit their reports to the palace archive.[123] Charlemagne's approaching end no doubt accounts for some of the eschatological interest for peace, unity and salvation at the heart of the programmes for reform – not unusual

---

[119] *Annales regni Francorum*, s.a. 809, p. 129.
[120] *Capitula tractanda cum comitibus episcopis et abbatibus* (811), c. 9, MGH Cap., 1, p. 161: 'quod nobis despiciendum est, utrum vere christiani sumus. Quod in consideratione vitae vel morum nostrorum facillime cognosci potest, si diligenter conversationem coram discutere voluerimus.' See J. Nelson, 'The Voice of Charlemagne', in R. Gameson and H. Leyser, eds., *Belief and Culture in the Earlier Middle Ages: Studies Presented to Henry Mayr-Harting* (Oxford, 2001), pp. 76–88. If there are any echoes of Pseudo-Methodius in Charlemagne's thought it is here: compare Pseudo-Methodius, *Sermo*, [12], 1, ed. W. J. Aerts and G. A. A. Kortekaas, *Die Apokalypse des Pseudo-Methodius. Die ältesten Grieschen und Lateinischen Übersetzungen* (Leuven, 1998), p. 157.
[121] Altfrid, *Vita Liudgeri*, I. 30, ed. W. Diekamp, *Vitae sancti Liudgeri* (Münster, 1888), p. 36. See also the comments in Chapter 6, p. 180.
[122] Einhard, *Vita Karoli*, c. 30, p. 34.
[123] *Annales regni Francorum*, s.a. 813, p. 138. Reports on the council were taken to the palace 'archive' (*archivum palatii*), which probably gave rise to the copy of the council records in Munich, Bayerische Staatsbibliothek, Clm 27246 (s. x).

for Church councils, but maybe more prominent.[124] Many provisions
addressed issues of order, discipline and practice. At Chalon-sur-Saône
the bishops, whose leader Leidrad of Lyon still had Felix of Urgell pris-
oner, praised Charlemagne's decision to order new schools because it
provided the education to resist heresy and Antichrist himself.[125] It is
a reminder that the Church had many interests and concerns, many of
which drew eschatological reflection, but few of which stimulated apocalyptic rhetoric like the threat of heresy.

Conclusion

Charlemagne's empire was, in many ways, the realisation of Gregory
of Tours's dreams for the *ecclesia Dei*. There was co-operation between
secular and ecclesiastical authorities, who pulled together for the salvation of society. They combated charismatics and unregulated 'popular
religion' because such things posed grave threats to the projects in hand.
Sometimes these popular figures seemed more apocalyptic or millenarian than the mainstream, as happened with Migetius. This did not, however, make Charlemagne's *ecclesia Dei* (or *castra Dei*) an anti-apocalyptic
institution. It shared with both Gregorys a deep sense of responsibility
which was generated by eschatological frames of reference, now coupled
more fully with political authority and action. Indeed, in Alcuin's *tempora
periculosa*, we can see the apocalyptic mood as argument, as an important advisor encouraged his king to act. In the fight against heresy, the
Carolingian Church was a universal institution pitched against pseudo-
prophets (and Elipandus of Toledo returned the favour by inverting the
roles in his response). The blending of political and religious authority
in labels such as *regnum Francorum*, *imperium Christianum* and *imperium
Romanorum* gave Daniel's scheme and St Paul's warnings more urgency
because pious Franks now held responsibility for looking after the Last
Empire until they handed it over to God or until they lost grace. In an
empire defined by prayer, the distinction between 'eschatology' and
'apocalyptic scenario' was less clear cut than modern commentators have

[124] *Concilium Arelatense* (813), pref., MGH Conc., 2. 1, pp. 248–9 and c. 1, p. 250; *Concilium
Remense* (813), pref., MGH Conc., 2. 1, p. 254; *Concilium Moguntinense* (813), pref.,
MGH Conc., 2. 1, p. 259 (especially snatching souls away from the Dragon [of Rev.
12?] to focus on paradise) and c. 5, p. 261 on peace as a route to the Heavenly Kingdom;
Concilium Cabillonense (813), c. 20, MGH Conc., 2. 1, p. 277 (on peace and concord)
and a significant emphasis on penitence. The *Concilium Turonense* (813), MGH Conc.,
2. 1, is more business-like but still encourages renouncing the Devil (c. 18, pp. 288–9)
and encourages peace (c. 32, p. 290).
[125] *Concilium Cabillonense* (813), c. 3, p. 275.

hoped. The consequence was that the apocalyptic was, slowly, becoming more political, even if it provided only one possible way for contemporaries to look at the idea of empire and reform.

Meanwhile, an important part of early apocalyptic tradition had broken: the Year 6000 had either passed (AM^I or AM^{II}) or been located so far in the future that it no longer mattered. It was not like in the East, where we have seen that people played with ideas of the world enduring 6,500 or 7,000 years. Fascination with the whole question faded in a mist of computistical confusion, to be replaced by interest in an 'Apocalyptic Year 1000' (Y1K) for which there was at least an actual scriptural basis. Bede and his intellectual predecessors had also already taught that the date was artificial and unimportant because the End could come at any time, whatever the occasional Beatus thought. An idea that barely qualified even as a prophecy in many eyes had led nowhere, so it is little surprise to find no indication of 'cognitive dissonance' unless one accepts the weak case for the shift from AM^{II} to the use of AD and, to a lesser degree, AM^{III}. As we shall see in the next chapter, predication still occurred but the Y6K problem had run its course in the West – and yet there was to be no shortage of apocalyptic hopes and fears in the century still to come.

6   A Golden Age in danger (*c. 820–c. 911*)

Charlemagne had left a deep legacy for the coming generations. Writing for the emperor's great-grandson Charles the Fat sometime between 885 and 887, Notker the Stammerer of St Gall proclaimed that:

> The omnipotent disposer of all things and the director of kingdoms and of the ages, when he had destroyed that wonderful statue with feet of iron or clay among the Romans, set up the golden head of another no less remarkable statue among the Franks through the illustrious Charlemagne.[1]

Toying with the Danielian scheme of world kingdoms, Notker had cast the Frankish empire as the 'kingdom which shall never be destroyed' (Dan. 2.44) – or at least which would never be scattered.[2] Notker, of course, knew that the Carolingian Empire had often been carved up since Charlemagne's death in 814 but in the new Charles, the third of that name, the empire had a new uniting power. Or at least it would have if Charles could learn the lessons of his predecessors. As Paul Dutton once argued, the ninth century was a time in which people could feel the breathless pace of change acutely – and that was without taking account of the obliteration of political organisation in nearby England at the hands of the Vikings in the 860s, where no doubt change was felt no less acutely.[3] There were new enemies and new heresies, but these were accompanied by new heights of creativity and cultural production. Charles had every advantage as well as challenges he could turn

---

[1] Notker, *Gesta Karoli*, I. 1, ed. H. Haefele, MGH SRG, n.s. 12 (Berlin, 1959), p. 1: 'Omnipotens rerum dispositor ordinatorque regnorum et temporum, cum illius admirandae statuae pedes ferreos vel testaceos comminuiesset in Romanis, alterius non minus admirabilis statuae caput aureum per illustrem Karolum erexit in Francis' (trans. D. Ganz, *Two Lives of Charlemagne* [Harmondsworth, 2009], p. 55).

[2] T. Siegrist, *Herrscherbild und Weltsicht bei Notker Balbulus: Untersuchungen zu den Gesta Karoli* (Zurich, 1963), pp. 109–23; B. McGinn, 'Eriugena Confronts the End: Reflections on Johannes Scottus's Place in Carolingian Eschatology', in M. Dunne and J. McEvoy (eds.), *History and Eschatology in John Scottus Eriugena and His Time* (Leuven, 2002), pp. 3–29 at pp. 10–12.

[3] P. E. Dutton, *The Politics of Dreaming in the Carolingian Empire* (Lincoln, NE, 1994), p. 1.

to his benefit. Within a couple of years of Notker's writing, however, the Carolingian Empire was emperor-less and seemingly in decline. Daniel's scheme was running out of incarnations.

'Decline' remains one of those relative terms which is often more apparent than real. Every other generation laments the state of the world while looking back to some Golden Age. Charlemagne's was a particularly recent and tangible one, reconceptualised and reprocessed repeatedly as soon as it had ended, as Matthew Gabriele and Anne Latowsky have recently shown.[4] But, as we saw, even Charlemagne's court ran through its last years with a sense of gloom – part genuine anxiety about standards and progress, part rhetorical strategy of motivation. In order to create and maintain order, one can find as much stimulation in energising optimism as one can in having to fight darker battles, particularly if the End could come at any moment. As Hrabanus Maurus wrote in the first half of the ninth century, quoting Bede: 'When it is said that "It is not for you to know", it shows that he should know always to be uncertain of the coming of Judgement, so they may live everyday as if it were another day for being judged.'[5] It is difficult not to remain critical, watchful, and uncertain, if that is your primary driving dynamic. There was no place for complacency and it therefore remained hard to be satisfied and not to look for how much better things could be. This was the 'political millenarian' mood inherited from Charlemagne's world.

The sense of agitation has struck modern historians as a crucial feature of the ninth century. Recent studies have highlighted a 'pentitentialism' in which correction was codified and came to govern aspects of high political behaviour.[6] There was a resurgence in the production of vision

[4] M. Gabriele, *An Empire of Memory: The Legend of Charlemagne, the Franks, and Jerusalem before the First Crusade* (Oxford, 2011), esp. ch. 1; A. Latowsky, *Emperor of the World: Charlemagne and the Construction of Imperial Authority, 800–1225* (Ithaca, NY, 2013).
[5] Hrabanus Maurus, *Expositio in Mattaeum*, VII (24), ed. B. Löfstedt, CCCM, 174A (Turnhout, 2000), p. 637, drawing on Bede, *In Marci evangelium exposition*, 4, ed. D. Hurst, CCSL, 120 (Turnhout, 1960), p. 590: 'Quando dicit: *Non est vestrum scire*, ostendit quod ipse sciat ... ut semper incerti de adventu judicis, sic quotidie vivant quasi alia die judicandi sint.' See also Hrabanus, *Ennarrationum in epistolas Beati Pauli*, PL, 112, 570 and Hrabanus, *Epistolae*, no. 13, ed. E. Dümmler, MGH Epp., 5 (Berlin, 1899), p. 401. On Hrabanus here, see J. Heil, '"Nos nescientes de hoc velle manere" – "We Wish to Remain Ignorant About This": Timeless End, or: Approaches to Reconceptualising Eschatology after AD 800 (AM 6000)', *Traditio*, 55 (2000), 73–103 at pp. 86–9. See also amongst Hrabanus's contemporaries Christian of Stablo-Malmedy, *Expositio super Librum Generationis*, c. 24, ed. R. B. C. Huygens, CCCM, 224 (Turnhout, 2008), p. 445 and Paschasius Radbertus, *Expositio in Matthaeo*, XII (24), ed. B. Paulus, CCCM, 56B (Turnhout, 1984), p. 1195 and Sedulius Scotus, *In evangelium Matthaei*, IV (24), ed. B. Löfstedt, Aus der Geschichte der lateinischen Bibel, 19 (Freiburg, 1991), p. 539.
[6] M. de Jong, *The Penitential State: Authority and Atonement in the Age of Louis the Pious, 814–840* (Cambridge, 2009); A. Firey, *A Contrite Heart: Prosecution and Redemption in the Carolingian Empire* (Leiden, 2009).

literature, some of which seemed designed to critique royal actions.[7] Regulation of the Church and a veneration of Benedictine monastic discipline continued, which in the process redrew the relationship between religious and lay communities.[8] At the same time, Frankish unity was undermined by conflict between the brothers Lothar, Louis the German and Charles the Bald in the 830s and 840s – a situation exacerbated, at least in the historical imagination, by the successes of the Vikings against the Franks (and English).[9] Whether the empire 'collapsed' into natural regions in response to this situation, historians now doubt, favouring a model in which all parties concerned negotiated their way into contingent new power and economic structures.[10] The combination of the new moral critique and the end of the Carolingian experiment with unified authority gave the impression of a Christian world mobilised, anxious and excited. Diffused apocalyptic tension such as Hrabanus's was rarely far away.

This is, in many ways, to propose that an events-based eschatology dominated ninth-century apocalyptic imaginations. The best account of this phase of Carolingian apocalyptic thought, by Johannes Heil, frames matters very much as a response to the Y6K 'failed prophecy', with clerics attempting to 'minimize the meaning of time' at the same time that they adopted AD dates and the lower Iro-Bedan AM reckoning.[11] But, as we saw at the end of Chapter 5, this can make too much of Y6K and not enough of psychological imminence and imperial apocalyptic. We can agree that prediction continued to be condemned because we have the (solitary) case of the 'pseudo-prophetess' Thiota in Hrabanus's Mainz: she predicted the imminent end of the world in 847 and was publicly flogged for her efforts (and, apparently, her admission of fraud)

[7] W. Levison, 'Die Politik in den Jenseitsvisionen des frühen Mittelalter', in his *Aus rheinischer und fränkischer Frühzeit* (Düsseldorf, 1948), pp. 229–46; Dutton, *The Politics of Dreaming*.
[8] R. McKitterick, *The Frankish Church and the Carolingian Reforms, 789–895* (London, 1977); M. de Jong, 'Carolingian Monasticism: The Power of Prayer', in R. McKitterick (ed.), *The New Cambridge Medieval History* II (Cambridge, 1995), pp. 622–53; J. Raaijmakers, *The Making of the Monastic Community of Fulda, c. 744–c. 900* (Cambridge, 2012).
[9] J. L. Nelson, *Charles the Bald* (London, 1992); W. Hartmann, *Ludwig der Deutsche* (Darmstadt, 2002); E. J. Goldberg, *Struggle for Empire: Kingship and Conflict under Louis the German, 817–876* (Ithaca, NY, 2006). For a good survey of the whole period see M. Costambeys, M. Innes and S. MacLean, *The Carolingian World* (Cambridge, 2011).
[10] S. Airlie, 'After Empire: Recent Work on the Emergence of Post-Carolingian Kingdoms', *Early Medieval Europe*, 2.2 (1993), 153–61; S. MacLean, *Kingship and Politics in the Late Ninth Century: Charles the Fat and the End of the Carolingian Empire* (Cambridge, 2003); S. Robbie, 'The Emergence of Regional Politics in Burgundy and Alemannia, c. 888–940: A Comparative Assessment', unpublished PhD thesis, University of St Andrews, 2012.
[11] Heil, 'Timeless End', p. 103.

after proving rather too popular amongst both anxious plebs and those in sacred orders.[12] Her condemnation was clearly an act of suppression yet, as with earlier attacks on charismatics, we should not assume the persecutor (here, Hrabanus) was 'anti-apocalyptic' rather than 'differently apocalyptic' since we have just seen him urging watchfulness. Definitions of the apocalyptic need to be reconsidered so that we can move beyond people being simply 'for' or 'against', because apocalypse was more than just about predicting dates. In what follows, we will need to understand the powerful combination of socio-political crisis and a heightened textualisation of the world in relation to scripture, in order to assess the role of apocalyptic thought in its broadest terms in the ninth century.

Accumulated apocalypticisms

Before we continue, it is necessary to stress a much overlooked point: we are moving to a point in intellectual history when libraries were archiving a vast array of texts which were not all strictly 'orthodox'. Modern studies of ideas or theology will often stress historical development in terms of the texts that were composed at the time, so a period like the ninth century will be judged strictly on its writers. In terms of apocalyptic tradition this means that scholars concentrate on gloomy annalists and biblical exegetes (and we will too, later). But we should not forget that libraries contained many of the texts we have encountered in previous chapters and indeed new copies were being produced on a regular basis. Augustine was copied many times over, but so too were the works of Orosius and Quodvultdeus which offered different takes on Augustine's ideas. Scribes copied and adapted the apocalyptic narrative of Pseudo-Methodius and added the millenarian treatise of Hilarianus to the Fredegar chronicles. And, of course, many of the more polemical texts by Augustine, Jerome or Bede actively delineated both their views and the views of their opponents, preserving multiple sides to debate. Carolingian libraries attest not necessarily to the suppression of certain kinds of apocalyptic thought, but often rather to the preservation of the different, the outdated and the potentially useful as part of a wider programme of vigilance and intellectual vigour.

Setting out the proof for this argument is complicated by the poor survival rates for manuscripts but it can be done for some centres. At the same

---

[12] *Annales Fuldenses*, s.a. 847, ed. F. Kurze, MGH SRG, 7 (Hanover, 1891), p. 37. Dutton, *Politics of Dreaming*, pp. 127–8; R. Landes, *Heaven on Earth: The Varieties of Millennial Experience* (Oxford, 2011), pp. 37–46; J. L. Nelson, 'Women and the Word in the Middle Ages', in her *The Frankish World 750–900* (London, 1996), pp. 199–222 at pp. 217–18.

time, it must also be true that different centres had different resources, so we should not treat one example as 'exemplary'. Below I provide just one partial list from the most extreme example, the library of St Gall, which housed many different apocalyptic and eschatological voices:

A selection of different eschatologies in St Gall in the ninth century[13]
Cosmography of Aethicus Ister (St Gall, Stiftsbibliothek, Cod. Sang. 133, *c.* 800)
Augustine, *On the City of God* (St Gall, Stiftsbibliothek, Cod. Sang. 178, *c.* 850)
Bede, *Commentary on Revelation* (St Gall, Stiftsbibliothek, Cod. Sang. 259, late s. viii or early s. ix)
Bede, *On the Reckoning of Time* (St Gall, Stiftsbibliothek, Cod. Sang. 248, from Laon, mid s. ix but then moved to St Gall)
Fredegar Chronicles including Hilarianus's *On the Duration of the World* (Leiden, Universitatsbibliothek, Voss. lat. Q. 5 and continued in BAV Reg. lat. 713, early s. ix)
Gregory the Great, *Dialogues* (St Gall, Stiftsbibliothek, Cod. Sang. 214 plus fragments, written in Northern France late s. viii but then moved to St Gall)
Gregory the Great, *Homilies on the Gospels* (St Gall, Stiftsbibliothek, Cod. Sang. 221, early s. ix)
Jerome, *On Ezekiel* (St Gall, Stiftsbibliothek, Cod. Sang. 117+118, between 820 and 830)
Orosius, *Seven Books of History against the Pagans* (St Gall, Stiftsbibliothek, Cod. Sang. 621, late s. ix)
Pseudo-Methodius (St Gall, Stiftsbibliothek, Cod. Sang. 225, late s. viii)
Quodvultdeus, *The Book of Promises* (St Gall, Stiftsbibliothek, Cod. Sang. 185, late s. viii)
See also various collections of visionary material, discussed below pp. 170–2.

These texts, as mentioned, cover a wide spectrum of thought from the radical to the conservative. The best interpretation is likely that the monks in St Gall were avid collectors of material regardless of its position relative to orthodoxy. It was all material for contemplation. This is a view which complicates, without necessarily contradicting, arguments about the 'Augustinian' tendencies of Carolingian intellectual life. Other centres might point in other directions: Corbie and Bobbio had similarly wide-ranging collections, for examples, but Auxerre, Cologne and Würzburg seem to have been more conservative. As we proceed, then, it will be necessary bear in mind the importance of local resources and attitudes.

The new empire

The Carolingian Empire changed dramatically in the decades after Charlemagne. Expansion had slowed and consolidation had begun

---

[13] Information and facsimiles of all these manuscripts can be found on either or both of www.stgallplan.org and www.e-codices.ch

already in Charlemagne's last days, but such processes were more pronounced under Louis the Pious.[14] Imperially supported efforts to convert Denmark were fitful and ultimately aborted, in contrast to the sustained campaigning in Saxony in the 770s–790s. Louis also signalled a new higher sense of Christian morality when he ejected his 'naughty sisters' from court, destroyed Charlemagne's copies of heroic verse, and supported Benedict of Aniane's refresh of Benedictine discipline.[15] Political realities upset any idealism, however, with Louis's sons Lothar and Louis openly rebelling against their father in the 830s over inheritance, in a conflict which spilled over into civil war against the sons' half-brother Charles the Bald on their father's death. In 843 the empire was divided into three kingdoms in the Treaty of Verdun with Lothar remaining emperor, at least nominally, over the whole. The brothers continued to compete and squabble, leaving the ideals of unity and morality undermined by the reality of division and unpopular rule. After Lothar's death in 855 and the division of his kingdom into two further parts, one chronicler in Cologne commented: 'As the prophet says: because of the sins of the land, many are its rulers [Prov. 28.2]. And at that time four kings were reigning in Charlemagne's former empire.'[16]

Reading the rich annalistic accounts of the period, it seems that this was part of a return to Gregory of Tours's world of civil war framed by natural disasters. Harsh winters and stormy, wet summers drew considerable comment.[17] Famine and disease were rarely far behind. Comets, eclipses and strange shapes were seen in the sky, while earthquakes brought disaster. In Germany, wolves grew as a problem, and in 873 the whole of Europe was beset by a plague of locusts. The response of many was surprisingly bloody-minded. When the Adriatic froze over in the winter of 859–60, for instance, merchants used it as an opportunity to get to Venice without paying for boats.[18] People ploughed on. Not everyone was as indifferent to the possible portentousness of the natural world

---

[14] T. Reuter, 'The End of Carolingian Military Expansion', in P. Godman and R. Collins (eds.), *Charlemagne's Heir: New Perspectives on the Reign of Louis the Pious (814–840)* (Oxford, 1990), pp. 391–405, a paper conceived alongside his 'Plunder and Tribute in the Carolingian Empire', *TRHS*, 5th series, 35 (1985), 75–94.

[15] Nithard, *Libri historiarum IIII*, I. 2, ed. G. Pertz, MGH SRG, 44 (Hanover, 1907) p. 2; Thegan, *Vita Hludowici*, c. 19, ed. E. Tremp, MGH SRG, 64 (Hanover, 1995), pp. 200–2; Astronomer, *Vita Hludowici*, c. 23, ed. Tremp, MGH SRG, 64, p. 352.

[16] *Annales Xantenenses*, s.a. 869(868), ed. B. von Simon, MGH SRM (Hanover and Leipzig, 1909), pp. 26–7: 'eo tempore, ut propheta ait: propter peccata terrae multi principes eius (Prov. 28.2), quattuor reges regnaverunt in regno quondam Karoli Magni.'

[17] M. McCormick, P. E. Dutton and P. A. Mayewski, 'Volcanoes and the Climate Forcing of Carolingian Europe, AD 750–950', *Speculum*, 82.4 (2007), 865–95.

[18] *Annales Fuldenses*, s.a. 860, p. 54.

as Charlemagne had been; Louis the Pious, upon observing a moving star in February 837, was moved to pray and give alms lest it be a sign of his impending death.[19] But, as with Gregory of Tours's writings, most historians who recorded signs did not explain them. The report on the freezing of the Adriatic (and associated blood-red snow) led into a notice on a peace treaty between the three Carolingian kings in the *Annales Fuldenses* but there was no explicit indication whether this was supposed to be a meaningful juxtaposition, although one could infer this by the narrative structure. We, like any medieval audience for these texts, are left with a degree of uncertainty concerning interpretation to match the instability of events.

The emendation of the Church stood throughout as a calculated exercise in striving for unity against the uncertainty of the world. At a general council in the imperial complex at Aachen in 819, Louis the Pious, 'divinely ordained emperor', set out a vision of his Holy Church peregrinating away from God, awaiting Judgement, but moved to make good for a time of peace.[20] Proclamations such as this lacked a definite sense of imminence beyond the brevity of life itself, yet drew extensively on the apocalyptic repertoire with its references to collective responsibility for correction, the inevitability of Judgement, the hope for peace, and struggle against the Devil. As under Charlemagne, diversity within unity was more than acceptable.[21] But the simple 'Good vs Evil' dynamic meant that canonists could detect the work of Antichrist in such things as lay interference in monastic discipline, or the *tempora periculosa* in incestuous unions.[22] Canon law here went beyond diagnostic statements because issuing it was itself a penitential act, a constituent action in the policing of the 'penitential state'.[23]

During all this there was a coming together of political discourse and biblical commentary which drove providential and eschatological readings of events. During Louis the Pious's troubles, Hrabanus Maurus – a

[19] Astronomer, *Vita Hludowici*, c. 58, p. 522. The star is often identified with Halley's Comet but the timing and movement seem wrong, making it more likely it was Mercury or a nova – see S. Ashley, 'What Did Louis the Pious See in the Night Sky? A New Interpretation of the Astronomer's Account of Halley's Comet, 837', *EME*, 21.1 (2013), 27–49.
[20] *Capitulare Aquisgranense generale*, ed. G. H. Pertz, MGH Leges, 1 (Hanover, 1835), pp. 204–5.
[21] McKitterick, *The Frankish Church*, p. 207. On some of the difficulties of reform under Louis, see J. Semmler, 'Benedictus II: Una regula, una consuetudo', in W. Lourdaux and D. Verhelst (eds.), *Benedictine Culture, 750–1050* (Louvain, 1983), pp. 1–49.
[22] Synod of Meaux-Paris (845), c. 10, ed. W. Hartmann, MGH Conc., 3 (Hanover, 1984), pp. 89–90; Synod of Douzy (874), ed. W. Hartmann, MGH Conc., 4 (Hanover, 1998), p. 582.
[23] De Jong, *The Penitential State*; Firey, *A Contrite Heart*, esp. p. 88.

former student of Alcuin and, at the time, abbot of Fulda – offered con-
solation and guidance for his emperor by composing a commentary on
the Book of Kings in 832.[24] Further gifts followed, also to Empress Judith,
Lothar and Louis the German, the two kings notably receiving commentaries on the prophets Jeremiah and Daniel as vehicles through which
Hrabanus could emphasise legitimate rule and responsibility in difficult
times. As Mayke de Jong has shown, such gifts added a heightened sense
of spiritual textualisation, as more powerful figures were encouraged to
contemplate the meanings of their actions in relation to scripture. This
meant that Hrabanus's actions were loaded with political resonance,
and indeed the commentary on Daniel he offered to Louis while having
'time out' for having supported Lothar during the civil war of 841–3.
(He was later raised to be archbishop of Mainz and so became one of
Louis's senior bishops.) Biblical exegesis had never been so worldly and
political.

Despite Hrabanus's unfair reputation as an unimaginative and conservative scholar, he was a master of subtlety when it came to turning
his source material to new ends.[25] The resonance of Daniel came mostly
from the situation in which it was issued, because in content his work
was mostly another repackaging of Jerome's with its weak Rome; at the
same time, however, the rearticulation of those words during Carolingian
instability must have stung.[26] Strikingly, Hrabanus urged Louis to consider Daniel alongside his commentary on Maccabees, an apocryphal
book he cast as a history of empire engaged in war and reform.[27] Even
with an ambiguous sense of imminence, Hrabanus did not hold back
from sketching out the apocalyptic struggle the Church faced here. King
Antiochus IV, for example, was described as a type of Antichrist (*typus
Antichristi*) who, through his persecutions of Jews, prefigured the last
enemy – but then, to amplify the contemporary resonance, Hrabanus
brought in the 'many antichrists' and pointed accusatorily at the 'heretics,

[24] M. de Jong, 'The Empire as *ecclesia*: Hrabanus Maurus and Biblical *historia* for Rulers',
in Y. Hen and M. Innes (eds.), *The Uses of the Past in the Early Middle Ages* (Cambridge,
2000), pp. 191–226 at p. 206. The text disseminated widely: https://risd.digication.com/
bvnedwards/Bibliography. On the manuscript traditions more generally see R. Kottje,
'Die handschriftliche Überlieferung der Bibelkommrnentaren des Hrabanus Maurus', in
P. Depreux, S. Lebecq, M. Perrin and O. Szerwiniack (eds.), *Raban Maur et sons temps*
(Turnhout, 2010), pp. 259–74.
[25] R. Kottje, 'Hrabanus Maurus: Praeceptor Germaniae?', *DA*, 31 (1975), 534–45; K.
Zechiel-Eckes, 'Ein Dummkopf und Plagiator? Hrabanus Maurus aus der Sicht des
Diakons Florus von Lyon', in Depreux *et al.*, *Raban Maur et son temps*, pp. 119–35; S.
Shimahara, 'Le *Commentaire sur Daniel* de Raban Maur', in Depreux *et al.*, *Raban Maur
et son temps*, pp. 275–91 at p. 277.
[26] Shimahara, 'Le *Commentaire*', pp. 288–9.
[27] Hrabanus, *Epistolae*, no. 35, p. 470.

schismatics and pagans' of his own day.[28] The 'limbs of Antichrist' (*membra Antichristi*) were a real and present threat to the unity of a Christian empire forged in scripture, and biblical commentaries for kings helped to explain this at the highest level.

We are, of course, only talking about one exegete here, and it is true that much other exegetical work was not as overtly political as this. Nevertheless, one finds no less political resonance in the works of the ninth century's other prolific exegete, Haimo of Auxerre.[29] Following John Contreni's reconstruction of his career, we can see Haimo as an ambitious monk frustrated by the standards around him, and possibly disappointed by the political use of Saint-Germain d'Auxerre by King Charles the Bald which ensured the monk never acquired its abbacy.[30] In his exegesis, Haimo did not work to commission, and he interpreted texts with more freedom than Hrabanus did.[31] On occasion, this freedom allowed him to posit some potentially incendiary thoughts. In his commentary on Ezekiel, for instance, he wrote that 'in our Jerusalem' (*in nostram Hierusalem*), people sinned because they followed the priests (*sacerdotes*) and secular leaders (*principes*).[32] In other words: the Carolingian world was corrupt from the top down. The 'public' for such comments might not always be apparent but we do at least know that Haimo traded books with Duke Conrad I the Elder, the kind of layman who sought books and moral advice from bishops (and who indeed later become lay abbot of St-Germain d'Auxerre).[33] Being monastic in focus did not

---

[28] Hrabanus, *Commentaria in libros Machabaeorum* 1, PL, 109. 1135. See de Jong, 'The Empire as *ecclesia*', p. 223; K. L. Hughes, *Constructing Antichrist: Paul, Biblical Commentary, and the Development of Doctrine in the Early Middle Ages* (Washington, DC, 2005), p. 138.

[29] For a survey of Haimo's work and the problems of identifying it, see D. Iogna-Prat, 'L'oeuvre d'Haymon d'Auxerre. État de la question', in D. Iogna-Prat, J. Colette and G. Lobrichon (eds.), *L'école carolingienne d'Auxerre de Murethach à Remi 830–908* (Paris, 1991), pp. 157–79, esp. 161–2 on the most relevant apocalyptic works. For a detailed study of *In Apocalypsin*, especially how Haimo amplified Ambrosius Autpertus's work, see R. Savigni, 'Il commentario di Aimone all'apocalisse', in R. E. Guglielmetti (ed.), *L'apocalisse nel medioevo* (Florence, 2011), pp. 207–66.

[30] J. Contreni, '"By Lions, Bishops Are Meant; by Wolves, Priests": History, Exegesis, and the Carolingian Church in Haimo of Auxerre's *Commentary on Ezechiel*', *Francia*, 29.1 (2002), 29–56.

[31] S. Shimahara, 'Exégèse et politique dans l'œuvre d'Haymon d'Auxerre', *Revue de l'histoire des religions*, 225.4 (2008), 471–86.

[32] Haimo, *In Ezechielem*, in Paris, Bibliothèque nationale, lat. 12302 (c. 1000), ff. 32v–33r; extract printed in Contreni, 'By Lions, Bishops Are Meant', p. 36 n. 31: 'similiter in nostram Hierusalem, hoc est in aecclesia, maxime aliquando ex culpa sacerdotum et principum pendet peccatum populi qui errorem illorum sequitur.'

[33] Contreni, 'By Lions, Bishops Are Meant', pp. 46–7. Conrad was sent a penitential at his request by Hrabanus Maurus: PL, 110. 467–94. For Conrad's political situation see Nelson, *Charles the Bald*, pp. 177–8.

always mean retreating from the world, because the world was still there to be influenced for the better.

Haimo's popular take on Revelation fitted into this *modus operandi* as he conceptualised society and the Church through the prism of *revelatio*.[34] He drew extensively on the meditations of Ambrosius Autpertus and Bede yet, unlike Bede, he was more concerned for a spiritual reading than a historical one.[35] Ecclesiological interpretation remained front and centre, with John's vision described as 'a prophecy about the state of the present and future Ecclesia'.[36] But whereas his enemies in Ezekiel had been dukes and bishops on the inside, and Northmen, Saracens and Slavs outwith, Haimo adopted a sense of typology more in keeping with Augustinian sensibilities. Repeatedly, general 'heretics, pagans, Jews, and False Christians/brothers' appear in conjunction, playing on the symbolism of the number four.[37] On the Fourth Seal, for example, he wrote (with a clear nod to contemporary politics):

Power is given to them over the four corners of the world, that is over all reprobates, who remain in the four corners of the Earth, namely in the East, West, North and South. Either in the four parts of the Earth we are able to discern the four principal kingdoms, that is of the Assyrians, Chaldeans, Medes and Persians, and Macedonians or Romans; or in the four corners of the Earth, in which the Devil received power, we discern heretics, pagans, Jews and false Christians. Over these four corners of the world, that is the lands of men, the Devil has power through the desired land of the inhabitants, and with this he fights against the one Church of Christ, which he is not able to divide, because it is united by the faith of Christ.[38]

---

[34] Professor van Name Edwards lists 146 manuscripts in his bibliography of Carolingian biblical exegesis: https://risd.digication.com/bvnedwards/Bibliography.

[35] G. Lobrichon, 'Stalking the Signs: The Apocalyptic Commentaries', in A. Gow, R. Landes and D. C. van Meter (eds.), *The Apocalyptic Year 1000: Religious Expectation and Social Changes, 950–1050* (Oxford, 2003), pp. 67–79 at p. 72.

[36] Haimo, *In Apocalypsin*, pref., PL, 117. 937: 'hanc prophetiam de statu praesentis et futurae Ecclesiae'. E. A. Matter, 'The Apocalypse in Early Medieval Exegesis', in R. Emmerson and B. McGinn (eds.), *The Apocalypse in the Middle Ages* (Ithaca, NY, 1993), pp. 38–50 at p. 49.

[37] This combination is absent from his commentary on Paul, although its presence in *In Apocalypsin* complicates the interpretation of J. Heil, 'Labourers in the Lord's Quarry: Carolingian Exegetes, Patristic Authority, and Theological Innovation, a Case Study in the Representation of Jews in Commentaries on Paul', in C. Chazelle and B. van Name Edwards, *The Study of the Bible in the Carolingian Era* (Turnhout, 2003), pp. 75–96 at p. 88.

[38] Haimo, *In Apocalypsin*, II. 6, PL, 117. 1028: 'Data est illi potestas super quatuor partes terrae, id est super omnes reprobos, qui in quatuor partibus terrae morantur, in oriente scilicet, occidente, aquilone et meridie. Vel per quatuor partes terrae, possumus intelligere quatuor regna principalia, Assyriorum videlicet et Chaldaeorum, Medorum et Persarum, Macedonum atque Romanorum. Sive etiam quatuor partes terrae, in quibus potestatem accepit diabolus, intelligamus haereticos, paganos, judaeos et falsos christianos. Super has quatuor partes terrae, id est terrenorum hominum, et per desiderium

In doing this Haimo generated a sense of how the Church was defined against all enemies collectively. Christian society itself he divided into 'priests, soldiers and farmers [*agricultores*]', where Roman society had been divided into 'senators, soldiers and farmers [*agricolae*]' (and in *On Ezekiel* it would be three camps marked for salvation: (1) apostles, evangelists, and holy martyrs, (2) celibates and good canons, and (3) good husbands).[39] Such a way of thinking provided an eschatological sketch of society's functional nature, marking out some of the parameters of salvation. In the process, Haimo exposed 'the gap between the ideal (of public order) and the reality (of political disorder)'.[40]

Living in the shadow of the End provided mixed messages on apocalyptic time for this eschatologically defined community. Writing about Paul's second epistle to the Thessalonians, Haimo of Auxerre warned people not to believe 'any interpreter or handler of the prophets' (*explanator et tractator prophetiarum*) who said that Judgement was imminent. But where some people have seen this as a classic anti-apocalyptic statement, it is worth noting that the warning only really covers Old Testament texts.[41] On Rev. 20.2 he began in a familiar Augustinian register: '[A thousand], on account of its perfection, is the whole of this present time, that is, from the Lord's Passion up to the end of the world, and this whole stands for the part.' 'Good Augustinians' would then be surprised to read 'because a thousand years are the amount squeezed into the time of Ecclesia, that is, up to the reign of Antichrist'.[42] Lobrichon saw here an element of 'repression or, rather, censure' because of the way that Haimo seemed to refuse to make explicit the apocalyptic implications of his statement, namely that Antichrist would come a millennium after Christ's ministry.[43] Certainly elsewhere Haimo preferred to play with

---

terram inhabitantium habet potestatem diabolus, et cum his contra unam Christi pugnat Ecclesiam, quam ideo scindere non potest, quia fide Christi est unita.'

[39] PL, 117. 953. *In Ezechielem* – Contreni, 'By Lions, Bishops are Meant', p. 34 n. 23. For the importance of Haimo's thoughts here, especially as a spiritual precursor to the later 'Three Orders', see D. Iogna-Prat, 'Le "baptême" du schéma des trois ordres fonctionnels. L'apport de l'école d'Auxerre dans la second moitié du IXe siècle', *Annales. économies, sociétés, civilisations*, 41.1 (1986), 101–26 and E. Ortigues, 'Haymon d'Auxerre, théoricien des trois ordres', in Lobrichon (ed.), *L'école carolingienne d'Auxerre*, pp. 181–215.

[40] G. Lobrichon, 'L'ordre de ce temps et les désordres de la fin. Apocalypse et société, du IXe à la fin du XIe siècle', in W. Verbeke, D. Verhelst and A. Welkenhuysen (eds.), *The Use and Abuse of Eschatology in the Middle Ages* (Leuven, 1988), pp. 221–41 at p. 233. See also Savigni, 'Il commentario', pp. 265–6.

[41] Cf Heil, 'Timeless End', p. 92.

[42] Haimo, *In Apocalypsin*, PL, 117. 1182: 'propter sui perfectionem omne significat tempus hoc praesens, a Domini scilicet passione usque ad finem saeculi, et hic totum pro parte positum est, quia mille anni quantumlibet tempus Ecclesiae exprimunt, id est usque ad regnum Antichristi.'

[43] Lobrichon, 'Stalking the Signs', p. 74.

the spiritual resonance of numbers rather than dabble in the arts of prediction. On 666, the Number of the Beast (Rev. 13.18), for example, he explained how God created the world in six days, there are six world ages, and so it stands for all time 'and it shows the wickedness of the Devil's fraud and the final end of the world'.[44] Concepts of time here were not being minimised (remembering Heil's thesis) but rather remained a treasure house of potential and multiple meanings.

His views on society and time set the scene for one of his most famous contributions to apocalyptic thought: an explanation of how the *discessio* promised by Paul (2 Thess. 2.3) had already happened and that Rome had indeed fallen. He wrote: 'The Lord will not come for Judgement before the defection of the human kingdoms – which we already see fulfilled – and the appearance in the world of Antichrist, who will kill the witnesses of Christ.'[45] Daniel Verhelst misunderstood Haimo on the basis of other statements as believing that Rome endured still; and indeed Adso, in the tenth century, decided to understand him this way.[46] But Hughes has argued that in the above quotation it is clear that Haimo drew a distinction between the Rome-still-to-fall of Paul's day and the fallen-Rome of his own.[47] This meant that, as Notker suggested too, Charlemagne's kingdom was *after* Daniel's sequence of four, which meant that the only remaining thing to come to pass was the coming of Antichrist, much as he would have known from reading Bede's non-imperial apocalyptic thoughts anyway. Since Haimo took inspiration from Pseudo-Methodius in his description of Antichrist, we can also see a rejection of the sermon's imperial eschatology here. The fate of empires was not going to determine anything about the timing of the End – all that was left was to prepare for final struggles and Judgement, whenever they might come.

One clear effect of this situation, as Levison and Dutton have argued, was a return to the moral revelation of visionary literature in order to articulate anxiety about the morality of political order.[48] Many took their

[44] Haimo, *In Apocalypsin*, PL, 117.1104: 'et diabolicae fraudis nequitiam, et finalem saeculi terminum ostendit.' There are also hints at earlier debates on the nature of eternity, when Haimo explained that time would not end so much as cease to change (Rev. 10.6) PL, 117.1064.
[45] Haimo of Auxerre, *In epistolam II ad Thessalonicenses*, 2, PL, 117.780: 'non prius venturum Dominum ad judicium, qui regni humani defectio fieret, quod iam nos impletum videmus, et Antichristum apparere in mundo qui interficiet Christi martyres' (trans. Hughes, *Constructing Antichrist*, p. 156).
[46] D. Verhelst, 'La préhistoire des conceptions d'Adson concernant l'Antichrist', *Recherches de théologie ancienne et médiévale*, 40 (1973), 52–103 at pp. 89–90. See also Heil, 'Timeless End', p. 94.
[47] Hughes, *Constructing Antichrist*, pp. 155–7.
[48] Levison, 'Die Politik', p. 245; Dutton, *The Politics of Dreaming*, p. 49. De Jong, *The Penitential State*, pp. 136–41 argues that this goes too far because the dreams are about collective responsibility for reform.

cues from tours of the afterlife, and indeed it is perhaps no coincidence that this is the period in which the manuscript tradition of the *Vision of St Paul* starts to take off.[49] The earliest 'dreams' featured Charlemagne being punished – in two, with his private parts being gnawed by animals as a symbol of his sexual excess.[50] The surprise revelation of finding such a great figure in torment was balanced by the emperor's predestined place in Heaven once he had completed his torments. Prayers for the dead were essential and indeed, in the *Vision of the Poor Woman of Laon*, Charlemagne's salvation was guaranteed if Louis the Pious provided seven memorial services – although Louis's status was far from assured on account of the scandalous manslaughter of his illegitimate nephew, Bernard of Italy.[51] The fate of the souls of figures living and dead were in danger, and action was required. The Gregorian *Dialogues* and similar works had begun to fashion a new mode of penitential political discourse unthinkable in the early sixth century.

The Alemannic manuscripts of these texts point towards an intersection of the visionary, the admonitory and the apocalyptic. In the earliest, Heito's *Vision of Wetti* and the Laon vision were paired together alongside Gregory's *Moralia in Job* (XXXI. xlv.87–90) on vices, picking up on a thematic unit in an earlier section of the manuscript which contained extracts on virtues and vices, the Caesarian-Augustinian sermon *On Judgement Day*, and the Visigothic *On the Seven Seals*.[52] Across Lake Constance in St Gall a similar approach to thematic compiling was observed with the same pair of visions plus the *Vision of Barontus* and Bede's *On Judgement Day*.[53] Similar compilations from the same region, it seems, have been

[49] L. Jiroušková, *Die Visio Pauli. Wege und Wandlungen einer orientalischen Apokryphe im lateinischen Mittelalter* (Leiden, 2006). Paris, Bibliothèque nationale, nouv. acq. lat. 1631 (Fleury, s. ix); St Gall, Kantonsbibliothek, VadSlg 317 (probably St Gall, s. ix²). There are also two full ninth-century witnesses to 'Redaction VI': Biblioteca Apostolica Vaticana, Pal. lat. 220 (Middle or Upper Rhineland, Lorsch provenance, s. ix); St Gall, Stiftsbibliothek, Cod. Sang. 682 (probably St Gall, s. ix¹).

[50] Heito, *Visio Wettini*, c. 11, ed. R. Pollard, p. 14 (http://sites.google.com/site/visiowet-tini/home/files). The name is given away in Walahfrid Strabo's poetic *Visio Wettini*, lines 446–65, ed. E. Dümmler, MGH Poetae, 2, pp. 318–19. See also *Visio Rotcharii*, ed. W. Wattenbach, 'Aus Petersburger Handschriften', *Anzeiger für Kunde der deutschen Vorzeit*, 22 (1875), 72–4 at p. 73, which rehabilitates Charlemagne in this context (C. Carozzi, *Le voyage de l'âme dans l'Au-delà d'après la littérature latine (Ve-VIIIe siècle)* [Rome, 1994], pp. 341–6).

[51] *Visio cuiusdam pauperculae mulieris*, ed. H. Houben, in *Zeitschrift für die Geschichte des Oberrheins*, 124, n.f. 85 (1976), 41–2.

[52] Karlsruhe, Badische Landesbibliothek, Aug. perg. 111 (Reichenau, s. ix¹). Caesarius, *Sermo*, no. 39, ed. G. Morin, CCSL, 103 (Turnhout, 1953), pp. 172–7; E. A. Matter, 'The Pseudo-Alcuinian *De septem sigillis*: An Early Latin Apocalypse Exegesis', *Traditio*, 36 (1980), 111–37. But note that no such 'apocalyptic logic' is evident in the Reichenau miscellany Zurich, Zentralbibliothek, Rh. Hist. 28 (Reichenau, late s. ix).

[53] St Gall, Stiftsbibliothek, Cod. Sang. 573 (late s. ix or early s. x).

lost, so these examples are just suggestive.[54] At St Gall we also find, suggestively, a shortened version of the *Vision of St Paul* copied in the middle of the collection of sermons, suggesting that sometimes this kind of material was intended to arm preachers.[55] When we add back in the actual composition of visionary texts at Reichenau too, alongside the compilation of a grand *liber vitae* listing people for intercessory prayer (see Dan. 12.1), it starts to mark the area out as having an unusually pronounced interest in collecting and archiving material on 'Last Things' as part of guiding the Christian community at large towards salvation.[56]

Such strategies may have had real effects on political behaviour. Despite the geographical detachment of the region, there were close and persistent connections with court. Heito specifically was a significant figure in the spiritual life of the Frankish court and his concerns for family solidarity and morality, reflected in the visions, could easily have been heard.[57] Louis, after a series of arguments about the nature of his office and the death of his key advisor, suddenly decided to undertake penance in 822 for his treatment, and one wonders if he had been aware of texts (or stories) such as that of the Laon woman.[58] Not that his sincerity was believed, and indeed the crime was thrown back at him in October 833 after revolts by his sons Pippin and Lothar.[59] Archbishop Agobard of Lyon had already, that Easter, defended Pope Gregory IV's opposition to him in a warning which built up to a Gregorian apocalyptic conclusion:

Deign to weigh, Your Prudence, what the Apostle said: 'In the Last Days, perilous times will come' (2 Tim. 3.1). These perils the blessed Pope Gregory [I] deplored in his own time, when the situation was then better than it is now … Alas! Alas! If then the ship of Ecclesia was rotten … what is it now?[60]

[54] Similar coherent collections because widespread – see examples discussed in P. Sims-Williams, 'A Recension of Boniface's Letter to Eadburg about the Monk of Wenlock's vision', in K. O'Brien O'Keefe and A. Orchard (eds.), *Latin Learning and English Lore: Studies in Anglo-Saxon Literature for Michael Lapidge* (Toronto, 2005), I. 194–214.
[55] St Gall, Stiftsbibliothek, Cod. Sang. 682, pp. 193–204; ed. T. Silverstein, *Vita sancti Pauli* (London, 1935), pp. 215–18.
[56] K. Schmid, 'Bemerkungen zur Anlage des Reichenauer Verbrüderungsbuches: Zugleich ein Beitrag zum Verständnis der 'Visio Wettini'', in his *Gebetsgedenken und adliges Selbstverständnis* (Stuttgart, 1977), pp. 514–31.
[57] Carozzi, *Le voyage*, pp. 322–3 and 340–1.
[58] Agobard of Lyon, *De dispensatione ecclesiarum rerum*, ed. L. van Acker, CCCM, 52 (Turnhout, 1981), pp. 119–22; *Annales regni Francorum*, s.a. 822, ed. Kurze, MGH SRG, 6, p. 158; *Annales Fuldenses*, s.a. 822, p. 22 (Louis with the counsel of all); de Jong, *The Penitential State*, pp. 28–9. On representations of the struggle see also P. Buc, 'Ritual and Interpretation: The Early Medieval Case', *EME*, 9.2 (2000), 190–1.
[59] MGH Cap., 2, no. 197, c. 1, p. 54; Paschasius Radbertus, *Vita Adalhardi*, c. 51, PL, 120. 1535; de Jong, *The Penitential State*, pp. 128–9.
[60] Agobard of Lyon, *De privilegio apostolicae sedis*, c. 6, ed. van Acker, CCCM, 52, p. 305: 'Dignetur sublimis prudentia vestra pie perpendere quod apostolus dicit: in novissimis diebus instabant tempora periculosa. Quae pericula beatus papa Gregorius suo iam

Carolingian kingship was being subjected to the old critiques as well as the new visionary ones.

One consequence of this kind of thinking was a particular eschatology which focussed on the Carolingian line itself. This is best represented by the *Visio Karoli Magni*, a late ninth-century text from Mainz, albeit one which circulated little, about a vision purportedly witnessed by Charlemagne himself in which he saw a sword inscribed with four Germanic words – *raht, radoleiba, nasg* and *enti*, resonating deeply with Daniel's providential 'writing on the wall' (5.25). These words the emperor and courtiers interpreted as symbolising, in order, a shift from days of abundance, to the end of abundance, to a time of confusion, and finally to some kind of end.[61] The nature of this ending is left open by the report: 'it is possible to understand this in two ways', states visionary-Charlemagne, 'either it will mean the end of the world or the end of our line, that is, that none of our descendants will thereafter rule over the Frankish people.'[62] The worry for the author in his own days was *nasg*, as he considered the Carolingian kings to have neglected their kingdoms so much, that even the pope decried that 'the holy Roman church, its patron and people are generally wounded, ripped apart, reviled, humiliated and annihilated'.[63] This is, of course, closely related to the views of the Cologne annalist we encountered earlier, and similar negative assessments of the divisions and *bellum civile* were provided by Audradus of Sens and Christian of Stavelot-Malmedy.[64] The trajectory of empire seemed pregnant with meaning again.

Louis the German, at least, may have been in tune with the ongoing mood. As we have seen, he was symbolically sent a commentary on Daniel by Hrabanus Maurus early on in his reign. In 874 he was also said to have had a vision of his father suffering from torments (*tormenta*) in

tempore, quando adhuc status idem multo et inconparabiliter melior erat quam nunc, ita deplorat … Heu heu, is tunc iam putrescebat navis Ecclesiae … quid nunc est?'
[61] P. Geary, 'German Tradition and Royal Ideology in the Ninth Century: The *Visio Karoli Magni*', in his *Living with the Dead in the Middle Ages* (Princeton, NJ, 1994), pp. 49–76 (with edition of text, pp. 74–6). On the Danielian resonances see Dutton, *The Politics of Dreaming*, pp. 202–6.
[62] *Visio Karoli Magni*, ed. Geary, p. 75: '[Enti] duobus modis intellegi potest: Aut enim finish seculi tunc erit aut stirpis nostrę; scilicet quod nullus de progenie nostra deinceps in gente Francorum regnaturus sit.'
[63] 'Sancta Romana aecclesia suusque patronus et populus generaliter sauciatur, diripitur, discerpitur, humiliatur, adnichilatur.' The letter of the pope was said to have been available in the archive of St Martin's, Mainz.
[64] Christian of Stablo-Malmedy, *Expositio super Librum Generationis*, c. 9 (on Matt. 9.34), pp. 211–12; Audradus Modicus, *Liber revelationum*, II and XI, ed. L. Traube, *Abhandlungen der philosophisch-philologischen Classe der königlich Bayerischen Akademie der Wissenschaften*, 19 (1892), 379 and 383–5. For a detailed analysis of Audradus, see Dutton, *The Politics of Dreaming*, pp. 128–56.

death which moved him to order intercessory prayers for him.[65] His personal library included an Old High German poem called *Muspilli*, about the fate of the soul and the destruction of the world. The poet recalled in particular how he had heard from the worldly-wise (*wërolt-rëhtwîs*) of the fight between Antichrist and Elijah to come, setting the scene for the Last Judgement itself and a warning that no sin can be concealed.[66] The poem is transmitted in only one manuscript, written in an 'inexpert' hand in space at the end of a copy of Quodvultdeus's *Sermon on the Creed against Jews, Pagans and Arians* around a dedication from Archbishop Adalramn of Salzburg to Louis in his youth.[67] As an addition, the poem shows not the workings of an organised scriptorium, but more likely the active use of the manuscript at court, possibly by Louis himself.[68] Quodvultdeus's sermon itself is relevant (but over-looked) context, as it deals with the pressures of office against the forces of the Devil, and even includes a version of the *Sibylline Prophecy* in which the world is also destroyed by fire but here interpreted as a metaphor for Christ's resurrection.[69] For Louis, this speaks volumes about the way in which a Carolingian king was encouraged to reflect upon his piety and actions, and not least in this case because Louis was a king with duties to protect Christendom and its moral fibre from the threats of non-Christian neighbours.

The visuality of divine and earthly order gave renewed voice to representations of power too. Charles the Bald, Louis's half-brother rival and in his name a clear heir of Charlemagne, favoured this more than most. His first Bible (the Vivian Bible) ended with an image of him enthroned, surrounded by his court, with the hand of God (*dextra Dei*) reaching down from above – some of which imagery would be repeated in his Psalter where, as he looked across at Jerome, he was described as being 'like Josiah and Theodosius [I] in equal measure'.[70] In his sacramentary his power was allegorised as a *dextra dei* reached down from Heaven with a crown and the king stood flanked by saints, followed by images including two images of

[65] *Annales Fuldenses*, s.a. 874, p. 82.
[66] Goldberg, *Struggle for Empire*, p. 37, draws the comparison with Carolingian legislation.
[67] Munich, Bayerische Staatsbibliothek, Clm 14098, ff. 119v–121v (with the dedication on 120r), text edited in W. Braun, *Althochdeutsches Lesebuch* (16th edn, Tübingen, 1979), pp. 86–9.
[68] B. Bischoff, 'Bücher am Hofe Ludwigs des Deutschen und die Privatbibliothek des Kanzlers Grimalt', in his *Mittelalterliche Studien*, III (Stuttgart, 1981), pp. 187–215 at p. 188, suggesting 'at court'; D. Geuenich, 'Die volksprachliche Überlieferung der Karolingerzeit aus der Sicht des Historikers', *DA*, 39 (1983), 104–30 at p. 129; and Goldberg, *Struggle for Empire*, p. 37, suggesting Louis.
[69] Quodvultdeus, *Contra Iudaeos, paganos et Arianos*, ed. R. Braun, CCSL, 60 (Turnhout, 1976), pp. 227–58; Munich, Bayerische Staatsbibliothek, Clm 14098, ff. 102r–103r.
[70] Paris, Bibliothèque nationale, lat. 1, f. 423r; Paris, Bibliothèque nationale, lat. 1152, f. 3v–4r.

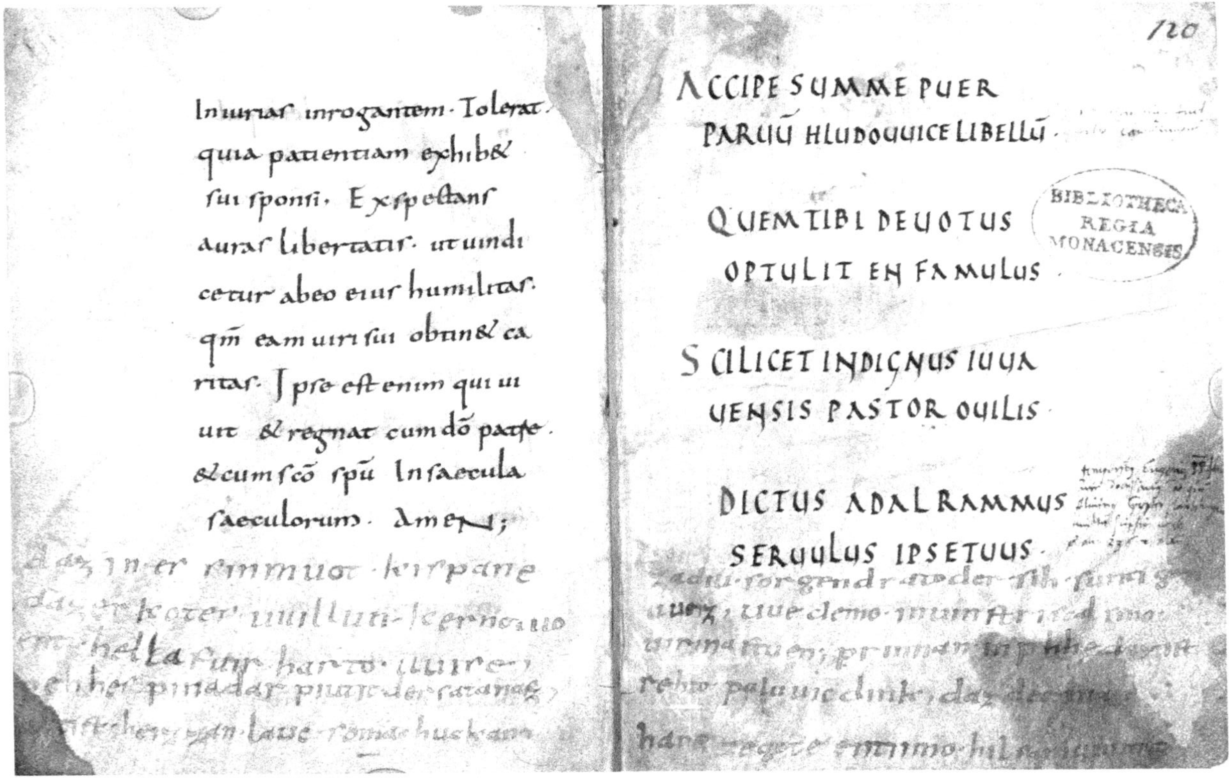
120
ACCIPE SUMME PUER
PARUU HLUDOUUICE LIBELLU
QUEM TIBI DEUOTUS
OPTULIT EN FAMULUS
SCILICET INDIGNUS IUUA
UENSIS PASTOR OUILIS
DICTUS ADALRAMMUS
SERUULUS IPSE TUUS
BIBLIOTHECA REGIA MONACENSIS

Figure 4 The Old High German *Muspilli*, copied into space in a manuscript belonging to King Louis the German.

the *maiestas Domini* and a celestial court, leaving no ambiguity of eschatological resonance.[71] Kingship was part of the spiritual fabric of the world. How tantalising, then, that his Bible contained an illustration of Revelation which presented the Seven Seals and the four evangelists, but with a depiction of the *rex regum* (Rev. 19.11–13) at the top where an earlier version of the same allegorical scheme had not.[72] It was an image entirely relevant to a court which sought to textualise and interpret kingship in relation to the Bible and reminded the reader that it was part of eschatological struggle. At the same time, it shows Charles's self-perceived strength in this narrative in contrast to his half-brother's anxiety.

Perhaps the most remarkable feature of the Carolingian order of things was how little any of the apocalyptic critiques and posturing had any noticeable effect on the end of the empire itself. After the long and action-packed reigns of Charles and Louis, there was a high turnover of rulers for twenty years – a 'slapstick mortality' which ended with the deposition of the much-maligned Charles the Fat and the five-fold division of the empire under non- or illegitimate Carolingians.[73] One Bavarian chronicler dismissed the new rulers as 'kinglets' (*reguli*) while, despite being positive in tone, the West Saxon court in southern England recorded the division as a counterpoint to its own growing unity and strength.[74] The Carolingians rallied in West Frankia under Charles the Straightforward (r. 898–923) but the empire as a going concern had gone. And yet no one proclaimed anxiety or hope at what this might mean about what little time there was left. Not for the first time, dark voices and predictions were made to look as if they were features of Golden Ages, of communities in strength, rather than a sign of the world undone.

Outsiders of the End Times

As Haimo's assessment of the Fourth Seal suggested, part of the problem with the Golden Age of Empire was that the Christian community

---

[71] Paris, Bibliothèque nationale, lat. 1141, f. 2v. On the eschatological symbolism of the *maiestas Domini*, see B. Kühnel, *The End of Time in the Order of Things* (Regensburg, 2003).

[72] Paris, Bibliothèque nationale, lat. 1, f. 415v – a similar character, if more ready for combat, to Valenciennes, Bibliothèque nationale, MS 99, f. 35r, clearly labelled *rex regum*. Compare London, British Library, Add. 10546, f. 449r (the Grandval-Moutier Bible, also produced in Tours). The image also bears an uncanny resemblance to the famous statuette of Charles on horseback in the Louvre.

[73] Costambeys *et al.*, *The Carolingian World*, p. 422.

[74] *Annales Fuldenses, continuatio Ratisbonensis*, s.a. 888, p. 116; *Anglo-Saxon Chronicle* (A), s.a. 887, ed. J. Bately (Woodbridge, 1986), p. 53; Asser, *Vita Alfredi*, c. 85, ed. W. H. Stevenson (London, 1904), pp. 71–2. See also Regino of Prüm, *Chronicon*, s.a. 888, ed. F. Kurze, MGH SRM, 50 (Hanover, 1890), p. 129, where the author blames division on competition and the inability of any one king to dominate.

Figure 5 Revelation in the Vivian Bible of King Charles the Bald.

was beset on all sides by its enemies. Worse still, many military and cultural clashes with these groups fed into apocalyptic disquiet.[75] In the 840s Agnellus of Ravenna, for example, cast Charlemagne's empire as a 'Frankish Rome', torn apart by a catalogue of biblical apocalyptic signs, with assaults of the Arabs on the coasts of Italy a key indicator of crisis.[76] Yet, elsewhere, it was Scandinavians in particular who stimulated apocalyptic reflection. First, they were pagan Viking raiders from the north with a particularly good track record at getting the better of rich Christians to the south, and so the prophecies of Joel, Ezekiel, Jeremiah and Revelation about providential scourges and Gog and Magog seemed active once more. Secondly, as they were pagans living on the edges of the known world, the Scandinavians invited engagement with the apocalyptic missionary imperative we encountered in Chapters 2 and 3 (Matt. 24.14). Pitched against a Western Christendom so strongly defined by biblical resonances, these apocalyptic outsiders would play a crucial role in changing perceptions of the world.

We need to understand the threat of Vikings in purely political terms first. One of the things which exposed the weaknesses of Christian kings time and time again was the success of (mostly pagan) Viking raids.[77] Louis the Pious and Lothar were embarrassed when, having sought great political capital out of the conversion of King Harald Klak of the Danes, his new ally lost his throne, took Christian lands and turned to piracy, Lothar subsequently giving him land to secure an allegiance.[78] Charles the Bald's strength was questioned after he paid Vikings to go away after they attacked Paris in 845, and forty years later Charles the Fat made the same mistakes in the eyes of contemporaries.[79] Only Louis III scored a decisive victory against any significant Viking attack, in the famous battle of Saucourt in 881 (although even that moment of glory was offset by the king's embarrassing death, racing into a house on a horse after a girl, a few months later).[80] Things were worse still across the Channel, where

---

[75] Some of the context here is discussed in J. T. Palmer, 'Apocalyptic Outsiders and Their Uses in the Early Medieval West' (forthcoming).

[76] Agnellus of Ravenna, *Liber pontificalis ecclesiae Ravennatis*, ed. D. M. Deliyannis, CCCM, 199 (Turnhout, 2006), p. 346; McGinn, 'Eriugena Confronts the End', pp. 6–7, rightly points out that this has nothing to do with Pseudo-Methodius.

[77] S. Coupland, 'From Poachers to Gamekeepers: Scandinavian Warlords and Carolingian Kings', *EME*, 7.1 (1998), 85–114.

[78] *Annales regni Francorum*, s.a. 826, 827, pp. 169–70, p. 173; *Annales Bertiniani*, ed. G. Waitz, MGH SRG, 5 (Hanover, 1883), s.a. 841, p. 26.

[79] *Annales Bertiniani*, s.a. 845, p. 32; *Annales Vedastini*, ed. B. von Simson, MGH SRG, 12 (Hanover and Leipzig, 1909), s.a. 887, p. 63 (and compare also *Annales Fuldenses*, s.a. 882, p. 99).

[80] *Annales Fuldenses* (Mainz continuation), s.a. 881, p. 96; *Annales Vedastini*, s.a. 881, pp. 50–1.

a great army in the 860s effectively brought down the long-lived kingdoms of Northumbria, East Anglia and Mercia, and nearly Wessex until
a change of fortune under Alfred the Great (r. 871–99).[81] Lamentations
about the poor state of the Christian world were, unsurprisingly, plenti-
ful, while Vikings could legitimately question why their neighbours considered themselves to be so strong.

Apocalyptic and providential tradition had predisposed Christian
commentators to bleak assessments of society's values before Viking
raids had proved much. Already, in mid-eighth-century Bobbio, the
satirical *Cosmography of Aethicus Ister* drew on Pseudo-Methodius to
paint the Danes and the north more generally in apocalyptic colours
(see Chapter 4).[82] The collected northern peoples were the antithesis of
civility for a start: 'immense in body and monstrous races, hardened by
the most savage folkways'.[83] Pseudo-Methodius's account of the peoples
locked behind Alexander's Gate with Gog and Magog loomed large, with
the author describing Dog-Heads living on Scandinavian islands along
with *Alani* and *Turci*.[84] Having redrawn apocalyptic geography for the
West, almost prophetically the author wrote:

Let them not at any time hear or learn of the most sweet and rich glory and
abundance of the world ... lest perchance they burst over the whole face of the
earth and tear and devour everything like bread. 'And you, O North / mother of
dragons / and nurse of scorpions / pit of vipers / and lake of demons', it was better
that an inaccessible enclosure like hell be within you than to beget such races.[85]

---

[81] *Anglo-Saxon Chronicle* (A), s.a. 865–s.a. 871, pp. 46–9.

[82] M. W. Herren, *The Cosmography of Aethicus Ister: Edition, Translation and Commentary*
(Turnhout, 2011), lxii–lxxiii. Just from Herren's manuscripts described on pp. c–cii or O.
Prinz, *Die Kosmographie des Aethicus*, MGH QQ zur Geistesgesch., 14 (Munich, 1993),
pp. 55–60, the text can be seen in Tours, St Amand, St Gall Murbach, and Freising by
the end of the ninth century.

[83] *Cosmographia*, ed. Herren, c. 29, pp. 28–9: 'inmania corpora inmanesque nationes, seuis-
simis moribus durate.'

[84] Dog-Heads: *Cosmographia*, c. 28, pp. 27–9. Turks: cc. 32–3, pp. 32–5. On the Dog-Heads
as illustrative of an 'intellectual frontier' see I. N. Wood, 'Categorising the *cynocephali*', in
R. Corradini, M. Gillis, R. McKitterick and I. van Renswoude (eds.), *Ego Trouble: Authors
and Their Identities in the Early Middle Ages* (Vienna, 2010), pp. 125–36, which draws out
a variety of influences and resonances but not in relation to Pseudo-Methodius.

[85] c. 33, pp. 34–5: 'ne quando audiant uel percipiant mellifluam et uberrimam mundi glo-
riam et abundantiam et regna inclita ... ne forte inruant in uniuersam superficiem terrae
et quasi panem cuncta decerpiant ac deglutiant. "O et tu aquilon!/mater draconum/et
nutrix scorpionum/fouea serpentium/lacusque demonum", facilius fuerat in te obtura-
tionem inaccessibilem fore uelut infernum quam tales gentes partuire.' Compare later
the alleged words of Ragnar, leader of the raid on Paris in 845, who said that he had
never seen a land so rich nor a people so cowardly: *Translatio sancti Germani*, c. 30. 1, ed.
C. de Smedt, *Analecta Bollandiana*, 2 (1893), 69–98 at p. 92.

But of course they did hear and learn. The very first properly documented attack – on the monastery of Lindisfarne in 793 – provoked Alcuin of York to proclaim that the raid was a warning and that it fulfilled the prophecy of Jeremiah 1.14 – 'out of the North an evil shall break forth'.[86] In the Frankish kingdoms Vikings were known almost exclusively as Northmen (*Nordmanni*) rather than *Dani*, thus ensuring their name had a prophetic ring to it, even though some – notably Haimo – found this distasteful and misleading when it led people to think of Revelation's Gog and Magog.[87] None of it necessarily meant that the world was about to end, but the resonance of evil from the north was hard to escape.

As with the fall of Rome and the Arab conquests, Viking attacks inspired visionary calls for moral reform. Alcuin wrote to warn people in Northumbria that the sack of Lindisfarne was a punishment for drinking, dressing up and general unbecoming behaviour. Bishops and clerics – perhaps aware of Alcuin's letters – cited Jeremiah again in the wake of the sack of Paris in 845 at a Church council, articulating the urgency of reform at the Synod of Meaux.[88] Also in the wake of the sack, Audradus of Sens adopted a prophetic voice to encourage reform, warning that God had granted only a ten-year reprieve.[89] Only a few years earlier a terrifying vision had been reported at the Frankish court from England, where a priest had experienced a dream in which names were written out alternately in black and blood in imitation of a *liber vitae*. When the priest asked the boys writing why, they told him that the Christian people lived in too much sin and that, unless they repented, they would be destroyed by pagans.[90] In Frisia, Heriberga, sister of Liudger of Münster (d. 809), had a dream about a sun being chased away by fog, which was interpreted as the coming persecutions of the Northmen in punishment for sin until the 'Sun of Justice' might return.[91] Notker, dimissively calling the *Nordmanni* 'Dog-Heads' (*cynocephali*), also saw providence at work in Charlemagne's failure to invade Denmark balanced against the Danes'

[86] Alcuin, *Epistolae*, no. 19, ed. E. Dümmler, MGH Epp., 4 (Berlin, 1895), p. 55.
[87] Haimo, PL, 117. 1186–7 and compare 117. 996 where he associates pagans with the cold of the North (Rev. 3.15). See also on a Gothic North (without Gog and Magog) Frechulf, *Chronicon*, I. 2. 25, ed. M. I. Allen, CCCM, 169 (Turnhout, 2002), pp. 134–9. On this image of the Northmen see S. Coupland, 'Rod of God's Wrath or the People of God's Wrath? The Carolingian Theology of the Viking Invasions', *JEH*, 42.4 (1991), 535–54.
[88] Synod of Meaux-Paris (845), MGH Conc., 3, p. 82.
[89] Audradus, *Liber revelationum*, IV, pp. 379–80; Dutton, *The Politics of Dreaming*, pp. 139–40.
[90] *Annales Bertiniani*, s.a. 839, pp. 18–19.
[91] Altfrid, *Vita Liudgeri*, I. 27, ed. W. Diekamp, *Vitae sancti Liudgeri* (Münster, 1888), pp. 32–3.

failure to invade the empire.[92] The end of the world might not quite have
been to hand, but the Vikings had inspired people to see divine revelations about punishment for sin; and this, as we have argued many times
now, was part of the same spectrum of moral reflection that encom-
passed apocalyptic thought.

Interest in the end of the world was more definite when it came to
evangelising the North. As some commentaries stressed, there were still
peoples (*gentes*) who had not heard the Gospel, and therefore the End
could not come yet.[93] But by the middle of the ninth century, Christian
of Stavelot-Malmedy doubted that this was still the case, not after the
Khazar Turks – 'in Gog and in Magog' and descended from the Huns –
converted to Judaism, just as the Bulgars converted to Christianity.[94]
And further north, people could see the same processes unfolding.
Paschasius Radbertus, writing in Corbie, saw the building of churches in
Scandinavia exactly as proof that scripture was being fulfilled: 'It will be
shown that there will be nowhere where there is not a church in future.
Indeed, how many have been built on islands in Ocean? Now for certain they receive the Gospel!'[95] The End was near, Paschasius continued,
even if it remained indefinable; and even the persistence of paganism
was no obstacle because Christ had spoken of preaching to 'all peoples' (*omnes gentes*) not converting 'all men' (*omnes homines*). The act of
preaching was of more importance than the success rate. Such interest in
the conversion of Scandinavia was by no means widespread, and it was
actively discouraged by Archbishop Hincmar of Rheims and Notker the
Stammerer because the Northmen were simply untrustworthy.[96] Altfrid
of Münster in *c.* 845 had cause to lament how Charlemagne had pre-
vented St Liudger from evangelising the Danes which, if true, likely had
more to do with border disputes and the ambitions of King Godefrid of
the Danes in the north than anti-apocalyptic tradition.[97] There was no

[92] Notker, *Gesta Karoli*, II. 13, pp. 75–6. As noted earlier in the chapter, there was also certainly a copy of Aethicus Ister in St Gall, so Notker may have had that text in mind.
[93] Ps.-Bede, *Expositio in Mattheum*, c. 24, PL, 92.102C.
[94] Christian of Stablo-Malmedy, *Expositio super Librum Generationis*, c. 24 (on Matt. 24.14),
p. 436.
[95] Paschasius, *Expositio in Mattheo*, XI, ed. Paulus, p. 1164: 'Hinc ostendit quod nulla relin-
quantur terrarum spatia ubi non sit future Ecclesia. Quarum quamplurimae insularum
in Oceano constitutae, iam pro certe Evangelium susceperunt.'
[96] *Annales Bertiniani*, s.a. 841, p. 25 and s.a. 876, p. 131; Notker, *Gesta Karoli*, II. 19,
pp. 89–90. J. T. Palmer, 'Rimbert's *Vita Anskarii* and the Failure of Scandinavian Mission
in the Ninth Century', *JEH*, 55.2 (2004), 235–56 at p. 253.
[97] Altfrid, *Vita Liudgeri*, I. 30, p. 36. For the trouble with Godefrid, see Einhard, *Vita Karoli*,
c. 14, p. 17 and *Annales regni Francorum*, s.a. 804 (pp. 118–19), s.a. 808 (pp. 125–6), s.a.
809 (pp. 128–9), and 810 (p. 131).

uniform position in the Carolingian world about the importance, or even desirability, of converting Scandinavia.

In the diocese of Hamburg-Bremen there was no debate, because it was founded expressly to evangelise the north. There, the apocalyptic and revelatory character of mission weighed strongly upon those involved.[98] In the midst of legal wrangles about the diocese's fraudulent claims to archiepiscopal status in the north, St Anskar (bishop 832–65) wrote down visions that he had experienced since his childhood which had set out his destiny as a missionary.[99] An early one at the monastery of Corbie – the community to which his successor, Rimbert, addressed the *Life of Anskar* – involved a vision of purgatorial fires and then the twenty-four elders of the Apocalypse in a scene reminiscent of the painted ceiling of Charlemagne's cathedral in Aachen.[100] The experience of promised judgement scared the boy into behaving better. Later, he had a vision of his deceased abbot Adalhard (Charlemagne's cousin) who reassured him when contemplating missionary work in Sweden, saying: '"You shall be salvation to them up to the extremes of the lands", because the end of the world lies in the northern parts of Sweden.'[101] Here in particular the geographical ends of the earth resonated with the temporal. Anskar's visions had strengthened his resolve but also revealed the divine approval for his work, which could then be broadcast through the circulation of texts.

A line between the apocalyptic geography of 'Aethicus Ister' and the work of Hamburg-Bremen can be traced. Early in his career, (Arch) Bishop Rimbert wrote to his friend Ratramnus of Corbie (d. 868) to inquire whether he thought that the Dog-Heads in the north were people in need of evangelisation or were instead animals who did not need to hear the word of God.[102] The question hints at the importance of universal mission as encouraged by Christ and the expectation that one might find Dog-Heads at the edges of the world, just beyond civilisation, just

<hr/>

[98] W. Haas, 'Foris apostulus intus monachus: Ansgar als Mönch und Apostel des Nordens', *Journal of Medieval History*, 11 (1985), 1–30 at pp. 11–15.
[99] *Epistolae variorum inde a saeculo non medio usque ad mortem Karoli II. imperatoris collectae*, no. 16, MGH Epp., 6, p. 163. The starting point for understanding this is now E. Knibbs, *Ansgar, Rimbert and the Foundations of Hamburg-Bremen* (Farnham, 2011).
[100] Rimbert, *Vita Anskarii*, c. 3, p. 22; Dutton, *The Politics of Dreaming*, pp. 52–4.
[101] Rimbert, *Vita Anskarii*, c. 25, p. 55: 'Eris illis in salutem usque ad extremum terrae, quia finis mundi in aquilonis partibus in Sueonum coniacet regionibus.' For further discussion see J. T. Palmer, 'Defining Paganism in the Carolingian World', *EME*, 15.4 (2007), 402–25 at pp. 424–5 and Wood, 'Categorising the *cynocephali*', pp. 133–4.
[102] In addition to Wood's 'Categorising the *cynocephali*', see S. Bruce, 'Hagiography as Monstrous Ethnography: A Note on Ratramnus of Corbie's Letter Concerning the Conversion of the *cynocephali*', in G. Wieland, C. Ruff and R. Arthur (eds.), *Sophiae Arcator: Medieval Latin Studies in Honour of Michael Herren on his 65th Birthday* (Turnhout, 2006), pp. 45–56.

as Aethicus Ister and Pseudo-Methodius had suggested. We are not so far away again from anxiety about whether to convert Gog and Magog who were, remember, the Dog-Heads' neighbours and also, through the Goths, associated with the island of Scandza. Sadly we have lost the details of Rimbert's letter. Ratramnus, however, replied on the basis of Isidore and the *Suffering of St Christopher* (for St Christopher was a Dog-Head), to argue in favour of their potential for humanity and therefore the need for evangelisation.[103] Such a socio-literary approach hardly announces apocalyptic imminence. The fact of the debate, on the other hand, points towards the kind of resonance that missionary work had relative to apocalyptic narrative and geography.

The Vikings provided a threat that was real, immediate and readily wrapped up in apocalyptic scripture. This should not cloud the fact that many ninth-century Christians actively sought to see apocalyptic conflict in the world. This has been well illustrated by Johannes Heil in the case of Carolingian attitudes towards Jews. Unlike in the case of the Vikings, there were probably very few Jews in the Carolingian Empire at all, and in all likelihood mostly in the Rhône valley.[104] Yet, in Heil's words, 'the conflict with Jews was an intellectual, not a social, reality' and 'if there had been no Jews living in the ninth-century Frankish empire, Carolingian theologians would have had to invent them'.[105] Carolingian biblical commentators are indeed more notable for writing about Jews as the antithesis of the Christian Church, with some writers (including Haimo) even denying the possibility of their redemption.[106] Where there were real Jews, attitudes were mixed. Louis the Pious employed a 'Master of the Jews' (*magister Iudaeorum*) and was prepared to offer legal protection to some, but the fact that they needed protection in the first place points towards anti-Jewish sentiments. In Lyon, these spilled over

[103] *Epistolae variorum inde a saeculo non medio usque ad mortem Karoli II. imperatoris collectae*, no. 12, MGH Epp., 6, pp. 155–7. Even the reference to Alexander is drawn from Isidore, *Etymologiae*, XI.5.3. Ratramnus also uses the *Vita et passio Christophori*, AASS, July VI, 25, 146–9. See Wood, 'Categorising the *cynocephali*', p. 132; Bruce, 'Hagiography as Monstrous Ethnography', pp. 53–5.
[104] J. Heil, 'Goldenes Zeitalter? Juden und Judentum in der Karolingerzeit', in R. Kampling (ed.), *Wie schön sind deine Zelte, Jakob, deine Wohnungen, Israel?* (Frankfurt-am-Main, 2009), pp. 99–114.
[105] Heil, 'Timeless End', pp. 98–9. There is an interesting contrast here with the analysis of G. Langmuir, *Towards a Definition of Antisemitism* (Ann Arbor, MI, 1996), esp. at pp. 303–4, where it is argued that such anti-Semitism – rather than a simpler anti-Judaism – was not present in the ninth century but only really developed at the end of the eleventh.
[106] In addition to Heil's 'Timeless End', see his *Kompilation oder Konstruktion? Die Juden in den Pauluskommentaren des 9. Jahrhunderts* (Hanover, 1998), summarised in 'Labourers in the Lord's Quarry', pp. 75–96.

into an apocalyptic mood, as Agobard of Lyon – his nose out of joint over a land dispute – complained to the emperor that collaboration between imperial envoys and the Jews was another sign of the promised *tempora periculosa*.[107] As is well recognised from the later period: anti-Jewish feeling and apocalyptic anxiety often developed hand-in-hand.[108]

Agobard's complaints against the Jews of Lyon highlighted an intensification of interest in the possible Jewishness of Antichrist. As opponents of Ecclesia, Agobard opined, the Jews were the many Antichrists prophesied by John (1 John 2.4).[109] His successor, Amulo, was no more moderate in his views.[110] In Auxerre, Haimo seized on passages he found in Jerome's commentary on Daniel and in the Pseudo-Methodian sermon to explain that *the* Antichrist himself would be Jewish, being a descendent of the tribe of Dan.[111] This was a crucial moment in the development of the biography of Antichrist, as it blended together different schools of interpretation, and provided a new one which would be fleshed out from these sources by Adso a century later (see Chapter 7). At the same time it highlights how many Christians in the Carolingian world had a pronounced tendency to turn benign otherness into part of a universal struggle.

The Carolingian experience was not unique, however, and we can find similar tendencies developing in ninth-century Córdoba.[112] As we have seen, Muslims had controlled much of the Iberian peninsula since the conquests of 711 and, as far as we can tell, Christian–Muslim tensions were at least partially defused because, as peoples of the Book, Christians were afforded the protected (but highly taxed) status of the *dhimma*. Christians continued to live and worship free from persecution. In the middle of the ninth century, however, things changed in a most unexpected way. In 850 a Christian called Isaac, who had once held the title of *exceptor reipublicae* (in Arabic, *kâtib adh-dhimam*) in Córdoba, scandalised both Muslims and Christians by visiting the local judge (*qâdî*) and vocally denouncing Islam. The dispute between the two escalated and Isaac was beheaded and hung upside-down on a boat as a warning. But

---

[107] J. Heil, 'Agobard, Amolo, das Kirchengut und die Juden von Lyon', *Francia*, 25.1 (1998), 39–76.

[108] See also in this context the ninth-century Spanish text, *Indiculus de adventum Henoc et Elie*, ed. J. Gil, in *Corpus scriptorum Muzarabicorum* (Madrid, 1974), pp. 126–33 which places conversion of the Jews centrally to the apocalyptic narrative.

[109] Agobard, *De Iudaicis superstitionibus et erroribus*, c. 19, ed. van Acker, p. 214.

[110] E. g. Amulo, *Adversus Iudeos*, c. 15 and c. 19, PL, 116. 150 and 153. B.-S. Albert, '*Adversus Iudeos* in the Carolingian Empire', in O. Limor and G. G. Stroumsa (eds.), *Contra Iudaeos: Ancient and Medieval Polemics Between Christians and Jews* (Tübingen, 1996), 119–42 at p. 132; Firey, *A Contrite Heart*, pp. 86–7.

[111] *In epistolam II ad Thessalonicenses*, PL, 117. 780.

[112] On Spain in this period see now R. Collins, *Caliphs and Kings: Spain, 796–1031* (Chichester, 2012).

this only inspired more Christians to break the harmony of Córdoban society and over the next decade, unprovoked, a couple of dozen more Christians became new martyrs.[113] While none of this on first sight looks particularly 'apocalyptic', the enthusiasm of the martyrs to upset social order has been explained by appeal to millenarian hopes.[114] And even if this is unproveable (as Kenneth Baxter Wolf has stressed), their apologists certainly saw a struggle here against the 'precursors of Antichrist'.[115]

The lead apologist was a priest named Eulogius who interpreted Islam essentially as a heresy, with much of the apocalyptic baggage that brought with it. He wrote for a Christian audience with whom he clashed so fundamentally at times that he was once arrested by city authorities in collaboration with Bishop Reccafredus of Seville as part of an attempt to contain the threat to good Muslim–Christian relations. His most famous work – begun whilst in prison – is a series of hagiographical sketches defending the actions of the martyrs. It was in his *Apology*, however, that he launched his own attack on the 'sect of Muhammad' and its pseudo-prophets. Muhammad himself he called *praecursor Antichristi*, before copying a polemical Latin *Life of Muhammad* he had found in Pamplona in the north which talked about the Prophet as a sinful heresiarch and false prophet.[116] The lack of miracles which accompanied the martyrdoms, which worried some, Eulogius also explained in relation to the Last Days, using the Gregorian idea that there would just be fewer miracles at that time.[117] These themes were taken up by Eulogius's friend and hagiographer Paul Alvar, whose own *apologeticus* took the form of an extended meditation on Daniel and Job.[118] For neither writer was the end of the world necessarily 'close', but for neither was that the issue anyway. Peace under Muslim dominion was not an option, even where it was effectively a reality, because the apocalyptic imagination ensured

[113] K. B. Wolf, *Christian Martyrs in Muslim Spain* (Cambridge, 1988); J. A. Coope, *The Martyrs of Cordoba: Community and Family Conflict in an Age of Mass Conversion* (Lincoln, NE, 1995). On the sources at a more technical level see E. P. Colbert, *The Martyrs of Córdoba (850–859): A Study of the Sources* (Washington, DC, 1962).

[114] A. Cutler, 'The Ninth-Century Spanish Martyrs' Movement and the Origins of Western Christian Missions to the Muslims', *Muslim World*, 55 (1965), 321–39 at pp. 329–39.

[115] Wolf, *Christian Martyrs*, p. 104.

[116] Eulogius, *Apologeticus martyrum*, c. 12 (*praecursor Antichristi*), cc. 15–16 (*Vita Muhammadi*), ed. J. Gil, in *Corpus scriptorum Muzarabicorum* (Madrid, 1974), pp. 482 and 483–6. A second version has survived in *Chronica prophetica*, 4, ed. Y. Bonnaz, in *Chroniques Asturiennes (fin IXe siècle)* (Paris, 1987), p. 5. The text might have had Greek origins and been influenced in the Latin revision by George of Mar Saba: J. Wasilewski, 'The "Life of Muhammad" in Eulogius of Córdoba: Some Evidence for the Transmission of Greek Polemic to the Latin West', *EME*, 16.3 (2008), 333–53.

[117] Wolf, *Christian Martyrs*, pp. 84–5.

[118] Paul Alvar, *Indiculus luminosus*, ed. J. Gil, in *Corpus scriptorum Muzarabicorum*, pp. 270–314.

that some Christians could only see dissonance in any mixed religious environment.

The influence of the Córdoba apocalyptically textualised worldview was mixed but evident. The martyrs themselves achieved moderate fame in the kingdom of Charles the Bald after they came to the attention of Usuard of Saint-Germain-des-Prés, but only as martyrs.[119] Uncoupled from the martyr stories, on the other hand, Eulogius's broader anti-Muslim invective apparently found a receptive audience at the court of Alfonso III of Léon, Asturias and Galicia (r. 866–910) along with the *Life of Muhammad*. In an addendum to the *Chronica Albendense* text called the *Prophetic Chronicle* (883), a writer at Alfonso's court reflected back on Isidore's *History of the Goths, Vandals and Suebi* and its association between the Goths and Ezekiel's Gog (see Chapter 3).[120] He extended the story into a providential narrative by explaining how the Goths had lost Spain on account of their sins but how they had now begun to redeem themselves (something which forms a nice parallel with Audradus claiming Charles had lost God's backing to reconquer Spain from the 'infidel').[121] This final notion is captured in a prophecy:

Christ is our hope that, when in the very near future, the 170 years have passed, the audacity of the enemy will be reduced to nothing and peace will be given to the holy church of Christ. The Saracens themselves have foreseen their destruction approaching in prodigies and signs in the stars, and have said that the kingdom of the Goths will be restored by our present prince. Also, this our prince, the glorious lord Alfonso, is foretold by the revelations and demonstrations of many Christians to be on the verge of ruling over all of Spain in the near future.[122]

These turned out to be famous last words. The narrative of our only source runs dry at this juncture but Alfonso's failure is self-evident as southern Spain remained firmly in Muslim hands for centuries more.

---

[119] J.L. Nelson, 'The Franks, the Martyrology of Usuard and the Martyrs of Cordoba', in D. Wood (ed.), *Martyrs and Martyrologies*, Studies in Church History, 30 (Woodbridge, 1993), pp. 67–80; A. Christys, 'St-Germain des-Prés, St Vincent and the Martyrs of Cordoba', *EME*, 7.2 (1998), 199–216.

[120] Collins, *Caliphs*, pp. 54–5 reasonably questions treating the *Chronica prophetica* as a text separate from the *Chronica Albendense* as the former is an extension of the later. Compare the treatment in Bonnaz, *Chroniques Asturiennes*.

[121] Audradus, *Liber revelationum*, XI, p. 384.

[122] *Chronica prophetica*, 2. 2, p. 3: 'Spes nostra Christus est: quod completis proximiori tempore CLXX annis, inimicorum audacia ad nicilum redigatur et pax Christi Ecclesiae Sanctae reddatur. Quod etiam ipsi Sarrazeni, quosdam prodigiis uel astrorum signis, interitum suum adpropinquare praedicunt, et Gothorum regnum restaurari per hunc nostrum principem dicunt. Etiam et multorum christianorum reuelationibus atque ostensionibus, hic princeps noster, gloriosus domnus Adefonsus, proximiori tempore in omni Spania praedicetur regnaturus'; trans. K. B. Wolf, http://pages.pomona. edu/~kbw14747/prophchr.htm.

How the failure of the prophecy hit cannot be known, but it may be telling that the northern kingdoms retreated for a less 'glorious' future.

By taking attitudes towards the Vikings, Jews and Muslims together we can see the wide-ranging, situational and discontinuous manifestations of the apocalyptic. End-focused thought explained, legitimised and provoked struggle. Successes and failures in dealing with 'others' could be understood in relation to various narratives so that their logic – tragic or comic – could be determined. Naturally this fostered a strong sense of community because the conflict involved reinforced core values while pointing out the threats that would promise negation. Social realities and polemical moods did not always coincide: some people did not care for Scandinavian mission, some people protected Jews and some people had no problem living in a mixed Christian–Muslim community. Apocalypse was not the only discourse available; it was, however, one option people could adopt to make sense of the changing world around them and their aspirations within it.

Conclusion

The diffused apocalypticism of the ninth century attests to many of the underlying currents we have encountered in previous chapters, while highlighting the importance of situational moments for determining their logic. Political Augustinianism meant that history had moved beyond Daniel's sequence of empires; only the coming of Antichrist remained. The providential mission of the Carolingian experiment provided a sense of purpose and importance within the shadow of the End. Here we perhaps see the maturation of the 'biblical turn' that first became apparent under the two Gregorys, with a wide spread of political and social action textualised in relation to scripture. What could be a higher realisation of this than the gifts of exegetical treatises to kings as part of their education? Yet the vagaries of history quickly meant that such articulations and legitimisations of power were simultaneously problematised by the same processes which enabled them. Civil wars and invasions were cultural events every bit as much as they were political ones, and they had the power to undermine strength by changing narrative and resonance. There was little room for sin or human weakness in the kingdom of God.

The apocalyptic discourse of Christian empire hinged on a constant state of redefinition. The critique of rulership and morals was the natural internal side of things. This was complemented by the discourse on outsiders as apocalyptic enemies and the antithesis of Ecclesia, either assaulting the faithful or else leading them astray. Again, the processes involved could be contradictory. On the one hand, people could understand punishment as a providential call to moral reform, so it had a reinforcing effect. On the other, it pushed some members of the faithful into conflict with Jews, Muslims and perceived 'heretics' in ways which threatened to destabilise the collective where others thought peace to be the better way forward. In such cases, apocalyptic rhetoric could be employed in an attempt to rally doubters. Part of the dialectic, of course, stemmed from the totalising view of the apocalyptic community, in which all peoples were potentially to be drawn into the fold. Difference plus apocalyptic narrative heightened the likelihood of conflict.

What this all meant was that the Carolingian experiment had led to a Christendom that was, as I suggested at the beginning, mobilised, anxious and excited. It agitated for reform programmes it could not complete, was torn between ideological unity and practical division, was inclusive yet discriminatory, and had rulers who could not live up to the religio-social standards they had set for themselves. Carolingian rulers and writers did not proclaim a predictable imminence of the End during this time, but their language, ideas and motifs drew heavily on the apocalyptic repertoire. Action was necessary and urgent, because every day had to be lived as if it was the last. And importantly, this had long been the case before the Apocalyptic Year 1000 started to creep onto the horizon.

7   The Year 1000 and other apocalypticisms (c. 911–c. 1033)

Was there a widespread expectation that the world would end around the millennial anniversary of Christ's Incarnation (1000/1) or Passion (1033/4)? As we saw at the beginning of this book, this is a question which has been fiercely contested for two centuries. In his revelation, John clearly foresaw a thousand-year reign of Christ and his saints, at the end of which Satan would be unleashed (Rev. 20.2–7). Even Augustine and his intellectual successors, studying typology and allegory in scripture, could see some kind of statement about duration here. Many writers in the late tenth and early eleventh centuries alluded to the Y1K problem. Yet, to complicate matters, few were explicit about apocalyptic expectations, many of the sources are scattered in time and space, and there was little of the mass hysteria modern scholars on both sides of the debate seem to have expected.[1] As a result, the modern debate has rather gone round in circles as people look for different kinds of proof using different criteria. In this last chapter I would like to pursue two ways forward: first, to move beyond the Y1K problem to analyse broader apocalyptic cultures as we have done so far in this book; and second, to pay more attention to similarities and differences between regions and individuals, rather than vainly trying to establish what a chimerical, singular 'medieval mind' believed.

With the second suggestion, scholars of the apocalyptic can continue to integrate their findings into a larger debate about the changing social

---

[1] J. Fried, 'Endzeiterwartung um die Jahrtausendwende', *DA*, 45 (1989), 381–473 and R. Landes, 'The Fear of an Apocalyptic Year 1000: Augustinian Historiography, Medieval and Modern', *Speculum*, 75.1 (2000), 97–145. A sustained polemic against them is offered in S. Gouguenheim, *Les fausses terreurs de l'an mil: Attente de la fin des temps ou approfondissement de la foi* (Paris, 1999) and T. Boiadjiev, 'Der mittelalterliche Apokalyptismus und der Mythos vom Jahre 1000', in J. A. Aertsen and M. Pickavé (eds.), *Ende und Vollendung. Eschatologische Perspektiven im Mittelalter* (Berlin and New York, 2002), pp. 165–78. A useful historiographical overview of the whole debate up to c. 1999 is E. Peters, 'Mutations, Adjustments, Terrors, Historians, and the Year 1000', in M. Frassetto (ed.), *The Year 1000: Religious and Social Responses to the Turning of the First Millennium* (New York, 2002), pp. 9–28.

189

and political nature of the Middle Ages: the 'Transformation of the Year 1000'.[2] If there was significant change around the Year 1000, what role did the apocalyptic play? Much of the debate has focused on France. The Mutation School, led by Georges Duby, posited that there was considerable continuity in Carolingian social and legal order until the end of the tenth century, when there was a spectacular and violent collapse of royal power, a rise in private violence, and apocalyptic angst was a reflex of these changes.[3] Against all this, Dominique Barthélemy argued that the most important thing that changed was actually the nature of documentary evidence, which obscured the essential continuity in the background.[4] In this model apocalypticism is less welcome because it suggests there was a crisis (although one could now entertain instead the idea of continuity in apocalyptic culture!). There are problems because some historians involved are talking about different things while engaging in grand generalisations and limited comparative study.[5] For this study, we need just content ourselves with considering how apocalypse contributed to discourses of power in the period, both in crisis and in stability.

The first suggestion – that we need to consider 'apocalyptic cultures' – is more central to our overarching argument. Our sources contain plenty of warnings about Antichrist, anxieties about the direction of empire, visions of the afterlife, and a sense of the inevitability of judgement soon. Efforts to shackle these to Y1K itself, even in Fried's 'weak thesis', have sometimes seemed forced, but at the same time there is too much evidence to warrant a complete dismissal. Both sides seek over-simplification. So, as we have done so far, it is important to take different traditions according to their own local logics, and in their manuscript contexts where possible, rather than lumping them all together indiscriminately. Y1K will still be important – more important perhaps than Y6K – but I will argue that it did not account for all apocalyptic expectation. Concern

---

[2] A useful and even-handed starting point is provided in S. MacLean, 'Apocalypse and Revolution: Europe around the Year 1000', *EME*, 15.1 (2007), 86–106.

[3] G. Duby, *La société aux XIe et XIIe siècles dans la region mâconnaise* (2nd edn, Paris, 1971) and his *L'an mil* (Paris, 1967). J. Poly and E. Bournazel, *The Feudal Transformation, 900–1200*, trans. C. Higgitt (New York and London, 1991). An important contribution is made by T. Bisson, 'The Feudal Revolution', *P&P*, 142 (1994), 6–42 and 'Reply', *P&P*, 155 (1997), 208–25.

[4] D. Barthélemy, *La société dans le comté de Vendôme de l'an mil au XVIe siècle* (Paris, 1993), p. 11 and throughout *L'an mil et la paix de Dieu. La France chrétienne et féodale 980–1060* (Paris, 1999), the collection of essays in translation with some additions as *The Serf, the Knight and the Historian*, trans. G. R. Edwards (Ithaca, NY, and London, 2009). See also now C. West, *Reframing the Feudal Revolution: Political and Social Transformation between Marne and Moselle c. 800 and c. 1100* (Cambridge, 2013).

[5] MacLean, 'Apocalypse and Revolution', esp. 92–6. On the difficulties and benefits of more comparative history here see the responses of Timothy Reuter and Chris Wickham to Bisson in *P&P*, 155 (1997), 177–208.

for an unpredictable Judgement, not so far away, continued to be a driving force for reorganising political, social and religious institutions.

Counting to 1,000

To begin, we need to address a technical point about the 'weak thesis' – the idea that the attempts to revise Dionysiac chronology gave an extended apocalyptic window of 979–1042 because that was the full window of time in which the millennial anniversary of the Incarnation or Passion could have fallen. Debate was triggered by the observation that astronomical data in Dionysiac tables did not fit with evidence in the Gospels. Abbo of Fleury (d. 1004) tried various solutions between 982 and his death, from a three-year recalibration of time so that the Incarnation fell in 3 BC (so then 997 = 1000), via more radical schemes, until he settled on placing the Incarnation in 21 BC (so now 979 = 1000).[6] Others engaged with the problem too, notably Herigar of Lobbes (d. 1007), who proposed shifting the Incarnation to 9 (so now 1009 = 1000).[7] It was this kind of tinkering with AD dates which first suggested to Fried that some people might have had their Y1K expectations orientated towards years other than our standard 1000 and 1033.[8] Anyone accepting Abbo's final calculation, for instance, could say Y1K had passed before Abbo had even conducted his inquiry. There are, however, a cluster of problems. For a start no one involved mentioned apocalypse in their calculations, just like in the last major debates on chronology (see Chapter 3). Secondly, only a few intellectuals adopted the revised dates, so most people would have remained working towards the standard 1000 and 1033. And finally, it is unclear whether such minor tinkering – three years, nine, twenty-one – would have had much effect on apocalyptic expectations. Fried's reframing of Y1K does not lead us very far.

[6] The root of the problem was the data in the Dionysiac Easter table, which on closer inspection did not fit the traditionally held conditions believed to have held on the day of Christ's Passion in 33 or 34, namely that there was a full moon (= *luna* 14) on the Thursday, with Christ crucified the next day (= *luna* 15) and resurrected on the Sunday (= *luna* 17), 27 March. Bede had in fact noticed this but in a clearly ironic passage he had argued that you could find the right data in a Dionysiac table (Bede, *De temporum ratione*, c. 47, ed. C. W. Jones, CCSL 123B (Turnhout, 1980), pp. 431–2). See P. Verbist, *Duelling with the Past: Medieval Authors and the Problem of the Christian Era, c. 990–1135* (Turnhout, 2010), esp. ch. 2 on Abbo. On the establishment of the Dionysiac era see A.-D. von den Brincken, 'Abendländischer Chiasmus um 1000? Zur Rezeption unserer christlichen Ära', in Aertsen and Pickavé (eds.), *Ende und Vollendung*, pp. 179–92.
[7] Edited in A. Cordoliani, 'Abbon de Fleury, Hérigar de Lobbes et Gerland de Besançon sur l'ère de l'Incarnation de Denys le Petit', *Revue d'historie ecclesiastique*, 44 (1949), 463–87 at 480–4.
[8] Fried, 'Endzeiterwartung', p. 423; Landes, 'The Fear', pp. 113, 122, 127.

There is, in the grand scheme of things, fair evidence that there were active apocalyptic beliefs in play connected to the millennium. The most explicit story is told by Abbo of Fleury. One day, when he was young, he had been to church in Paris, where he had heard a preacher predict that the end of the world would fall in the Year 1000.[9] Appalled, presumably at the non-Augustinian tenor of such ideas, Abbo had stood up in the middle of the church and debated the matter with the priest. That, disappointingly for us, is the end of the matter as it is related in the sources. What it means, on the other hand, has been the subject of much enthusiastic amplification and argument. The story does demonstrate that some people believed in an apocalyptic Year 1000, and that others were prepared to argue against them. But we do not know enough about the priest or the beliefs of his colleagues, congregation or neighbours to make much of a guess about whether this was a one-off incident or not, or what people other than Abbo would have made of it, or if it even happened. At the same time it would seem to be stretching the evidence of such an isolated story to say that Abbo challenging the sermon is representative of large-scale efforts to suppress non-Augustinian thought on the End. The story by itself raises more issues than it can resolve.

Strikingly Y1K had real cross-cultural resonance, which helps us to appreciate its importance. In Byzantium, a scribe noted the birth of Antichrist in 995 (their AD 1000 plus three years).[10] In England, another announced this in 999, while shortly afterwards Abbo's English pupil Byrhtferth of Ramsey noted that a thousand years had been completed so it was down to the Saviour's discretion when time would end.[11] Ralph Glaber, writing in Burgundy, produced a chronicle of anxiety and hope that included only two dates, 1000 and 1033, and reference to the fulfilment of prophecy that Satan would be released after a thousand years. (His equally anxious contemporary Ademar of Chabannes avoided reference to the date or was not interested in it compared to the signs

[9] Abbo, *Apologeticus ad Hugonem et Rodbertum reges Francorum*, PL, 139. 472. Fried, 'Endzeiterwartung', pp. 422–3; Landes, 'The Fear', pp. 123–4.

[10] P. Magdalino, 'The Year 1000 in Byzantium', in P. Magdalino (ed.), *Byzantium in the Year 1000* (Leiden, 2002), pp. 233–70 at p. 269 amongst other evidence; W. Brandes, 'Liudprand von Cremona (*Legatio* Cap. 39–40) und eine bisher unbeachtete Westöstliche Korrespondenz über die Bedeutung des Jahres 1000 A.D.', *Byzantinische Zeitschrift*, 93 (2000), 435–63 at p. 462.

[11] London, British Library, Cotton Tiberius B V (part 1), f. 15r; Byrhtferth, *Enchiridion*, IV. 2, eds. P. S. Baker and M. Lapidge (Cambridge, 1995), p. 236. M. Godden, 'The Millennium, Time, and History for the Anglo-Saxons', in A. Gow, R. Landes and D. van Meter, *The Apocalyptic Year 1000: Religious Expectation and Social Change, 950–1050* (Oxford, 2003), pp. 155–80.

around him.)[12] Later in the eleventh century at Hildesheim, one annalist looked back at the appropriate juncture in their work and wrote, 'accordingly it is read that the millennial year surpasses and transcends all'.[13] (Where this was read is unknown.) A contemporary apocalyptic context might be hinted at in the subsequent negative account of Otto III visiting Charlemagne's tomb, as we shall see below, although the negativity may have much to do with later Saxon hostility to German emperors.[14] Safe distance could elicit other kinds of response too. Adam of Bremen, in about 1075, wrote after an account of the conversion of Norway that 'meanwhile, the thousandth year since the Incarnation of the Lord was completed happily'.[15] As a narrative moment, however, it was the calm before the storm, as the following year Otto died and 'the kingdom remained under contention'.[16] The year spoke of turning points, and turning points came.

Examples could be multiplied and will be. Together, they prove that the millennial anniversaries were considered meaningful, but at the same time it is difficult to prove that that meaning was purely apocalyptic, millenarian, or anything else. It changed with individual perspective, no doubt. Many could have believed in an imminence that was unpredictable, as in the vision of a monk of St Vaast who was symbolically shown an unreadable end date in the afterlife.[17] One could list signs from the

---

[12] On Ademar's perceived aversion to chronology see R. Landes, *Relics, Apocalypse, and the Deceits of History: Ademar of Chabannes, 989–1034* (Cambridge, MA, 1995), esp. pp. 295–9. On his apocalyptic imagination see D. Callahan, 'Adémar of Chabannes, Apocalypticism and the Peace Council of Limoges of 1031', *Revue bénédictine*, 101 (1991), 32–49 and his 'Adémar of Chabannes, Millennial Fears and the Development of Western Anti-Judaism', *JEH*, 46.1 (1995), 19–35. Barthélemy misses the point by thinking Glaber and Ademar should have behaved the same if they had similar influences (*The Serf*, p. 288).

[13] *Annales Hildesheimenses*, s.a. 1000, ed. G. H. Pertz, MGH SS, 3 (Hanover, 1839), pp. 91–2: '[millesimus annus supercrescens statuit computationis numerum,] secundum illud quod legitur scriptum: millesimus exsuperat et transcendit omnia annus.' Apocalyptic reading: R. Landes, 'Sur les traces du Millennium: La via negativa', *Le Moyen Age*, 99 (1993), 5–26 at pp. 16–17, and compare Gouguenheim, *Les fausses terreurs*, pp. 68–9, who makes it a simple expression of Tyconian perfection.

[14] K. Görich, *Otto III. Romanus Saxonicus et Italicus. Kaiserliche Rompolitik und sächsische Historiographie* (Sigmaringen, 1993), p. 93; M. Gabriele, 'Otto III, Charlemagne, and Pentecost AD 1000: A Reconsideration using Diplomatic Evidence', in Frassetto (ed.), *The Year 1000*, pp. 111–32 at pp. 112–13.

[15] Adam of Bremen, *Gesta Hammaburgensis ecclesiae pontificum*, II. 40 (42), ed. B. Schmeidler, MGH SRG, 2 (Hanover, 1917), p. 101: 'interea millesimus ab incarnatione Domini annus feliciter impetus est.'

[16] Adam of Bremen, *Gesta Hammaburgensis*, p. 102: 'post mortem eius regnum in contentione remansit.'

[17] Hugh of Flavigny, *Chronicon*, ed. G. H. Pertz, MGH SS, 8 (Hanover, 1848), p. 390. Pertz's text has recently been corrected by Mathias Lawo: www.mgh.de/datenbanken/die-chronik-des-hugo-von-flavigny/.

period to make the approach of the Year 1000 look more portentous but there is no way to tell which ones were reported *because* of Y1K and which ones just happened to have been reported when Y1K was close.[18] When, anyway, were portentous signs actually at a premium? If signs were as commonly reported between 950 and 1050 as they were between 850 and 950 – and they were! – then it proves that signs are always interesting, not that people attached importance to one date in the middle.[19] But we must also be careful not to fall into the sceptics' trap of believing that signs are meaningless because they are so common. The way to proceed is to look at the circumstances of apocalyptic thought, signs and crisis and to take them on their own terms, rather than to subordinate them all to the proximity of Y1K. As Paul Magdalino observed for Byzantium, this might still mean that the proximity of Y1K was crucial in some cases – just not in every case. With this in mind we shall turn to one of the most popular 'apocalyptic' texts of the period, written with no apparent concern for Y1K at all but with a significant impact upon contemporary eschatology and soaked in Sibylline tradition: Adso's *On Antichrist*.

Adso and the restabilisation of the West

Stability was far from certain in the West Frankish world in the tenth century.[20] After the death of Charles the Fat (d. 888), Carolingian kings did reign from 898 to 922, and then from 936 to 987. Dynastic claims, however, were not enough any more. On three occasions members of the Robertine family were elected king at the expense of a Carolingian: Odo in 888, Robert in 922, and Hugh Capet in 987; and on each occasion it was because they were considered more effective leaders than the Carolingian alternative. Duke Raoul (or Radulf) of Burgundy also enjoyed over a decade of kingship from 923 to 936. The magic of the Carolingians withered only slowly, however, and in 936 the Robertine

---

[18] Even the report of an earthquake in 1000 (Valenciennes, Bibliothèque municipale, MS 343, f. 47v), which concludes 'his namque et aliis signis quae praenuntiata fuerunt opere completis, hinc iam fit nostra spes certior omni visu, de his quae restant ordine complendis', is only at best ambiguously *about* Y1K and could just be referring to an accumulation of signs including that one. Compare Landes, 'The Fear', p. 131 (who may nevertheless be right).

[19] www.mille.org/scholarship/1000/1000-dos.html compiled by Richard Landes is nevertheless a useful resource.

[20] The tenth century is a century more passed through than studied in detail. Recent collections and studies include T. Reuter (ed.), *The New Cambridge Medieval History*, III (Cambridge, 1999); C. Leyser, D. Rollason and H. Williams (eds.), *England and the Continent in the Tenth Century* (Turnhout, 2010).

duke Hugh 'the Great' himself was responsible for bringing Louis IV out of exile in England to succeed Raoul, although he then provided active competition for Louis which included imprisoning the king in 945–6. What few narrative sources there are present little sense of anxiety in the midst of such a complicated political situation. Moreover, contrary to the view of Verhelst and others, it actually seems to have been at the height of Louis IV's reign years later that his wife, Queen Gerberga, sought Adso's thoughts on Antichrist.[21]

With the uncertain political backdrop in mind, the political tone of Adso's letter is striking. 'As long as the kings of the Franks, who should hold the *imperium* of the Romans, endure', Adso assured Gerberga, 'the dignity of the Roman Empire will not perish altogether, because it remains in its kings.'[22] But of course, even when the Robertines or Raoul had reigned, this had been true, because they were still *reges Francorum* (kings of the Franks).[23] The diversification of leadership had devalued both dynasty and any institutional rendering of 'imperial authority'. Moreover, as Verhelst argued, Adso's perception of a persisting order under the Franks created an optimistic stance on the state of the world which opposed the imminence of the End.[24] But at the same time, Adso was concerned to stress how it was the unifying power of the last ruler which would define them, not their job title.[25] 'Certain of our teachers', Adso wrote, 'say that one of the kings of the Franks will hold the Roman Empire [or 'Roman authority'] in its entirety, and he will come in the Last Time and will be the greatest and last of all kings.'[26] It was unity, not

---

[21] D. Verhelst, 'Adso of Montier-en-Der and the Fear of the Year 1000', in Gow *et al.*, *The Apocalyptic Year 1000*, pp. 81–92 at pp. 84–5. See also Fried, 'Endzeiterwartung', pp. 420–2 and Landes, 'The Fear', pp. 118–19. The starting point for context should now be S. MacLean, 'Reform, Queenship and the End of the World in Tenth-Century France: Adso's "Letter on the Origin and Time of the Antichrist" Reconsidered', *Revue Belge de Philologie et d'Histoire*, 86 (2008), 645–75. Useful examination in C. Carozzi, *Apocalypse et salut dans le christianisme ancien et médiéval* (Paris, 1999), pp. 13–26 although whether it is 'paradoxical' (p. 18) should be queried. See also H. D. Rauh, *Das Bild des Antichrist im Mittelalter: Von Tyconius zum deutschen Symbolismus* (Münster, 1973), pp. 153–64.

[22] Adso, *De Antichristo*, ed. D. Verhelst, CCCM, 45 (Turnhout, 1976), p. 26: 'quandiu reges Francorum durauerint, qui Romanum imperium tenere debent, Romani regni dignitas ex toto non peribit, quia in regibus suis stabit.'

[23] Cf. Landes, 'The Fear', p. 119.

[24] Verhelst, 'Adso of Montier-en-Der', pp. 84–5.

[25] M. Gabriele, *An Empire of Memory: The Legend of Charlemagne, the Franks, and Jerusalem before the First Crusade* (Oxford, 2011), p. 110.

[26] Adso, *De Antichristo*, p. 26: 'Quidam vero doctores nostri dicunt, quod unus ex regibus Francorum, Romanum imperium ex integro tenebit, qui in novissimo tempore erit et ipse erit maximus et omnium regum ultimus.'

disorder, which would bring about the scenario leading up to Judgement. Peace was paramount but distant.

In keeping with this scenario, Adso developed his Last King figure squarely as a prelude to the coming of Antichrist, just as his source Pseudo-Methodius had done.[27] Here, Adso took odds and ends from the traditions surrounding Antichrist and created the first full biography of him, or an 'anti-hagiography' as Richard Emmerson has called it.[28] Indeed, Adso's Antichrist is very much the inverted Christ his name suggests. He would be a normal person, born to a mother and father rather than to a virgin, but because of the influence of the Devil he would be corrupt even in the womb. He would be born in Babylon, to contrast with Christ's birth in Bethlehem; and he would travel to Jerusalem, seduce the people – torturing the unconvertible – and rebuild the temple of Solomon. By this point, rather than being the opposite of Christ, he would be behaving like him, but with evil intentions and false miracles. The prophets Enoch and Elijah would then come and challenge Antichrist but they would be killed, paving the way for a continuation of persecution and the Parousia, when Christ would come and kill Antichrist with his breath. As a whole, there was not much radical here except the biography. The wider historical point, however, was that all this would happen far away and in the future. Current turbulence in France was no guide to apocalyptic events – as long as there was a Frankish king.

Precisely how this answered Gerberga's questions is anybody's guess. Adso's work may have had a reformist undercurrent as Gerberga was active on this front, and their mutual acquaintance Rorico of Laon was involved in a circle which explicitly identified 'antichrists' as the enemies of reform.[29] The letter could therefore be a piece of rallying rhetoric, strengthening the queen's resolve as a champion of good against evil. On the other hand it could be suggested that Gerberga may have been comforted by the unspoken confirmation that she was unlikely to give birth to

---

[27] R. Konrad, *De ortu et tempore Antichristi. Antichristvorstellung und Geschichtsbild des Abtes Adso von Montier-en-Der* (Kallmünz, 1964), pp. 33–4; B. McGinn, *Antichrist: Two ThousandYears of the Human Fascination with Evil* (San Francisco, 1994), p. 312. Doubts expressed about Adso's knowledge of Pseudo-Methodius in D. Verhelst, 'La préhistoire des conceptions d'Adson concernant l'Antichrist', *Recherches de théologie ancienne et médiévale*, 40 (1973), 52–103 at p. 101 and M. Rangheri, 'La *Espistola ad Gerbergam reginam de ortu et tempore Antichristi di Adsone* di Montier-en-Der e le sue fonti', *Studi Mediaevali*, 3rd series, 14 (1973), 677–732 at pp. 711–12.

[28] R. K. Emmerson, 'The Significance of Abbot Adso's *Libellus de Antichristo*', *American Benedictine Review*, 30 (1979), 175–90. 'Biographie' also in Rauh, *Das Bild des Antichrist*, p. 164.

[29] H. Löwe, '*Dialogus de statu sanctae ecclesiae*: Das Werk eines Iren im Laon des 10. Jahrhunderts', *DA*, 17 (1961), 12–90 at p. 76. MacLean, 'Reform, Queenship and the End of theWorld', pp. 655–6.

Antichrist with the millennial anniversary of Christ's Incarnation coming onto the horizon, but this is rather too speculative a line of thought.[30] Whatever answers she found, she seems to have played a role in circulating the text beyond Louis's spheres of authority, as indicated by a popular paraphrasing of the title 'description of a certain wise man … to Queen Gerberga, daughter of the most noble king, Henry of the Saxons' (although the oldest witness coming from Lyon, in the south, rather than Germany).[31] Here, as Verhelst observed, the text was at least proving adaptable in the face of shifting political realities and its own reception.

The place of *On Antichrist* in the spectrum of active Christian thought is apparent if one considers how it is juxtaposed with other texts. The Gerberga-version, for example, can be found in an early eleventh-century penitential from Worcester where it forms chapter 72 of a *Book of Sparks*, providing a conclusion to a list of virtues which builds up to a reflection on death and Judgement, possibly initially collected by Wulfstan.[32] This was but one such re-employment of the text, to judge by Alboin the Hermit's use of it in his compendium of virtues and vices produced for Archbishop Heribert of Cologne (d. 1021).[33] Slightly later, a theological collection from St Emmeram's, Regensburg, betrayed similar concerns, with the *sermo*-version of *On Antichrist* copied towards the end, after extracts on topics such as baptism, as part of a series on simony, judgement, fornicating priests, lapsed priests, penance, and alms-giving.[34] Placed so, the warnings about Antichrist are an integral part of reflecting upon sin and correction. To that end, Alboin encouraged Heribert to 'make copies often, so that many people may have them … lest I am sorry to impose such great labour upon them [as penance]'.[35]

The role that *On Antichrist* found in penitential thought blurred the distinction between personal and collective eschatologies, because it meant people were contemplating both together. In the process, Adso's work began to influence high-level political discourse. The examples of the Worcester manuscript and the redaction for Heribert begin to reveal

[30] P. Skinner and E. van Houts (eds.), *Medieval Writings on Secular Women* (Harmondsworth, 2011), pp. 4 and 10.
[31] *Descriptio*, ed. Verhelst, pp. 43–9, with comment on the paraphrase at p. 34; Lyon, Bibliothèque municipale, MS 620, f. 110v.
[32] Cambridge, Corpus Christi College, MS 190, pp. 281–91, with problematic contents page at ix–x: see M. Bateson, 'A Worcester Cathedral Book of Ecclesiastical Collections, Made c. 1000 AD', *EHR*, 10 (1895), 712–31 at pp. 715–20.
[33] Verhelst, CCCM, 45, p. 81.
[34] Munich, Bayerische Staatsbibliothek, Clm 14569, ff. 135–40.
[35] *Incipit liber scintillarum collectus ab Albuino heremita*, ed. Verhelst, p. 81: 'tunc sepius facite rescribere, ut plures illum habeant, ne me penitet tantum imposuisse laborem super eum.'

the active use of the text in powerful circles: Worcester was the one-time home of Archbishop Wulfstan of York, who as we shall see worked with kings of England, while Heribert was one of Emperor Otto III's closest advisors. But before we pursue these case studies, we need to pay attention to the rise of Sibylline tradition because of the way it intersected with Adso's work.

The rise of the Sibyls

Stories about the oracles of the Sibyls enjoyed renewed prominence under the Ottonians, the ducal Saxon family who had held the East Frankish throne since 912.[36] This seems to have occurred as a consequence of the actions of Otto I (r. 936–73), who not only reinvigorated the office of emperor in 962 after conquering Italy and 'restoring' the papacy, but also pursued legitimisation through a marriage alliance between his son, Otto II, and a Byzantine imperial princess. The doors were open for a reorientation of imperial thought with stronger Byzantine influences, particularly once Emperor Nikephoros II Phokos (r. 963–9) had been deposed by John I Tzimiskes (r. 969–76) and a certain thawing of East–West relations helped Otto to secure the emperor's niece Theophanu as a wife for his son.[37] This was important for apocalyptic tradition because Bishop Liudprand of Cremona (d. 972), one of the emissaries involved in negotiations, noted that 'the Greeks and the Saracens have books that they call oracles or visions of Daniel, and I call Sibylline books' when he reported back to Otto I, Otto II and Queen Adelheid on his initial failures.[38] A particularly Eastern apocalyptic tradition was about to head West.

The traditions Liudprand referred to can be found in a number of interrelated texts of the ninth and tenth centuries. While most presented themselves as 'dreams of Daniel', they offered expansions or elaborations of the kind of prophecy first found in Pseudo-Methodius's still-popular revelations (see Chapter 4). Still present were hopes that the Saracens would be defeated, and that an emperor would bring peace, but also that afterwards the trials and tribulations of the End Times, with the reign of Antichrist and the attacks of the unclean nations, would inevitably come. The most notable 'innovation' was the expansion of the sequence of rulers leading up to the End Times, much as one could find earlier in the

[36] G. Althoff, *Die Ottonen. Königsherrschaft ohne Staat* (2nd edn, Stuttgart, 2005).
[37] A. von Euw and P. Schreiner (eds.), *Kaiserin Theophanu: Begegnung des Ostens und Westens um die Wende des ersten Jahrtausends* (2 vols, Cologne, 1991).
[38] Liudprand, *Relatio de legatione Constantinopolitana*, c. 39, ed. P. Chiesa, CCCM, 156 (Turnhout, 1998), p. 195: 'Habent Greci et Saraceni libros, quos ὁράσεις sive visiones, Danielis vocant, ego autem Sibyllanos.'

Oracle of Baalbek.[39] Detailed prophecies would be harder to fulfil – yet, at least according to Liudprand, they also encouraged people to speculate over whether prophecy was on the way to being fulfilled and so to act accordingly. Emperor Nikephoros, at least, had been encouraged to attack the Saracens because of them.

Liudprand's extended comments on the subject of prophecy were dismissive but at least informed. At one point, to underline his thoughts on the matter, he recounted how he had met astronomers who were capable of cold reading, able to tell him accurately about his past and to make predictions about the future which came true; but he cared not for such 'lies' (*mendacia*).[40] He did, however, make much polemical use of a prophecy of a 'certain Hippolytus': 'the lion and the cub together shall exterminate the wild donkey'.[41] At Nikephoros's court, Liudprand asserted, this was understood to mean that the emperor (the lion) and Otto (the cub) would conquer the Arabs (associated symbolically with donkeys after Gen. 16.12). Liudprand did not appreciate the assumed similarity between Nikephoros and Otto here because he found nearly everything about the emperor distasteful, and so he argued that the lion and cub were really Otto I and Otto II taking down donkey-loving Nikephoros.[42] Here Liudprand recorded a prophecy by the same Hippolytus that it would be the Franks rather than the Greeks who would defeat the Saracens, which the bishop gave hope for by pointing out the failure in 964 of a Byzantine attempt to secure Sicily. Liudprand clearly used this discussion of prophecy to denigrate Nikephoros and two reasons – not exclusive of each other – can be put forward: on the one hand, Liudprand could show his failure to secure a Byzantine bride for Otto II as a slice of fortune, while on the other, he could legitimise Otto's ambitions to secure Byzantine-dominated southern Italy for himself.[43]

While Liudprand's discussion of Sibylline traditions superficially focused on the prophetic over the apocalyptic, evidence has emerged which seems to suggest that apocalyptic thought was not so far from his mind either. One text in particular reveals discussion between intellectuals in the East and West about the Year 1000 and its implications.

[39] For an example see L. Rydén, 'The Andreas Salos Apocalypse: Greek Text, Translation and Commentary', *Dumbarton Oaks Papers*, 28 (1974), 197–261, discussed at pp. 229–46.
[40] Liudprand, *Relatio*, c. 42, p. 198. In modern predictive thought, this is probably 'cold reading'.
[41] Liudprand, *Relatio*, c. 40, p. 196: 'Leo et catulus simul exterminabunt onagrum'.
[42] The whole prophetic section of the text follows a story about Nikephoros owning donkeys: *Relatio*, c. 38, p. 195.
[43] H. Mayr-Harting, 'Liudprand of Cremona's Account of His Legation to Constantinople (968) and Ottonian Imperial Strategy', *EHR*, 116.467 (2001), 539–56 at p. 553.

In the first half of the tenth century, Niketas (David) the Paphlagonian addressed a letter to 'Western bishops', who had approached him concerning the authenticity of Revelation, the meaning of a 'thousand-year reign', and whether there were really only fifty years left to complete the millennium.[44] Niketas, drawing on Theophanios's calculations, took these issues seriously. Brandes notes that Bishop Siegfried of Parma and Liudprand himself were both in Constantinople towards the end of 944 when Niketas was active and so it is likely they who were the Western bishops in question.[45] If nothing else, knowledge of Greek in the tenth-century West was so rare that is hard to identify an alternative audience.[46] We are at least still afforded a glimpse of the role of East–West communication in the course of contemplation about possible apocalyptic scenarios.

With this background, it is unsurprising to discover that someone in Ottonian Italy composed a new Sibylline text, drawing on a Syrian or Greek original. In form, it was a variation on the Tiburtine Sibyl which generated the *Oracle of Baalbek* (Chapter 1), with the Sibyl interpreting a dream about nine suns to the people of Rome as a prophetic history leading up to the End Times. Anke Holdenried has shown convincingly that the popularity of the text lay not a little bit in the fact that the Sibyl – a pagan character – was said to have prophesied the first coming of Christ.[47] Modern scholars have nevertheless repeatedly fixated on lists of letters denoting kings and emperors, which represent retrospective prophetic histories of Italian rule from the Lombards through to the Ottonian conquests (possibly the end of one interpolation) and the Salians up to Henry III (the oldest complete version).[48] The lists are so unsystematically arranged that the text cannot represent a coherent 'apocalyptic history' and perhaps rather attests to the text's status as something repeatedly toyed with and re-edited in response to a variety of situations, now largely unrecoverable.[49] The result, on the other hand, established Italian political history as the background to the rise of the

---

[44] Letter edited by L. G. Westerink, 'Nicetas the Paphlagonian on the End of the World', in *Essays in Memory of Basil Laourdas* (Thessalonica, 1975), pp. 177–95.

[45] Brandes, 'Liudprand', p. 457.

[46] W. Berschin, *Greek Letters and the Latin Middle Ages: From Jerome to Nicholas of Cusa*, trans. J. C. Frakes (2nd edn, Washington DC, 1988); P. Squatriti, *The Complete Works of Liudprand of Cremona* (Washington, DC, 2007), pp. 16–17.

[47] A. Holdenried, *The Sibyl and Her Scribes: Manuscripts and Interpretation of the Latin Sibylla Tiburtina, c. 1050–1500* (Aldershot, 2006). See esp. *Oracula Tiburtina*, ed. E. Sackur, *Sibyllinische Texte und Forschungen* (Halle, 1898), p. 179.

[48] *Oracula Tiburtina*, pp. 181–4. For Sackur's reconstruction of the original names see *Sibyllinische Texte*, pp. 129–37.

[49] A. Holdenried, 'Many Hands without Design: The Evolution of a Medieval Prophetic Text', *The Mediaeval Journal*, 4.1 (2014), 23–42.

last 'King of the Greeks and Romans', whose cleansing reign would set the scene for the reign of Antichrist in Jerusalem. The West was being rewritten into an Eastern-style apocalyptic tradition.

Further proof of this development lies in the legend that Charlemagne himself would return as the Last Emperor. The Tiburtine Sibyl contained an old prophecy that the Emperor Constans would come in the Last Days to unite Christendom, destroy paganism, and pave the way for the conversion of the Jews and the coming of Antichrist (see Chapter 4).[50] Almost immediately, at least one reader thought this resonated with Adso's *On Antichrist*. The two texts were brought together at Fécamp in Normandy – the Normans, of course, also being firmly entrenched in Italy at this time – where they were combined with a copy of Ralph Glaber's *Life of William of Volpiano* to provide ominous commentary on the unsettled political scene of the 1030s.[51] The author of a new recension of Adso's text went one further and integrated the Constans-Vaticinium, recasting Constans as 'C', a Frankish *rex Romanorum* who would reign for 112 years, destroy Gog and Magog, and give over his authority, his *imperium*, at the end.[52] This 'C' could only really be Charlemagne, which shows how Charlemagne's eschatological vision of unity had continued to resonate and develop since his death. Possibly the figure most inspired by these developments early on was a man living within the shadow of the Year 1000: Emperor Otto III (d. 1002).

Otto III and imperial spirituality

Otto III stands out as the most troubled and troubling of the Ottonian emperors, in terms of both real politics and apocalyptic tradition.[53] The young Otto was raised to the purple aged only three, whereupon he was guided for over a decade by his Greek mother, Theophanu, and an assortment of nobles. His personal reign was characterised by his romanticisation of the Roman Empire and Charlemagne, and a curious piety which saw him take an interest in the ascetic holy man Romuald of Ravenna, pilgrimage to Jerusalem, and the conversion of Bohemia and Hungary. In outline there is nothing necessarily exceptional about such fancies in a medieval ruler. Otto, however, died in 1002 aged only

[50] *Oracula Tiburtina*, p. 185.
[51] Paris, Bibliothèque nationale, lat. 5390, ff. 222–35.
[52] *De tempore Antichristi*, ed. Verhelst, pp. 135–6; Gabriele, *An Empire of Memory*, pp. 123–5. See also the Cummaen tradition: C. Erdmann, 'Endkaiserglaube und Kreuzzugsgedanke im 11. Jahrhundert', *Zeitschrift für Kirchengeschichte*, 51 (1932), 384–414 at pp. 398–402.
[53] G. Althoff, *Otto III*, trans. P. G. Jestice (University Park, PA, 2003).

twenty-one, having apparently generated the impression that he was little more than a politically negligent youthful romantic or, to later scholars, 'an unbalanced religious mystic'.[54] A more positive recent reassessment by Gerd Althoff presented the king as a dynamic young man open to novelty. But Althoff's intention was to show that political life in tenth-century Germany was dominated by symbolic communication and ritual, underpinned by *Spielregeln* ('rules of the game'); and as such, Otto's spirituality, and possible apocalypticism, figure little in his account. As a number of historians have stressed, most recently Levi Roach, to exclude the apocalyptic is to misunderstand the young emperor and the rules by which he played.[55]

It is, for a start, possible that Otto considered himself to be a LastWorld Emperor figure – a model he could easily have encountered in discussion withTheophanu (for a Greek view) or Heribert (for Adso). Certainly he was deeply interested in *renovatio imperii Romanorum* – the renewal of Roman authority – but obviously this was a many-sided objective.[56] Yet, on the day of his imperial coronation in 996, in Rome, Otto allegedly wore a mantle 'on which the whole of Apocalypse was marked out in gold'.[57] Here would have been a public statement of some note, binding together imperial authority and reflection on Judgement.[58] Accounts recorded the ceremony as a straightforward imperial coronation, even in the letter drafted by Gerbert of Aurillac (later Pope Sylvester II) for Otto reporting on his coronation to his grandmother, so we might want to think about the situational importance of the mantle rather than any

---

[54] This is the characterisation of Otto in the literature as summarised by Landes, 'The Fear', p. 99.

[55] B. Arnold, 'Eschatological Imagination and the Program of Roman Imperial and Ecclesiastical Renewal at the End of theTenth Century', in Gow *et al.*, *The Apocalyptic Year 1000*, pp. 271–88; Gabriele, 'Otto III'; H. Möhring, 'Die *renovatio imperii* Kaiser Ottos III. und die Antichrist-Erwartung der Zeitgenossen an der Jahrtausendwende von 1000/1001', *Archiv für Kulturgeschichte*, 93.2 (2011), 333–50; L. Roach, 'Otto III and the End ofTime', *TRHS*, 6th series, 23 (2013), 75–102.

[56] P. E. Schramm, *Kaiser, Rom und Renovatio. Studien zur Geschichte des römischen Erneuerungsgedankens vom Ende des karolingischen Reiches bis zum Investiturstreit*, I (Leipzig and Berlin, 1929); Görich, *Otto III*.

[57] *Miracula Alexii*, c. 9, ed. J. Pien, AASS July IV (Paris and Rome, 1868), p. 259: 'in quo omnis Apocalipsis erat auro insignita.' Comparisons can be made to Henry II's star mantle but so different must they have been that I doubt much light is shed on the form or function of the apocalypse mantle.

[58] Compare Gouguenheim's minimisation of the mantle's importance on the grounds that, despite its unique nature, it merely illustrated common symbols of power (*Les fausses terreurs de l'an mil*, pp. 136–7). P. Klein, 'Medieval Apocalypse Cycles and Eschatological Expectations: The So-Called "Terrors" of the Year 1000', in R. E. Guglielmetti (ed.), *L'apocalisse nel medioevo* (Florence, 2009), pp. 267–301 at pp. 273–4 also finds the choice of apocalypse illustration completely without any apocalyptic resonance.

universal significance.[59] This is, after all, a garment known about only because it is mentioned as one of Otto's gifts to his favoured monastery of Ss Bonifacius and Alexios on the Aventine in Rome. The story goes that the abbot Adalbert – possibly the later bishop of Prague – swapped it for something else because he did not feel that it was of use to his community.[60] When the matter came to the attention of a judge, he confiscated the mantle for the treasury rather than returning it to the monastery; and so Adalbert brought upon himself the vengeance of the saints as he fell ill until, prompted by a series of visions, the garment could be returned. From the perspective of the eleventh-century author, presumably in Ss Bonifacius and Alexios itself, the mantle had come to represent a rich gift from a beneficent emperor, more than it remained a symbolic part of a ritual setting. Moreover, from Otto's perspective, it seems that the mantle did not have a place in how he continued to represent himself publicly, if it was something of which he could make a gift. The story of Otto's apocalyptic mantle confirms that we are dealing with an individual alive to the drama of public statement, but also open to playing with different ideas and models which could shift meaning depending on context.

Some of these issues about visual apocalypse carry over into analysis of the Bamberg Apocalypse – a beautiful illuminated copy of Revelation likely made for Otto III at Reichenau.[61] On the whole, in terms of its image scheme, it moves things on little from Carolingian illuminated apocalypses, which provided literal representations of scenes from Revelation.[62] In an unusual Last Judgement scene, however, we do see what seems to be a young, crowned Otto III standing next to a woman (Theophanu?) and being pulled towards Hell, while looking diagonally

[59] Accounts in Thietmar, *Chronicon*, IV. 47 (29), ed. R. Holtzmann, MGH SRG, n.s. 9 (Berlin, 1935), pp. 184/186; *Annales Quedlingburgenses*, s.a. 996, ed. M. Giese, MGH SRG, 72 (Hanover, 2004), p. 491. *Die Briefsammlung Gerberts von Reims*, no. 215, ed. F. Weigle, MGH Briefe der deuschen Kaiserzeit, 2 (Weimar, 1966), pp. 256–7.

[60] *Miracula Alexii*, c. 9, p. 259–60. The identification of *Adalbertus abbas* with Adalbert of Prague is suggested by I. N. Wood, *The Missionary Life: Saints and the Evangelization of Europe 400–1050* (Harlow, 2001), p. 214.

[61] Bamberg, Staatsbibliothek, Msc. Bibl. 140. For interpretation and context H. Mayr-Harting, 'Apocalyptic Book Illustration in the Early Middle Ages', in C. Rowland and J. Barton (eds.), *Apocalyptic in History and Tradition* (London and New York, 2002), pp. 179–82 and more generally his *Ottonian Book Illumination: An Historical Study* (2 vols., London, 1991–9); Fried, 'Endzeiterwartung', p. 429. Klein, 'Medieval Apocalypse Cycles', pp. 275–8 argues that the apocalyptic aspects are carefully muted.

[62] On the Carolingian cycles see P. Klein, 'The Apocalypse in Medieval Art', in R. K. Emmerson and B. McGinn, *The Apocalypse in the Middle Ages* (Ithaca, NY, 1993), pp. 175–9 and J. Snyder, 'The Reconstruction of an Early Christian Cycle of Illustrations for the Book of Revelation – The Trier Apocalypse', *Vigiliae Christianae*, 18 (1964), 146–62.

Figure 6 Judgement Day in the Bamberg Apocalypse.

upwards towards his own salvation (f. 53r).[63] The manuscript also ends with an image of Otto enthroned at the end of time (ff. 59v–60r). What we do not know about this kind of manuscript is exactly how it was to be used: was it for private meditation, for impressing people at court, or both? Whichever way, the combination of penitentialism and triumphalism in the face of the Last Judgement reveals much about how Otto considered himself as a non-static figure before Christ.[64]

[63] For this interpretation of the scene see G. Lobrichon, 'Jugement sur la terre comme au ciel. L'étrange cas de l'Apocalypse millénaire de Bamberg', *Médiévales*, 37 (1999), 71–9.
[64] S. E. von Daum Tholl, 'Visualizing the Millennium: Eschatological Rhetoric for the Ottonian Court', in Gow, Landes and van Meter, *The Apocalyptic Year 1000*, pp. 231–8 at p. 237.

The mantle and Bamberg Apocalypse provide 'clues', but much of the thought-world behind them remains obscured for us. Much scholarly attention has focused on how Otto, at Pentecost in the all-important Year 1000, opened up the tomb of Charlemagne – something, it has been suggested, which shows Otto inheriting the apocalyptic role from his illustrious predecessor because Charlemagne seemed to be sleeping, waiting to be recalled to action.[65] Otto would have made a good heir, being a half-Greek *rex Romanorum*, interested in converting pagans, restoring Rome and even heading to Jerusalem, as we shall see. He fitted the Tiburtine prophecy surprisingly well. Objections can be raised, however, since the sources are rather vague. Maybe Otto was just interested in Charlemagne, maybe even in canonising him.[66] Did Otto even know any Sibylline prophecies? One may have to concede at least that, if Otto opened the tomb secretly, only so much political capital could have been gained from an act with no spectacle.[67] His motivations remain unclear. Indeed, it is perhaps telling that Thietmar introduced his version of the story by noting that Otto 'did much that was understood differently by different people' (*multa faciebat, quae diversi diverse sentiebant*). Even if Otto's mind had been on apocalyptic matters, he was failing to control the conversation about his actions.

Charters show that it was not for want of trying. Many of these, as Hartmut Hoffmann has shown, he dictated himself, which means that they provide a teasing insight into the emperor's view of his authority.[68] One striking example comes in a document Otto issued while reforming the monastery of Farfa in 999, which is unusual not only for including a spiritual justification, but also for insisting that anyone who violated his vision would have to answer to the coming Christ 'when he comes to judge the age with fire'.[69] (Teasingly, this is more than a little reminiscent

[65] Gabriele, 'Otto III', p. 119; Gabriele, *An Empire of Memory*, pp. 120–1. R. Folz, *Le souvenir et la légende de Charlemagne dans l'empire germanique médiéval* (Paris, 1950), pp. 92–3 (but without the apocalypse).
[66] K. Görich, 'Otto III öffnet das Karlsgrab in Aachen: Überlegungen zu Heiligenverehrung, Heiligsprechung und Traditionsbildung', in G. Althoff and E. Schubert (eds.), *Herrschaftsrepräsentation im ottonischen Sachsen* (Sigmaringen, 1998), pp. 381–430, supported by Althoff, *Otto III*, pp. 105–6.
[67] Thietmar, *Chronicon*, IV. 47 (29), p. 184; Görich, 'Otto III öffnet das Karlsgrab', pp. 388–9. Gabriele is probably right to suggest that Görich's polarisation of 'political' and 'holy' purpose is too simplistic in this case ('Otto III', p. 114).
[68] H. Hoffmann, 'Eigendiktat in den Urkunden ottos III. und Heinrichs II.', *DA*, 44 (1988), 390–423 at 392–9.
[69] *Diplomata Ottonis III*, no. 331, ed. T. Sickel, MGH Diplomatum regum et imperatorum Germaniae, 2. 2 (Hanover, 1893), pp. 759–60: 'dum venerit iudicare saeculum per ignem.' On the context see Roach, 'Otto III', pp. 87–9.

of a phrase from Recension 3 of Pseudo-Methodius from Novara.)[70]
Shortly before he entered Charlemagne's tomb, Otto granted the town of
Salz to Würzburg and ordered that 'objections be held off until the end of
time and the Day of Judgement'.[71] Otto liked an eschatological flourish to
reinforce his will and may even have performed them, reading them out to
his audience. After the Aachen trip, Otto also seems to have preferred to
call himself 'servant of Jesus Christ and, after the will of God, our saviour
and liberator, august Roman emperor', which gave him an unusual
quasi-apostolic character that might have resonated with a Last Emperor
schtick.[72] None of this has been enough to convince Gouguenheim that
there was anything more going on here than mild spins on old formulae
for threatening people and for self-aggrandisement.[73] Yet it was idiosyncratic and it does draw attention to Otto's models for piety.

A more public dynamic of Otto's spirituality, and again one with apocalyptic analogues, is his association with pilgrimage. Pilgrimage is a complex phenomenon at the best of times, with any single instance of travel
open to multiple (re)interpretations, states, destinations and constituent ritual acts.[74] Otto himself undertook three. In the first, in 998, Otto
undertook a penitential pilgrimage to Monte Gargano and the shrine of
St Michael – slayer of Antichrist in some stories – to visit the aged holy
man St Nilus and to make a show of his remorse for the harsh treatment
of the rebel Crescentius and antipope John Philagathos, even though
some thought them to be 'ministers of Satan'.[75] Only a few months later,
setting out late in 999, Otto undertook what appears to have been a pilgrimage from Rome to the shrine of his martyred friend St Adalbert of
Prague; but, as Gerd Althoff observes, contemporary reporters saw not
a penitential pilgrimage but rather an opportunity for the emperor to be
seen and received with honour by many north of the Alps.[76] Indeed, the

[70] Karlsruhe, Badische Landesbibliothek, Aug. perg. 254, f. 209v: 'Et cum uenerit Dominus postea iudicare seculum per ignem, tunc apparebit crux ante eum sicut dixit apostolus ad arguendum prophetia in fidelium.'
[71] *Diplomata Ottonis III*, no. 361, pp. 790–1: 'obiectione usque finem seculi et diem iudicii longe remota.'
[72] Gabriele, 'Otto III', pp. 119–20.
[73] Gouguenheim, *Les fausses terreurs*, pp. 138–9.
[74] On Otto III in this context, see S. Hamilton, 'Otto III's Penance: A Case Study of Unity and Diversity in the Eleventh-Century Church', *Studies in Church History*, 32 (1996), 83–94.
[75] Althoff, *Otto III*, pp. 71–81. *Vita Nili*, c. 91, ed. and trans. M. Carophylus, AASS, Sept VII (Antwerp, 1760), p. 337. Also *Annales Quedlingburgenses*, s.a. 998, pp. 497–8. More posi-tive on Otto's treatment of Crescentius and Philagathos is the assessment of Thietmar, *Chronicon*, IV. 30 (21), pp. 167/169. On the cult of St Michael see D. Callahan, 'The Cult of St Michael the Archangel and the "Terrors of the Year 1000"', in Gow et al., *The Apocalyptic Year 1000*, pp. 181–204.
[76] Althoff, *Otto III*, p. 98. See for example *Annales Quedlingburgenses*, s.a. 999, p. 511.

emperor's travels were to be dominated by the establishment of good relations with the Polish ruler Boleslav Chrobry, who accompanied Otto back from St Adalbert's shrine to Aachen just before the opening of Charlemagne's tomb. Pilgrimage, here, established a moving political stage with different spiritual meanings at different stages.

It is the third of Otto's planned pilgrimages that is the most curious, because, just as in the Last World Emperor legends, it involved a plan to retire to Jerusalem. According to Bruno of Querfurt, in his last days Otto had become so disillusioned with worldly things because of opposition to him that he announced: 'after three years, during which I shall correct the faults of my empire, I shall relinquish my kingdom to someone better than me and, distributing the money my mother left me as an inheritance, I shall follow Christ with my soul stripped bare.'[77] The terse response from Romuald of Ravenna was, correctly, that he would be dead within a year, but Otto's mind was made up, and in conversation later in the story the monks Benedict and Bruno discuss how Otto wanted to retreat to hermitage as a monk in Jerusalem 'to philosophize'.[78] This, Fried suggests, ties in with prophecies about the Last World Emperor, even if it does so in a rather unspecific manner.[79] Yet within this generality, it seems that Bruno was specifically moved to write in praise of Otto's piety; and indeed Otto's actions are 'for the love of the eternal life', bringing to mind Adalbert of Prague's homily on St Alexios which encouraged the faithful to imitate the saint by relinquishing earthly things to become a *peregrinus* and earn eternal life.[80] Indeed, the two early *vitae* about Adalbert – one written by Bruno – say that Adalbert was en route to Jerusalem on pilgrimage when Nilus convinced him against the necessity for a *peregrinus* to travel to specific places, leading him to enter a stable exile in the monastery of Ss Bonifacius and Alexios instead.[81] All this fits into long-running debates about acceptable and appropriate forms of pilgrimage relative to the monastic life, which Bruno acknowledges by explicitly citing Jerome's comment to Paulinus of Nola that 'it is not laudable to go to Jerusalem, but to have lived well in Jerusalem'.[82] Travel

---

[77] Bruno, *Vita quinque patrum*, c. 2, ed. R. Kade, MGH SS, 15. 2 (Hanover, 1887), p. 719: 'post tres annos, intra quos imperii mei errata corrigam, meliori me regnum dimittam et, expensa pecunia, quam mihi mater pro hereditate reliquit, tota anima nudus sequar Christum.'

[78] Bruno, *Vita quinque patrum.*, c. 3, pp. 720–1.

[79] Fried, 'Endzeiterwartung', p. 431.

[80] Adalbert of Prague, *Homilia*, ed. J. Pien, AASS, July IV, pp. 257–8, especially c. 6, p. 258. The homily is based upon Bede's homily for Benedict Biscop.

[81] John Canaparius, *Vita Adalberti*, cc. 14–15, ed. G. H. Pertz, MGH SS, 4 (Hanover, 1841), pp. 586–8; Bruno, *Vita Adalberti*, cc. 12–13, ed. Pertz, MGH SS, 4, pp. 601–2.

[82] Bruno, *Vita Adalberti*, c. 13, p. 601; Jerome, *Epistola*, no. 58. 2, ed. I. Hilberg, CSEL 54 (Vienna, 1996), p. 529. On the resonance of these debates for Adalbert, see Wood, *The*

meant nothing without the conversion of the soul. Nevertheless, it seems from Bruno that Otto did intend to 'live well in Jerusalem' by dedicating himself to philosophy in a hermitage instead of simply going through the motions of visiting the holy places. Our one source for Otto's renunciation of imperial honour, then, fits within a close social and textual network which clearly suggests that Adalbert's spirituality was a defining influence on Otto in his final years. The Last World Emperor legend may still have had 'resonance', particularly for Otto himself, but it was one influence amongst many.

Assessing the 'Emperor of the Year 1000' will never satisfy everyone. There are too many unusual resonances in Otto's behaviour for some historians to dismiss any apocalyptic interests out of hand, but at the same time things are not so clear in the sources as to convince the sceptics. Maybe the ambiguities are exactly what we should expect. People are often not consistent, or at least are subject to a complex mix of influences, while the societies in which they live tend not to be homogenous. Apocalyptic discourse would then have been more useful to Otto at some points than others, and on top of that he might have felt the pull of tradition at some points more than others. Believing in some degree of imminence of Judgement still left a complicated life to lead. Even if it did not dominate everything and in every way, apocalypse had a place here.

Wulfstan's England in crisis

Otto's penitentialist behaviour, and the mood of his empire, can usefully be compared to events in England around the same time.[83] Comparison between Germany and England is particularly apposite because of the close connections between the two, even if their political trajectories look somewhat different. Otto I, Gerberga's brother, was married to Eadgyth (Edith), the sister of King Æthelstan, the first king of all the English.[84] Memories of such connections lingered naturally, encouraging Eadgyth's granddaughter, Abbess Matilda of Essen, to request a 'family history'

Missionary Life, p. 214. For background see J. T. Palmer, *Anglo-Saxons in a Frankish World, 690–900* (Turnhout, 2009), chs. 1 and 7.

[83] Fried, 'Endzeiterwartung', pp. 434–6; S. Keynes, 'Apocalypse Then: England AD 1000', in P. Urbańczyk (ed.), *Europe around the Year 1000* (Warsaw, 2001), pp. 247–70; Godden, 'The Millennium'; L. Roach, 'Apocalypse and Atonement in the Politics of Æthelredian England', *English Studies* 95 (2014). For wider context on theology and belief see now H. Foxhall Forbes, *Heaven and Earth in Anglo-Saxon England: Theology and Society in an Age of Faith* (Farnham, 2013), esp. ch. 3.

[84] On the context see S. Foot, 'Dynastic Strategies, The West Saxon Royal Family in Europe' in D. Rollason, C. Leyser and H. Williams (eds.), *England and the Continent in the Tenth Century: Studies in Honour of Wilhelm Levison (1876–1947)* (Turnhout, 2010), pp. 237–54.

from her distant relative Ealdorman Æthelweard towards the end of the century, even as connections 'thinned'.[85] But most of all, England was another place where Adso's work became popular, where the king engaged in public displays of penitence, and there was open speculation about Antichrist and the significance of Y1K. This was an anxious time. Danes, led by their king Svein Forkbeard, greatly unsettled the kingdom by raiding which only subsided briefly during a famine in 1005. In 1009 a huge fleet landed at Sandwich, and over the next five years Svein set about conquering England, eventually forcing King Æthelred II 'Unræd' – the 'ill-counselled' – into exile.[86] As the stock of the English fell, Archbishop Wulfstan of York called them to penance and berated them all with his famous *Sermon of the Wolf to the English*:

Beloved men, know that which is true: this world is in haste and it nears the end. And therefore things in this world go ever the longer the worse, and so it must needs be that things quickly worsen, on account of people's sinning from day to day, before the coming of Antichrist. And indeed it will then be awful and grim widely throughout the world.[87]

In practice, there was a long-soaked mood of diffused apocalypticism in England stretching back at least to the middle of the tenth century. An outbreak of plague in London in 962, followed by the burning down of St Peter's, seems to have triggered the popular use of a proem in charters which addressed the urgency of action with the end of the world approaching.[88] King Edgar issued a new law code in response to the sense of crisis, addressing various matters, but introduced with a statement about how present troubles were divine punishment for sin.[89] Homilists

[85] J. Roberts, 'Saint Oswald and Anglo-Saxon Identity in the *Chronicon Æthelweardi*: The Correspondence of Æthelweard and Abbess Matilda', in H. Sauer and J. Story (eds.), *Anglo-Saxon England and the Continent* (Tempe, AZ, 2011), pp. 163–78; K. Leyser, 'The Ottonians and Wessex', in T. Reuter (ed.), *Communication and Power in Medieval Europe* (London, 1994), pp. 73–104.

[86] S. Keynes, 'An Abbot, an Archbishop, and the Vikings Raids of 1006–7 and 1009–12', *Anglo-Saxon England*, 36 (2007), 151–220, esp. pp. 186–8 on penance.

[87] Wulfstan, *Sermo Lupi ad Anglos*, ed. D. Bethurum, *The Homilies of Wulfstan* (Oxford, 1957), p. 267: 'Leofan men gecnawað þæt soð is: ðeos worolde is on ofste & hit nealæcð þam ende. & þy hit is on worolde aa swa leng swa wyrse, & swa hit sceal nyde for folces synnan fram dæge to dæge, ær antecristes tocyme, yfelian swyþe. & huru hit wyrð þænne egeslic & grimlic wide on worolde.' The text may now be dated to the crisis of 1009 rather than to 1014: see Keynes, 'An Abbot, an Archbishop', pp. 212–13. On Wulfstan's homilies and eschatology see J. T. Lionarons, *The Homiletic Writings of Archbishop Wulfstan* (Woodbridge, 2010).

[88] R. H. Bremmer, 'The Final Countdown: Apocalyptic Expectations in Anglo-Saxon Charters', in G. Jaritz and G. Moreno-Riaño (eds.), *Time and Eternity: The Medieval Discourse* (Turnhout, 2003), pp. 501–14 at pp. 509–10.

[89] Edgar III (the Andover Code), ed. F. Liebermann, *Die Gesetze der Angelsachsen* (3 vols., Halle, 1903), I. 200.

including Ælfric of Eynsham made great capital of the imminence of the world's end and the coming of Antichrist, in part inspired by Gregory the Great, as they cajoled their audiences into taking care of their souls.[90] It is not surprising in such a context to find an Old English translation of the *Vision of St Paul* in circulation, with its repertoire of punishments for sins ahead of the Last Judgement. Indeed, elements were incorporated into the Blickling Homilies to encourage reflection while alluding to imminence.[91] Anxiety and reform again sat side by side. None of this was explicitly in reference to Y1K, or indeed even representative of a consistent line of thought, so again we might prefer to see an events-focused eschatology in play alongside speculation about chronology.

The fostering of a penitential mood came to the fore under troubled Æthelred.[92] Vikings assaults continued to destabilise and unsettle the kingdom, while the king's own actions included widespread abuses in the Church, from the devastation of the see of Rochester in 986 to the sale of Church lands and even the monastery of Abingdon. In 993, just as a great Danish army was mustering, Æthelred began a campaign of remorse and atonement for his 'youthful indiscretions'.[93] In part, the king moved to make good losses of the Church directly, as recorded in diplomas which laid great rhetorical stress on penitence – some, in his last decade or so, also putting stress on the approaching End.[94] But the issuing of these charters tied into a high-risk series of public declarations, starting with a council at Winchester that year, convened so that Æthelred could be freed from curses issued in response to the abuses. Risk lay in appearing weak, which can only have raised the stakes in the face of the Danish attacks and, in 1005, the worst famine for a generation.[95] No one seemed to blame the king directly, but as Svein's army began the conquests that would ultimately bring down the king, Æthelred encouraged the whole

---

[90] Godden, 'The Millennium'.

[91] M. McC. Gatch, 'Eschatology in the Anonymous Old English Homilies', *Traditio*, 21 (1965), 117–65 at pp. 127–8. Gouguenheim may be right that there is 'everyday eschatology' here (*Les fausses terreurs*, pp. 77–8) but that is still a form of psychological imminence as Gatch stresses at 130. See also Foxhall Forbes, *Heaven and Earth*, pp. 101–5, especially on Ælfric's objections to the *Visio s. Pauli*.

[92] This paragraph draws particularly on C. Cubitt, 'The Politics of Remorse: Penance and Royal Piety in the Reign of Æthelred the Unready', *Historical Research*, 85.228 (2012), 179–92.

[93] 'Youthful indiscretions' from S. Keynes, *The Diplomas of King Æthelred 'The Unready', 978–1016: A Study in Their Use as Historical Evidence* (Cambridge, 1980), pp. 176–86.

[94] Compare Bremmer ('The Final Countdown') who denies that Æthelred had much interest in apocalyptic thought because he worked with an incomplete set of Æthelred's charters. Godden, 'The Millennium', p. 156 clearly sees the statements as mere rhetoric.

[95] Æthelred's situation begs at least some comparison with the situation of Louis the Pious: see Chapter 6.

kingdom to penitence and Wulfstan warned of Antichrist's reign.[96] Again, eschatological concern for salvation shaped political discourse, and again we can see this cutting across Y1K as an issue.

Yet, in the writings of Wulfstan, we can see politics and time intersect. Indeed, Wulfstan addressed the matter directly in his latest eschatological homily, *According to Mark*:

> A thousand years and also more have now passed since Christ was among people in human form, and now Satan's bonds are very loose, and Antichrist's time is well at hand. And thus it is in the world always the longer the weaker. People are deceitful, and the world is worse, and that injures us all. And indeed it must henceforth become more oppressive for the righteous and the innocent; now the evil and the deceitful spread widely throughout the world against the coming of the greatest evil that will come to men. That is the archfiend Antichrist himself.[97]

It is nonsense to think that the passing of 1000 was in any way comfort to Wulfstan here, and he made that much clear: prophecy had not failed but rather put people on their guard. And, as we have already seen, other contemporaries of Wulfstan in England were interested in the apocalyptic implications of Y1K. At the same time, if the ministry of Antichrist were to mirror the ministry of Christ, then it was the 1030s which were to mark the period of greatest battle, and this might be what Wulfstan was alluding to.[98] The mood of under-defined Gregorian imminence – 'we know *for certain* it is near', but not when – was underscored by references to how some people might yet live to see Antichrist and, of course, how no one could actually know the hour or the moment.[99] The rhetoric walked a fine line between non-millenarian, non-predicitive apocalyptic expectation on the one hand, and political agitation on the other.

Wulfstan's eschatological arguments made full use of Antichrist as a character in ways which highlight the receptiveness of audiences to Adso's ideas. In his earliest eschatological homilies, on the Little Apocalypse, Wulfstan portrayed Antichrist coming amongst liars and false prophets as the lead deceiver, the person to whom false Christians would bow

---

[96] VIIa Æthelred, ed. Lieberman, *Die Gesetze*, I. 262.
[97] *Secundum Marcam*, ed. Bethurum, pp. 136–7 (trans. Lionarons, http://webpages.ursinus.edu/jlionarons/wulfstan/Wulfstan.html): 'Þusend geara 7 eac ma is nu agan syððan Crist wæs mid mannum on menniscan hiwe, 7 nu syndon Satanases bendas swyðe toslopene, 7 Antecristes tima is wel gehende, 7 ðy hit is on worulde a swa leng swa wacre. Men syndon swicole 7 woruld is þe wyrse, 7 þæt us dereð eallum; 7 huru hit sceal hefegian heonanford þearle rihtwisan þearfan 7 ðam unbealafullum. Nu ða yfelan 7 ða swicelan swa oferlice swyðe brædað on worulde ongean þæt mæste yfel þe mannum is towerd; ðæt is se þeodfeond Antecrist sylfa'.
[98] Godden, 'The Millennium', p. 171.
[99] *De Antichristo*, ed. Bethurum, pp. 113–15; Lionarons, *The Homiletic Writings*, pp. 46–7.

down eagerly and serve. It is, of course, striking that Wulfstan should have introduced Antichrist to the Gospel readings given that he is not a figure found in Matthew or Luke. The synthesised End Times narrative was essential to establishing a focused mood of struggle and a call to action: 'beloved people, let us do what is needful for us, protect ourselves earnestly against that terror and help ourselves while we may and might, lest we die when we least expect to.'[100] Neither of these two homilies suggests that Wulfstan had yet read Adso's treatise, but his subsequent compositions did. Once he had, he expanded Antichrist's role, not just as a force of evil to be resisted, but as a source of cleansing persecution.[101] Reform and providence stood close.

Wulfstan's combination of eschatology and penitentialism defined not only his homiletic voice but also the way he approached law as a leading advisor to both Æthelred and Cnut. Wulfstan's references to the importance of steadfastly maintaining God's law (*godes lare*) here take on a double meaning, pointing to both a general preservation of faith and the worldly adherence to Christian laws. In the homilies Wulfstan talked about the ubiquitous presence of injustice and tribulation, and the need for everyone to turn from sin, most prominently in the different versions of the *Sermon of theWolf* in which he talked about the communal failure to ensure justice and faithfulness. He also drafted laws for Cnut which shared the mood: 'we earnestly enjoin all men to have the fear of God constantly in their hearts and day and night to be in terror of sin, dreading the Day of Judgement and shuddering at the thought of hell and ever expecting their last day to be close at hand.'[102] It is moments in the law codes like this that remind us that many of the laws were likely 'preached' by Wulfstan to his king – either of them – to exhort them to be good and to raise their standards.[103] Indeed in one mid-eleventh-century manuscript, which might be copied from aWorcester collection, we find the homilies, laws and other material about reform and penance

[100] Wulfstan, *Secundum Lucam*, ed. Bethurum, p. 126 (trans. Lionarons): 'Eala, leofan men, utan don swa us þearf is, beorgan us georne wið þæne egesan 7 helpan ure sylfra þa hwile þe we magan 7 motan, þe læs we forweorð þonne we læst wenan.' This sermon contains Wulfstan's most developed account of Antichrist: Lionarons, *The Homiletic Writings*, pp. 67–70.
[101] Especially *De temporibus Antichristi*, ed. Bethurum, p. 129–30 for the cleansing persecution.
[102] Cnut I, c. 25, *Die Gesetze*, p. 304: '7 we lærað eac georne manna gehwylcne, þæt he Godes ege hæbbe symle on his gemynde, 7 dæges 7 nihtes forhtige for synnum, Domdæg onræde 7 for helle agrise, 7 æfre him gehende endedæges wene'; trans. A. J. Robertson, *The Laws of the Kings of England from Edmund to Henry I* (Cambridge, 1925), p. 173.
[103] M. K. Lawson, 'Archbishop Wulfstan and the Homiletic Element in the Laws of Æthelred II and Cnut', *EHR*, 107/426 (1992), 565–86. For a wider perspective on penance and law see Foxhall Forbes, *Heaven and Earth*, pp. 114–19.

copied together.[104] For all Æthelred's laws and penitence, he was still said only to have been welcomed back after exile in 1014 on condition that he rule 'more lawfully' (*rihtlicor*), which makes one wonder about the efficacy and genuineness of his strategies.[105] Lack of trust in government combined with Viking raids, on the other hand, clearly occasioned the use of the apocalyptic and eschatological amongst other strategies of persuasion.[106]

But where were the English's 'Gog and Magog' if the Northmen afflicted them so badly? Wulfstan and Ælfric of Eynesham had no qualms about associating Vikings, ominously, with the 'nation rising against nation' of Matthew (24.7), just as Gregory had done with the Lombards; but there is no Gog and Magog.[107] Here we might have a case which underlines the importance of Pseudo-Methodius and its reception on the continent. There is little evidence that Pseudo-Methodius was known in Britain before the twelfth century, let alone any of Aethicus Ister, Ambrosius or Haimo.[108] The first (twelfth-century) text which might suggest any knowledge of Pseudo-Methodius, mainly focusing on Antichrist, states at one point:

It says in holy books, that after a course of years it will thus come to pass, that the whole world will be oppressed by the nation of heathens, and shall be so troubled and oppressed by their captivity that any orthodox man will not easily be able to bless himself or dare to sign himself with the heavenly king's sign. We are now able to perceive these afflictions much greater in looking to ourselves than by learning about them in books.[109]

It is worth quoting fully because it highlights a key issue here, which is actually having the 'books' to hand to underpin certain kinds of interpretation. Ælfric, similarly, had appealed to 'old books', possibly to distance himself from their failed prophecies.[110] Wulfstan's homilies, and

[104] Cambridge, Corpus Christi College, MS 201.
[105] *Anglo-Saxon Chronicle* (C), s.a. 1014, ed. K. O'Brien O'Keefe (Cambridge, 2001), p. 98; *Anglo-Saxon Chronicle* (E), s.a. 1014, ed. S. Irvine (Cambridge, 2004), p. 71.
[106] It is hard in this context to see 'immediate reality' as a distraction from 'apocalyptic fantasies', as is suggested by Keynes, 'Apocalypse Then', p. 260.
[107] Cf. Keynes, 'Apocalypse Then', p. 268.
[108] S. Pelle, 'The *Revelations* of Pseudo-Methodius and *Concerning the Coming of Antichrist* in British Library Ms Cotton Vespasian D. xiv', *Notes & Queries*, 56.3 (2009), 324–30. See also Godden, 'The Millennium', p. 177.
[109] Pelle, 'The *Revelations*', 327 (text and translation): 'Hit sægð on halgen bocan, þæt æfter gearan ymbryne swa gewurðen scyle, þæt eall middaneard mid hæðenra þeode geðrynge, 7 mid heoran hæftnysse swa swyðe gedrecced 7 gedrefod wurðeð, þæt hine uneaðe ænig riht gelefed mann mid þan heofolicen kinges tacne gebletsigen mote, oððe gesenigen durre. þas geswæncennysse we mugen nu mycele mare on us sylfen ongyten, þonne we hit on bocan leornigen.'
[110] Godden, 'The Millennium', p. 160.

other texts elsewhere in England, demonstrate a clear debt to Adso's *On Antichrist*, which is striking because Adso chose to omit Gog and Magog in favour of describing a more general persecution of Christians instigated by Antichrist himself.[111] No earlier sources – not Gregory the Great, not Bede – were going to make good this resource gap. English communities had a different repertoire of apocalyptic thought from many of their Frankish and German counterparts, which contributed alongside good social, political and cultural factors to the Northmen seeming less ominous than they might have done.

This last point underlines the importance of taking into account difference and discontinuity in apocalyptic tradition as one compares different regions. It is perhaps telling that the Winchester translator of Adso's work into Old English omitted the arguments about Rome and Frankish kingship – the *regnum Anglorum* was insulated against that particular anxiety because it was politically separate.[112] At the same time, as Emmerson pointed out, this meant that there were no political barriers to apocalypse, not that there had been back when Bede had outlined his End Times scenario either.[113] This suited the recasting of Adso's work as a homily and as a work of exhortation. And there we have another key difference: English eschatology was experienced more through homiletic culture compared to on the continent (at least, almost as crucially, as far as the surviving evidence indicates). Whether or not Y1K and Antichrist seemed important in Europe will be distorted with the English evidence, then, because the cultural process was different from, say, Ottonian Italy. Common concerns gave different results. Otto's audience for imperial ritual and charters, for example, was never going to be the same as Wulfstan's audience for an eschatological sermon – and certainly the situation in which the messages would have been consumed would have been quite different. Through all the complexity, however, one thing is again clear: apocalypse had a clear part to play in reform and the pursuit of power here.

---

[111] On the process of adopting Adso into Old English see R. K. Emmerson, 'From "Epistola" to "Sermo": The Old English Version of Adso's *Libellus de Antichristo*', *Journal of English and Germanic Philology*, 82.1 (1983), 1–10.

[112] Homily 42, ed. A. Napier, *Wulfstan: Sammlung der ihm zugeschiebenen Homilien nebst Untersuchungen über ihre Echtheit* (Berlin, 1883), pp. 191–205. The location of the translator is suggested in J. Wilcox, 'Napier's "Wulfstan" Homilies XL and XLII: Two Anonymous Works from Winchester?', *Journal of English and Germanic Philology*, 90.1 (1991), 1–19. One editor of Ælfric's homilies did make use of Adso's argument that the Roman Empire persisted, so it was meaningful to some: see *Homilies of Ælfric: A Supplementary Collection*, no. 28, ed. J. C. Pope (2 vols., Oxford, 1967–8), II. 784. My thanks to Professor Cubitt for bringing this to my attention.

[113] Emmerson, 'From "Epistola" to "Sermo"', pp. 8–9.

Peace and revolution in France

By coincidence, the French king of the Year 1000 was another peni-
tent facing troubled times, notably when he was excommunicated for
incest.[114] Robert II (r. 987–1031), 'the Pious', was only the second king
of the Capetian family that had supplanted the Carolingians in 987. But,
in the assessment of Jean Dunbabin (and many others) 'royal powers had
declined to almost nothing'.[115] Kings could command few, offered little,
and stood scarcely above their leading nobles. Such perceived weakness
at the centre underpins many different models of the 'Transformation
of the Year 1000' because it has helped historians to explain increases
in private violence, the rise of the Peace of God, and more generally the
circumstances which gave rise to feudalism, anarchy and the first populist heresies. Weakness, of course, is relative and depends what you are
looking for, and Robert did have his admirers.[116] And so it has gone, that
the more crisis historians have imagined in France around the Year 1000,
the more apocalypse they have detected, and vice versa. The important
thing for us will be to bear in mind the complexities of the political, social
and religious situations developing in relation to apocalyptic discourse –
especially as the transformations in religious practice here mark a real
difference compared to the German and English kingdoms.

First, it is worth noting that little about any perceived political crisis
was directly cited as an apocalyptic sign. The excommunication of Robert
by Pope Gregory V could have been a moment of considerable unrest but
was managed swiftly and effectively by Abbo of Fleury. The most alarm-
ing thing raised directly in relation to the king was when, in 1027, blood
rain was experienced and Abbot Gauzlin of Fleury wrote to him to say
that 'it clearly seems to us from histories that blood rain always portends

---

[114] Helgaud, *Epistoma vite regis Rotberti pii*, c. 17, ed. and trans. R.-H. Bautier and G.
Labory, Sources d'Histoire Médiévale, 1 (Paris, 1965), pp. 92–7; Gregory V, *De synodo
Papiensi*, c. 2, ed. G. H. Pertz, MGH SS, 3, p. 694; council in P. Labbé, *Sacrosancta
concilia ad regiam editionem* (Paris, 1671), IX. 772–4. On Robert: C. Pfister, *Études sur
le règne de Robert le Pieux (996–1031)* (Paris, 1885); J. Glenn, *Politics and History in the
Tenth Century: The Work and World of Richer of Rheims* (Cambridge, 2004).

[115] J. Dunbabin, *France in the Making 843–1180* (2nd edn, Oxford, 2000), p. 137 citing
Adalbero, *Poème au Roi Robert*, ed. and trans. C. Carozzi (Paris, 1979), p. 30, line 390:
'Francorum primus tu seruus in ordine regum.'

[116] Little had changed here according to Barthélemy (*L'an mil*, esp. pp. 214–31), who illus-
trates a number of ways in which Robert's position was typical of the previous century.
Good grounds for not exaggerating Robert's weakness are provided in T. Riches, 'The
Peace of God, the Weakness of Robert the Pious, and the Struggle for the German
Throne, 1023–5', *EME*, 18. 2 (2010), 202–22. Fond memories of Robert in Ralph
Glaber, *Historiarum libri quinque*, III. ii. 7, ed. and trans. J. France (Oxford, 1989), pp.
106–9.

the sword, civil war, or the rising of nation against nation (Matt. 24.7; Mark 13.8)'.[117] Fulbert of Chartres, in a separate response to the same query, talked about the judgement 'of the most imminent judge' (*praesentissimi iudicis*) and 'general catastrophe' (*publica strages*) the rain signified, even while remaining unsure how much time was left.[118] But still, it had taken something quite extraordinary to provoke this discussion, and even then nothing was put forward that was not explicitly grounded in the eschatology of the two Gregorys 400 years earlier. Perhaps Adso's text had defused Frankish imperial apocalyptic a little, or else it had been deflected onto the Ottonians, as this was all far more conservative than one would have found even in the ninth century. Royal weakness had not notably intensified speculation amongst anyone whose writings survive.

Antichrist still seemed to be in the air when it came to affairs of the high Church. The big crisis in the last years under Hugh Capet and the early years of Robert's reign focused on the contested election of Arnulf as archbishop of Rheims in 989.[119] In a letter to the papacy asking to have Arnulf removed – which may or may not have been faked by one of the protagonists – bishops complained that their voices were not being heard: 'Antichrist is sitting in the temple of God and showing himself as if he were God.' The *discessio*, they argued, would be the churches abandoning papal Rome, not imperial Rome.[120] When Arnulf was deposed in favour of Gerbert of Aurillac in 991 without papal approval, Abbot Leo of Ss Bonifacius and Alexios in Rome wrote furiously on Pope John's behalf accusing the kings of fulfilling John's prophecy that in the Last Days there would be many antichrists for supporting such disobedience.[121] The pope's hands had been tied until Otto had sorted out Crescentius. Nevertheless, Robert and the bishops slowly withdrew support from Gerbert, who himself withdrew to become Pope Sylvester II at Otto III's request. No one in the course of this exchange seems to have thought that they were prophesying the actual advent of Antichrist. Rather, the rhetoric of central authority in the Church and its absence

[117] Gauzlin, *Epistula ad Robertem regem*, ed. R.-H. Bautier and G. Labory (Paris, 1969), p. 160: 'hoc nobis ex historiis aperte patet, quod sanguis semper gladium, aut civile bellum, aut gentem super gentem exurgere portendit.' On this and the letter of Fulbert below see Fried, 'Endzeiterwartung', pp. 382–4.

[118] Fulbert of Chartres, *Letters and Poems*, no. 125, ed. and trans. F. Behrends (Oxford, 1976), pp. 224–7.

[119] Glenn, *Politics and History*, ch. 6.

[120] *Gerberti acta concilii Remensis*, c. 28, ed. G. H. Pertz, MGH SS, 3 (Hanover, 1839), pp. 672 and 676.

[121] *Leonis abbatis et legati ad Hugonem et Robertum reges epistola*, ed. Pertz, MGH SS, 3, p. 686. Leo's apocalyptic rhetoric here is particularly notable given the place of his monastery under Otto III: see above p. 203.

had generated some apocalyptically framed arguments. In the wake of Adso's work, Antichrist-motifs were becoming a powerful weapon.[122] A different example takes us closer to the heart of the feudal revolution debate. In an account of the miracles surrounding the relics of St Foy, Bernard of Angers also made great play of the enemies of the Church being antichrists in the context of the despoiling of churches by laypeople:

And so at that time there were many who we can justly call antichrists who, with blind ambition, dared to violate the laws of the Church, so that officials of the holy ministry were not revered in any way, but they assailed them with insults and beatings, and killing some ... We have seen bishops, some condemned with proscription, some expelled without cause from bishoprics, others cut down by swords, and even burned by Christians in terrible flames for the defence of church laws – if indeed one could call them Christians, who attack the order of the Christian religion. They stand in everything as enemies to Christ and to truth. Because they are not inflicted with punishment in present times, they are not terrified by celestial vengeance – on the contrary, some hope there will be no such thing and there will prove to be no future Judgement.[123]

Clearly this is not about apocalyptic prophecy but rather about concern for salvation, and indeed the story continues with St Foy taking revenge on thieves, before Bernard promised anyone who escaped punishment in life to receive a worse punishment in death. Barthélemy has argued that sources such as this are really rhetorical pieces that overdramatise change in the period.[124] Nevertheless, it remains that antichrist rhetoric was not common before the second half of the tenth century, so we are dealing with a real cultural change in which the language of opposition has shifted to incorporate more apocalyptic motifs. Competition for lordship and resources may or may not have been increasing, but violence and

[122] See also here Gregory VII: T. Struve, 'Endzeiterwartungen als Symptom politisch-sozialer Krisen im Mittelalter', in Aertsen and Pickavé (eds.), Ende und Vollendung, pp. 207–26.
[123] Bernard of Angers, Miracula s. Fidis, I. 11, ed. L. Robertini, Biblioteca di Medioevo Latino, 10 (Spoleto, 1994), p. 106: 'namque hoc tempore permulti sunt, quos merito antichristos nominare possumus, qui tam ceca ambitione iura ecclesiastica invader audent, ut sacri ministerii officiales non modo non revereantur, sed etiam modo contumeliis et verberibus appetent, modo morte afficiant ... Vidimus episcopos, alios proscriptione damnatos, alios sine causa episcopio pulsos, alios vero ferro trucidatos, alios et etiam atrocibus flammis pro ecclesiastici iuris defensione a christianis combustos, sit amen christianos dici fas est, qui christiane religionis ordinem impugnantes, Christo per omnia contrarii extant veritatisque inimici. Hi quia in presentiarum nullo plectuntur supplicio, celeste vindictam nihil formidant, immo nullam aliquando sperant existuntque future increduli iudicio.'
[124] D. Barthélemy, 'Antichrist et blasphémateur', Médiévales, 37 (1999), 57–70 at 68–9. More widely on the complexities of Bernard's text see K. Ashley and P. Sheingorn, Writing Faith: Text, Sign, and History in the Miracles of Ste Foy (Chicago, 1999).

church despoliation were a reality that was finding new expression here. It would be cavalier indeed to dismiss changes in how people saw the world as mere rhetoric with no real historical bite. After all, Bernard told his story precisely to motivate reform and to rally people to the defence of the Church, and it seems that many followed such advice.

Changes in rhetoric, then, need to be seen in conjunction with the changes in popular piety which began to change the logic of apocalyptic thought.[125] The rise of popular heresy is a good example. Before the eleventh century, most debates about heresy had concerned Christology or the veneration of icons, and they had been conducted at an institutional level. The False Christ of Bourges, Aldebert and Thiota were one-offs. The millennial generation, however, witnessed an increase in localised unrest which was more theologically and ritually radical.[126] In 1017/18 a puritanical sect appeared in Aquitaine which attracted much support, until it was destroyed in Toulouse.[127] Adherents caused upset in Orléans and in 1022 became the first heretics on record to be burned.[128] Soon afterwards, in 1028, their fate was shared by heretics in Monforte near Turin, who promoted chastity and fasting and who refused to recognise the institutional Church.[129] Some 'heresies' were apparently more individual, notably that of the peasant Leutard, from Vertus near Châlons-sur-Marne, who separated from his wife, smashed a cross in church, and argued against tithes (all while possessed by bees in a story curiously reminiscent of Gregory's account of the False Christ). These incidents all hint at an increased and widespread appetite for reform after the millennium.[130] Whether they can be considered 'millennial' in any more than a loose sense is doubtful, because they focus on transformation but not

[125] R. Fulton, *From Judgment to Passion: Devotion to Christ and the Virgin Mary, 800–1200* (New York, 2002) discusses some of the issues involved but places the Landesian Y1K thesis uncritically at the heart of her argument for when and why piety changed (see esp. pp. 74–8). As ever one must ask whether piety also changed apocalypse, and whether the simple division of people 'for or against' apocalypse is too simplistic. See also the discussions listed in the following note.

[126] Poly and Bournazel, *The Feudal Transformation*, ch. 9. Compare R. I. Moore, 'The Birth of Popular Heresy: A Millennial Phenomenon?', *Journal of Religious History*, 24. 1 (2000), 8–25 (importance of distance between elites and non-elites) and R. Landes, 'The Birth of Popular Heresy: A Millennial Phenomenon', *Journal of Religious History*, 24.1 (2000), 26–43 (importance of millenarianism).

[127] Ademar of Chabannes, *Chronicon*, III. 49, ed. P. Bourgain, CCCM, 129 (Turnhout, 1999), p. 170 and III. 59, p. 180.

[128] Ademar of Chabannes, *Chronicon*, III. 59, p. 180; Ralph Glaber, *Historiarum libri quinque*, III. viii. 31, p. 150; John of Ripoll, *Epistola ad Olibam*, ed. ed. R.-H. Bautier and G. Labory (Paris, 1969)), pp. 180–3.

[129] Landulf, *Historia Mediolanensis*, II. 27, eds. W. Wattenbach and L. Bethmann, MGH SS, 8 (Hanover, 1858), pp. 65–6

[130] On this point Barthélemy, *The Serf*, p. 283 is surely correct.

apocalyptic imminence, charismatic leaders and other features popularly associated with the phenomenon.

Heresy was bound together with a rise in anti-Semitic feeling in some quarters.[131] And, as we saw with Antichrist's developing biography, hostility towards Jews was part of the fabric of apocalyptic anxiety. Glaber, as background to the story of the Orléans heresy, told of how it was Jews from the city who had convinced al-Hakim, caliph of Cairo, to destroy the Holy Sepulchre in 1009.[132] A similar story was told by Ademar of Chabannes, both writers drawing associations between al-Hakim's regime and the anti-Christian kingdom of Babylon to intensify the sense that the enemies of Christ were uniting.[133] In the West this inaugurated a surge in violence against Jews, with King Robert ordering forced conversions, while in Mainz, under Henry II, Jews were expelled from the city as heresy was condemned. One later account drew together the threads saying:

In the year 1009, the land of Jerusalem was invaded ... and in that year many Jews converted to Christianity for fear of their lives. In the year 1010, in many places throughout the world, a rumour spread that frightened and saddened many hearts, that the End of the World approached. But those sounder of mind turned themselves to correcting their own lives.[134]

The mood was for purification and reform but clearly this was not being handled quite as soberly as some people would have liked. In France,

---

[131] R. Chazan, '1007–1012: Initial Crisis for Northern European Jewry', *Proceedings of the American Academy for Jewish Research*, 39 (1971), 101–7; R. Landes, 'The Massacres of 1010: On the Origin of Popular Anti-Jewish Violence in Western Europe', in J. J. Cohen (ed.), *From Witness to Witchcraft: Jews and Judaism in Medieval Christian Thought* (Wolfenbüttel, 1996), pp. 79–112, esp. pp. 96–102 on the apocalyptic undercurrent.

[132] Ralph Glaber, *Historiarum libri quinque*, III. vii. 24, pp. 132–7. D. Callahan, 'The Cross, the Jews, and the Destruction of the Church of the Holy Sepulcher in the Writings of Ademar of Chabannes', in M. Frassetto (ed.), *Christian Attitudes Toward the Jews in the Middle Ages: A Casebook* (London, 2007), pp. 15–24; J. Fried, '"999 Jahre nach Christi Geburt: der Antichrist." Wie die Zerstörung des Heiligen Grabes zum apokalyptischen Zeichen wurde und die Denkfigur universaler Judenverfolgung hervorbrachte', in R.-J. Lilie (ed.), *Konfliktbewältigung vor 1000 Jahren: Die Zerstörung der Grabeskirche in Jerusalem im Jahre 1009* (Berlin, 2011), pp. 99–136; J. Heil, 'Die Juden um das Jahr 1000 und die antijüdischen Reaktionen auf die Jerusalemer Krise', in Lilie, *Konfliktbewältigung*, pp. 195–220.

[133] Ademar of Chabannes, *Chronicon*, c. 47, p. 166.

[134] William Godell, *Chronica*, ed. M. Bouquet, *Receuil des historiens des Gaules et de la France*, 10 (Paris, 1874), p. 262: 'Anno Domini MIX terra Jerosolimorum, permittente Deo, ab immundis Turcis invasa ... Judaei multi eo anno prae timore baptizati sunt. Anno Domini MX in multis locis per orbem tali rumore audito, timor et moeror corda, plurimorum occupavit, et suspicati sunt multi finem saeculi adesse: sanioris animi quique de vitae suae correctione attentius studuerunt salubti consili utentes'; trans. and discussion in Landes, *Heaven on Earth*, p. 49.

religious action was being driven by greater participation in religion across society and more often.

This is no more apparent than in the mass pilgrimage of 1033, the millennial anniversary of Christ's Passion. Ralph Glaber tells a terrifying series of stories in Book IV of his *Five Books of History*, in which he details deaths, famine, floods, descent into madness, cannibalism in Mâçon, and the stripping of churches, all of which unsurprisingly seemed to foretell the end of mankind.[135] The reaction of the masses in his story was positive. After first holding peace councils (on which more below) many of them set off on pilgrimage to Jerusalem – and many apparently said 'cautiously enough' (*satis caute*) that Antichrist might be expected to arrive.[136] Antichrist's arrival into Jerusalem, of course, is not in the Bible but is rather an intellectual confection of the kind that hyper-sceptics think was reserved for 'experts', not 'the people' in general.[137] But we saw in England that this was precisely the kind of thing that was being preached there by the experts to their people. In the case of this very pilgrimage, in the case of France, it is notable that apocalyptically minded Ademar of Chabannes – author of many eschatological sermons – was one of the travellers we are supposed to imagine not talking to people.[138] No – it is hard to imagine communication of ideas not occurring. And if people were not setting out on pilgrimage to Jerusalem from other areas of Latin Europe at this time, then we have a vivid illustration of the particular local factors which affected apocalyptic expectations and behaviour.[139]

As so often, the clerical reports provided rather than suppressed the apocalyptic mood which surrounded this popular religosity. Indeed, while there was little which directly suggests that the heretics or persecutors of Jews were guided by their millenarian hopes, there are unambiguous condemnations of unorthodox beliefs which invoke the coming Last Judgement. It was Ademar who denounced heretics as 'messengers of Antichrist' (*nuntii Antichristi*) in his chronicle.[140] And it was Glaber who ended his summary of 'recent' heresies with the words 'all this accords with the prophecy of St John, who said that the Devil would be freed

[135] Ralph Glaber, *Historiarum libri quinque*, IV. 4. 9, pp. 184–93. Gouguenheim, *Les fausses terreurs*, pp. 172–3 finds the pilgrimage suspiciously under-documented.
[136] Ralph Glaber, *Historiarum libri quinque*, IV. 4. 21, pp. 204–5. See Landes, *Relics*, pp. 320–1.
[137] Barthélemy, *The Serf*, pp. 290–6, especially at p. 290 the phrase 'experts' apocalypse'.
[138] *Chroniques de Saint-Martial de Limoges*, s.a. 1034, ed. H. Duplès-Agier (Paris, 1874), p. 47.
[139] There is, for example, no indication that anything so interesting was going on in Herman the Lame, *Chronicon*, s.a. 1033–4, ed. G. H. Pertz, MGH SS, 5 (Hanover, 1849), pp. 121–2.
[140] Ademar, *Chronicon*, III. 49, p. 170; Landes, *Relics*, p. 175.

after a thousand years'.[141] Glaber's tone varies throughout and he never came back to discuss these things as he promised, but in general he can be seen writing with what Ortigues and Iogna-Prat called 'une conception deutéronomiste de l'histoire' in which people would be punished until they accepted the law of God.[142] Apocalyptic fears were not the preserve of the frenzied masses but rather of their critics.[143] Some critics kept their 'discourse within more moderate bounds' – or perhaps just different ones – and launched their attacks without reference to the apocalyptic.[144] Yet even this just proves that there was variety and difference within 'tiers' of society.

A number of issues came together in the Peace councils, held predominantly in Aquitaine and Burgundy in the fifty years or so from 980.[145] Episcopal and comital powers, with enthusiastic popular support and the parading of saints' relics, came together to establish protection for churchmen and property in the face of a perceived increase in violence. The idea was spearheaded by Bishop Guy (Wido) of Le Puy, who gathered 'knights and rustics' (*milites et rustici*) to swear oaths and, when they initially refused to do so, he also had to hand his own militia to force the issue.[146] As the Peace developed, it was accompanied in some quarters by rhetoric which sought to invoke a millenarianesque harmony of earth, with the participants often as New Israelites entering a Promised Land.[147] We might doubt just how radical and surprising this

[141] Ralph Glaber, *Historiarum libri quinque*, II. xii. 23, pp. 92–3: 'quod presagium Iohannis prophetie congruit, quia dixit Sathanam soluendum, expletis mille annis.'

[142] E. Ortigues and D. Iogna - Prat, 'Raoul Glaber et l'historiographie clunisienne', *Studi Medievali*, 26 (1985), 537–72 at p. 541.

[143] Gouguenheim, *Les fausses terreurs*, pp. 166–77, anxious that too much weight is put on Glaber by historians.

[144] Quotation from G. Lobrichon, 'The Chiaroscuro of Heresy: Early Eleventh-Century Aquitaine as Seen from Auxerre', in T. Head and R. Landes (eds.), *The Peace of God: Social Violence and Religious Response in France around the Year 1000* (Ithaca, NY, and London, 1992), pp. 80–103 at p. 100.

[145] Classic studies of the Peace of God include Head and Landes, *The Peace of God* and H. Hoffmann, *Gottesfriede und Treuga Dei* (Stuttgart, 1964). A list of councils is provided in T. Head, 'Peace and Power in France around the Year 1000', *Essays in Medieval Studies*, 23 (2006), pp. 1–17 at pp. 5–6. This is different from the list supplied by Hoffmann, and in H.-W. Goetz, 'Protection of the Church, Defence of the Law, and Reform: On the Purposes and Character of the Peace of God 989–1038', in Head and Landes, *The Peace of God*, pp. 259–79 at p. 262, because Head identified a number of overlooked meetings and discounted a number possibly invented by Ademar.

[146] *Chronicon monasterii s. Petri Aniciensis*, no. 413, in U. Chevalier (ed.), *Cartulaire de l'abbaye de Saint-Chaffre du Monastier* (Paris, 1864), p. 152; Head, 'Peace and Power', pp. 3–4.

[147] *Chartes et documents pour servir à l'histoire de l'abbaye de Charroux*, ed. P. de Monsabert (Poitiers, 1910), pp. 36–7; (Ademar sermon) PL, 141. 188; Andrew of Fleury, *Miracula s. Benedicti*, V. 2, ed. E. de Certain (Paris, 1858), p. 193; Fulbert of Chartres, *Letter and Poems*, no. 149, pp. 262–3; D. Callahan, 'The Peace of God and the Cult of the Saints

development was overall, given some of the utopian currents evident in earlier reform movements (see especially Chapter 5). But its success at rallying popular feeling was not lost on contemporaries, even if it is too much to equate popularity with class struggle as some historians have done.[148] Ralph Glaber famously described the movement spreading from Aquitaine, then to Arles and Burgundy, and then to the rest of France; and how people signalled their covenant with God by shouting 'Peace! Peace! Peace!' (straying close to the deceitful peace declared in Jeremiah 6.14).[149] The new millennium seemed to have brought renewed hope for the future.

Here, there is some debate about exactly what kind of social dynamic was at work. Was it revolutionary and led from below or conservative and led from above? It is certainly easy to see the Peace as a response to growing violence and weakening royal justice. Yet Dominique Barthélemy has stood at the fore of a critique which has sought to deny that there was any deep social crisis, and certainly not one which can be equated with millenarianism.[150] For Barthélemy, the Peace of God represented little more than a development in traditional Carolingian legislative activity, not least because at a legal level little radical or new was promoted other than the protection of property rights. The rhetorical dimensions of the Peace from this perspective are just that – 'mere' rhetoric, locked into the mysterious and secretive discourses of an 'expert's apocalypse' in which the clergy speculated about obscure meanings while an unreceptive and uninterested laity got on with their lives. So: no social crisis, no apocalypse. It is true, as Barthélemy observes, that one could exaggerate providential-prophetic talk, such as references to a New Israel, to make them sound apocalyptic when really they belong an Old Testament mode of threatening punishment for sin.[151] The Peace of God could then look more traditional and less ridden with anxiety. This would be, however, a conclusion which sits uneasily with some of the evidence we have already encountered, as well as running the risk of minimising the apocalyptic power of providential discourses too.

A different approach has been sketched out by Thomas Head, who argued that the institution of the Peace in Aquitaine gained much of

in Aquitaine in the Tenth and Eleventh Centuries', in Head and Landes, *The Peace of God*, pp. 165–85 at pp. 171–2; R. Landes, 'Between Aristocracy and Heresy: Popular Participation in the Limousin Peace of God (994–1032)', in Head and Landes, *The Peace of God*, pp. 184–219 at pp. 190 and 199–202.

[148] On this see Barthélemy, *The Serf*, pp. 260–2 – although the lack of classic 'class struggle' defuses neither struggle in society nor apocalyptic culture.

[149] Ralph Glaber, *Historiarum libri quinque*, IV. v. 14–16, pp. 194–6.

[150] Barthélemy, *L'an mil*, p. 140.

[151] Barthélemy, *The Serf*, pp. 297–9.

its attraction from its specific local conflicts and efforts by everyone
to resolve them. It was not quite revolution, but neither was it merely
shuffling the deck. Fights such as that between Gerald, the viscount of
Limoges, and Boso I in the last quarter of the tenth century threatened
the safety of both lay and ecclesiastical lands, and so helped to foster
the Peace as a response which blurred secular and sacred authority.[152]
Barthélemy has taken the collaborative nature of the Peace shown here to
undermine Landes's view of it as a popular millenarian uprising, but in
practice it does little to erase any eschatological overtones. Indeed, Head
has pointed out that the urgency of salvation was an important issue
seized upon by all parties to cajole and coerce – such as with threats of
excommunication – and to make sure that they played the game fully. A
number of powerful figures, such as Duke William IV (d. 994), died as
monks *ad succurrendum*, and many more undertook penitential pilgrimages – not as mere capitulations to Church demands, but as efforts to
take responsibility for individual souls while remaining on or near the
political scene. Quite possibly some people were 'playing the game' by
behaving this way. But even so, it shows the importance eschatological
thought had in shaping both communal ideals and strategies for corrective action within society.

Any clear distinction between 'everyday eschatology' and apocalyptic
expectation is at least problematized by some of the same charters which
help to reconstruct the political culture behind the Peace in Aquitaine.
As Callahan and Landes have highlighted, there are a significant number
of these which refer to the approaching end of the world.[153] Does this
too, then, point towards the Peace being a symptom of a society dealing with its apocalyptic expectations (and with not much hysteria)? The
matter is complicated, however, as most draw on stock phrasing, as in
this example:

With the end of the world approaching, and with its disasters becoming widespread, now sure signs are becoming manifest. And for that reason in the name
of God I, Gunden, considering the cause of human frailty, and having confidence
in the great mercy and goodness of God, I give [this land] by letter of dona-
tion and I wish [it] to given in perpetuity, for the remedy of my soul and of my
parents'.[154]

[152] T. Head, 'The Development of the Peace of God in Aquitaine (970–1005)', *Speculum*,
74.3 (1999), 656–86 at pp. 662–6.
[153] Callahan, 'The Peace of God', p. 171; Landes, 'The Fear', pp. 128–9.
[154] *Chartes et documents pour servir a l'histoire de L'Abbaye de Saint-Maixent*, no. 47, ed.
A. Richard (Poitiers, 1886), pp. 63–4: 'mundi termino appropinquante, ruinisque eius
crebescentibus, iam certa signa manifestantur. Idcirco ego in Dei nomine Gundenus,
considerans casum humane fragilitatis, de tanta Dei misericordia et pietate confisus,

Gunden himself is, sadly, of no great importance to any unfolding dramas, and even the record of his gift to Saint-Maixent in Poitou in 970 falls over a century after the same formula was first used in a charter at nearby Nouillé.[155] But the use of this formula tells us two important things about Poitevin society, because it reveals a clear connection between apocalyptic expectation and personal eschatology leading to remedial action, and it shows that this was one perfectly acceptable option in the repertoire for expressing the moral cause for gift-giving. Even as a commonplace formula, its use required that someone chose it over other non-apocalyptic phrases in use, thus exposing its perceived potency as a way of explaining the related grants to both God and local society. In the case of Gunden, he was making this grant, as far as one can tell from the charter itself, standing before the grave of St Maxentius, surrounded by priests of the church, one of whom probably wrote the charter. Apocalyptic expectations were both part of everyday eschatology here and part of a language of power.

Being sensitive to regional variation, there are some points that need to be stressed. Apocalypse was meaningful to some people, even if that does not mean it was important to everyone, everywhere; and it does not mean that it was all to do with Y1K even if it was for some people. Apocalyptic discourse seems to have had more utility and more presence in Aquitaine than in some other regions and we should be comfortable with that as a conclusion. It does not even mean there was more crisis there, just that the way people dealt with change was different. Also we have plenty of indications that there was space for an 'experts' apocalypse' with people in other contexts taking an interest too. No doubt careful study of other commonplaces in medieval culture would produce similar results. Apocalypse made sense of things and conceptualised history. It offered a language which could be used to direct situations. Apocalypse does not prove that there was the unprecedented crisis Landes and others have believed, nor can it be reduced to 'everyday eschatology' and 'mere rhetoric' as simply as Barthélemy or Gouguenheim would like. Confronted with perceptions of change, violence *and opportunity*, many people naturally engaged with End Times thought to address their situation in different ways. The changing world of France *c.* 1000 neatly illuminates the

per hanc epistolam donationis dono donatumque in perpetuum esse volo, pro remedio animae meae et parentum meorum.'
[155] *Chartes de l'Abbaye de Nouillé de 678 à 1200*, no. 18, ed. P. de Monsabert (Poitiers, 1936), p. 34 (863–6), with similar sentiments expressed in no. 17, p. 31 (857). See also no. 35, p. 63 (906, 908 or 912), which also pre-dates Callahan's first example, which is no. 54, pp. 93–4 (942). The history is indeed longer: Boiadjiev, 'Der mittelalterliche Apokalyptismus', pp. 169–70 – but that does not mean that it was meaningless.

complexity of cause and effect in human societies – and with that, the power of apocalypse.

Conclusion

Much ground has been covered in this chapter and, if we have got away from a simple confirmation or denial of the veracity of the Y1K problem, then that is because that was the point. There were people who looked at the millennial anniversaries of the Incarnation and Passion with some anxiety. Then there were others who saw other kinds of signs which seemed portentous with or without the passing of either date, especially when those dates were not all that close at hand. Some people did not want to think about such things; some people did not think about such things *all of the time*. Apocalypse was a scenario people were in (or might be in), and a language people could use to argue about the world around them. The important point throughout this study has been that it is an ever-present part of Christian culture in the early Middle Ages, whether Y1K was close or not. The only satisfying analyses must proceed on the basis that there were many ideas in play, but not all at once, and not always coherently.

Such conclusions seem to be reinforced by treating the material comparatively rather than as different parts of a single whole. Fried's initial survey of apocalyptic anxiety around the turn of the Year 1000 was important for bringing so much material from Germany, France, Spain and more together to show that there was too much evidence to ignore. The way to develop Fried's conclusions is to work on the differences too. To repeat some observations: the Ottonian *Reich* unsurprisingly was more fertile ground for imperial eschatology than other areas, in England under invasion from Danes there was greater stress on moral correction and preaching, and in France there was a greater role for populist expressions of piety. Even then, as the French example showed, we might sometimes have to look for units smaller than kingdoms, because Aquitaine was not like, say, Maine (any more, one suspects, than Saxony was like Lombardy in the *Reich*). Modern enthusiasm to make all-or-nothing cases has made the worst of regional variation.

There is, I think, one last point which needs to be made about apocalypse and change, particularly with the 'feudal revolution' debate in the air. It is this: apocalyptic traditions and rhetoric are about directing and conceptualising change and so they are as much part of 'strength' as they are of 'weakness'. The misunderstanding posed even by the mere phrase 'terrors of the Year 1000' is that apocalyptic anxiety is irrational, hysterical and representative of crisis. Far from it, as Fried argued. Aquitaine could have had a population living in fear of imminent Judgement regardless of whether it was experiencing socio-political crisis or confidently undergoing change ably led by champions of justice. The penitential streak in tenth-century kingship would have been a curious (collective) admittance of hopelessness if it did not also have positive transformational properties. And how can one even contemplate the meaning and function of the Bamberg Apocalypse in imperial circles unless one accepts that apocalyptic can be a statement about standing and fighting on the correct side of Christ in anticipation of Judgement Day? Medieval apocalyptic, like modern apocalyptic, was a powerful force because it was much bigger, more subtle, and more engrained in human experience than fearing that tomorrow might not come.

Conclusion: the end (*c.* 400–*c.* 1033)

The argument of this book has been that apocalyptic thought was an important cultural resource used in the early Middle Ages for changing the world. Christ himself had promised that the End would come, soon but unexpectedly, so it would have taken an unusual Christian in these important centuries to deny Christ on the matter. The issue that mattered was how apocalypse called the mind's attention to reform. Speculation – second-guessing God – was forbidden. Beyond that, apocalypse provided the language, the incentive and the time-frame which helped to stimulate people to strive for better things. Crises came: Rome 'fell', external forces attacked, members of the Church could become corrupt, heresies could rise, the weather and stars could prove less than predictable. Experts offered frameworks for interpretation which encouraged action motivated by the greatest of hopes and fears – but fears that were to be responded to with bravery, not despondency. None of this is to say that the early Middle Ages was uniquely beset by terrible crises. Rather, what I hope to have provided is an extended case study on the ways in which people have used anxiety and reflection on finality to make a difference, to mobilise and to stimulate change. In this brief conclusion, I shall try and bring some of the threads together.

What is the End?

There would be only one ending. Whichever way one got there, the Last Judgement and the destruction of the current physical world were inevitable. The moral dimension of this was equally clear because the very fact of Judgement ensured that Christians knew they would eventually have to be accountable for their sins and would (hopefully) act accordingly. What followed, beyond the End, was unchanging perfection for the saved or eternal damnation for those who could not make amends. Apocalypse and eschatology were parts of a body of thought – singular but complex – which explained to people how they would get from pre-Judgement to post-Judgement, from history to post-history. The whole

227

package revolved around visionary material, either entering into the spirit of, or carefully explaining, the mystical symbolism and oblique predictions espoused by the Old Testament prophets, Christ, John of Patmos and the apocryphal revelations of Paul, Timothy and others. Visions of the End and their interpretation fundamentally communicated future expectations to prepare people for their inescapable fate.

The key question is one of imminence. Did people think that the end of the world was upon them? If they did, people could be affected; if not, then apocalypse was an empty promise. This is the central debate in much modern scholarship. Yet it can easily misrepresent the situation. 'Predictable End' versus 'certain but unknowable End' was a more important issue, complicated by many agnostics believing that they lived in the shadow of the End, whenever it might come. Indeed, denials of imminence are strikingly rare, while an impressive parade of mainstream figures from emperors to monks actively appealed to apocalyptic ideas, fearing for the present but hopeful for the future. Matters were complicated further by the threat of personal mortality: even if people were unlikely to live to see the actual end of the world en route to the Last Judgement, they could still die at any moment, possibly face some kind of intermediate station of existence, and eventually arrive at the Last Judgement anyway. Denying the imminence of the end of the world still left people with much to be anxious and excited about. The conclusion we must arrive at is this: psychological imminence and personal eschatology ensured that there were persistent imperatives to act, even where simple predictive apocalypticism was weak. There might be differences in action depending on the nature of eschatology (e.g. a dying man giving his wealth to a church compared to a bishop holding a reformist council). Nevertheless, anxious uncertainty, combined with imperial apocalyptic and fear of outsider persecutors, is the fundamental reason why apocalyptic thought does not just focus on Y6K, Y1K or millenarianism.

Time

The history of time and chronology still framed much early apocalyptic thought. Nevertheless, we have also seen that this history was not solely determined by traditions about the end. Early beliefs that the world would end in its 6,000th year informed expectation that the world could end around 500, and this did worry people in the East and a few in the West. The fall of Rome and the subsequent dominance of Augustinian-Hieronymian theology, however, began to uncouple any shared Eastern and Western expectations. The 'more accurate' chronology of Eusebius promoted within this framework moved the apocalyptic goalposts, but certainly as much by virtue of its perceived accuracy and Jerome's seal of approval as by any desire to sidestep the Y6K problem. We saw that similar factors affected the shift from the Eusebian world age to the 'Hebrew Truth' in the eighth century: scholars such as Bede recognised problems with Eusbius's calculations, derived from comparisons of Greek and Hebrew texts, and changed the age of the world accordingly. Such a move may have helped quell any 'fears of a Year 6000' – for we saw plenty of hints of such fears earlier, either side of 700 – but we cannot say that the change was in any way enacted because of apocalyptic expectation. Besides, the point underlined by Augustine and more so by Bede was that the date did not matter, because the end could come at any time.

The situation was quite different when it came to the Year 1000. There had been no real scriptural basis for attaching importance to 6,000 years of the world, as Bede pointed out. John of Patmos's revelation, on the other hand, did talk of a thousand-year-long reign of Christ and his saints and a thousand-year-long binding of Satan. Tyconius, Augustine, Bede and others did not fully defuse any implication that a real duration might be meant when they discussed the symbolism of numbers, because they insisted that the thousand was both perfection and the fullness of time. Could that thousand years of duration have been counted from the Incarnation or Passion, announcing changing times around 1000 or 1033? Yes, the evidence is not always overwhelming, but there is enough unambiguous evidence that we must conclude that some people *did* believe in the cosmic significance of the millennial anniversaries, even if some people did not – Abbo of Fleury neatly exemplifying both categories with his grumbles about the Parisian preacher in his youth. Again, it is hard to see that anti-apocalypticism drove efforts to redate Christ's life, because scholars were reacting to a concrete problem (in this case, following Bede, recognising that Dionysiac Easter tables gave the wrong luni-solar data in the accepted year of Christ's Passion). Fried's extended chronological window for anxiety, based on these calculations, may be a false friend: it looks like it explains the chronological spread of the evidence, but the work of the chronologers had very little influence outside of the most limited intellectual circles.

What kind of impact these apocalyptic dates had is unclear (hence the modern debates). I do think that the evidence points to apocalyptic concerns around 500 and 800 – and indeed other non-apocalyptic matters – that transcend questions concerning the date, so it is hard to see much in, say, the behaviour of Anastasios I or Charlemagne that is linked exclusively to Y6K rather than, say, more pervasive imperial apocalyptic anxieties. On the other hand, there are some indications that the date was a more pronounced factor in stimulating popular piety across Western

Europe (and in the East to an extent) around the Year 1000, but only as part of a wider package of issues. Paul Magdalino's wise assessment of Byzantine apocalypticism likely holds true for the West too: this was about much more than numbers, but the numbers could play a role in stimulating hopes and anxieties in the right circumstances.

Crucially – and this is the issue which set me writing this book in the first place – historians have failed to appreciate the profound changes in attitudes towards time and history in the early Middle Ages. In recent scholarship it was the late Arno Borst who did more than anyone to expose how, in the centuries after the fall of Rome, the development of calendars, Easter tables and natural sciences led to profound rationalisations of time. Time could be more linear, objective and measurable than many scholars would give credit. Thanks to Hiberno-Irish models, even Augustine's mystical views on the subject quickly looked completely at odds with the scientific compendia that quoted him in Carolingian monasteries. On the back of this, we cannot simply say that medieval people were lost in the cycles of liturgical time, aware of little more than the rhythms of the seasons and feasts, and so indifferent to what year it was. Nor can we think of medieval people having under-evolved 'temporal consciousnesses', or just being 'simple'. The universalization of Church time – won only at length and through crises such as the Synod of Whitby in 664 – regularised the rhythms of Christian life deeply and on the basis of considerable learning, and in doing so pointed the flow of history in one direction only: towards the Last Judgement. If specific dates had only ambiguous apocalyptic implications, the progress of time and history more generally remained reminders of where things were going.

Imperial apocalyptic

Around and between apocalyptic dates, the fate of political communities provided numerous causes for reflection and constant re-evaluation. Christianity and the Roman Empire, for a start, had grown up with an uneasy relationship, which shaped much of the imagery in John's revelation. After the conversion of Constantine, the rapid Christianisation of the empire briefly brought optimism, even if anxieties remained that Rome was the doomed, brutal last kingdom from the Book of Daniel. The collapse of old state structures in the West again firmly detached Eastern and Western apocalyptic. In 410 the sack of Rome prompted some concern for the coming of Antichrist but most of the anxiety focused on the barbarians and heretics (and barbarian heretics) who challenged the way things were being done. Few people in the West even seem to have 'noticed' that the empire had fallen and it remained a non-issue, even during the Justinianic wars, until the Carolingian experiment got under way in the late eighth century. The complicating factor then, however, was that Charlemagne's New Rome was not really a resurrection of the old empire or even its authority, because the centrality of the Church defined his kingdom so much. It also sat outside the Pseudo-Methodian narrative of the *rex Romanorum sive Gregorum*, which had started to spread only slowly. To some commentators in the ninth century, the Carolingian empire existed after Daniel's four kingdoms and after Paul's prophesied *discessio*, the 'falling away' of imperial authority, leaving people to await not a 'fall' but perhaps nothing more than the arrival of Antichrist himself. By the tenth century, in Adso's *On Antichrist*, this idea was being sold so that only the kings of the Franks – the heirs of Rome – were holding back Antichrist's arrival. One way or another, no one was prepared to let symbolic-Rome fall. How this could be achieved, on the other hand, depended on circumstance.

The apocalyptic role of Rome helped to foster a sense of responsibility. Charlemagne and Louis the German were both sent commentaries on the Book of Daniel which stressed the world-historical importance of executing their duties as king well. Kings and emperors needed little encouragement not just to sponsor Church reform but to lead councils and make proclamations on doctrine, or to sponsor missionary activity unto the ends of the earth. Many flirted with apocalyptic imagery in order, yes, to bolster their authority, and to make statements about how important they were in the scheme of things. Yet, what seemed natural for Justinian or Charles the Bald eventually seemed unbearable to Otto III, who considered fleeing his destiny. Some rulers needed to be reminded, if not outright convinced, as we see in the letters of Cathwulf and Alcuin to Charlemagne. One problem was the evolution of apocalyptic imperial thought. Where the Bible was vague about political leadership in the Last Times, Sibylline texts and Pseudo-Methodius were not, promising good rulers and bad rulers, but always one last one who would fulfil the destiny of the Christian community to find peace in the world before the last assaults and Judgement itself.

Apocalypse may have been a source of strength for many rulers but it could also add pressure where there were weaknesses. Gregory of Tours could see the civil wars of his times as little more than a sign of the disorder of the end, and the author of the *Suffering of Leudegar* a century later saw little different in his own, except that he was more convinced that Antichrist was close. The return of large-scale internal strife in the civil wars of the ninth century encouraged similar judgements, and under Robert the Pious this led Fulbert of Chartres just to appeal back to the authority of Gregory. By now, however, visionary literature was growing in prominence as a moral-critical tool in the arsenal of polemicists, eager to expose the dangers of loose morals for kings, bishops and others who had lost their way by showing them torments in hell and mystical dreams. This, really, was where John of Patmos had started, when he had appealed to mystical revelations as a way of attacking the Roman Empire and the Pauline mission so as to defend his own vision of the Judaeo-Christian community. A fundamental purpose of reflecting upon hopes and fears for the future was to expose how far from perfect things were now.

Outsiders, identities and reform

Imperial apocalyptic was one side of a coin. The universal Christian community defined by that body of thought also needed its antitheses, its enemies, those peoples who would lead persecutions or lead the faithful astray. This was a broad category of out-groupers pitched against the in-group, set to include non-Romans (especially Goths and Huns), heretics, Jews, Muslims and pagans. They could be geographically external, or they could be living amongst Christians; they just had to be sufficiently 'different'. The 'us vs. them' dynamic, importantly, was often part of a process rather than a static thing because definitions of community and belief were not stable. The Goths started as outsiders associated with Gog and Magog and, despite Jerome and Augustine arguing against the link, they never escaped it, even as they forged a new Christian community in Spain. But then, first with Isidore, and later with the so-called *Prophetic Chronicle* in the ninth century, Gog became a symbol of their antiquity as a people and indeed of their strength. Where the cultural-social logic of apocalypse no longer worked, it could change. In the meantime the 'borealisation' of tradition in the West moved Gog and Magog of Revelation into the North – perhaps influenced by Pseudo-Methodius – just in time to cast the Vikings as a portentous providential scourge. Apocalypse helped to explain changing circumstances as Christendom expanded into 'strange' new places and conflict followed.

Heresy was perhaps the greatest apocalyptic concern of all. Indeed, as we saw in Chapter 1, all of the earliest Western commentaries on Revelation were composed in the midst of disputes about doctrine, so it is no surprise to find that most subsequent commentators preferred to see Gog and Magog as symbols of heretics – the secret enemies within – rather than as invading foreigners. The idea of Antichrist coalesced around similar ideas because 'there will be many antichrists' (1 John 2.18) in the Last Days and Antichrist's great deception would be to appear Christ-like while leading people to damnation. There was a long history of Christians calling their opponents 'Antichrist' because they were getting the message wrong, particularly during highly charged disputes such as Gregory of Tours's condemnation of charismatics, the Carolingian fight against Adoptionism, and especially after Adso's treatise. Associations between Antichrist and Jews or Muslims tended to be restricted, for now, to where there was direct contact with those religious groups. Even then, the vilification of them derived from the same kinds of concerns as drove the attacks on heresy: these groups had heard the Gospel but refused to accept the Catholic position.

Fears about antichrists, pseudoprophets, and attacking foreigners fed into desires to reform morals and the Church. The project of reform was, in some ways, impossible to complete, because vigilance was required right up until the End. Seducers of the faithful could appear at any time, but particularly in the Last Days. A number of Carolingian reformers were good at seizing on this kind of rhetoric and it was even enshrined in Charlemagne's *Admonitio generalis* in 789. At the same time, an integral part of this reforming process involved striving for a vision of peace like Gregory's *ecclesia Dei* with bishops and kings working together for the good of the Christian community – another reason why civil war and violence was an apocalyptically charged issue, and later why one finds the Peace of God promoting the absence of violence as a spiritual mode of being.

With the last examples, we begin to highlight some of the problems of talking about millenarianism in the early Middle Ages. The belief in a literal thousand-year-long reign of Christ and his saints on earth is virtually unattested after the fourth century, except through the transmission of texts such as Hilarianus's *On the Duration of the World* or by Landesian 'implication'. There are, on the other hand, plenty of illustrations of what Cohn called 'liberal' millenarianism, with people seeking transformations on earth. We are naturally tempted to point at the occasional charismatic such as the False Christ of Bourges or Aldebert of Soissons, radicalising popular piety in the face of a conservative and suppressive mainstream Church. And yet it was their critics, Gregory and Boniface, who added the apocalyptic colour by labelling them 'precursors of Antichrist' or similar, and they did so precisely because such figures were disrupting their own attempts to reform Church and society in relation to their own vision of peace. Glaber's famous account of Liuthard's bees around the Year 1000 is no different. One might want to hold back from labelling all Church reform 'millenarian', but it is important to recognise that tension between charismatics and the Church was as much about method as vision.

Apocalypse and authority in the early Middle Ages

In the end, then, apocalypse really was about the imperative to pursue change. Apocalyptic scripture helped to define the nature and destiny of the Christian community, in the process fostering identity and exposing the nature of opposition in the world. As part of the same body of thought as 'everyday eschatology', it encouraged urgent correction now, before it was too late; and thereafter it promoted constant vigilance because the ending – individual or collective – could come at any time. Apocalyptic thought also helped people to conceptualise, make sense of and generally deal with change, by explaining the nature of time, evil and authority in the grand scheme of things and what to do about them. This all ran much deeper than whether people believed the world was about to end and whether such beliefs were rational or not. It is certainly not about hysteria – the crucial point in Fried's thesis which is often overlooked. Rather, apocalypse was an integral and central part of how Christians imagined and textualised the world and, in being so, a powerful tool in stimulating and directing action.

The nature of apocalypse means that it is fundamentally about power in and over the world, as we have seen throughout this study. First, it provided a particular language – a rhetoric which added authority to chastisement or encouragement in any sort of situation. Act soon or be caught out; destiny is at hand. This was a language, however, which had to be developed because it was only from the sixth century onwards that the Bible was *the* universal reference point in society, and even then the oblique nature of many passages meant that expertise needed to be developed, both through institutional status and the systematic, line-by-line interpretation of words and imagery. Secondly – and sometimes independently of the first point – there was power in being able to identify oneself or others in scripture, because it grounded the world in the authority of the book that textualised the Christian imagination. The fourth kingdom must give way to the last; pseudo-prophets must be resisted. And finally, it really did make people act. They built and joined churches and monasteries, gave away money, made art, gave sermons, wrote histories and letters, engaged in missionary work, went on pilgrimage, reformed institutions and fought wars. Yes, there were other reasons for action, but rarely in human history does any individual, let alone a whole society, do anything for a single all-pervading reason, and that is something which has been abundantly clear with each case study. Power, we should remember, is as much about establishing the potential for action, its justification, and its meaning in relation to other things.

For the early Middle Ages, this all meant that apocalypse was at the heart of the development of Christendom. It gave people identity, purpose and direction. None of that was necessarily coherent or consistent from context to context, but then we are dealing with complex and varied thought in complex and varied societies, before we even factor in idiosyncratic individuals. But in its many forms and expressions, apocalypse helped to give vision to the religious and political communities which grew out of the crises of the fifth century, and in every incarnation thereafter. It did not matter that the End never actually came, because people had prepared just in case.

Select bibliography

The present study covers a wide geographical and chronological range and a full list of literature used would be huge. I list here only the most important or directly relevant works.

PRINTED PRIMARY SOURCES

Additamenta Coloniensia ad Chronica, ed. A. Borst, *Schriften zur Komputistik im Frankenreich von 721 bis 818*, MGH QQ zur Geistesgeschichte, 21 (3 vols, Hanover, 2006), II, pp. 780–94.

Ademar of Chabannes, *Chronicae*, ed. P. Bourgain and R. Landes, CCCM, 129 (Turnhout, 1999).

Agobard of Lyons, *Opera omnia*, ed. L. van Acker, CCCM, 52 (Turnhout, 1981).

Alcuin, *Epistolae*, ed. E. Dümmler, MGH Epp., 4 (Berlin, 1895), pp. 1–481.

Expositio Apocalypsin, PL, 100. 1055–156.

Annales Fuldenses, ed. F. Kurze, MGH SRM, 7 (Hanover, 1891).

Annales Quedlingburgenses, ed. M. Giese, MGH SRG, 72 (Hanover, 2004).

Apringus, *Tractatus in Apocalypsin*, ed. R. Gryson, CCSL, 107 (Turnhout, 2003), pp. 33–97.

Audradus Modicus, *Liber revelationum*, ed. L. Traube, *Abhandlungen der philosophisch-philologischen Classe der königlich Bayerischen Akademie der Wissenschaften*, 19 (1892), pp. 374–92.

Augustine, *De civitate Dei*, eds. B. Dombart and A. Kalb, CCSL, 48–9 (2 vols, Turnhout, 1955).

Enchiridion, ed. E. Evans, CCSL, 46 (Turnhout, 1969).

De Genesi contra Manichaeos, ed. D. Weber, CSEL, 91 (Vienna, 1998).

Beatus of Liébana, *Tractus in Apocalipsin*, ed. R. Gryson, CCSL, 107A (Turnhout, 2012).

Beatus of Liébana and Eterius of Osma, *Adversus Elipandum libri duo*, ed. B. Löfstedt, CCCM, 59 (Turnhout, 1984)

Bede, *Epistola ad Pleguinam*, ed. C. W. Jones, CCSL, 123C (Turnhout, 1980), pp. 615–26.

In epistolas septem catholicas, ed. D. Hurst, CCSL, 121 (Turnhout, 1983), pp. 180–342.

Expositio Actuum Apostolorum, ed. M. Laistner, CCSL, 121 (Turnhout, 1983), pp. 2–99.

Expositio Apocalypseos, ed. R. Gryson, CCSL, 121A (Turnhout, 2001).

Historia ecclesiastica, ed. M. Lapidge, Italian trans. P. Chiesa (2 vols, Rome, 2008–10).

In Lucae evangelium expositio, ed. D. Hurst, CCSL, 120 (Turnhout, 1960), pp. 1–425.

In Marci evangelium exposition, ed. D. Hurst, CCSL, 120 (Turnhout, 1960), pp. 427–648.

De temporum ratione, ed. C. W. Jones, CCSL 123B (Turnhout, 1980).

Bruno, *Vita quinque patrum*, ed. R. Kade, MGH SS, 15. 2 (Hanover, 1887), pp. 709–38.

Caesarius of Arles, *Expositio de Apocalypsi sancti Iohannis*, ed. G. Morin, Sancti Caesarii episcopi Arelatensis Opera Omnia, 2 (Maredsous, 1942), pp. 209–77.

Sermones, ed. G. Morin, CCSL, 103–4 (2 vols, Turnhout, 1953).

Christian of Stablo-Malmedy, *Expositio super Librum Generationis*, ed. R. B. C. Huygens, CCCM, 224 (Turnhout, 2008).

Chronica prophetica, ed. Y. Bonnaz, in *Chroniques Asturiennes (fin IXe siècle)* (Paris, 1987), pp. 1–9.

Commemoratorium, ed. R. Gryson, CCSL 107 (Turnhout, 2003), pp. 161–229.

Columbanus, *Opera*, ed. G. S. M. Walker, Scriptores Latini Hiberniae, 2 (Dublin, 1970).

The Cosmography of Aethicus Ister, ed. and trans. M. Herren, Publications of the Journal of Medieval Latin, 8 (Turnhout, 2011).

De enigmatibus, ed. R. Gryson, CCSL 107 (Turnhout, 2003), pp. 233–95.

Elipandus, *Epistulae*, ed. J. Gil, in *Corpus scriptorum Muzarabicorum* (Madrid, 1974), pp. 67–112.

Eulogius, *Apologeticus martyrum*, ed. J. Gil, in *Corpus scriptorum Muzarabicorum* (Madrid, 1974), pp. 475–94.

Eusebius, *Historia ecclesiastica*, ed. E. Schwartz, Die Griechischen christlichen Schriftsteller der ersten drei Jahrhunderte: Eusebius Werke, 2 (Leipzig, 1903)

Eusebius (-Jerome), *Canones*, ed. R. Helm, Die Griechischen christlichen Schriftsteller der ersten drei Jahrhunderte: Eusebius Werke, 7 (Berlin, 1956).

Fredegarii Chronicae, ed. B. Krusch, MGH SRM, 2 (Hanover, 1888).

Fulbert of Chartres, *Letters and Poems*, ed. and trans. F. Behrends (Oxford, 1976).

Gildas, *De excidio et conquestu Britanniae*, ed. T. Mommsen, MGH AA, 13 (Berlin, 1888).

Gregory the Great, *Dialogi*, ed. A. de Vogüé, SC, 251, 260, 265 (3 vols, Paris, 1978–80).

Homilia in Evangelia, ed. R. Étaix, CCSL, 141 (Turnhout, 1999).

Homilia in Hiezechihelem prophetam, ed. M. Adriaen, CCSL 142 (Turnhout, 1971).

Moralia in Job, ed. M. Adriaen, CCSL, 143 (3 vols, Turnhout, 1979–85).

Registrum, ed. D. Norberg, CCSL, 140 (2 vols, Turnhout, 1982).

Gregory of Tours, *Historiae*, ed. B. Krusch and W. Levison, MGH SRM, 1.1 (Hanover, 1951).

Haimo of Auxerre, *In Apocalypsin*, PL, 117. 937–1220.

In epistolam II ad Thessalonicenses, PL, 117. 777–83.

Hrabanus Maurus, *Expositio in Mattaeum*, ed. B. Löfstedt, CCCM, 174A (Turnhout, 2000).

Hydatius, *Chronicon*, ed. and trans. R. W. Burgess (Oxford, 1993).

Indiculus de adventu Enoch et Elie, ed. J. Gil, in *Corpus scriptorum Muzarabicorum* (Madrid, 1974), pp. 125–34.

Isidore of Seville, *Chronica maiora*, ed. J. C. Martín, CCSL, 112 (Turnhout, 2003).

Historia Gothorum, Vandalorum et Suevorum, ed. C. Rodríguez Alonso (Léon, 1975).

Jerome, *Commentariorum in Mathaeum libri iv*, eds. D. Hurst and M. Adriaen, CCSL, 77 (Turnhout, 1969).

Commentarius in Apocalypsin, ed. J. Haussleiter, CSEL, 49 (Vienna and Leipzig, 1916).

Epistolae, ed. I. Hilberg, CSEL, 54–6 (4 vols., Vienna, 1996).

In Danielem, ed. F. Glorie, CCSL, 75A (Turnhout, 1964).

In Hezechielem, ed. F. Glorie, CCSL, 75 (Turnhout, 1964).

Julian of Toledo, *Opera omnia*, ed. J. N. Hillgarth, CCSL, 115 (Turnhout, 1976).

Liudprand of Cremona, *Opera omnia*, ed. P. Chiesa, CCCM, 156 (Turnhout, 1998).

Miracula Alexii, ed. J. Pien, AASS July IV (Paris and Rome, 1868), pp. 258–62.

The Oracle of Baalbek, ed. and trans. P. J. Alexander (Washington, DC, 1967).

Oracula Tiburtina, ed. E. Sackur, in *Sibyllinische Texte und Forschungen* (Halle, 1898), pp. 177–87.

Paschasius Radbertus, *Expositio in Matthaeo*, ed. B. Paulus, CCCM, 56B (Turnhout, 1984).

Patrick, *Confessio*, ed. L. Bieler, in *Libri epistolarum sancti Patricii episcopi* (Dublin, 1993), pp. 56–90.

Paul Alvar, *Indiculus luminosus*, ed. J. Gil, in *Corpus scriptorum Muzarabicorum* (Madrid, 1974), pp. 270–314.

Primasius, *Commentarius in apocalypsin*, ed. A. W. Adams, CCSL, 92 (Turnhout, 1985).

Pseudo-Ephraim, *Scarpsum*, ed. D. Verhelst, in R. Lievens, E. van Mingroot and W. Verbeke (eds.), *Pascua Mediaevalia*, Historica Lovaniensia, 155 (Leuven, 1983), pp. 518–28.

Pseudo-Methodius I, eds. W. J. Aerts and G. A. A. Kortekaas, *Die Apokalypse des Pseudo-Methodius. Die ältesten Grieschen und Lateinischen Übersetzungen* (2 vols., Leuven, 1998).

Pseudo-Methodius II, ed. O. Prinz, 'Eine frühe abendländische Aktulaisierung der lateinischen Übersetzung des Pseudo-Methodius', *Deutsches Archiv für Erforschung des Mittelalters*, 41 (1985), 1–23 at pp. 6–17.

Ralph Glaber, *Historiarum libri quinque*, ed. and trans. J. France (Oxford, 1989).

Quintus Julius Hilarianus, *Libellus de mundi duratione*, cc. 17–18, PL, 13. 1097–106.

Quodvultdeus, *Opera*, ed. R. Braun, CCSL, 60 (Turnhout, 1976).
Salvian, *De gubernatione Dei*, ed. C. Halm, MGH AA, 1. 1 (Berlin, 1877).
Transitus beati Fursei, ed. C. Carozzi, in *Le voyage de l'âme dans l'au-delà, d'après la littérature latine (Ve–XIIIe siècle)* (Rome, 1994), pp. 679–92.
Tyconius Afer, *Expositio Apocalypseos*, ed. R. Gryson, CCSL, 107A (Turnhout, 2011).
Liber regularum, ed. F. C. Burkitt (Cambridge, 1894); ed. and French. trans. J.-M. Vercruysse, *Tyconius. Le livre des règles*, Source chrétiennes, 488 (Paris, 2004).
Visio Baronti, ed. W. Levison, MGH SRG, 5 (Hanover, 1910), pp. 377–94.
Visio cuiusdam pauperculae mulieris, ed. H. Houben, in *Zeitschrift für die Geschichte des Oberrheins*, 124, n.f. 85 (1976), 41–2.
Visio Pauli, ed. M. R. James, in *Apocrypha Anecdota* (Cambridge, 1893), pp. 11–42.
Wulfstan, *Homilies*, ed. D. Bethurum (Oxford, 1957).

SECONDARY LITERATURE

Aertsen, J. A. and M. Pickavé (eds.), *Ende und Vollendung. Eschatologische Perspektiven im Mittelalter* (Berlin and New York, 2002).
Alberi, M., 'The Evolution of Alcuin's Concept of the *Imperium Christianum*', in J. Hill and M. Swan (eds.), *The Community, the Family and the Saint: Patterns of Power in Early Medieval Europe* (Turnhout, 1998), pp. 3–18.
'"Like the Army of God's Camp": Political Theology and Apocalyptic Warfare at Charlemagne's Court', *Viator*, 41.2 (2010), 1–20.
Alexander, P. J., *The Byzantine Apocalyptic Tradition*, ed. D. Abrahamse (Berkeley, CA, 1985).
'Byzantium and the Migration of Literary Works and Motifs: The Legend of the Last Roman Emperor', *Medievalia et Humanistica*, n.s. 2 (1971), 47–68.
'The Medieval Legend of the Last Roman Emperor and Its Messianic Origin', *Journal of the Warburg and Courtauld Institutes*, 41 (1978), 1–15.
Arnold, B., 'Eschatological Imagination and the Program of Roman Imperial and Ecclesiastical Renewal at the End of the Tenth Century', in Gow, Landes and van Meter, *The Apocalyptic Year 1000*, pp. 271–88.
Barthélemy, D., *L'an mil et la paix de Dieu* (Paris, 1999).
'Antichrist et blasphémateur', *Médiévales*, 37 (1999), 57–70.
La mutation de l'an mil a-t-elle eu lieu? (Paris, 1997); trans. G. R. Edwards as *The Serf, the Knight, and the Historian* (Ithaca, NY, 2009).
Bischoff, B., 'Wendepunkte in der Geschichte der lateinischen Exegese in Frühmittelalter', in his *Mittelalterliche Studien* (3 vols., Stuttgart, 1966), I. 205–73.
Bisson, T., 'The Feudal Revolution', *P&P*, 142 (1994), 6–42.
Boiadjiev, T., 'Der mittelalterliche Apokalyptismus und der Mythos vom Jahre 1000', in Aertsen and Pickavé, *Ende und Vollendung*, pp. 165–78.
Bonner, G., 'Saint Bede in the Tradition of Western Apocalypse Commentary', Jarrow Lecture (Jarrow, 1966).
Borst, A., *Die karolingische Kalenderreform*, MGH Schriften, 48 (Hanover, 1998).

Brandes, W., 'Anastasios ὁ Δίκορος. Endzeiterwartung und Kaiserkritik in Byzanz um 500 n.Chr.', *Byzantinische Zeitschrift*, 90 (1997), 24–63.

'Liudprand von Cremona (*Legatio* Cap. 39–40) und eine bisher unbeachtete West-Östliche Korrespondenz über die bedeutung des Jahres 1000 A.D.', *Byzantinische Zeitschrift*, 93 (2000), 435–63.

'"Tempora periculosa sunt." Eschatologisches im Vorfeld der Kaiserkrönung Karls des Großen', in R. Berndt (ed.), *Das Frankfurter Konzil von 794. Kristallisationspunkt karolingischer Kultur* (Mainz, 1997), I. 49–79.

Brandes, W. and F. Schmieder (eds.), *Endzeiten. Eschatologie in den monotheistischen Weltreligionen* (Berlin and New York, 2008).

Bremmer, R. H., 'The Final Countdown: Apocalyptic Expectations in Anglo-Saxon Charters', in G. Jaritz and G. Moreno-Riaño (eds.), *Time and Eternity: The Medieval Discourse* (Turnhout, 2003), pp. 501–14.

Brown, P., 'The Decline of the Empire of God: Amnesty, Penance, and the Afterlife from Late Antiquity to the Middle Ages', in C. W. Bynum and P. Freedman (eds.), *Last Things: Death and the Apocalypse in the Middle Ages* (Philadelphia, PA, 2000), pp. 41–59.

The Rise of Western Christendom: Triumph and Diversity AD 200–1000 (2nd edn, Oxford, 2002).

Through the Eye of a Needle: Wealth, the Fall of Rome, and the Making of Christianity, 350–550 AD (Princeton, NJ, 2012).

Burgess, R. W., 'Hydatius and the Final Frontier: The Fall of the Roman Empire and the End of the World', in R. Mathiesen and H. Sivan (eds.), *Shifting Frontiers in Late Antiquity* (Aldershot, 1996), pp. 321–32.

Burr, G. L., 'The Year 1000 and the Antecedents of the Crusades', *American Historical Review*, 6.3 (1901), 429–39.

Callahan, D., 'Ademar of Chabannes, Millennial Fears and the Development of Western Anti-Judaism', *JEH*, 46.1 (1995), 19–35.

'The Cross, the Jews, and the Destruction of the Church of the Holy Sepulcher in the Writings of Ademar of Chabannes', in M. Frassetto (ed.), *Christian Attitudes toward the Jews in the Middle Ages: A Casebook* (London, 2007), pp. 15–24.

'The Cult of St Michael the Archangel and the "Terrors of the Year 1000"', in Gow, Landes and van Meter, *The Apocalyptic Year 1000*, pp. 181–204.

'The Peace of God and the Cult of the Saints in Aquitaine in the Tenth and Eleventh Centuries', in Head and Landes, *The Peace of God*, pp. 165–85.

Carozzi, C., *Apocalypse et salut dans le christianisme ancien et médiéval* (Paris, 1999).

'Apocalypse et temps de l'église selon Bède le vénérable', in Guglielmetti, *L'apocalisse*, pp. 115–32.

Le voyage de l'âme dans l'Au-delà d'après la littérature latine (Ve–VIIIe siècle) (Rome, 1994).

Cavadini, J., The *Last Christology of the West: Adoptionism in Spain and Gaul, 785–820* (Philadelphia, 1993).

Cohn, N., *In Pursuit of the Millennium: Revolutionary Millenarians and Mystical Anarchists of the Middle Ages* (2nd edn, London, 1970).

Contreni, J., '"By Lions, Bishops are Meant; by Wolves, Priests": History, Exegesis, and the Carolingian Church in Haimo of Auxerre's *Commentary on Ezechiel*', *Francia*, 29.1 (2002), 29–56.

'"Building Mansions in Heaven": The *Visio Baronti*, Archangel Raphael, and a Carolingian King', *Speculum*, 78.3 (2003), 673–706.

Costambeys, M., M. Innes and S. MacLean, *The Carolingian World* (Cambridge, 2011).

Coupland, S., 'Rod of God's Wrath or the People of God's Wrath? The Carolingian Theology of the Viking Invasions', *JEH*, 42.4 (1991), 535–54.

Cubitt, C., 'The Politics of Remorse: Penance and Royal Piety in the Reign of Æthelred the Unready', *Historical Research*, 85.228 (2012), 179–92.

Dagens, C., 'La fin de temps et l'Église selon Saint Grégoire le Grand', *Recherches de science religieuse*, 58 (1970), 273–88.

Daley, B., *The Hope of the Early Church: A Handbook of Patristic Eschatology* (Cambridge, 1991).

Darby, P., *Bede and the End of Time* (Farnham, 2012).

'Bede's Time Shift of 703 in Context', in Wieser *et al.*, *Abendländische Apokalyptik*, pp. 619–40.

Dutton, P. E., *Charlemagne's Mustache and Other Cultural Clusters of a Dark Age* (New York, 2005).

The Politics of Dreaming in the Carolingian Empire (Lincoln, NE, 1994).

Eicken, H. von, 'Die Legende von der Erwartung des Weltunterganges und der Wiederkehr Christi im Jahre 1000', *Forschungen zur Deutschen Geschichte*, 23 (1883), 303–18.

Emmerson, R. K., 'From "Epistola" to "Sermo": The Old English Version of Adso's *Libellus de Antichristo*', *Journal of English and Germanic Philology*, 82.1 (1983), 1–10.

'The Significance of Abbot Adso's *Libellus de Antichristo*', *American Benedictine Review*, 30 (1979), 175–90.

Emmerson, R. K. and B. McGinn (eds.), *The Apocalypse in the Middle Ages* (Ithaca, NY, 1992).

Firey, A., *A Contrite Heart: Prosecution and Redemption in the Carolingian Empire* (Leiden, 2009).

Flori, J., *L'Islam et la fin des temps. L'interprétation prophétique des invasions musulmanes dans la chrétienté médiévale* (Paris, 2007).

Foxhall Forbes, H., '*Diuiduntur in quattuor*: The Interim and Judgement in Anglo-Saxon England', *Journal of Theological Studies*, 61.2 (2010), 659–84.

Heaven and Earth in Anglo-Saxon England: Theology and Society in an Age of Faith (Farnham, 2013).

Frassetto, M. (ed.), *The Year 1000: Religious and Social Responses to the Turning of the First Millennium* (New York, 2002).

Fredriksen, P., 'Apocalypse and Redemption in Early Christianity: From John of Patmos to Augustine of Hippo', *Vigiliae Christianae*, 45.2 (1991), 151–83.

'Tyconius and Augustine on the Apocalypse', in Emmerson and McGinn, *The Apocalypse in the Middle Ages*, pp. 20–37.

'Tyconius and the End of the World," *Revue des études augustiniennes*, 28 (1982), 59–75.

Fried, J., *Aufstieg aus dem Untergang. Apokalyptisches Denken und die Entstehung der modernen Naturwissenschaft im Mittelalter* (Munich, 2001).

'Die Endzeit fest im Griff des Positivismus? Zur Auseinandersetzung mit Sylvain Gouguenheim', *Historische Zeitschrift*, 275 (2002), 281–322.

'Endzeiterwartung um die Jahrtausendwende', *DA*, 45.2 (1989), 381–473.

Karl der Große: Gewalt und Glaube. Eine Biographie (Munich, 2013).

'Papst Leo III. besucht Karl den Großen in Paderborn oder Einhards Schweigen', *Historische Zeitschrift*, 272 (2001), 281–326.

Gabriele, M., *An Empire of Memory: The Legend of Charlemagne, the Franks and Jerusalem before the First Crusade* (Oxford, 2011).

'Otto III, Charlemagne, and Pentecost AD 1000: A Reconsideration using Diplomatic Evidence', in Frassetto, *The Year 1000*, pp. 111–32.

García Moreno, L. A., 'Expectatives milenaristas y escatolólogicas en la España tardoantigua (ss. V–VIII)', in *Spania. Estudis d'Antiguitat Tardana oferts en homenatge al professor Pere de Palol I Salellas* (Barcelona, 1996), 103–9.

Garrison, M., 'The Bible and Alcuin's Interpretation of Current Events', *Peritia*, 16 (2002), 68–84.

Gatch, M. McC., 'Eschatology in the Anonymous Old English Homilies', *Traditio*, 21 (1965), 117–65.

Gil, J., 'Los terrores del ano 6000', in *Actas del simposio para el estudio de los codices del 'Comentario al apocalypsis' de Beato de Liebana* (Madrid, 1978), pp. 217–47.

Godden, M., 'The Millennium, Time, and History for the Anglo-Saxons', in Gow, Landes and van Meter, *The Apocalyptic Year 1000*, pp. 155–80.

Goffart, W., *The Narrators of Barbarian History AD 550–800: Jordanes, Gregory of Tours, Bede and Paul the Deacon* (Princeton, NJ, 1988).

Gouguenheim, S., *Les fausses terreurs de l'an mil: Attente de la fin des temps ou approfondissement de la foi* (Paris, 1999).

Gow, A., R. Landes and D. C. van Meter (eds.), *The Apocalyptic Year 1000: Religious Expectation and Social Changes, 950–1050* (Oxford, 2003).

Greenwood, T., 'Sasanian Echoes and Apocalyptic Expectations: A Re-Evaluation of the Armenian History Attributed to Sebeos', *Le Muséon*, 115.3–4 (2002), 323–97.

Guglielmetti, R. E (ed.), *L'apocalisse nel medioevo* (Florence, 2011).

Halsall, G., 'The Preface to Book V of Gregory of Tours' Histories: Its Form, Context and Significance', *EHR*, 122.496 (2007), 297–317.

Hartmann, W., *Karl der Große* (Stuttgart, 2010).

Head, T., 'The Development of the Peace of God in Aquitaine (970–1005)', *Speculum*, 74.3 (1999), 656–86.

'Peace and Power in France around the Year 1000', *Essays in Medieval Studies*, 23 (2006), 1–17.

Head, T. and R. Landes (eds.), *The Peace of God: Social Violence and Religious Response around the Year 1000* (Ithaca, NY, 1992).

Heil, J., '"Nos nescientes de hoc velle manere" – "We Wish to Remain Ignorant About This": Timeless End, or: Approaches to Reconceptualising Eschatology after AD 800 (AM 6000)', *Traditio*, 55 (2000), 73–103.

Heinzelmann, M., *Gregory of Tours: History and Society in the Sixth Century*, trans. C. Carroll (Cambridge, 2001).

Hen, Y., 'The Structure and Aims of the *Visio Baronti*', *Journal of Theological Studies*, n.s. 47 (1996), 477–97.

Hillgarth, J. N., 'Eschatological and Political Concepts in the Seventh Century', in J. Fontaine and J. N. Hillgarth (eds.), *Le septième siècle: Changements et continuités* (London, 1992), pp. 212–35.

Himmelfarb, M., *The Apocalypse: A Brief History* (Chichester, 2010).

Holdenried, A., 'Many Hands without Design: The Evolution of a Medieval Prophetic Text', *The Mediaeval Journal* 4.1 (2014), 23–42.

The Sibyl and Her Scribes: Manuscripts and Interpretation of the Latin Sibylla Tiburtina, c. 1050–1500 (Aldershot, 2006).

Hughes, K. L., *Constructing Antichrist: Paul, Biblical Commentary, and the Development of Doctrine in the Early Middle Ages* (Washington, DC, 2005).

Innes, M., 'Immune from Heresy: Defining the Boundaries of Carolingian Christianity', in P. Fouracre and D. Ganz (eds.), *Frankland: The Franks and the World of the Early Middle Ages* (Manchester, 2008), pp. 101–25.

Iogna-Prat, D., 'Le baptême du schéma des trois ordres fonctionnels: L'apport de l'école d'Auxerre dans la second moitié du IXe siècle', *Annales – économies, sociétés, civilisations*, 41.1 (1986), 101–26.

Jiroušková, L., *Die Visio Pauli. Wege und Wandlungen einer orientalischen Apokryphe im lateinischen Mittelalter* (Leiden, 2006).

Jong, M. de, 'The Empire as *ecclesia*: Hrabanus Maurus and Biblical *historia* for Rulers', in Y. Hen and M. Innes (eds.), *The Uses of the Past in the Early Middle Ages* (Cambridge, 2000), pp. 191–226.

The Penitential State: Authority and Atonement in the Age of Louis the Pious, 814–840 (Cambridge, 2009).

Kelly, J., 'Bede and the Irish Exegetical Tradition on the Apocalypse', *Revue Bénédictine*, 92 (1982), 393–406.

Keynes, S., 'An Abbot, an Archbishop, and the Vikings Raids of 1006–7 and 1009–12', *Anglo-Saxon England*, 36 (2007), 151–220.

'Apocalypse Then: England AD 1000', in P. Urbańczyk (ed.), *Europe around the Year 1000* (Warsaw, 2001), pp. 247–70.

Kitchen, T. E., 'Apocalyptic Perceptions of the Roman Empire in the Fifth Century', in Wieser *et al.*, *Abendländische Apokalyptik*, pp. 641–60.

Klein, P., 'The Apocalypse in Medieval Art', in Emmerson and McGinn, *The Apocalypse in the Middle Ages*, pp. 159–99.

'Medieval Apocalypse Cycles and Eschatological Expectations: The So-Called "Terrors" of the Year 1000', in Guglielmetti, *L'apocalisse*, pp. 267–301

Kühnel, B., *The End of Time in the Order of Things* (Regensburg, 2003).

Landes, R., 'Between Aristocracy and Heresy: Popular Participation in the Limousin Peace of God (994–1032), in Head and Landes, *The Peace of God*, pp. 184–219.

'The Birth of Popular Heresy: A Millennial Phenomenon', *Journal of Religious History*, 24.1 (2000), 26–43.

'The Fear of an Apocalyptic Year 1000: Augustinian Historiography, Medieval and Modern', *Speculum*, 75.1 (2000), 97–145.

Heaven on Earth: The Varieties of the Millennial Experience (Oxford, 2011).

'Lest the Millennium Be Fulfilled: Apocalyptic Expectations and the Pattern of Western Chronography, 100–800 CE', in Verbeke, Verhelst and Welkenhuysen, *The Use and Abuse of Eschatology*, pp. 137–211.

'*Millenarismus absconditus*: L'historiographie augustinienne et l'An Mil', *Le Moyen Age*, 98 (1992), 355–77.

'Owls, Roosters, and Apocalyptic Time: A Historical Method for Reading a Refractory Documentation', *Union Seminary Quarterly Review*, 49 (1996), 165–85.

Relics, Apocalypse, and the Deceits of History: Ademar of Chabannes (989–1034) (Cambridge, MA, 1995).

'Sur les traces du Millennium: La via negativa', *Le Moyen Age*, 99 (1993), 5–26.

Levison, W., 'Die Politik in den Jenseitsvisionen des frühen Mittelalter', in his *Aus rheinischer und fränkischer Frühzeit* (Düsseldorf, 1948), pp. 229–46.

Leyser, C., *Authority and Asceticism from Augustine to Gregory the Great* (Oxford, 2000).

Lionarons, J. T., *The Homiletic Writings of Archbishop Wulfstan* (Woodbridge, 2010).

Lobrichon, G., 'The Chiaroscuro of Heresy: Early Eleventh Century Aquitaine as Seen from Auxerre', in Head and Landes, *The Peace of God*, pp. 80–103.

'Jugement sur la terre comme au ciel. L'étrange cas de l'Apocalypse millénaire de Bamberg', *Médiévales*, 37 (1999), 71–9.

'L'ordre de ce temps et les désordres de la fin. Apocalypse et société, du IXe à la fin du XIe siècle', in Verbeke, Verhelst and Welkenhuysen, *The Use and Abuse of Eschatology*, pp. 221–41.

'Stalking the Signs: The Apocalyptic Commentaries', in Gow, Landes and van Meter, *The Apocalyptic Year 1000*, pp. 67–79.

Lössl, J., '"Apocalypse? No." The Power of Millennialism and Its Transformation in Late Antique Christianity', in A. Cain and N. Lenski (eds.), *The Power of Religion in Late Antiquity* (Aldershot, 2009), pp. 31–44.

McGinn, B., *Antichrist: Two Thousand Years of the Human Fascination with Evil* (New York, 1994).

'The End of the World and the Beginning of Christendom', in M. Bull (ed.), *Apocalypse Theory and the End of the World* (Oxford, 1995), pp. 58–89.

'Eriugena Confronts the End: Reflections on Johannes Scottus's Place in Carolingian Eschatology', in M. Dunne and J. McEvoy (eds.), *History and Eschatology in John Scottus Eriugena and His Time* (Leuven, 2002), pp. 3–29.

Mackay, T., 'Apocalypse Commentary by Primasius, Bede and Alcuin: Interrelationship, Dependency and Individuality', *Studia Patristica*, 36 (2001), 28–34.

MacLean, S. 'Apocalypse and Revolution: Europe around the Year 1000', *EME*, 15.1 (2007), 86–106.

'Reform, Queenship and the End of the World in Tenth-Century France: Adso's "Letter on the Origin and Time of the Antichrist"', *Revue Belge de Philologie et d'Histoire*, 86 (2008), 645–75.

Magdalino, P. 'The History of the Future and Its Uses: Prophecy, Policy and Propaganda', in R. Beaton and C. Roueché (eds.), *The Making of Byzantine History: Studies Dedicated to Donald M. Nicol on his Seventieth Birthday* (Aldershot, 1993), 3–34.

'The Year 1000 in Byzantium', in P. Magdalino (ed.), *Byzantium in the Year 1000* (Leiden, 2002), pp. 233–70.

'The End of Time in Byzantium', in Brandes and Schmieder, *Endzeiten*, pp. 119–34.

R. A. Markus, *Saeculum: History and Society in the Theology of St Augustine* (Cambridge, 1970).

Gregory the Great and His World (Cambridge, 1997).

'Living within Sight of the End', in C. Humphrey and M. Ormrod (eds.), *Time in the Medieval World* (York, 2001), pp. 23–34.

'Gregory and Bede: The Making of the Western Apocalyptic Tradition', in *Gregorio Magno nel XIV centenario della morte* (Rome, 2004), pp. 247–55.

Matter, E. A., 'The Apocalypse in Early Medieval Exegesis', in Emmerson and McGinn, *The Apocalypse in the Middle Ages*, pp. 38–50.

'The Pseudo-Alcuinian *De septem sigillis*: An Early Latin Apocalypse Exegesis', *Traditio*, 36 (1980), 111–37.

Mayr-Harting, H., 'Apocalyptic Book Illustration in the Early Middle Ages', in C. Rowland and J. Barton (eds.), *Apocalyptic in History and Tradition* (London and New York, 2002), pp. 179–82.

Meier, M., 'Eschatologie und Kommunikation im 6. Jahrhundert n. Chr. – oder: Wie osten und Westen beständig aneinander vorbei redeten', in Brandes and Schmieder, *Endzeiten*, pp. 41–73.

Meter, D. C. van, 'Christian of Stavelot on Matthew 24:42 and the Tradition that the World will End on a March 25th', *Recherches de théologie ancienne et médiévale*, 63 (1996), 68–92.

Milo, D., 'L'an mil: un problème d'historiographie moderne', *History and Theory*, 27.3 (1988), 261–81.

Möhring, H., 'Karl der Große und die Endkaiser-Weissagung: Der Sieger über den Islam kommt aus dem Westen', in B. Z. Kedar, J. Riley-Smith and R. Hiestand (eds.), *Montjoie: Studies in Crusade History in Honour of Hans Eberhard Mayer* (Aldershot, 1997), 1–20.

'Die *renovatio imperii* Kaiser Ottos III. und die Antichrist-Erwartung der Zeitgenossen an der Jahrtausendwende von 1000/1001', *Archiv für Kulturgeschichte*, 93.2 (2011), 333–50.

Der Weltkaiser der Endzeit. Entstehung, Wandel und Wirkung einer tausendjährigen Weissagung (Stuttgart, 2000).

Moore, R. I., 'The Birth of Popular Heresy: A Millennial Phenomenon?' *Journal of Religious History*, 24.1 (2000), 8–25.

Moreira, I., *Dreams, Visions and Spiritual Authority in Merovingian Gaul* (Ithaca, NY, and London, 2000).

Heaven's Purge: Purgatory in Late Antiquity (Oxford, 2010).

Nie, G. de, *Views from a Many-Windowed Tower: Studies of Imagination in the Works of Gregory of Tours* (Amsterdam, 1987).

O'Hara, A., 'Death and the Afterlife in Jonas of Bobbio's *Vita Columbani*', *Studies in Church History*, 45 (2009), 64–73.

O'Leary, S., *Arguing the Apocalypse: A Theory of Millennial Rhetoric* (Oxford, 1994).

Ortigues, E. and D. Iogna-Prat, 'Raoul Glaber et l'historiographie clunisienne', *Studi Medievali*, 26 (1985), 537–72.

Palmer, J. T. 'Calculating Time and the End of Time in the Carolingian World, *c.* 740–*c.* 820', *EHR*, 523 (2011), 1307–31.

'Computus after the Paschal Controversy of 740', in D. Ó Cróinín and I. Warntjes (eds.), *The Easter Controversy of Late Antiquity and the Early Middle Ages* (Turnhout, 2011), pp. 213–41.

'The Ordering of Time', in Wieser *et al.*, *Abendländische Apokalyptik*, pp. 605–18.

Pelle, S., 'The *Revelations* of Pseudo-Methodius and *Concerning the Coming of Antichrist* in British Library Ms Cotton Vespasian D. xiv', *Notes & Queries*, 56.3 (2009), 324–30.

Peters, E., 'Mutations, Adjustments, Terrors, Historians, and the Year 1000', in Frassetto, *The Year 1000*, pp. 9–28.

Plaine, F., 'Les prétendues terreurs de l'an mille', *Revue des questions historiques*, 13 (1873), 145–64.

Podskalsky, G., *Byzantinische Reichseschatologie. Die Periodisierung der Weltgeschichte in den vier Grossreichen (Daniel 2 und 7) und dem tausend-jährigen Friedensreihe (Apok. 20). Eine Motivgeschichtliche Untersuchung* (Munich, 1972).

Pollard, R. M., 'One Other on Another: Petrus Monachus' *Revelationes* and Islam', in M. Cohen and J. Firnhaber-Baker (eds.), *Difference and Identity in Francia and Medieval France* (Farnham, 2010), pp. 25–42.

Potestà, G. L., '*The Vaticinium of Constans*: Genesis and Original Purposes of the Legend of the Last World Emperor', *Millennium-Jahrbuch*, 8 (2011), 271–89.

Rangheri, M., 'La *Espistola ad Gerbergam reginam de ortu et tempore Antichristi di Adsone* di Montier-en-Der e le sue fonti', *Studi Mediaevali*, 3rd series, 14 (1973), 677–732.

Rauh, H. D., *Das Bild des Antichrist im Mittelalter: Von Tyconius zum deutschen Symbolismus* (Münster, 1973).

'Pseudo-Methodius und die Legende vom römischen Endkaiser', in Verbeke, Verhelst and Welkenhuysen, *The Use and Abuse of Eschatology*, pp. 82–111.

Reinink, G. J., 'Pseudo-Methodius: A Concept of History in Response to the Rise of Islam', in A. Cameron and L. I. Conrad (eds.), *The Byzantine and Early Islamic East: Problems in the Literary Source Material* (Princeton, NJ, 1992), pp. 149–87.

Roach, L., 'Otto III and the End of Time', *TRHS*, 6th series, 23 (2013), 75–102.

Rouche, M., *L'Aquitaine dès Wisigoths aux Arabes, 418–781* (Paris, 1979).

Rubenstein, J., *Armies of Heaven: The First Crusade and the Quest for Apocalypse* (Philadelphia, PA, 2011).

Rydén, L., 'The Andreas Salos Apocalypse: Greek Text, Translation and Commentary', *Dumbarton Oaks Papers*, 28 (1974), 197–261.

Savigni, R., 'Il commentario di Aimone all'apocalisse', in Guglielmetti, *L'apocalisse*, pp. 207–66.

Savon, H., 'L'Antéchrist dan l'oeuvre de Grégoire le Grand', in J. Fontaine (ed.), *Grégoire le Grand* (Paris, 1986), pp. 389–404.

Schieffer, R., *Neues von der Kaiserkrönung Karls der Großen*, Bayerische Akademie der Wissenschaften, Philosophisch-historische Klasse, Jahrgang 2004, Heft 2 (Munich, 2004).

Scott, R. D., 'Malalas, *The Secret History*, and Justinian's Propaganda', *Dumbarton Oaks Papers*, 39 (1985), 99–109.

Shimahara, S., 'Le *Commentaire sur Daniel* de Raban Maur', in P. Depreux, S. Lebecq, M. Perrin and O. Szerwiniack (eds.), *Raban Maur et sons temps* (Turnhout, 2010), pp. 275–91.

'Exégèse et politique dans l'œuvre d'Haymon d'Auxerre', *Revue de l'histoire des religions*, 225.4 (2008), 471–86.

Slyke, D. van, *Quodvultdeus of Carthage: The Apocalyptic Theology of a Roman African in Exile* (Strathfield, NSW, 2003).

Snyder, J., 'The Reconstruction of an Early Christian Cycle of Illustrations for the Book of Revelation – The Trier Apocalypse', *Vigiliae Christianae*, 18 (1964), 146–62.

Southern, R., 'Aspects of the European Tradition of Historical Writing: 3. History as Prophecy', *Transactions of the Royal Historical Society*, 5th series, 22 (1972), 159–80.

Troncarelli, F., 'Il consolato dell'Anticristo', *Studi Medievali*, 3rd series, 30.2 (1989), 567–92.

Verbeke, W., D. Verhelst and A. Welkenhuysen (eds.), *The Use and Abuse of Eschatology in the Middle Ages* (Leuven, 1988).

Verbist, P., *Duelling with the Past: Medieval Authors and the Problem of the Christian Era, c. 990–1135* (Turnhout, 2010).

Verhelst, D., 'Adso of Montier-en-Der and the Fear of the Year 1000', in Gow, Landes and van Meter, *The Apocalyptic Year 1000*, pp. 81–92.

'La préhistoire des conceptions d'Adson concernant l'Antichrist', *Recherches de théologie ancienne et médiévale*, 40 (1973), 52–103.

von den Brincken, A.-D., 'Abendländischer Chialasmus um 1000? Zur Rezeption unserer christlichen Ära', in Aertsen and Pickavé, *Ende und Vollendung*, pp. 179–92.

Wallis, F., *Bede: Commentary on Revelation* (Liverpool, 2013).

Bede: On the Reckoning of Time (Liverpool, 1999).

Warntjes, I., 'A Newly Discovered Prologue of AD 699 to the Easter Table of Victorius of Aquitaine in an Unknown Sirmond Manuscript', *Peritia* 21 (2010), 254–83.

Whalen, B., *Dominion of God: Christendom and Apocalypse in the Middle Ages* (Cambridge, MA, 2009).

Wieser, V., C. Zolles, C. Feik, M. Zolles and L. Schlöndorff (eds.), *Abendländische Apokalyptik. Kompendium zur Genealogie der Endzeit* (Berlin, 2013).

Williams, J., 'Purpose and Imagery in the Apocalypse Commentary of Beatus of Liébana', in Emmerson and McGinn, *The Apocalypse in the Middle Ages*, pp. 217–33.

Wood, J., 'Individual and Collective Salvation in Late Visigothic Spain', *Studies in Church History*, 45 (2009), 74–86.

Index of manuscript references

General index

Aachen, 142, 149, 156, 165, 182, 207
Abbo of Fleury, abbot, 191, 192, 215
Adam of Bremen, 193
Ademar of Chabannes, 192, 219, 220
Adso of Montier-en-Der, 7, 109, 118,
    129, 170, 184, 194, 195–8, 201,
    202, 209, 211, 212, 214, 216, 217,
    231, 233
Ælfric of Eynsham, 210, 213
Æthelbald, king of Mercia, 111
Æthelberht, king of Kent, 65–6, 101
Æthelred II 'Unræd', king of England,
    209, 210–11, 213
'Aethicus Ister', 120, 124–5, 163,
    179, 182
Agathias, 1–2, 21
Agnellus of Ravenna, 178
Agobard of Lyon, archbishop, 155,
    172, 183–4
Alaric I, Gothic leader, 25, 30–1
Alcuin of York, 132, 135, 136, 138–40,
    141, 146, 154, 155, 157, 166,
    180, 231
Alemannia, 83, 94, 122,
    see also Reichenau; St Gall
Alexander the Great, 32, 112–13, 114,
    116, 122, 123, 124, 125, 126, 179
Alexander, Paul, 109, 114
Alfred the Great, king of the English,
    34, 179
al-Hakim, caliph, 219
Ambrosius Autpertus, 114, 120, 125–6,
    168, 213
Anastasios I, emperor, 30, 48, 229
Anskar of Hamburg-Bremen, (arch)
    bishop, 182
Antichrist, 4, 7, 9, 22, 24, 29, 30, 31, 33,
    34, 37, 41, 44, 48, 53, 54, 59, 64,
    71, 73, 75, 86, 88, 101, 103, 109,
    118, 122, 123, 124, 138, 148, 149,
    150, 151, 152, 153, 155, 157, 165,
    166–7, 169, 170, 174, 184, 185,

187, 190, 192, 195, 196, 197, 198,
    201, 206, 209, 211–12, 213, 214,
    216–18, 219, 220, 230, 231, 232–3
Apringus of Beja, 40
Arabs, 3, 23, 107, 108, 110–17, 122, 123,
    126–7, 129, 151, 168, 178, 180,
    184–7, 199
Arnulf of Rheims, archbishop, 216
Audradus of Sens, 173, 180, 186
Augustine of Canterbury, archbishop, 66
Augustine of Hippo, bishop, 8, 14, 15, 16,
    19, 22, 23, 25, 26, 27, 32, 37, 38,
    39, 42, 45–6, 49, 53, 54, 55, 56,
    57, 59–60, 67, 68, 78, 79, 87, 90,
    93, 99, 101, 105, 107, 108, 109,
    112, 153, 155, 162, 171, 189, 229,
    230, 232
    On the City of God, 31–2, 38–9, 163
    Enchiridion for Laurentius, 51–2
Avitus of Vienne, bishop, 36

Balthild, 84, 121
Barthélemy, Dominique, 7, 190, 217, 222,
    223, 224
Beatus of Liébana, 92, 141–2, 145,
    152–4, 158
Becher, Matthias, 6
Bede, 9, 16, 39, 65, 68, 80, 95–105, 111,
    135, 141, 142, 143, 144, 155, 158,
    160, 162, 168, 170, 214, 229
    Commentary on Revelation, 22, 105,
    108, 163
    Ecclesiastical History of the English People,
    95, 96–8, 101, 103
    On Judgement Day, 96, 171
    Letter to Plegwine, 95, 99–100
    On the Reckoning of Time, 95, 98, 99,
    101, 102, 103, 143, 163
Bernard of Angers, 7, 217–18
Blickling Homilies, 210
Bobbio, monastery, 119, 124, 163, 179
Boniface IV, pope, 82

250